STRENGTH THROUGH JOY

Based on extensive archival research, this is the first major book on the Nazi leisure and tourism agency, Strength through Joy (KdF). The Third Reich aimed to unify Germans in preparation for war and the acquisition of "living space." Yet it was also sensitive to German consumers, whose wish for higher living standards threatened national cohesion and rearmament. The leisure organization Strength through Joy became the Nazi regime's most determined attempt to ease the tension between collective goals and individual desires, as well as between "guns and butter." Its factory beautification, organized sports, cultural events, and mass tourism sought to raise the status of workers and integrate them in the nation, while keeping its costs low so that its clientele could afford its programs without wage increases that compromised rearmament. Nevertheless, if KdF did attract workers, it also drew the middle classes, which sought adventure, personal comfort, and pleasure – especially through its tourism. Although the motivations of Strength through Joy's constituencies often diverged from the Nazi ideal of a united, politicized "racial community" (*Volksgemeinschaft*), KdF's accommodation to consumer expectations made it the regime's most popular institution. KdF mitigated present sacrifices while presenting visions of a prosperous future once "living space" was acquired. As a privilege extended to racially acceptable Germans, it segregated the Nazi regime's victims from the German "racial community."

Shelley Baranowski is Professor of History at the University of Akron. Her previous books include *The Confessing Church: Conservative Elites and the Nazi State* (1986) and *The Sanctity of Rural Life: Nobility, Protestantism, and Nazism in Weimar Prussia* (1995). She has also co-edited *Being Elsewhere: Tourism, Consumer Culture, and Identity in Modern Europe and North America* (2001) with Ellen Furlough.

The führer on vacation
Source: Kraft durch Freude Gau Sachsen, *Urlaubsfahrten 1936,*
frontispiece.

STRENGTH THROUGH JOY

CONSUMERISM AND MASS TOURISM
IN THE THIRD REICH

SHELLEY BARANOWSKI
University of Akron

CAMBRIDGE
UNIVERSITY PRESS

CAMBRIDGE UNIVERSITY PRESS
Cambridge, New York, Melbourne, Madrid, Cape Town
Singapore, São Paulo, Delhi, Tokyo, Mexico City

Cambridge University Press
The Edinburgh Building, Cambridge CB2 8RU, UK

Published in the United States of America by
Cambridge University Press, New York

www.cambridge.org
Information on this title: www.cambridge.org/9780521705998

First published 2004
First paperback edition 2007

A catalogue record for this publication is available from the British Library

Library of Congress Cataloguing in Publication data
Baranowski, Shelley.
Strength through Joy : consumerism and mass tourism in the Third Reich /
Shelley Baranowski.
    p. cm.
Includes bibliographical references and index.
ISBN 0-521-83352-3
1. Nationalsozialistische Gemeinschaft "Kraft durch Freude" – History.
2. Germany – Politics and government – 1933–1945.   3. Consumption
(Economics) – Germany – History – 20th century.   4. Tourism – Government
policy – Germany – History – 20th century.   I. Title
DD256.5.B324 2004
339.4'7'094309043 – dc22   2003060603

ISBN 978-0-521-83352-3 Hardback
ISBN 978-0-521-70599-8 Paperback

For Mary and Ed Baranowski

Contents

Illustrations and Table

Table

Acknowledgments

It is my pleasure to recognize those many whose support and encouragement have contributed to this book. The University of Akron Faculty Research Committee awarded me two summer fellowships and one smaller grant, which allowed me the extended travel to archives necessary to this project's completion. In addition, a Fellowship for University Teachers from the National Endowment for the Humanities in 2001–2002 was indispensable to composing the first draft of my manuscript. I especially thank my chair, Walter Hixson, and my dean, Roger Creel, for providing matching funds for my NEH grant, which allowed me the luxury of a year's leave from teaching. The history department staff, especially Carol Brantley and Kym Rohrbach, have responded generously to my numerous requests to photocopy interlibrary loan materials. It is my good fortune to have received such a wonderful combination of internal and external support.

During the gestation of *Strength through Joy*, many friends and colleagues have benefited me with their criticisms of earlier presentations of my work. Hasso Spode, who invited me to present the results of my research at the Institut für Tourismus in Berlin, David Abraham, Celia Applegate, Michael Burleigh, Alon Confino, Victoria de Grazia, Jeffrey Herf, Konrad Jarausch, Rudy Koshar, and Arno Mayer helped me conceptualize a project that was initially difficult to grasp. How does one, after all, make the connection between leisure, especially tourism, and horror? What did the existence of Strength through Joy mean in the context of the Third Reich's quest for living space? I am also grateful to Omer Bartov, James Retallack, Thomas Ertman, Young-Sun Hong, and John K. Walton, who invited me to give talks at the Center for Historical Analysis at Rutgers, the Department of History at the University of Toronto, the Minda de Gunzberg Center for European Studies at Harvard, the Northeast Working Group on German Women's History and Culture at its meeting at Vassar, and a major conference on tourism at University of Central Lancashire respectively.

Because of her own work on French consumerism and tourism, Ellen Furlough was the first to encourage me to write a book on Strength through Joy, and her critiques of my work at various stages facilitated my grasp of subjects far from my earlier work on German Protestantism and Prussian landowners. Stephen Harp, who was my valued colleague for ten years, offered insightful comments on the first draft of my manuscript. I was also fortunate to have received the detailed and thoughtful evaluations of Joshua Hagen, Kristin Semmens, and Richard Steigmann-Gall, who tolerated my interruptions to their own work while I picked their brains. Paul Betts generously shared his own chapter on the Beauty of Labor, which sharpened my analysis of Strength through Joy's shop floor activities. My graduate students at Kent State University and the University of Akron, Jordan Broderick, Mark Cole, Rose Eichler, Monika Flaschka, Sandy Hopwood, Sharyn Koosed-Boyce, Chris Van Hauter, and Shawn Walker, were generous in the praise but (fortunately) incisive in their criticisms. Finally, I very much appreciate the support that my project has received from my editor at Cambridge University Press, Frank Smith, and his assistant, Barbara Chin, whose professionalism stands out in my experience with academic publishing. I benefited from the outstanding copyediting of Lee Young of TechBooks. I have especially valued the comments of Cambridge's anonymous readers, who I hope will see evidence of their perceptive suggestions in this book. It is customary and appropriate for authors to assume responsibility for the contents of their work, yet I could not have completed *Strength through Joy* without the feedback of others.

Because of the destruction of Strength through Joy's headquarters during the war, I traveled widely in search of archival and primary source material. As a consequence, I am indebted to many archives and libraries. I very much appreciate the warm assistance of the staffs at the Auswärtiges Amt Politisches Archiv (Bonn), the Bayerisches Hauptstaatsarchiv (Munich), the Bergbau-Archiv (Bochum), the Bundesarchiv Berlin–Lichterfelde, and the Bundesarchiv Militärarchiv (Freiburg), the Deutsche Bücherei (Leipzig), the Institut für Tourismus (Berlin–Dahlem), the Institut für Zeitgeschichte (Munich), the Landeshauptarchiv Magdeburg, the Landeshauptarchiv Koblenz, the Niedersächsisches Hauptstaatsarchiv Hannover, the New York Public Library, the Ohio State University Library (Columbus), the Sächsisches Wirtschaftsarchiv (Leipzig), the Staatsbibliothek Preussischer Kulturbesitz (Berlin), and the Wirtschaftsarchiv Baden–Württemberg (Stuttgart). Frau Köhne-Lindenlaub and Dr. Jens Hohensee at the Historisches Archiv Krupp and Ruth Beck Perrenoud at the Olympic Studies Center in Lausanne went out of their way not only to help me navigate their collections, but also to introduce me to other scholars working in their archives. Herbert Böhner of the Siemens-Archiv in Munich graciously gave me a copy of a two-volume history of the company. Gabriele Unverwerth of the Stiftung Westfälisches Wirtschaftsarchiv in Dortmund referred me to other resources in the region and allowed me to reproduce a slide at no cost. Randall Bytwerk of Calvin College generously lent me primary materials from his large collection of German propaganda from the Third Reich and the German Democratic Republic. Finally, Sarah Akers, who heads interlibrary loan at the Bierce Library of the University of Akron, managed to track down nearly everything I needed, no matter how obscure.

Lastly, there are friends and family whose support has been beyond measure. My husband Ed, not only endured my long research trips, but also acquired Strength through Joy literature for me, designed many of the images in this book, helped me negotiate the copyright laws that applied to them, and otherwise supported me with his love. Youlandia Peak and Earl Hull have provided essential support at home during the academic year, and especially during my travels abroad. On two occasions, Diana Tisher graciously photocopied my entire manuscript. My parents, Robert and Ann Osmun, my brother David, and my sister Marion have followed this project from the beginning, happily reading article-length versions of it. Finally, I could not imagine having better, more loving, in-laws than Mary and Ed Baranowski, to whom this book is dedicated.

Abbreviations

AA/PA	Auswärtiges Amt Politisches Archiv (Foreign Ministry Political Archive, Bonn)
AOG	Gesetz zur Ordnung der nationalen Arbeit (National Labor Law)
APK	Akten der Partei-Kanzlei der NSDAP (Files of the NSDAP Chancellery, Munich)
AWI	Arbeitswissenschaftliches Institut (Institute for the Science of Labor)
BdA	Bank der deutschen Arbeit (Bank of German Labor)
BAB	Bergbau-Archiv Bochum (Mining Archive, Bochum)
BAL	Bundesarchiv Berlin–Lichterfelde (Federal Archive, Berlin–Lichterfelde)
BA-MA	Bundesarchiv-Militärarchiv (Federal Military Archive, Freiburg)
BHA	Bayerisches Hauptstaatsarchiv München (Bavarian State Archive, Munich)
DAF	Deutsche Arbeitsfront (German Labor Front)
Dinta	Deutsches Institut für technische Arbeitsschulung (German Institute for Technical Labor Training)
DNVP	Deutschnationale Volkspartei (German National People's Party)
HA Krupp	Historisches Archiv Krupp (Historical Archive Krupp, Essen)
IfT	Institut für Tourismus (Insitute for Tourism at the Free University, Berlin)
IfZ	Institut für Zeitgeschichte (Institute for Contemporary History, Munich)
ILO	International Labour Office, Geneva
KdF	Kraft durch Freude (Strength through Joy)

KPD	Kommunistische Partei Deutschlands (German Communist Party)
LHAM	Landeshauptarchiv Magdeburg (central archive of the state of Saxony-Anhalt, Magdeburg)
LK	Landeshauptarchiv Koblenz (central archive, state of the Rhineland–Palatinate, Koblenz)
NHH	Niedersächsisches Hauptstaatsarchiv Hannover (central regional archive of the state of Lower Saxony, Hanover)
NSBO	Nationalsozialistische Betriebszellenorganisation (National Socialist Factory Cell Organization)
NSDAP	Nationalsozialistische Deutsche Arbeiterpartei (National Socialist German Workers' Party)
OSC	Olympic Studies Center, Lausanne
RSA	*Reden, Schriften, Anordnungen* (Hitler's writings, speeches, and directives)
SA	Siemens-Archiv (Siemens Archive, Munich)
SdA	Schönheit der Arbeit (Beauty of Labor)
SD	Sicherheitsdienst (Security Service)
SPD	Sozialdemokratische Partei Deutschlands (German Social Democratic Party)
Sopade	Deutschland-Berichte der Sozialdemokratischen Partei Deutschlands (Situation reports of the SPD executive in exile)
SWA	Sächsisches Wirtschaftsarchiv (Business Archive of Saxony, Leipzig)
WABW	Wirtschaftsarchiv Baden–Württemberg (Business Archive of Baden–Württemberg, Stuttgart)
WWA	Stiftung Westfälisches Wirtschaftsarchiv (Business Archive of Westphalia, Dortmund)

Note on Translations and Citations

I have translated *Volksgemeinschaft* as "racial community" rather than the more commonly used "national" or "people's community" to underscore the Nazi regime's ethnic and racial understanding of the "nation." The inclination of individuals to sacrifice themselves for the common good was, especially in Hitler's view, constitutive of racial superiority. On the other hand, I have left *Volk* and *völkisch* untranslated because without the noun "community," the logical English renderings, "race" and "racial," have a more specific application than the admixture of blood, ethnicity, and culture that the Nazi terms conveyed.

Due to the reorganization of the German Federal Archives, one of the collections that I consulted in the archive at Potsdam (formerly the Zentralstaatsarchiv of the German Democratic Republic and now dissolved), the Reich Main Security Office (Reichssicherheitshauptamt, or RSHA), has been moved to the archive in Berlin–Lichterfelde. Having confirmed that the RSHA documents are in their new location, I have named Berlin–Lichterfelde rather than Potsdam in the relevant citations. My format for archival citations is as follows: a description of the document followed by the date, the name of the archive, the specific holding, file number, and (if available) document number.

Introduction

Josef Nösler and Josef Amediet at first thought the news was a joke. When the two Krupp miners learned from their supervisors that they would sail to the Portuguese island of Madeira on an all-expenses paid cruise organized by the Nazi leisure-time organization, Strength through Joy (Kraft durch Freude, or KdF), they could scarcely believe their luck. After returning from their trip, the two workers contributed an article about their adventure to the Krupp newspaper, their prose conveying their enchantment with their sojourn on the island. With its bountiful banana trees, lush foliage and flowers, and the sparkling lights at night in its port city, Funchal, Madeira appeared to the authors as an exotic and pleasurable "fairy tale land." Nevertheless, the poverty of the Madeirans disrupted the magical impression that the island had left. While the gardens and villas of the wealthy were majestic and colorful, the miners recalled, the hovels of workers, who huddled in the slums near the harbor reminded them of how much their own lives differed from the Portuguese. Such conditions could hardly be imagined in Germany, they implied. Thanks to the führer, who understood what German workers wanted – a subtle reference to the "failure" of the Social Democrats and Communists to address the needs of wage earners – Nösler and Amediet had earned the experience of a lifetime. They had won the opportunity to travel and the chance to compare their standard of living with that in a Strength through Joy port of call.[1]

The miners' report contained the customary ingredients of the tourist recollections, which Strength through Joy and industry periodicals regularly published. Few words of criticism about the trip emerged. Rather, the workers' article expressed amazement that wage earners could enjoy a pastime once the privilege of the middle and upper classes. Moreover, it conveyed the dreamlike qualities of the voyage, especially because of

---

1 "Nochmals zwei Madeirafahrer. Zwei Kumpels von Hannover-Hannibal fahren zu den glücklichen Inseln," *Krupp: Zeitschrift der Kruppischen Betriebsgemeinschaft* 27, no. 19 (1 July 1936): 19.

1

the cruise's "exotic" destination. And, it included the observation as to the low living standards of the workers of the host nation, in contrast to the superiority of Germany's way of life under Adolf Hitler. Although an advertisement for the harmonious "plant community" (*Betriebsgemeinschaft*) at Krupp, reflected in the management's willingness to subsidize vacation trips for its workers, the article also attested to the success of Nazi social policy and the Nazi regime's ability to deliver a high standard of living to working-class Germans. As an agency that at low cost to its consumers sold the cultural practices that signified middle-class standing – concerts, plays, the opera, art exhibits and the theater, riding, sailing, and tennis lessons, and vacation travel – Strength through Joy testified to the Nazi regime's desire to convince its racially "valuable" citizens that it enhanced their well being.

Since the 1960s the social history of the Third Reich has overturned the image of Nazi rule that emerged during the early Cold War period, especially in the West. According to that view, Nazism terrorized the majority of Germans into submission befiting a "totalitarian" regime that controlled the public and private lives of its citizens, save for the heroic few who resisted at the cost of their lives.[2] Although acknowledging Nazism's persecution of political and racial "undesirables" and "deviants," historians highlight the limits of the regime's ability to indoctrinate, while recognizing the unforced popularity of its policies. Periodic opposition and nonconformity coexisted with the widespread acceptance of the Third Reich, which prevented the emergence of sustained opposition to the regime's most lethal goals.[3] Even renewed attempts to describe the Nazi regime as "totalitarian" – to describe its invasions of the private sphere, its abrogation of individual rights and the rule of law, and its attempts to remake civil society into a racial utopia – appreciate the support that the regime acquired from Germans regardless of class, who grasped at its millenarian solutions to contemporary crises.[4] If the knowledge of the regime's brutality was pervasive, encouraging the majority to avoid behavior that would result in their denunciation, the collaboration of

2 For a good example of this perspective, see the work of the emigré historian, Hans Rothfels, *The German Opposition to Hitler* (Hindale, Illinois: Henry Regnery, 1948).

3 Although more inclined to stress the relative immunity of individuals and groups to Nazi ideology than active popular consent, the multivolume social history of Bavaria, Martin Broszat, et al., *Bayern in der NS-Zeit*, 6 vols. (Munich and Vienna: Oldenbourg, 1977–83), opened a new lens through which to study the regime's impact on Germans. For an analysis of the scholarship on popular opinion, see Ian Kershaw, *The Nazi Dictatorship: Problems and Perspectives of Interpretation*, 4th ed. (London: Edward Arnold, 2000), 183–217.

4 Michael Burleigh's *The Third Reich: A New History* (New York: Hill and Wang, 2000) is the most thoroughgoing attempt to reintroduce the concept of totalitarianism to the Third Reich. See also Konrad H. Jarausch and Michael Geyer, *Shattered Past: Reconstructing German Histories* (Princeton and Oxford: Princeton University Press, 2003), 149–62.

many Germans in the regime's criminality have been abundantly documented.[5] For many if not most, the regime's "achievements," defined as the restoration of "order" against the parliamentary logjams and social conflict of Weimar, the rollback of the Versailles "humiliation," economic recovery, and the ostracizing of social outsiders outweighed the limitations on personal freedom and the sporadic grievances of subcultures and institutions.

Nevertheless, historians have devoted little attention to a major problem which preoccupied the Nazi leadership, that of mass consumption.[6] The Nazi party's awareness of a nascent consumer culture in Germany drew the Hitler movement into a controversy that became especially animated after World War I, despite and even because of the Weimar Republic's continuing crises.[7] Confronted by the emergence of the United States, which mass produced goods for private acquisition and material well

5   Emblematic of this position is Robert Gellately's *The Gestapo and German Society: Enforcing Racial Policy 1933–1945* (Oxford: Oxford University Press, 1990). Even Eric Johnson, Gellately's strongest critic, denies neither the significance of popular denunciation nor the selectivity of repression. See his *Nazi Terror: The Gestapo, Jews, and Ordinary Germans* (New York: Basic Books, 1999).

6   This despite Timothy W. Mason's attempt in his *Sozialpolitik im Dritten Reich: Arbeiterklasse und Volksgemeinschaft*, 2nd ed. (Opladen: Westdeutscher Verlag, 1978), subsequently translated as *Social Policy in the Third Reich: The Working Class and the "National Community,"* trans. John Broadwin and ed. Jane Caplan (Providence and Oxford: Berg, 1993), to analyze the regime's sensitivity to consumption and its contribution to the outbreak of war. Because Mason's argument as to the role of working-class discontent in the regime's decision to launch its Blitzkrieg was unconvincing, his awareness of the significance of consumption produced little follow through until recently. Hans-Dieter Schäfer's *Das gespaltene Bewußtsein: Über deutsche Kultur und Lebenswirklichkeit* (Munich, Vienna: Carl Hanser Verlag, 1981) and Detlev J. K. Peukert's *Inside Nazi Germany: Conformity, Opposition, and Racism in Everyday Life*, trans. Richard Deveson (New Haven and London: Yale University Press, 1987) were exceptions to that rule. A new appreciation for consumption, however, has arisen in Hartmut Berghoff's book that incorporates the Nazi era, *Zwischen Kleinstadt und Weltmarkt: Hohner und die Harmonika 1857–1961: Unternehmensgeschichte als Gesellschaftsgeschichte* (Paderborn: Schöningh, 1997), in the special issue of *German History* 19, no. 2 (2001), coedited by Alon Confino and Rudy Koshar, and in Michael Geyer's recent articles, which suggest the relationship between consumption and violence. See, for example, "The Stigma of Violence, Nationalism, and War in Twentieth-Century Germany," *German Studies Review* 16, no. 2 (1993): 75 ff.; "Restorative Elites, German Society and the Nazi Pursuit of War," in *Fascist Italy and Nazi Germany: Comparisons and Contrasts*, ed. Richard Bessel (Cambridge: Cambridge University Press, 1996): 134–64; and "Germany, or the Twentieth Century as History," *South Atlantic Quarterly* 94, no. 4 (Fall 1997): 663–702. Nevertheless, we still lack a work that is as ambitious as Mason's, yet more successful in exploring the Nazi regime's approach to consumption in all its complexity.

7   Following Michael Geyer, I distinguish between mass consumption, which clearly existed during the interwar period, and consumer culture, which did not emerge full blown until after World War II. The ambivalence toward proliferation of goods became gradually less evident in the postwar West as consumer cultures eliminated barriers of taste in the purchase of goods, while asserting the right to consume as a badge of citizenship and consumption as a source of happiness independent of work. See "In Pursuit of Happiness: Consumption, Mass Culture, and Consumerism," in *Shattered Past*, especially 306–14.

being,[8] and alternatively by the left's endorsement of collective entitlement that the Soviet Union newly embodied, Weimar debates on consumption exacerbated the Republic's deep political and social fissures. From the mid-twenties, as the Nazi party grew into a mass movement that sought power by legal means, its leadership rejected the socialist and American or "Fordist" routes to raising living standards through consumption. The Marxist presumption of class conflict was anathema to the Nazis, for it violated their vision of a unified racial community, while distribution according to need affronted the desire of Nazi leaders to reward "performance" (*Leistung*) in service to the nation. Fordism, on the other hand, represented commercialism, the denigration of German "quality" work, the "materialist" worship of commodities, and instant gratification of individual wants.

Yet, despite the party's suspicion of consumption, Hitler envisioned a future of material abundance once the obtainment of "living space" (*Lebensraum*) assured Germany's continental domination and biological survival. To be sure, the Nazi regime aggressively promoted production over consumption after 1933, for only rearmament and in all likelihood war would bring empire. It discriminated against consumer production and curtailed imports of consumer goods, following the führer's insistence that future prosperity derived from present sacrifice. Still, the regime needed to accommodate the party's diverse constituencies, who expected a better life after the privations of Weimar, for appeals to sacrifice would not suffice. To meet that need and simultaneously rearm, the Third Reich fashioned a paradoxical blend of belt tightening measures and foretastes of the good life for the "master race" (*Herrenvolk*).

Founded in November 1933 ten months after Hitler's assumption to power, Strength through Joy best embodied the Third Reich's attempts to improve German living standards until living space could be achieved.[9] By

---

8   On this point see Victoria de Grazia and Ellen Furlough, *The Sex of Things: Gender and Consumption in Historical Perspective* (Berkeley and London: University of California Press, 1996), 5.

9   Despite existing dissertations and articles on KdF, which include detailed analyses of the social bases of KdF's clientele and KdF's contributions to the regime's foreign policy, Strength through Joy has eluded a book-length study that links it to the Nazi regime's strategies to raise German living standards. The dissertations include Bruno Frommann, "Reisen im Dienste politischer Zielsetzungen: Arbeiter-Reisen und 'Kraft durch Freude' Fahrten" (Diss: Stuttgart, 1993); Laurence Van Zandt Moyer, "The *Kraft durch Freude* Movement in Nazi Germany, 1933–1939" (Diss: Northwestern, 1967), and the oft-cited Wolfhard Buchholz, "Die nationalsozialistische Gemeinschaft *Kraft durch Freude*: Freizeitgestaltung und Arbeiterschaft im Dritten Reich" (Diss: Munich, 1976). On KdF's relationship to Nazi foreign policy and to the Italian Fascist leisure organization "After Work" (Dopolavoro), see Daniela Liebscher's "Mit KdF 'die Welt erschliessen': Der Beitrag der KdF-Reisen zur Aussenpolitik der Deutschen Arbeitsfront, 1934–1939," in *1999: Zeitschrift für Sozialgeschichte des 20. und 21. Jahrhunderts* 14, no. 1 (March 1999): 42–72, and "Organisierte Freizeit als Sozialpolitik: Die faschistische Opera

mediating between its clientele and market-based leisure to keep its costs low, KdF strove to open the cultural practices of the middle and upper classes to workers, thus ameliorating their quality of life while compensating for wage freezes, longer working hours, and the restrictions on private consumption. As much the product of the hypercompetitive environment of the Third Reich, in which KdF appropriated the space available to it, as the result of deliberate design, KdF provided leisure activities on a scale that no other party or state agency could rival. Yet Strength through Joy also submitted to the regime's campaign for higher productivity. Although acknowledging that workers deserved recreation and vacations, KdF's leaders and operatives argued that work inspired individual creativity and national resurgence, the sustenance of the harmonious racial community (*Volksgemeinschaft*). Thus they maintained that KdF was no mere leisure-time organization. Rather, its programs, which included its workplace beautification project, the Beauty of Labor (Schönheit der Arbeit, or SdA), embraced the totality of workers' "creative lives." They would improve the work environment, guide workers to purposeful and restorative leisure that stimulated productivity, and deepen workers' attachment to nation and race.

For KdF to have linked leisure to productivity meant that it rejected a commonplace, if increasingly contested, assumption that the "standard of living" meant exclusively the possession of economic goods, whether the basic necessities of food, clothing, and housing, or other commodities and services that satisfied individual desires.[10] Adhering to the Nazi party's opposition to mass consumption and mass culture that it had articulated while bidding for power, KdF promoters expanded the definition of a "high" standard of living to incorporate the personal

Nazionale Dopolavoro und die NS-Gemeinschaft Kraft durch Freude 1925–1939," in *Faschismus und Gesellschaft in Italien*, ed. Jens Petersen and Wolfgang Schieder (Cologne: SH Verlag, 1998): 67–90. Finally, see the pioneering essays of Hasso Spode, "'Der deutsche Arbeiter reist!' Massentourismus im Dritten Reich," in *Sozialgeschichte der Freizeit: Untersuchungen zum Wandel der Alltagskultur in Deutschland*, ed. Gerhard Huck (Wupperthal: Peter Hammer Verlag, 1980): 281–306; "Arbeiterurlaub im Dritten Reich," in *Angst, Belohnung, Zucht, und Ordnung: Herrschaftsmechanismen im Nationalsozialismus*, ed. Carola Sachse (Opladen: Westdeutscher Verlag, 1982): 275–328; and "Ein Seebad für zwanzigtausend Volksgenossen: Zur Grammatik und Geschichte des fordistischen Urlaubs," in *Reisekultur in Deutschland: Von der Weimarer Republik zum "Dritten Reich,"* ed. P. J. Brenner (Tübingen: Max Niemeyer Verlag, 1997): 7–47. While building on Buchholz's detail regarding the social bases of KdF tourism, Spode analyzes it better. The paucity of archival material on Strength through Joy, the result of the destruction of its headquarters by Allied bombing, has contributed to the dearth of scholarship on KdF.

10   For a contemporary critique of mass consumption and materialist definitions of the standard of living, see the work of the German–American rural sociologist, Carle Zimmerman, *Consumption and Standards of Living* (New York: Arno Press, 1976). This edition is a reprint of the original, published in 1936. (Oxford: Oxford University Press, 2001).

satisfaction that workers derived from contributing to collective ends and the nonmaterial recognition that they obtained in return. Harmonizing the interests of employers and workers, a goal that Nazi leaders shared with conservative social theorists, the "joy" of work and the "honor" accorded to manual labor signified a "high" standard of living, which consisted of hierarchical but paternalistic shop floor "communities," the nonalienated relationship between workers and their products, and the integration of workers in the racial community. If rearmament entailed the postponement of material reward, KdF would still give wage earners a priceless source of happiness and fulfillment, the recognition of their "creativity" as producers and their contributions to national revival. Likewise Strength through Joy used its leisure programs, especially tourism which it developed to provide respite from the workaday environment, to reward work performance and enhance productivity once the worker returned to the job. Eschewing hedonistic pleasure seeking, Strength through Joy joined the self-improving high mindedness of middle-class travel with the promotion of the racial community through package tours.

Nevertheless, KdF's vacation trips compromised its productivism, even as KdF promoted the noncommercial goals of its leisure. Strength through Joy catered to consumer expectations as economic recovery ended unemployment and raised family incomes, recognizing that individual pleasure and autonomy mattered as much as the collective experience of cultural uplift and national renewal. While KdF directed its low-cost, noncommercial consumption toward collective ends, it simultaneously embedded visions of future prosperity in the dream worlds of the present, advertising material "luxuries" to appeal to its audience. If KdF distinguished its definition of the "standard of living" from the "materialist" hunger for consumer goods, it nonetheless delivered purchasable cultural practices with consumerist implications. Strength through Joy's tourism, in fact, became attractive because it offered opportunities for pleasure and self-realization similar to those advertised by the promoters of commercial leisure. Its willingness to allow popular desires to seduce it enhanced its popularity and that of the regime that sponsored it.

Given the Nazi regime's sensitivity to popular opinion, it is not surprising that Strength through Joy had to deliver more than regimentation or even cultural enrichment that KdF tourists sought along with relaxation and pleasure. Nor is it surprising that KdF evolved through the interplay of its aims and those of its clientele. Even the Third Reich's network of repression spread its tentacles in the course of an insidious dialogue between the Nazi leadership and popular opinion.[11] To recognize, however,

---

11 See Gellately, *Backing Hitler: Consent and Coercion in Nazi Germany* (Oxford, 2001), especially 35–69, for the compatibility between the Nazi press and popular prejudices.

that consumption emerged as a significant means of negotiation between the Nazi regime and its racially "valuable" citizens acknowledges a crucial component of the regime's legitimacy. In a less direct but subtler way than popular denunciations to the Gestapo, KdF's management of consumption exacerbated the exclusions that defined the Third Reich. KdF's mélange of respite, self-discovery, and fellowship gave racially acceptable Germans positive experiences of the Third Reich, which the regime's victims did not share.

Nazism was not unique in the industrialized world in viewing market-based consumption and the unregulated leisure that helped to sustain it as a threat to production. Nor did it stand alone in defining the "standard of living" as more than the possession of material things for personal gratification. Nor was it unusual, finally, in pursuing collective goals over individual needs, fearing that private consumption threatened social cohesion.[12] Nevertheless, KdF's dream worlds modified its productivism, antimaterialism, *völkisch* collectivism, and gospel of delayed gratification. Moreover, Hitler's permanent solution for guaranteeing a German standard of living suitable for a "master race" departed radically from the lamentations of conservative critics of mass consumption and mass culture in Germany and elsewhere, who sought the permanent containment of desires.[13] Expansion and the subordination, exploitation, or extermination of racial "inferiors" would assure the racial community's biological reproduction *and* material abundance. The good life would thrive in the New Order along with the honor accorded to labor and the provision of culture for all. As Nazi leaders availed themselves of the rewards of power in an orgy of conspicuous consumption, suppressing their pre-1933 contempt for "materialism," KdF manufactured dreams of future prosperity for the master race, which German occupiers carried out after 1939. KdF's noncommercial consumption provided the transition between Nazism's condemnations of consumerism prior to 1933 and the greed mixed with violence that flourished with the expropriation of German Jewish property in 1938 and again with total war.

I have organized *Strength through Joy* to chart the evolution of its aims as they translated into practice. Opening in Chapter 1 with a discussion of the debates on consumption during the Weimar, I describe the Nazi party's rejection of the two prevailing modes of mass consumption, the Marxist model of collective entitlement and the American, or "Fordist,"

---

12 Evidence of this could be found even in the heartland of mass consumption, the United States, as revealed in Zimmerman's critique *Consumption and Standards of Living*.

13 On this topic see Wolfgang König, *Geschichte der Konsumgesellschaft* (Stuttgart: Franz Steiner Verlag, 2000), 441–50. On the defeat of "democratic leisure" in the West, see Gary Cross, *Time and Money: The Making of Consumer Culture* (London and New York: Routledge, 1993).

methods of mass production and distribution to satisfy private needs. I then turn in Chapter 2 to the emergence of Strength through Joy as the Nazi regime's short-term solution to mass desires after 1933 until living space could be acquired. Strength through Joy's rise occurred in the context of the international debate on the "problems" of work, consumption, and leisure, the power struggles of the Nazi regime, and the priority that the Third Reich accorded to rearmament. As an agency that adhered to the leader principle (*Führerprinzip*) and a militarized, disciplined, and hierarchical structure, KdF stressed the indivisibility of work and leisure consistent with its productivist definition of the standard of living. It thus ruled out individualistic and autonomous leisure practices that fostered unlimited desires. Like the imperatives of the regime that spawned it, Strength through Joy believed that it "honored" workers according to their ability to produce for nation and race. By improving the conditions of their labor, affording them cultural experiences comparable to those accorded to the middle class, and integrating them in the Nazi racial community, KdF would contribute its share to eliminating class conflict and the appeal of Marxism. The range of KdF's offerings, the millions that it impacted, the social diversity of its clientele which included workers, and the international recognition that KdF acquired testified to its success in carving out a place for itself in the social Darwinian climate of the Third Reich.

Nevertheless as I make clear in Chapter 3, Strength through Joy's emphasis on the workplace as the key to regulating leisure time and disciplining consumption, most clearly illustrated by the Beauty of Labor (SdA), came under stress due to the inherent coercion of SdA's plant communities. Although solidifying the power of employers that the Weimar system had once limited and convincing many wage earners of the regime's commitment to improving conditions on the shop floor, SdA proved less able to build popular support for the regime. Thus, I then turn my attention to Strength through Joy's domestic and international tourism, devoting Chapter 4 primarily to the perspective of KdF's leaders and Chapter 5 to the perspective of its participants. Tourism became KdF's most determined attempt to create a non-Marxist, non-Fordist, and characteristically Nazi mode of consumption. By exploiting tourism's less overtly "material" character as a concatenation of images, fantasies, and experiences, it successfully purveyed the noncommercial consumption of culture, which muted the conflict between consumption and rearmament. While promoting an edifying tourism that would bind its participants to the Nazi racial community, it increasingly encouraged self-fulfillment, pleasure seeking, and individual choice, which together would be satisfied through KdF's increasing emphasis on "luxury." Especially by exposing German tourists to the lower material living standards in its southern European and North African destinations, which encouraged tourists to compare their lives favorably with those they observed, Strength through Joy contributed significantly to the Third Reich's popular support.

Although forced to curtail its tourism during the war, Strength through Joy's civilian and troop entertainment, as seen in Chapter 6, became integral to the German war effort, reflecting the Nazi regime's fear of repeating the collapse of popular morale that took place during World War I. KdF substantially, if indirectly, contributed to the blend of racism and consumption that characterized Nazi-occupied Europe, and especially the extermination of the Jews. The defeat of the Nazi regime revitalized the competition between the Marxist and American-style roads to mass consumption, while eliminating the "German consumption" embodied in KdF. As I describe in the Epilogue, the postwar Germanys became unsuitable environments for a KdF style mediation between the market and consumers, albeit for different reasons. In any case, market-based consumption ultimately triumphed over the Soviet Bloc's vision of mass entitlement, thus ending a battle that had begun after World War I.

Strength through Joy encompassed many programs besides tourism, including its effort to increase popular access to the performing and visual arts. Nevertheless for two reasons, this book concentrates on the Beauty of Labor and tourism. Those ventures provide the clearest illustration of KdF's attempt to define the standard of living as accelerated production and noncommercial consumption by recognizing work and leisure as complementary aspects of workers' "creative" lives. Arguably, the Beauty of Labor and tourism also constituted KdF's most ambitious projects. In SdA, aestheticizing the shop floor meant eliminating class conflict and creating the plant community, as well as reconstructing the identities of workers so that they would become full-fledged members of the racial community. In addition to generating most of KdF's revenue, tourism became KdF's most impressive instrument of propaganda for foreign and domestic consumption. Not surprisingly, the evidence regarding the reception of KdF's workplace aestheticization and its tourism, so crucial to assessing the manner in which Nazism's attention to consumption resonated below, is the richest for those two programs. In addition to the situation reports of the Social Democratic Party in Exile (Sopade) and other underground leftist organizations, such as New Beginning (Neu Beginnen), the surveillance reports of SD and Gestapo agents, who monitored KdF tourists, provide invaluable insights into popular attitudes.[14]

---

14 *Deutschland-Berichte der Sozialdemokratischen Partei Deutschlands (Sopade) 1934–1940*, 7 vols. (Frankfurt am Main: Verlag Petra Nettelbeck, 1980); *Berichte über die Lage in Deutschland: die Lagemeldungen der Gruppe Neu Beginnen aus dem Dritten Reich, 1933–1936*, ed. Bernd Stöver (Bonn: Dietz, 1996). Gestapo and SD surveillance reports on KdF vacation trips are found in the Bundesarchiv, Berlin-Lichterfelde (BAL), in the files of the Reich Security Main Office (Reichssicherheitshauptamt, or RSHA), R58 943–50 and 609.

I integrate KdF's other programs into my narrative where appropriate, not least because factory beautification and tourism are capacious enough to accommodate them.

The issues that Strength through Joy addressed – the relationship between work and leisure, the introduction of paid vacations, and the social consequences of mass production and consumption – were widely discussed throughout the industrialized world. Although the product of a chauvinistic and autarkic regime, KdF participated in the international debate regarding the "problems" of leisure and consumption during an era of social conflict, economic hardship and conservative fears of individualism, democracy, and declining work discipline. As the product of Nazism's competition with socialism and Fordism, Strength through Joy's leaders hoped to demonstrate that the Third Reich "cared" for workers. For that reason, however, KdF revealed the ugly distinctiveness of the National Socialist approach to raising the standard of living. Its noncommercial consumption protected rapid rearmament and expansion, while reinforcing and even widening the gulf between racially "valuable" Germans and persecuted minorities. Its tourism forecasted a German imperium while confirming the racism of its vacationers and the regime's own legitimacy. KdF's wartime entertainment revealed Germany's dependence on living space at the expense of Germany's neighbors to secure prosperity for the racially acceptable. Although aesthetically pleasing workplaces and smiling tourists appear tangential to emergency decrees, concentration camps, and genocide, Strength through Joy exposed Nazism's fusion of pleasure and violence.

1

Nazism, Popular Aspirations, and Mass Consumption on the Road to Power

Adolf Hitler's assumption to power on January 30, 1933 resulted from the Nazi party's ability to build an unstable but formidable coalition of elite and popular supporters. As the Weimar Republic succumbed to economic crisis and political fragmentation, the Nazi movement collected a diverse electorate frustrated with economic hardship, social conflict, and parliamentary impasse. Needing mass support to pursue an authoritarian alternative to the Weimar "system," Germany's conservative agrarian, military, bureaucratic, and business leaderships suppressed their misgivings toward Nazism's populist radicalism to form a government of "national concentration" with Hitler as chancellor. Nazism's promises to restore German power and undermine the post–World War I settlements, promote economic recovery and self-sufficiency, destroy Weimar democracy and with it the political leverage of the Socialists and Communists, contributed to the party's success. Yet the NSDAP distinguished itself among Weimar political parties as much by the skill with which it unified incompatible interests as by its platforms. The competition among Nazism's constituencies fueled the brutal competition and greed that exacerbated the Third Reich's genocidal dynamism.[1]

Nazism's vision of a harmonious, synchronized, racial community (*Volksgemeinschaft*) unified its campaign platforms.[2] The Nazi party imagined an integrated, racially purified nation as an alternative to the

1 Despite their contrasting evaluations regarding the social bases of the Nazi electorate and membership, the following are indispensable to understanding the Nazi party's emergence as a mass movement: Thomas Childers, *The Nazi Voter: The Social Foundations of Fascism in Germany, 1919–1933* (Chapel Hill and London: University of North Carolina Press, 1983); Jürgen Falter, *Hitlers Wähler* (Munich: C.H. Beck, 1991); Richard Hamilton, *Who Voted for Hitler?* (Princeton: Princeton University Press, 1982); Michael Kater, *The Nazi Party: A Social Profile of Members and Leaders, 1919–1945* (Cambridge, Massachusetts and London: Harvard University Press, 1983); and Peter Manstein, *Die Mitglieder und Wähler der NSDAP 1919–1933* (Frankfurt am Main, New York: Peter Lang, 1989).
2 See Peter Fritzsche, *Germans into Nazis* (Cambridge, Massachusetts and London: Harvard University Press, 1998) for his discussion of the populist nationalism inherent in the Nazis' appeal.

11

class, regional, and religious divisions that survived the unification of Germany in 1871, and sharpened after World War I in the wake of defeat, revolution, hyperinflation, and then the Depression. All deepened the yearning for the "return" of the "front experience," the common purpose that fighting in the trenches had supposedly produced, which provided the racial community's intellectual rationale. Paradoxically Nazism encouraged individual achievement to accommodate popular expectations of a higher standard of living and popular resentment against class distinctions, at the same time that it promoted the common good over private interest. While demanding that individuals sacrifice their private interests to an ethnically exclusive nation, the Hitler movement promised to reward achievement (*Leistung*) and encourage upward mobility. Although the party enunciated it more stridently than did the population at large, antisemitism articulated present grievances and future aspirations.[3] Nazism's emphasis on social mobility through individual merit, combined with its campaign to erode class and regional particularism, exerted a powerful appeal amidst the divisive politics of late Weimar Germany.[4] To reconcile the clash between personal achievement and devotion to the "racial community," the NSDAP claimed that talent and ambition in service to the nation would bring Germany's independence from foreign enemies and "international Jewry," and its emergence as a global power.

3   Despite the claim of Daniel Jonah Goldhagen in his *Hitler's Willing Executioners: Ordinary Germans and the Holocaust* (New York: Alfred A. Knopf, 1996) as to a pervasive "eliminationist" antisemitism in German culture, the scholarship on the Nazi rise to power has generally maintained that other issues proved more immediate to the German electorate than anti-Jewish hatred. For surveys of that scholarship, see Oded Heilbronner, "The Role of Nazi Antisemitism in the Party's Activity and Propaganda: A Regional Historiographical Study," *Leo Baeck Institute Yearbook* 35 (1991): 397–439, and Jill Stephenson, "The Rise of the Nazis: *Sonderweg* or Spanner in the Works?" in *German History since 1800*, ed. Mary Fulbrook (London: Edward Arnold, 1997): 298–317. Nevertheless, we cannot overlook the utility of antisemitism as a catchall diagnosis of Germany's misfortunes. See John Weiss, *Ideology of Death: Why the Holocaust Happened in Germany* (Chicago: Ivan R. Dee, 1996), 271–87.

4   In recent years, scholars who stress the diversity of the Nazi electorate have emphasized the Nazis' ability to attract wage earners. See especially Falter, *Hitlers Wähler*, 198–230; and Conan Fischer, ed., *The Rise of National Socialism and the Working Classes in Germany* (Providence, Oxford: Berghahn Books, 1996). On the other hand, Claus-Christian Szejnmann, *Nazism in Central Germany: The Brownshirts in "Red" Saxony* (New York, Oxford: Berghahn Books, 1999), especially 92–141, and Michael Schneider, *Unterm Hakenkreuz: Arbeiter und Arbeiterbewegung 1933–1939* (Bonn: J.H.W. Dietz Nachf., 1999), 145–59, suggest to the contrary that Nazism's ability to undercut the left was more limited than recent claims suggest. Still, there can be no denying Nazism's appeal to workers who sought upward mobility, and who in turn contributed to a broad populist Nazi constituency. See William Brustein, *The Social Origins of the Nazi Party, 1925–1933* (New Haven and London, Yale University Press, 1996), 156–8.

Between Scarcity and Abundance: Mass Consumption in the Weimar Republic

Despite Weimar's economic weakness, the popular expectations of upward mobility and improved material well being testified to Germany's emergence as Europe's most advanced economy, having already overtaken Great Britain before World War I.[5] Nevertheless, it also reflected the post-war extension of mass culture and mass consumption, especially between 1924 and 1929, Weimar's post-stabilization years. The cinema's commercial success among moviegoers of all classes revealed Hollywood's dominance in the production and distribution of films and its influence in defining a broad consensus of taste. The popularity of Hollywood films and "movie stars" enjoying lives of luxury fascinated the movie-going public to such an extent that the commercial impact of cinematic alternatives, German expressionism, the "new objectivity" (*neue Sachlichkeit*), and the didactic films of the left paled in comparison. Jazz, swing, pulp fiction, and spectator sports appealed to the young, while the radio developed well-defined markets, especially among women, that blurred the lines between public and private.[6] Formidable barriers prevented the rapid increase in the ownership of automobiles, including the delayed introduction of assembly-line techniques by German car manufacturers. Yet the middle-class purchase of cars, stimulated by newspaper and magazine advertisements, automobile shows, and automobile clubs, bore witness to the desire for commodities once exclusively the possession of the wealthy, as means of personal empowerment and self-identification. Propelled by the images of motorized warfare from World War I, the motorcar symbolized speed, individual autonomy, and self-definition, dissipating the

---

5 Volker Berghahn, "Demographic Growth, Industrialization and Social Change," in *German History since 1800*, ed. Mary Fulbrook (London: Arnold, 1997): 171–2.

6 Hollywood's ascendancy after World War I in Europe was rapid and irreversible. See Victoria de Grazia, "Mass Culture and Sovereignty: The American Challenge to European Cinemas, 1920–1960," *Journal of Modern History* 61, no. 1 (March 1989): 53–87; and Richard Pells, *Not Like Us: How Europeans Have Loved, Hated, and Transformed American Culture since World War II* (New York: Basic Books, 1997), 13–19. For Hollywood's impact in Germany and the extension of radio listening, see Thomas Saunders, *Hollywood in Berlin: American Cinema and Weimar Germany* (Berkeley, London: University of California Press, 1994), especially 241–50; Bruce Murray, *Film and the German Left in the Weimar Republic: From Caligari to Kuhle Wampe* (Austin: University of Texas Press, 1990); Anton Kaes, Martin Jay, and Edward Dimendberg, eds., *The Weimar Republic Sourcebook* (Berkeley: University of California Press, 1994): 393–411, 594–616, 617–35, and 655–72; Heide Fehrenbach, *Cinema in Democratizing Germany: Reconstructing National Identity after Hitler* (Chapel Hill and London: University of North Carolina Press, 1995), 26–41; and Kate Lacey, *Feminine Frequencies: Gender, German Radio, and the Public Sphere, 1923–1945* (Ann Arbor: University of Michigan Press, 1996), 17–95.

antiautomobile protests of the Wilhelmine period.[7] Increases in the production of household appliances and cameras, in addition to the advertisements in the mass media for cosmetics, stockings, cigarettes, fashions, and Coca Cola, created and reflected the desire for consumer goods as badges of status and self-expression.[8]

Although a less tangible commodity than other consumer goods, tourism as a blend of advertised services, cultural experiences, and anticipated pleasures also contributed to the Weimar Republic's reputation as the incubator of "modern" lifestyles, which celebrated self-gratification and individual choice.[9] Stimulated by the deployment of mass conscripted armies during World War I, domestic and foreign travel attracted constituencies besides the educated middle classes, who composed the principal market for leisure trips prior to 1914. Package tours put together by an expanding infrastructure of travel agencies, hotels, pensions, and shipping lines became commonplace among civil servants, teachers, and white-collar workers in the service sector, especially single female white-collar workers, whose disposable income allowed a degree of freedom from rigidly defined gender roles. Because two-thirds of salaried employees and nearly all civil servants acquired paid vacations before World War I, those groups composed a ready market for the promotions of tourism entrepreneurs. The extension of paid vacations through wage agreements to blue-collar workers after 1918, although concentrated in urban areas and disproportionately in public sector employment, enabled tourism to attract still broader social constituencies. By the late twenties, the

7 For automobiles in Germany before and after World War I, see Uwe Fraunholz, *Motorphobia: Anti-automobiler Protest in Kaiserreich und Weimarer Republik* (Göttingen: Vandenhoeck and Ruprecht, 2002); Barbara Haubner, *Nervenkitzel und Freizeitvergnügen: Automobilismus in Deutschland, 1886–1914* (Göttingen: Vandenhoeck and Ruprecht, 1998); Kurt Möser, "World War I and the Creation of Desire for Automobiles in Germany," in *Getting and Spending: European and American Consumer Societies in the Twentieth Century*, ed. Susan Strasser, Charles McGovern, and Matthias Judt (Cambridge: Cambridge University Press, 1998): 195–222; Ulrich Kubisch, *Das Automobil als Lesestoff: Zur Geschichte der deutschen Motorpresse 1898–1998* (Berlin, 1998); and Rudy Koshar, "On the History of the Automobile in Everyday Life, *Contemporary European History* 10, no. 1 (2001): 143–54.

8 Compared to the scholarship on consumerism in the United States and Western Europe, the development of consumer culture has only recently begun to attract the attention of historians of Germany. Pioneering in this regard was Detlev J. K. Peukert's *The Weimar Republic: The Crisis of Classical Modernity*, trans. Richard Deveson (New York: Hill and Wang, 1987), 174–7. The special issue of *German History*, "Régimes of Consumer Culture: New Narratives in Twentieth-Century German History," vol. 19, no. 2 (2001), put together by Alon Confino and Rudy Koshar, attests to the emerging interest in consumption in Germany.

9 For the relationship between tourism and consumption, see Shelley Baranowski and Ellen Furlough, eds., *Being Elsewhere: Tourism, Consumer Culture, and Identity in Modern Europe and North America* (Ann Arbor: University of Michigan Press, 2001): 6–7.

attention that the General Federation of German Trade Unions and especially the Social Democratic party (SPD) devoted to vacations and tourism for workers attests to their importance for the leaders of organized labor. The Socialists and the unions raised horizons among a sector of the population once least able and least likely to take advantage of those practices. Workers composed ten percent of the total number of tourists, significantly above the percentage prior to 1914. Women too composed a large proportion of the working-class travelers, in marked contrast to female underrepresentation in working-class sports clubs. All told, a diverse group of tourism promoters, including state and local agencies, the producers of guidebooks, labor organizers, and travel agents, catered to more diverse clienteles than those who had toured before the war, Baedecker guides in hand.[10]

Weimar consumerism did not compare to that in the United States where because of the adoption of mass production and distribution, the right to consume became a badge of citizenship along with the ability to produce. Nor did it remotely resemble the vibrant consumer culture that took hold during the West German "economic miracle" of the fifties and sixties. The gospel that triumphed after World War II, that "getting and spending" defined economic success, broke irrevocably from the ethic of saving and limits on desire that characterized the interwar period.[11] A telescopic view from the end of World War I to the currency reform of 1948 shows that the budgets of working-class families left little flexibility beyond the essentials of food, clothing, and rent, and modest expenditures for recreation and sport. Aside from day outings, visits to the cinema, or other cultural activities, luxuries such as vacation travel remained a rare experience, so unusual that one miner's son from the Ruhr, who in 1928 served as a delegate to the International Socialist Youth Convention

10 For discussions of Weimar tourism, see Christine Keitz, *Reisen als Leitbild: Die Entstehung des modernen Massentourismus in Deutschland* (Munich: Deutscher Taschenbuch Verlag, 1997), 21–190, and Rudy Koshar, *German Travel Cultures* (Oxford and New York: Berg, 2000), 65–114.

11 Arne Andersen, *Der Traum vom guten Leben: Alltags- und Konsumgeschichte vom Wirtschaftswunder bis Heute* (Frankfurt and New York: Campus Verlag, 1999), 257; and Konrad H. Jarausch and Michael Geyer, *Shattered Past: Reconstructing German Histories* (Princeton and Oxford: Princeton University Press, 2003), 311–13. For the American experience, see Charles McGovern, "Consumption and Citizenship in the United States, 1900–1940"; and Meg Jacobs, "The Politics of Plenty in the Twentieth-Century United States," in *The Politics of Consumption: Material Culture and Citizenship in Europe and America*, ed. Martin Daunton and Matthew Hilton (Oxford and New York: Berg, 2001): 223–39; and especially Lisabeth Cohen, *A Consumers' Republic: The Politics of Mass Consumption in Postwar America* (New York: Alfred A. Knopf, 2003), 17–61. For a comparison of mass consumption in the United States and Germany, see Wolfgang König, *Geschichte der Konsumgesellschaft* (Stuttgart: Franz Steiner Verlag, 2000), 108–22.

in Hamburg, considered his trip equivalent to a voyage around the world.[12]

Moreover, if all classes in Weimar Germany considered thrift a cardinal virtue in the face of scarcity and economic crisis, spending habits and consumer choices varied according to class as they had before 1914.[13] Despite promoting tourism for workers and advocating mass consumption as means of achieving social equality, Social Democrats defined consumption less as the possession of consumer durables than the assurance of the necessities of food, clothing, and shelter. The proposals of home economists, government officials, and housewives' associations to create modern, efficient households did not project the benefits of labor saving appliances onto working-class women, nor did they envision increases in working-class household consumption. Rather, in a position the Nazi regime would itself come to adopt, the "rationalized" household practiced austerity in the interests of economic recovery.[14] The psychological and material impact of hardship partially explains why the popularity of the inexpensive leisure-time activities that Strength through Joy promoted did not reemerge in the postwar Federal Republic, when rising incomes and sustained prosperity deadened painful experiences of scarcity and defeat.

Yet if the need for sacrifice constrained popular hopes for higher levels of consumption, it did not eradicate them. The hardships that the home front endured during World War I in which consumers organized to combat shortages and high prices, Weimar's weak economy relative

12 Michael Zimmermann, "Aufbruchshoffnungen: Junge Bergleute in den dreißiger Jahre," in *"Die Jahre weiß man nicht, wo man die heute hinsetzen soll": Faschismus-Erfahrungen im Ruhr-Gebiet*, vol. 1, *Lebensgeschichte und Sozialkultur im Ruhrgebiet 1930 bis 1960*, ed. Lutz Niethammer (Bonn: J.H.W. Dietz Nachf., 1983): 100. For working-class expenses, see Heinrich-August Winkler, *Der Schein der Normalität: Arbeiter und Arbeiterbewegung in der Weimarer Republik 1924 bis 1930* (Berlin and Bonn: Verlag J.H.W. Dietz Nachf., 1985), 81–90; Michael Wildt, *Vom kleinen Wohlstand: Eine Konsumgeschichte der fünfziger Jahre* (Frankfurt am Main: Fischer Taschenbuch Verlag, 1994), 14–23; Karen Hagemann, "'Wir hatten mehr Notjahre als reichliche Jahre . . .' Lebenshaltung und Hausarbeit Hamburger Arbeiterfamilien in der Weimarer Republic," in *Arbeiter im 20. Jahrhundert*, ed. Klaus Tenfelde (Stuttgart: Klett-Cotta, 1991): 200–40; and W. L. Guttsman, *Workers' Culture in Weimar Germany: Between Tradition and Commitment* (New York, Oxford, Munich: Berg, 1990), 116–17.
13 Klaus Tenfelde, "Klassenspezifische Konsummuster im Deutschen Kaiserreich," in *Europäische Konsumgeschichte: Zur Gesellschafts-und Kulturgeschichte des Konsums (18. bis 20. Jahrhundert)*, ed. Hannes Siegrist, Hartmut Kaeble, Jürgen Kocka (Frankfurt: Campus Verlag, 1997): 245–66.
14 See Victoria de Grazia's remarks in *The Sex of Things: Gender and Consumption in Historical Perspective*, ed. de Grazia and Ellen Furlough (Berkeley, London: University of California Press, 1996): 151–61; and especially Mary Nolan, *Visions of Modernity: American Business and the Modernization of Germany* (New York, Oxford: Oxford University Press, 1994), 206–26; and Nancy Reagin, "Comparing Apples and Oranges: Housewives and the Politics of Consumption in Interwar Germany," in *Getting and Spending*, ed. Strasser, McGovern, and Judt: 241–61.

to the prosperity of the Wilhelmine era, and the Depression which created pent-up demand fueled dreams of a more prosperous future. The republic's economic burdens even encouraged practices such as tourism because of their perceived economic benefit.[15] The prospect of earning revenue encouraged communal and state governments to develop their towns, cities, and regions for the consumption of tourists, while the desire to achieve a favorable balance of payments to compensate for reparations payments stimulated efforts to make Germany attractive to foreign travelers.[16] Thus, consumer expectations infiltrated domestic political debates, sharpening the social and ideological polarization of interwar Germany, for those debates frequently alluded to the two most prevalent models for increasing mass consumption, American-style capitalism and socialism.[17] The impact of the United States and the emergence of the Soviet Union as the first successful Marxist revolution raised compelling questions. Did models from abroad, as many suggested, provide viable ways to improve German living standards, and in the process, did they promise increased national strength and independence through material prosperity? Or, as the German right repeatedly insisted, did they intensify Germany's postwar victimization by outside forces?

The Politics of Mass Consumption: Fordism and Socialism

The emergence of the United States as a global industrial power in the early twentieth century and its decisive intervention in the Great War engendered among Europeans a mixture of envy, admiration, and fear. While identifying its "modernity" as the source of its economic success, many sought to repel or at least contain America's economic and cultural

15 For consumer behavior during the war, see Belinda Davis, *Home Fires Burning: Food, Politics, and Everyday Life in World War I Berlin* (Chapel Hill and London: University of North Carolina Press, 2000). On Weimar's disappointments, consult Richard Bessel's *Germany after the First World War* (Oxford: Clarendon Press, 1993). Gary Cross's *Time and Money: The Making of Consumer Culture* (London and New York: Routledge, 1993), 128–53 underscores the Depression's impact on demand throughout the industrialized world. Finally for Weimar's burgeoning "mass consumption of culture," see Geyer, in Jarausch and Geyer, *Shattered Dreams*, 286–93.

16 Keitz, *Reisen als Leitbild*, 54–69; Rudy Koshar, *Germany's Transient Pasts: Preservation and National Memory in the Twentieth Century* (Chapel Hill and London: University of North Carolina Press, 1998), 145.

17 The discussion that follows has benefited greatly from Victoria de Grazia's essay, "Changing Consumption Regimes in Europe, 1930–1970: Comparative Perspectives on the Distribution Problem," in *Getting and Spending*, ed. Strasser, McGovern, and Judt: 59–83. Although de Grazia focuses less on the left as having provided a consumption model than I do, she provides a profitable way to understand the political and social conflicts of interwar and post–World War II Europe.

power.[18] In interwar Germany, the widely used term "Americanism" (*Amerikanismus*) encompassed the economic and business innovations which politicians, intellectuals, and corporate managers deemed crucial to America's wealth and productivity. These included the methods of increasing labor efficiency encapsulated in the theory of "scientific management" which the engineer Frederick Winslow Taylor advocated before World War I. By precisely correlating the placement of materials with the movements required for a particular task, Taylor's time–motion studies promised increased productivity, greater corporate profits, higher wages for productive workers without collective bargaining, and harmony between employers and employees. Americanism also referred to the mechanized mass production, product standardization, and mass advertising of inexpensive consumer goods, captured in the term "Fordism" (*Fordismus*) after the auto baron Henry Ford, the pioneer of the mechanized assembly line, whose autobiography became a best seller in Germany during the twenties. Although directed toward the entirety of production rather than the narrower issue of labor efficiency, Fordism shared with Taylorism the assumption that enhanced productivity and higher wages for workers would raise purchasing power and eliminate scarcity.[19] The American model for raising living standards gave rise to the expression "economic miracle" (*Wirtschaftswunder*) that referred to the sources of American ascendancy; a term that described the hothouse West German economy after World War II.[20]

German employers and managers selectively adapted American production techniques to fit their needs. Stripped of its potential for yielding high wages but not the principle of scaling wages by task and productivity, scientific management became most acceptable to them. Industrialists believed that time–motion studies and other efficiencies would eliminate jobs, reduce labor costs, increase profits, and undermine working-class solidarity on the shop floor. Fordism on the other hand proved less

18   On the ability of the French to nationalize "Americanism," see Stephen L. Harp, *Marketing Michelin: Advertising and Cultural Identity in Twentieth-Century France* (Baltimore and London: Johns Hopkins University Press, 2001), especially 187–224.

19   For a succinct discussion of Ford's production methods and labor policies, see Stephen Meyer, III, *The Five Dollar Day: Labor Management and Social Control in the Ford Motor Company, 1908–1921* (Albany: State University of New York Press, 1981). On the fascination with Ford in Germany, see Nolan, *Visions of Modernity*, 30–57. For European and German responses to and modifications of Taylorism, Charles Maier's "Society as Factory," in *In Search of Stability: Explorations in Historical Political Economy*, ed. C.S. Maier (Cambridge: Cambridge University Press, 1987), especially 19–53, is indispensable, as is Anson Rabinbach's, *The Human Motor: Energy, Fatigue, and the Origins of Modernity* (New York: Basic Books, 1990), 238–88.

20   Jennifer Loehlin, *From Rugs to Riches: Housework, Consumption and Modernity in Germany* (Oxford and New York: Berg, 1999), 31–2. See also König, *Geschichte der Konsumgesellschaft*, 33–90, for the technical aspects of American rationalization and mass production.

enticing. In addition to resisting the higher wages that would match Ford's five dollar a day wage and profit-sharing plan, German business ruled out price reductions for goods and the stimulation of mass consumption. The concentration of German industry, in which cartels set prices to accommodate their least efficient partners, prohibited the transfer of gains in productivity to consumers. Furthermore, Fordist standardization compromised flexibility in production and affronted the deeply ingrained bias against the "inferior" quality of mass-produced goods.[21] Despite accelerated mechanization and output, mass production did not become routine in Germany until the rearmament boom after 1936, and especially after 1941. The demands of total war and glaring shortages in military hardware forced the modernization of production and the allocation of labor according to factory capacity and available machinery, overcoming the entrenched resistance in the armed forces to assembly-line standardization.[22]

Yet the meaning of "Americanism" encompassed more than production techniques. It comprised the celebration of a mass culture centered on the proliferation of material goods and dream-inducing cultural artifacts such as film, which erased the boundaries between high and low culture. To German admirers and critics both, America encouraged a vision of happiness independent of work, individual freedom from bourgeois standards of privacy and deportment, the blurring of once well-defined gender roles, the elimination of class-specific consumption patterns, and participation across class lines in similar leisure-time and cultural pursuits. Owing to the influx of American loans, corporate investment, and consumer goods after the resolution of the Ruhr crisis and the stabilization of the mark,[23] intellectuals, economists, technocrats, and politicians of different political

---

21 See Nolan, 131–53, and Volker R. Berghahn, "Fordism and West German Industrial Culture, 1945–1989," in *The German-American Encounter: Conflict and Cooperation between Two Cultures, 1800–2000*, ed. Frank Trommler and Elliott Shore (New York and Oxford: Berghahn Books, 2001): 148. On the limits of "rationalization" in specific industries and firms, see Thomas von Freyberg, *Industrielle Rationalisierung in der Weimarer Republik: Untersucht an Beispielen aus dem Maschinenbau und der Elektroindustrie* (Frankfurt, New York: Campus Verlag, 1989); Rüdiger Hachtmann, *Industriearbeit im 'Dritten Reich'* (Göttingen: Vandenhoeck und Ruprecht, 1989); Heidrun Homburg, *Rationalisierung und Industriearbeit: Arbeitsmarkt-Management-Arbeiterschaft im Siemens-Konzern Berlin 1900–1939* (Berlin, 1991); Tilla Siegel and Thomas von Freyberg, *Industrielle Rationalisierung unter dem Nationalsozialismus* (Frankfurt am Main: Campus Verlag, 1991); and Carola Sachse, *Siemens, der Nationalsozialismus und die moderne Familie. Eine Untersuchung zur sozialen Rationalisierung in Deutschland im 20. Jahrhundert* (Hamburg: Rasch und Röhring, 1990).

22 R. J. Overy, "Rationalization and the 'Production Miracle' in Germany during the Second World War," in *War and Economy in the Third Reich*, ed. R. J. Overy (Oxford, New York: Oxford University Press): 343–75.

23 Daniel T. Rogers, *Atlantic Crossings: Social Politics in a Progressive Age* (Cambridge, Massachusetts and London: the Belknap Press of Harvard University Press, 1998), 367–91.

persuasions debated the cultural and social impact of standardization and mass distribution.[24]

If mass production proved difficult to implement in the workplace, mass consumption conjured up more disturbing social and cultural nightmares for conservative and right radical intellectuals, the Protestant and Catholic clergy, and bourgeois politicians, especially those of the antirepublican German National People's Party (DNVP).[25] Despite differences in emphasis, they collectively despaired over the triumph of "soulless" rationalism, the triviality, materialism, and distractions of mass culture, democracy and the social leveling that supposedly accompanied it, and the "mammonism" of consumerism which the Weimar "system" tolerated. Visions of American Jewish "finance capital" that colonized Germany in the wake of its prostration by the Entente saturated conservative fears of American-style cultural leveling. For sure, the distribution of mass-produced commodities might have promised a broadly middle-class standard of consumption on the American model and, given the deep fissures in German society, offered the prospect of social peace. The angst of cultural conservatives did not include the rejection of technology, which promised industrial expansion and increased productivity. Nevertheless, the individualism, materialism, and implicit cultural and economic egalitarianism of mass consumption raised the ire of the right, which adhered to elitist and racially tinged notions of taste. Increasingly abandoning monarchism and older notions of aristocratic rule, they fused a populist communitarianism with the vision of leadership by the talented, well trained, and cultivated.[26]

---

24 For the meanings of "Americanism," consult Detlev Peukert, *Die Weimarer Republik: Krisenjahre der Klassische Moderne* (Frankfurt am Main: Suhrkamp, 1987), 178–81; Philipp Gassert, "Amerikanismus, Antiamerikanismus, Amerikanisierung: Neue Literatur zur Sozial-, Wirtschafts- und Kulturgeschichte des amerikanischen Einflusses in Deutschland und Europa," *Archiv für Sozialgeschichte* 39 (1999): 535–7; Victoria de Grazia, "Amerikanisierung und wechselnde Leitbilder der Konsum-Modern (consumermodernity in Europa)," in *Europäische Konsumgeschichte*: 114–23; and Nolan, *Visions of Modernity*, 108–27.

25 For a similar typology, see Adelheid von Saldern, "Popular Culture: An Immense Challenge in the Weimar Republic," in *The Challenge of Modernity: German Social and Cultural Studies, 1890–1960*, ed. A. von Saldern, trans. Bruce Little (Ann Arbor: University of Michigan Press, 2002): 254–74.

26 The literature on Weimar conservatism is enormous. On intellectuals, see *The Weimar Republic Sourcebook*, 330–87 for the excellent selection of primary sources, as well as Fritz Stern, *The Politics of Cultural Despair: A Study in the Rise of Germanic Ideology* (Garden City, New York: Doubleday Anchor, 1965); and Walter Struve's *Elites against Democracy: Leadership Ideals in Bourgeois Political Thought in Germany, 1890–1933* (Princeton: Princeton University Press, 1973). For a rethinking of the "antimodernism" of German conservatives, see Jeffrey Herf, *Reactionary Modernism: Technology, Culture, and Politics in Weimar and the Third Reich* (Cambridge: Cambridge University Press, 1984), and despite his downplaying the links between conservative critics of modernity and Nazism, Thomas Rohkrämer's *Eine andere Moderne? Zivilisationskritik, Natur und Technik in Deutschland 1880–1933* (Paderborn: Ferdinand Schöningh,

In addition to drawing on antisemitism, the right's fear of the cultural consequences of "Americanism" equated mass culture with the "feminization" that arose from the seeming radical transformation in gender roles. The short-skirted, bobbed-haired, cigarette-smoking, Charleston-dancing, cosmetics indulging, and alcohol-consuming "new" woman sitting astride her motorcycle or perched in the rumble seat seat of a motorcar assumed mythical proportions. "She" symbolized the domination of women over men that presumably characterized gender relations in the United States. That the number of women who conformed to the "new woman" stereotype were few in number, or that employed women did not enjoy a glamorous lifestyle as conservatives glumly assumed, mattered less than the "new woman's" usefulness in personifying the destabilization of war, revolution and inflation. Identified with the cities and especially Berlin, where traditional forms of social control were limited, she celebrated her autonomy derived from her own income, consumed with abandon, and reshaped her identity in nonconformist ways. Simultaneously frigid and sexually libertine, her masculine clothing and appearance asserted the new woman's willingness to sacrifice her reproductive and nurturing role for the sake of personal pleasure, a near obsession for the German right after World War I. "It is high time that sound male judgment take a stand against these odious fashions, the excesses of which have been transplanted here from America," warned the *Berliner Illustrierte Zeitung*. "And the masculinization of the female face replaces its natural allure with, at best, an unnatural one: the look of a sickeningly sweet boy is detested by every real boy or man."[27] Even though the campaign to liberalize laws against abortion failed, due in large measure to the opposition of the churches, the unsettling potential of autonomous women fueled Weimar's culture wars.[28]

1999). On the antisemitic and anti-colonial rhetoric of Weimar conservatives, see Dan Diner, *America in the Eyes of the Germans: An Essay on Anti-Americanism*, trans. Allison Brown (Princeton: Markus Wiener Publishers, 1996), 53–77.

27 "Enough is Enough! Against the Masculinization of Women," *Berliner Illustrierte Zeitung* (March 29, 1935): 389, in *The Weimar Republic Sourcebook*, 659.

28 For Weimar debates on abortion, contraception, and the "new woman," consult Atina Grossman, *Reforming Sex: The German Movement for Birth Control and Abortion Reform 1920–1950* (New York and Oxford: Oxford University Press, 1995); and *Girlkultur*, or Thoroughly Rationalized Female: A New Woman in Weimar Germany?" in *Women in Culture and Politics*, ed. Judith Friedlander et al. (Bloomington: Indiana University Press, 1986): 62–80; Eve Rosenhaft, "Lesewut, Kinosucht, Radiotismus: Zur (geschlechter-) politischen Relevanz neuer Massenmedien in den 1920er Jahren, in *Amerikanisierung: Traum und Alptraum im Deutschland des 20. Jahrhunderts*, ed. Alf Lüdtke and Inge Marßolek, (Stuttgart: Steiner, 1996): 119–43; Adelheid von Saldern, "Überfremdungsängste. Gegen die Amerikanisierung der deutschen Kultur" in the same volume: 221–27; *The Weimar Republic Sourcebook*, 195–219 and 693–717; and Cornelie Usbourne, *The Politics of the Body in Weimar Germany: Women's Reproductive Rights and Duties* (Ann Arbor: University of

Americanism was not the only entry, however, in the discussion regarding mass consumption and culture. The Socialists and Communists offered alternatives of their own. Regardless of the poisonous conflicts between them, they converged on socializing the means of production to guarantee work and the dignity of the worker, and to ensure a decent collective subsistence. The Social Democratic party, which before World War I articulated worker discontent with the class structure and economic inequalities of imperial Germany, emerged as the largest and best-organized socialist party in Europe.[29] Despite the SPD's permanent division in 1917 over whether to support Germany's continuation of the war, the Majority Social Democrats spearheaded the formation of the Weimar Republic and its comprehensive welfare state. Following one of its leading economists, Rudolf Hilferding, who at the party's congress in 1927 put forth the theory of "organized capitalism," the SPD adhered to the view that public ownership of the means of production would evolve from the increasing concentration of capital, especially after the Social Democrats attained majority rule in the democratic state.[30]

The Social Democrats and the intransigently anti-Weimar Communist party (KPD) remained unreconciled throughout the republic's lifetime. Although Socialists and Communists belonged to the same unions and voluntary associations, their constrasting approaches to a new society – the evolution toward socialism through parliaments and organized capitalism favored by Social Democrats and immediate armed revolution by the Communists – proved unbridgeable. Nevertheless, both parties presupposed the catalytic role of the working class in effecting a fundamental change in property relations and the redistribution of material resources. Moreover, in sharp contrast to employers who rejected mass production, the Socialists and Communists maintained that socialism could harness Fordism for its own ends. Certainly neither party envisioned a future of consumerist abundance. Desite the claim of cultural conservatives, who linked the degenerative effects of consumption to the "Marxist" republic, the Socialist and Communist leaderships disparaged commercialized mass leisure, especially the Socialists for whom commercial pleasure palaces

Michigan Press, 1992). Germany was hardly alone in debating this "problem," which became a European-wide discourse. Yet its high level of urbanization magnified it in the mind of conservatives. Cf. Victoria de Grazia, *How Fascism Ruled Women: Italy, 1922–1945* (Berkeley, Los Angeles, Oxford: University of California Press, 1992), 128–40, 207–10.

29 David Blackbourn, *The Long Nineteenth Century. A History of Germany, 1780–1918* (New York, Oxford: Oxford University Press, 1998), 412.

30 On Hilferding's theory, see Donna Harsch, *German Social Democracy and the Rise of Nazism* (Chapel Hill and London: University of North Carolina Press, 1993), 33; Stefan Berger, *Social Democracy and the Working Class in Nineteenth and Twentieth Century Germany* (London: Longman, 2000), 124–9; and Nolan, *Visions of Modernity*, 173–4.

violated the long-held regard for self-improvement and purposeful recreation befitting the dignity of labor. Still, the leaderships of both parties expected that mass production in service to socialism would improve working-class lives.[31]

The Bolshevik Revolution became a powerful model to many for the achievement of social equality, progress, extensive social welfare, material well being, and cultural opportunity even though it had hastened the division of the European and German left into social democratic and communist wings. Having emancipated women and Jews and instituted a welfare state of then unprecedented scale, the Bolsheviks restructured property relations, subjugated or eliminated the tsarist elite, attacked the Russian Orthodox church, expropriated land, and encouraged the advancement of thousands of peasants and workers. The Bolshevik assault on privilege extended to tourism as well. Operating through the factories, party promoters organized workers' tours to the Black Sea, the Caucasus, the Crimea, and various tsarist palaces, such that by 1935, four million Soviets would tour annually, over one hundred thousand of them on longer trips to such locales as the Dnieper, the Baltic, and the White Sea Canal. If in retrospect the devastation in Russia reaped by war, revolution, and the ensuing civil war render perceptions of Soviet success from outside as sanguine at best, European and German communists articulated them frequently enough to testify to the Soviet Union's iconic status.[32]

If the German right disliked Americanism, it displayed an even greater loathing of "Marxism," a capacious term that covered all strands of socialism from the Bolsheviks and antirepublican German Communists to the pro-republican Social Democrats. The Social Democrats' leverage within the Weimar system, which remained strong even during the years between 1924 and 1928 when ruling coalitions drew from the bourgeois center and right, resulted in a significant redistribution of income. Wage increases arising from collective bargaining, expanded social insurance, municipal housing projects, youth welfare programs, enhanced maternity and public health benefits, and unemployment compensation together constituted an impediment to corporate profitability and a principal cause

31 Nolan, *Visions of Modernity*, 41, 47–8. See also Geoff Eley, "Cultural Socialism, the Public Sphere, and the Mass Form: Popular Culture and the Democratic Project, 1900 to 1934," in *Between Reform and Revolution: German Socialism and Communism from 1840 to 1990*, ed. David E. Barclay and Eric D. Weitz (New York and Oxford: Berghahn Books, 1998): 315–42; and von Saldern, "An Immense Challenge," 280–92.

32 Bruno Frommann, "Reisen im Dienste politischer Zielsetzungen: Arbeiter-Reisen und 'Kraft durch Freude'-Fahrten," (Diss: Stuttgart, 1993), 93–5. For German communist perceptions of the Soviet Union as the land of peace and prosperity, see Eric D. Weitz, *Creating German Communism, 1890–1990: From Popular Protests to Socialist State* (Princeton: Princeton University Press, 1997), 234–42, and Szejnmann, *Nazism in Central Germany*, 63.

of increased taxation. The SPD's advocacy of higher wages as the means of stimulating domestic consumption provided additional grounds for the right, and business especially, to seek the dismantling of the Weimar system.[33] In addition, the rapid growth of the Communist party during the Depression became the worst nightmare of conservatives, who feared the imposition of the Bolshevik experiment at home. That harbingered not just the socialization of the means of production, but also a cultural apocalypse, which included the destruction of religion and the ruination of the family through the legalization of divorce, abortion rights, and the creation of state-run nurseries and kindergartens.

In truth, the left was less formidable than the right believed. The divisions between the Socialists and Communists, the competition that commercial leisure posed to the organized variety of the left, and the growing separation between leaders and the rank and file undermined class cohesion. Together they prevented the formation of a decisive counterweight to the emergence of right radicalism.[34] Nevertheless, the right had grown accustomed since 1918 to linking moral breakdown with the revolution, the republic, and an undifferentiated left; seeing Weimar as the incubator of baleful cultural consequences such as the "new woman."[35] Moreover, the parties and voluntary associations of the left remained significant obstacles to the right and even to the Nazis, who after 1928 successfully supplanted the other bourgeois parties in their quest to attract the disaffected. Socialist consumer cooperatives, pioneers in mass advertising and mass distribution, remained formidable alternatives to market-based

33 For the impact of the Social Democrats on the *Sozialpolitk* of the Weimar Republic, see David Abraham, *The Collapse of the Weimar Republic: Political Economy and Crisis*, 2nd ed. (New York: Holmes and Meier, 1986), 220–318. By contrast, other historians tend to identify the causes for the SPD's failure to salvage the republic as internal, particularly its inability or unwillingness to reach beyond its working-class base. See Wolfram Pyta, *Gegen Hitler und für die Republik: Die Auseinandersetzung der deutschen Sozialdemokratie mit der NSDAP in der Weimarer Republik* (Düsseldorf: Droste, 1990); Harsch, *German Social Democracy*; and Heinrich-August Winkler's three-volume work, *Arbeiter und Arbeiterbewegung in der Weimarer Republik* (Bonn, Berlin: J.H.W. Dietz Nachf., 1983–7).

34 On the KPD's intransigence, see Weitz, *Creating German Communism*, 233–79. On the left's approach to commercial leisure, see Eley, "Cultural Socialism, the Public Sphere, and the Mass Form" in *Between Reform and Revolution*, ed. Barclay and Weitz: 315–40; Guttsman, *Workers' Culture*, especially 254–86; Dieter Langewiesche, "Das neue Massenmedium Film und die deutsche Arbeiterbewegung in der Weimarer Republik" in *Von der Arbeiterbewegung zum modernen Sozialstaat*, ed. Jürgen Kocka, Hans-Jürgen Puhle, and Klaus Tenfelde (Munich: Saur 1994): 114–30; Adelheid von Saldern, "Arbeiterkulturbewegung in Deutschland in der Zwischenkriegs-Zeit," in *Arbeiterkulturen zwischen Alltag und Politik: Beiträge zum europäischen Vergleich in der Zwischenkriegszeit*, ed. Friedhelm Boll (Zurich: Europa-Verlag, 1986) and James Wickham, "Working-Class Movement and Working-Class Life: Frankfurt am Main during the Weimar Republic," *Social History* 8 (1983): 315–43, especially 338–42.

35 For a discussion of post–World War I moral concerns, see Bessel, *Germany after the First World War*, 220–53.

consumption and a force for working-class solidarity. Along with selling goods at "fair" prices, they distributed profits to their members according to purchases made rather than shares owned.[36] The strong institutional network of the left challenged the Nazi party's claim that its racial community, not class conflict, would provide workers with a better life.

Taming Mass Consumption: Nazism's "German" Capitalism

Before the Nazi movement was outlawed in the aftermath of Hitler's imprisonment for his part in the 1923 Munich putsch, the party's "twenty-five point" program of 1920 transmitted its views to a broader public in Bavaria, a hotbed of right radicalism between 1918 and stabilization. Despite the "socialism" in its name, the party adhered to a version of capitalism, larded with racism and antisemitism, which catered to small producers while promising benefits for workers. In addition to demanding living space for resettling Germany's "excess" population, the destruction of the Versailles settlement, the revocation of German citizenship for Jews, the ban on the immigration of non-Germans, and the insistence on the common good before the good of the individual, the Nazi platform demanded the nationalization of industries and banks that put profits and dividends before popular needs. It further advocated land reform, the confiscation of the ill-gotten gains of war profiteers, the lease of wholesale enterprises at favorable rates to small retailers, the extension of old-age pensions, and the reduction of prices to allow every German to share in the national wealth.[37] In 1925, after Hitler's release from prison when the Nazi party was once again legalized, it redefined its organization and extended its reach beyond its Bavarian homeland, despite occupying the political margins as the stabilization of the mark and American loans jump started the Weimar economy.

The Nazi leadership in the south continued to enunciate the assumptions embedded in the 1920 program. It reaffirmed the conceptualization of capitalism originally coined by the engineer and probable author of the party program, Gottfried Feder, and applied it to Germany's postwar

---

36 See Szejnmann, *Nazism in Central Germany*, 62–3, and Brett Fairbairn, "The Rise and Fall of Consumer Cooperation in Germany," in *Consumers against Capitalism? Consumer Cooperation in Europe, North America, and Japan, 1840–1900*, ed. Ellen Furlough and Carl Strikwerda (Lanham, Maryland: Rowman and Littlefield, 1999): 267–302.

37 "The Program of the NSDAP," in *Nazi Ideology before 1933: A Documentation*, trans. Barbara Miller Lane and Leila J. Rupp (Austin, London: University of Texas Press, 1978): 40–3.

dilemma – the confrontation with Americanism and socialism as alternative models of social transformation. Consistent with the endeavor of conservative intellectuals during Weimar period, Werner Sombart especially, to racialize the distinction between capitalist production and exchange, the Nazis revealed that a root-and-branch "anticapitalism" less characterized their program, however "socialist" its planks, than the party's differentiation between "creative" (*schaffendes*) and "rapacious" (*raffendes*) capitalism. The first variant produced for the well being of the nation, contributing to the common good through the "creative" labor of managers and workers acting selflessly to generate employment and national wealth. The party described the second variant, international finance capitalism, as exploitative, usurious, speculative, and parasitic. Because it operated through the colonial enslavement inflicted by Germany's enemies, it was therefore "Jewish." If the Nazi party championed social "justice" for workers and the expropriation of property that failed to serve the common good, it had little difficulty finding German big business compatible with the capitalism that benefited the nation.[38] The party's attack on international capitalism as "Jewish" allowed it to mount its dual, seemingly incompatible, assaults against "Marxism" and "capitalism" that arose in its campaign speeches. The party's qualified critique of capitalism accorded with Hitler's strategic commitments after 1923 – the abandonment of putschism and the adoption of legal means to achieve power. Hitler's new tactics anticipated his party's cooperation with Germany's military and economic establishments to destroy the republic.[39]

To be sure, following the collapse of the Munich putsch, a contingent of the Nazi leadership, a "working group" of district leaders in the north centered around Goebbels and the Strasser brothers, Gregor and Otto, stressed the party's "national socialism" at the expense of its "national capitalism." Although not contesting Hitler's leadership, the group offered an alternative to his anti-socialism and that of the party cadre in Bavaria. The latter, traumatized by the Munich soviet in 1919 and the horror stories of anti-Bolshevik refugees, notably Alfred Rosenberg, had made anti-Bolshevism the centerpiece of their worldviews. Desiring to popularize Nazism in north Germany to compete with the Socialists and Communists for working-class support, Goebbels and the Strassers advocated a "national Bolshevism," which codified proposals then widely

38 See Herf, *Reactionary Modernism*, 130–51 and 189–90. For Nazi economics before 1933, see Avraham Barkai, *Nazi Economics: Ideology, Theory, and Policy*, trans. Ruth Hadass-Vashitz (New Haven and London: Yale University Press, 1990), especially 22–6. For Feder's gloss on the twenty-five point program, see the English version of a pamphlet that Feder published in 1927, *Hitler's Official Programme and Its Fundamental Ideals* (New York: Howard Fertig, 1971), especially 82–107.
39 Ian Kershaw, *Hitler 1889–1936: Hubris* (New York and London: W.W. Norton, 1998), 218.

circulated on the right. Despite the working group's espousal of the corporatist representation of interests that had little in common with the Soviet experience, it proposed the establishment of a dictatorship, the public ownership of the means of production, and the protection of small-scale property, particularly that belonging to the peasantry. They admired what they understood as the Russian nationalism of the Bolsheviks, who accomplished socialism, for in their view Lenin freed Russia from international economic domination and the internationalism of Marxism.[40] At a time when the Weimar Republic had reached a partial accommodation with the West through the Locarno agreement, the working group proposed an alliance with the Soviet Union, believing that the Soviet example would best serve the interests of the German proletariat.[41]

The decision of the Goebbels–Strasser group in early 1926 to support a referendum to expropriate royal property forced Hitler to convene a crucial meeting in the Nazi stronghold of Bamberg in upper Franconia. Hitler's charismatic leadership, arising from his ability to resurrect the party from its disarray during his imprisonment, asserted itself, as the führer rejected the referendum and an alliance with the Soviet Union. Although resistant at first, Goebbels succumbed to Hitler's authority despite his visceral anticapitalism, as did Gregor Strasser whom Hitler subsequently named Reich organization leader.[42] The desire to achieve power by the only means possible, garnering a mass electorate, proved decisive to resolving the controversy. Hitler believed that the party's success could only come from a broad-based social coalition; one that included workers, but one that also extended to the middle classes and accommodated itself to Germany's elite. Thereafter, Hitler's views remained unassailable.[43]

In common with the right, Hitler supposed that a suffocating entrapment encumbered Germany's domestic economy and international position, wedged between two forces, the Soviet Union and the Entente

---

40 See in particular, Joseph Goebbels, "National Socialism or Bolshevism?" *NS-Briefe* (October 25, 1925), in *The Weimar Republic Sourcebook*, 127–29.

41 See the documents in Lane and Rupp, *Nazi Ideology*, 74–94, as well as the discussions of Gregor Strasser's ideology in Udo Kissenkötter, *Gregor Strasser und die NSDAP* (Stuttgart: Deutsche Verlags-Anstalt, 1978), 22–7, and Peter Stachura, *Gregor Strasser and the Rise of Nazism* (London and Boston: Allen and Unwin, 1983), 51–60.

42 For the Bamberg episode, consult Kershaw, *Hubris*, 270–79; Dietrich Orlow, *The History of the Nazi Party: 1919–1933* (Pittsburgh: University of Pittsburgh Press, 1969), 62–72; and Joseph Nyomarsky, *Charisma and Factionalism in the Nazi Party* (Minneapolis: University of Minnesota Press, 1967), 71–109. For Goebbels' "road to Damascus," see his version of Bamberg in *Die Tagebücher von Joseph Goebbels* (hereinafter cited as *Tagebücher) sämtliche Fragmente*, Part I: *Aufzeichnungen 1924–1941*, vol. I, 27.6.1924–31.12.1930, ed. Elke Fröhlich and Institut für Zeitgeschichte (Munich and New York: K.G. Saur, 1987): 160–63.

43 Ian Kershaw, "'Working towards the Führer': Reflections on the Nature of the Hitler Dictatorship," in *Stalinism and Nazism: Dictatorships in Comparison*, ed. Ian Kershaw and Moshe Levin (Cambridge: Cambridge University Press, 1997): 94–5.

dominated by United States. Germany, in his view, had become a colony of international Jewish finance capitalism, which by operating through the Entente and Bolshevism destroyed the sovereignty and economic well being of nations. "Western democracy on the one hand and Russian Bolshevism on the other," he asserted, shaped "the forms in which the contemporary Jewish world domination finds its expression; wherein, however, the former must be considered only as the forerunner of the latter."[44] In Russia, Bolshevism not only destroyed the creators of the national economy and eliminated the tsarst elite, much of it composed of nobles of German descent. It also betrayed the interests of the proletariat who initially welcomed it, mortgaging Russia's forests, mines, and factories to Jewish financiers at the expense of better working and living conditions for the masses.[45] In Germany "Marxism" unleashed the November Revolution, sold out the army in surrendering to the Entente, delivered workers into the hands of "international loan capitalism," and subordinated the national economy to foreign interests, while exacerbating class conflict and parliamentary immobility.[46] Similarly, the Nazi party's campaign literature underscored the dual outcomes of Germany's imprisonment at the "command of world Jewry." "Democracy and Bolshevism are two means which serve the same end," proclaimed one Nazi leaflet, "Jewish money and Jewish world dictatorship." In addition to subsidizing the Red Army's plunder of Russia, the "Jewish world-octopus" imposed the Versailles Treaty, installed Social Democracy and parliamentarianism, and dissapated the national wealth.[47] The Dawes Plan, the prime channel for American economic power instituted in 1924 to stabilize the Reichsmark after the hyperinflation and the French occupation of the Ruhr, "put the creative German people into the chains of international high finance, i.e., of world Jewry."[48] In addition to expressing the führer's deeply held conviction, antisemitism explained Germany's victimization at the hands of powerful external forces, American capitalism and Soviet communism, however antagonistic to each other those alternatives remained.

Beyond condemning international capitalism and socialism, Hitler subsumed economics to politics, avoiding concreteness so as not to alienate potential supporters. According to Gauleiter Alfred Krebs of Hamburg,

---

44 Adolf Hitler, *Hitler: Reden, Schriften, Anordnungen* [hereinafter cited as *RSA* with volume number] *Februar 1925 bis Januar 1933*. Vol I: *Die Wiedergründung der NSDAP Februar 1925–Juni 1926*, ed. Institut für Zeitgeschichte (Munich, London: KG. Saur, 1992): 153.
45 *RSA*, vol. I, 121–2, 191–2.   46 *RSA*, vol. I, 87–90.
47 "The Command of World Jewry," leaflet issued by the party's Central Propaganda Department in Munich, in Simon Taylor ed. *Prelude to Genocide: Nazi Ideology and the Struggle for Power* (New York: St. Martin's Press, 1985): 41–3.
48 "2000 Oxen," leaflet in Taylor, *Prelude to Genocide:* 50.

an advocate of the north German strategy, the führer believed in swaying the public with simple emotional slogans rather than specific policies that would threaten his goal of achieving a broad electoral coalition.[49] Despite adopting that tactic to preserve Hitler's image as the charismatic leader above the fray, the party laid the groundwork for the interventionism, including large-scale public works projects, that the Nazi regime would put in place after 1933 to ensure that German capitalism served the regime's immediate and long-term goals. As a party that sought worker support, even after it broadened its reach to the peasantry and the middle classes, the Nazi movement promised state investment in economic development, full employment, and future prosperity.[50]

The Nazi party's populist economic platforms brought it unavoidably into the debate on mass consumption. Despite its promise of full employment, however, the party's diverse electorate complicated its attempts to deal coherently with the issue. At bottom lay the support that the NSDAP drew from small retailers, who resented department and single-price chain stores, mass distribution warehouses, and Socialist-sponsored consumer cooperatives. Such large-scale enterprises serviced mass constituencies and their economies of scale threatened to undermine the economic viability of small shopkeepers. They also affronted the hierarchies of taste and consumption to which small establishments catered, for they normally eschewed the mass distribution of goods at low cost.[51] To be sure, Nazi policy after 1933 disappointed small retailers as least as often as it satisfied them. Rearmament favored large-scale, war-related industries while discriminating against small producers in the allocation of raw materials, credit, and labor. Department stores remained largely untouched until 1938, when the "Crystal Night" (*Kristallnacht*) pogrom resulted in the arrest and murder of countless Jews and in the expropriation of their property.[52] Yet before taking power, the two available routes to a higher material standard of living – socialism and Fordism – threatened a constituency with whom the Nazis sympathized.

49 *The Infancy of Nazism: The Memoirs of Ex-Gauleiter Albert Krebs, 1923–1933,* ed. and trans. William Sheridan Allen (New York, London: New Viewpoints, 1976): 181–2.

50 Against the view that the Nazi party's economic proposals were incoherent, Barkai, *Nazi Economics,* 21–70, argues convincingly to the contrary. Local studies suggest that Nazism's appeals to workers lent urgency to formulating interventionist platforms that would satisfy their interests. See Szejnmann in particular, *Nazism in Central Germany,* 43–91.

51 See de Grazia, "Changing Consumption Regimes in Europe": 69–78.

52 On politics and economics in the Third Reich, consult Ian Kershaw, *The Nazi Dictatorship: Problems and Perspectives,* 4th ed. (London: Edward Arnold, 2000): 47–68. See also Pierre Ayçoberry, *The Social History of the Third Reich, 1933–1945,* trans. Janet Lloyd (New York: The New Press, 1999), 145–51.

The Nazi party's core ideological convictions intervened as well. Socialism, which included the consumer cooperation movement of the left, certainly sold goods at low cost. If small-scale retailing catered to bourgeois tastes, however, consumer cooperation reflected a quite different, and from the Nazi perspective, unacceptable class bias that grounded the party's hostility toward "Marxism." The financial support that the cooperatives funneled to the Socialists, not to mention their predominantly working-class members, who depended on those outlets for inexpensive necessities and additional income from dividends on shares, preserved the class divisions that the Nazi racial community wished to dissolve. Furthermore, the left's emphasis on the working class as the primary agent of social and economic transformation smacked of "class egoism." Once in power and especially after the outbreak of war, the regime could not eliminate the consumer cooperatives entirely, opting instead to incorporate them in the German Labor Front (Deutsche Arbeitsfront, or DAF). Their financial assets, market share, strong consumer loyalty, and the dependence of some regions on their systems of distribution necessitated a shift in policy.[53] Nonetheless before 1933, the party's deep-seated hostility to the left meant its equally consistent opposition to leftist modes of consumption. Moreover, not only did the popularity of the cooperatives antagonize small retailers, the Socialists' campaign for low food prices to aid working-class consumers provoked resentment among peasants, another source of Nazi support.[54]

Fordism, on the other hand, seemed a more promising solution because it held the potential to realize the populist and social integrationist presuppositions of the Nazi "racial community." Mass production and product standardization could mute class divisions because they offered popular access to a broad spectrum of goods that appealed to consumers. In Hitler's opinion, American mass production and distribution weakened communism's appeal to workers because the shorter workday and the low cost of consumer durables, such as automobiles and homes, achieved the very goal that Hitler sought for Germany – the fusion of nationalism and

---

53   The Reich Economics Ministry argued that some consumer cooperatives had to remain. See the communication (document 199) from the ministry to regional governments from 17 July 1933 in *Akten der Reichskanzlei: Regierung Hitler 1933–1938, Part I: 1933/34*, vol. 1, ed. Konrad Repgen (Boppard am Rhein: Harald Boldt Verlag, 1983): 699–701. The war continued to protect them from dissolution. Robert Ley, "Die Konsumverein und Verbrauchergenossenschaften," 27 February 1941, Bundesarchiv Berlin-Lichterfelde (hereinafter cited as BAL), R43II/32b, 102–8. As leader of the German Labor Front, Ley limited the "synchronization" of cooperatives to those that lacked economic viability.

54   On the political and economic difficulties of agriculture, see Abraham, *Collapse of the Weimar Republic*, 42–105 and 171–219; and Heinrich Becker, *Handlungsspielräume der Agrarpolitik in der Weimarer Republik Zwischen 1923 und 1929* (Stuttgart: Franz Steiner Verlag, 1990).

socialism.[55] In asserting as much, he attested to the attractiveness of the emerging consumerism of the twenties. Hitler's admiration for Henry Ford and his desire subsequent to taking power to replicate Ford's accomplishment in the mass production of a "people's car" testified to his awareness that Nazism's public reception depended on its ability to "deliver the goods," literally and figuratively.[56] In his "second" book published in 1928, Hitler acknowledged that modern networks of communication had made Germans acutely aware of the high standard of living in America, the result of the ingenuity of Nordic settlers, who had extended the nation's boundaries to its continental limits. Yet, he warned, Germans presently aspired to a level of material well being that their present living space did not merit. Only living space acquired through racial invigoration, Hitler insisted, would bring to Germany the living standards that the United States enjoyed.[57]

Regardless, neither Hitler nor other prominent Nazi ideologues accepted Fordism. In common with the bourgeois right, they bemoaned the consequences of mass consumption as evidence of democratic leveling, "Jewish" corruption, and Bolshevism. Apart from alienating retailers, who appreciated the party's condemnation of "the single-price system thought up by the American Woolworth chain,"[58] mass production, mass advertising, and consumerism promoted the corruption of "Jewish" mammonism. Nazi leaders identified mass consumption as emblematic of the "Jewish" form of capitalism, which undermined the welfare of the national community. "The large retail stores, all in the hands of Jews ... depend on 'charm,' 'display,' 'bluff,' and the awakening of wholly unnecessary 'demands' for 'luxuries,'" complained Gottfried Feder, who despite having placed Henry Ford in his pantheon of employers of "moral worth" along with such names as Krupp, Kirdorf, and Siemens, despised the institutions that best exemplified mass consumption:

> Great palaces, of enormous proportions, built with all the
> refinements of art, invite the public to purchase apparently
> cheap, but for the most part quite useless, articles, and by
> offering easy conditions of payment they entice their customers

55 *RSA*, vol. I, 368.
56 To this extent I agree with Rainer Zitelmann's emphasis on America's significance for Hitler. See his *Hitler: Selbstverständnis eines Revolutionärs: Zweite, überarbeitete und ergänzte Auflage* (Stuttgart: Klett-Cotta, 1989), 306–78. Yet one does not have to downplay Nazism's racist core, as Zitelmann does, to understand that. See Hans Mommsen with Manfred Grieger, *Das Volkswagenwerk und seine Arbeiter im Dritten Reich* (Düsseldorf: Econ Verlag, 1996), 53–91.
57 *Hitler's Secret Book*, introduction by Telford Taylor, trans: Salvator Attansio (New York: Grove Press, 1961), 95, 98.
58 "Middle Classes and Small Traders," leaflet from 1928/29, in Taylor, *Prelude to Genocide*: 57.

to spend all manner of sums on pure luxuries. Rest-rooms are provided to enable people to spend a long time in the stores, which thus become mere hotbeds of extravagance, for let no one imagine that he gets anything as a present.[59]

Beginning with Hitler, the Nazi leadership's hostility to mass consumption contributed to artistic conservatism and cultural autarky, indicative of the party's dislike of Americanism. Insisting that Aryans had created all great music and even the best of modern technology, Hitler rejected artistic internationalism. "The Tango, the shimmy, the jazz band, they are international, but they're not art," he exclaimed in a rally in Munich in 1927. Like the department stores of Jews and the shoddy, undistinguished modern hotels in Berlin, they reflected the "Bolshevization" of culture, which had contributed to Germany's sorry state.[60] In 1928, Alfred Rosenberg, the editor of the party's newspaper, the *Völkischer Beobachter*, spearheaded the Combat League for German Culture (Kampfbund für deutsche Kultur), which advocated the protection of German culture against the decadent "Jewish–Bolshevik" influences of musical and artistic modernism, including "nigger jazz." Although originally a conservative rather than Nazi organization, with a membership that favored the educated middle class and aristocracy, its gradual subordination to the party took place well before the Nazi takeover. The Combat League articulated the party's support of high culture as the true expression of the German nation against cultural modernism and the budget cutbacks that threatened German cultural institutions.[61]

Even Joseph Goebbels, who distinguished himself in the party by the relative favor he bestowed on modern art, had no peer in condemning the consumerism that he observed in Berlin, where he served as gauleiter after the resolution of the controversy over "national Bolshevism." Goebbels contrasted the glittering mélange of fancy cars, cinemas, women in their fancy clothes and sparkling jewelry, and the bustling night scene on the Kurfürstendamm, with the sober dignity of the Kaiser Wilhelm Memorial

59 Feder, *Hitler's Official Programme*, 84–7.
60 *RSA*, vol. II, part 1, 229; Adolf Hitler, *Mein Kampf* (Boston: Houghton Mifflin Company, 1939), 363.
61 On the Combat League and on the party's cultural campaigns, see Reinhard Bollmus, *Das Amt Rosenberg und seine Gegner: Studien zum Machtkampf im nationalsozialistischen Herrschaftssystem* (Stuttgart: Deutsche Verlags-Anstalt, 1970), 30–1; Michael H. Kater, *The Twisted Muse: Musicians and Their Music in the Third Reich* (New York and Oxford: Oxford University Press, 1997), 14–17; Alan Steinweis, *Art, Ideology, and Economics in Nazi Germany: The Reich Chambers of Music, Theater, and the Visual Arts* (Chapel Hill and London: University of North Carolina Press, 1993), 20–31, and "Weimar Culture and the Rise of National Socialism: The *Kampfbund für deutsche Kultur*," *Central European History* 24, no. 4 (1991): 402–23; and finally Karl-Christian Führer, "German Cultural Life and the Crisis of National Identity during the Depression, 1929–1933," *German Studies Review* 24, no. 3 (2001): 461–86.

Church that stood "alien in this noisy life." "Like an anachronism left behind," he rued, "it mourns between the cafés and cabarets, condescends to the automobiles humming around its stoney body, and calmly announces the hour to the sin of corruption." Goebbels further connected the "repulsive pseudoculture" of the Kurfürstendamm, Berlin's commercial center, to the exploitation of the "Israelites" and Berlin's cosmopolitanism: "The German people is alien and superfluous here. To speak in the national language is to be nearly conspicuous. Pan-Europe, the *Internationale*, jazz, France and Piscator – those are the watchwords."[62] Goebbels proved crucial to harnessing the Combat League to the party, transferring its offices from Munich to Berlin to the detriment of Rosenberg. After the Nazi takeover, the book-burning that Goebbels initiated as propaganda minister and his rigid control of the press achieved what right-wing agitation had previously failed to accomplish; a ban against the commercial production of "filth and trash" literature that allegedly corrupted youth.[63]

In addition to its distaste for commercialized cosmopolitanism, the allegedly soulless degradation of work arising from mass production occupied a central place in the Nazi party's critique of international capitalism. As an American invention and symbol of American power, the assembly line stood for the cutthroat international economy that "enslaved" Germany in the role of borrower and exporter of both goods and emigrants; a role that the party rejected in favor of autarky. As advocates of the "creativity" of "German" work and the autonomy of the national economy, Nazi party ideologues, like other intellectuals of the right, stressed the "honor" of labor, be it manual or mental, and the "spiritual" rewards arising from it. They emphasized pride in workmanship, the construction of quality products, and the transcendent capacities of material objects. As the results of human creativity rather than inanimate machines, they simultaneously refuted the deskilling of Fordist mass production and Marxist presumptions of alienated labor. For that reason Nazi leaders claimed to eliminate the distinction between workers of the "head" (*Stirn*) and "fist" (*Faust*), be they manual laborers or managers. Both collaborated in the ethical task of "creating" products for the common good.[64] Nazi leaders adhered not only to conviction, but also to

---

62   "Around the Gedächtniskirche," originally published in *Der Angriff* (23 January 1928), in *The Weimar Republic Sourcebook*, 560–2.

63   Steinweis, *Art, Ideology, and Economics*, 24–5. See Winfried Speitkamp, "Jugendgesetz und kommerzielle Interessen: Schunddebatte und Zensur in der Weimarer Republik," in *Konsumpolitik: Die Regulierung des privaten Verbrauchs im 20. Jahrhundert*, ed. Hartmut Berghoff (Göttingen: Vandenhoeck und Ruprecht, 1999): 47–75.

64   See Joan Campbell, *Joy in Work, German Work: The National Debate, 1800–1945* (Princeton and London: Princeton University Press, 1989), 312–36. The "reanimation" of manufactured objects, which became a central theme in the Nazi regime's attempt to revalorize labor, emerges as a prominent theme in Paul Betts, *The Authority of Everyday*

political calculation, for they strove to build a movement that cut across class divisions. Aside from appropriating antisemitism, anti-Marxism, and the productivism of the right, they catered to the symbolic world of wage earners and labor leaders, which celebrated the nobility of work.[65]

Despite his growing estrangement from the führer, even Gregor Strasser, who in May 1932 proposed job creation programs and state-generated full employment as the party emerged as a serious contender for power, never intended higher working-class living standards to mean the satisfaction of unbounded consumer desires. The task of the "national economy," as Strasser argued as early as 1926 in agreement with Gottfried Feder, was to satisfy the basic needs of the people. Against both "Marxists" and "capitalists," he asserted that "Speculative production" resulted in

> artificial need, a betrayal of human labor, of human life! For artificially stimulated covetousness creates ever-increasing aspirations, and increased aspirations *double human slavery, which is slavery of the mind, which instead of the soul has taken up mastery over life!* . . . What do people know today about life?! They run around and tire themselves out, torment themselves, strive and drudge like galley slaves – in order to lead a life of horrifying emptiness! *It is not that this new economic system which we want produces more. What is at stake is certainly not higher production*, which Marxism demands, *but the human soul!!*"[66]

Merging Taylorist and Nazi principles, Strasser rejected distribution according to need and across-the-board wage levels. He argued instead that wages be tied to individual achievement measured in increased productivity, maintaining that competition in the struggle for survival would assure racial supremacy.[67] Although Strasser resigned from the party at the end of the year, having been unable to resolve his tactical and ideological disagreements with Hitler, the sources of the conflict bore no relationship to the issue of consumption, which little distinguished Strasser from the rest of the party leadership.[68]

Objects: A Cultural History of West German Industrial Design, 1930–1965 (Berkeley and Los Angeles: University of California Press, 2004), Ch. 1.

65 For more on this topic, see Alf Lüdtke's pioneering essay, "'Ehre der Arbeit': Industriearbeiter und Macht der Symbole. Zur Reichweite symbolischer Orientierungen im Nationalsozialismus," in *Arbeiter im 20. Jahrhundert*, ed. Klaus Tenfelde (Stuttgart: Klett-Cotta, 1991): 343–92.

66 "Thoughts about the Tasks of the Future," in Lane and Rupp, *Nazi Ideology*, 89–90.

67 Campbell, *Joy in Work*, 317.

68 Kershaw, *Hubris*, 398–9; Orlow, *History of the Nazi Party*, 239–98, and Hans Mommsen, *The Rise and Fall of Weimar Democracy*, trans. Elborg Foster and Larry Eugene Jones (Chapel Hill and London: University of North Carolina Press, 1996), 498–511. Strasser's alienation resulted primarily from Hitler's refusal to countenance a

Aside from the Nazi party's cultural reservations, the assumption embedded in Fordism that workers needed a wage sufficient to purchase mass-produced goods presented a more serious problem, even though Henry Ford's intention, to assuage dissatisfaction that encouraged unionization, complimented the Nazis' own desire to transform industrial relations from an arena of class conflict to a replication of the racial community. Increasing wages not only smacked of "Marxism," for doing so was a key Social Democratic demand. It also fundamentally conflicted with Hitler's primary goal, the acquisition of living space in the east, which would become the center of gravity of a future German empire, and which would require rearmament and eventually war to obtain.

To be sure, sales of nonessential consumer goods continued throughout the thirties to accommodate middle-class demand. Radios, record players, cameras, harmonicas, camping equipment, refrigerators, automobiles, and cigarettes found ready markets. The regime's pronatalist policies, especially its marriage loans, encouraged the purchase of household furnishings. In 1936, the launching of the "people's car" or Volkswagen, which the führer imagined would provide every worker with an affordable mass-produced car, spoke to the regime's intention to "motorize" the masses. Regardless, the Third Reich privileged military spending and barred imports of raw materials and foodstuffs that consumer goods producers needed. Private consumption remained low relative to public investment to stimulate rearmament, and despite the savings accounts that proliferated toward the purchase of Volkswagen, not a single one made it into private hands.[69] If publicly the führer promised that the regime would "increase the buying power of the masses," he more often demanded sacrifice.[70] If most Germans perceived that their material quality of life improved under Nazism, the distortion of the economy to benefit rearmament left them less well off than the British and French, and especially the Americans, despite increases in the production of consumer

power-sharing arrangement between the Nazi party and Kurt Schleicher. To avoid a civil war that Schleicher feared would endanger the army, Schleicher proposed to incorporate the trade unions in his government, yet deny Hitler the office he had long sought.

69 Kershaw, *Hubris*, 444–6; Barkai, *Nazi Economics*, 196–7. For a nuanced treatment of the status of consumer production in the Third Reich, see Hartmut Berghoff, "Konsumgüterindustrie im Nationalsozialismus: Marketing im Spannungsfeld von Profit – und Regimeinteressen," *Archiv für Sozialgeschichte* 36 (1996): 293–322, and "Enticement and Deprivation: The Regulation of Consumption in Pre-War Nazi Germany," in *Politics of Consumption*, ed. Daunton and Hilton: 165–84. On the low consumer payoff of the Volkswagen, see Ronald Smelser, *Robert Ley: Hitler's Labor Front Leader* (Oxford, New York, and Hamburg, 1989), 173.

70 See his speeches of September 1933, one of them to Autobahn workers, in Max Domarus, *Hitler's Speeches and Proclamations 1932–1945: The Chronicle of a Dictatorship*, vol. 1, *The Years 1932–1934*, trans. Mary Fran Gilbert (London: I.B. Taurus, 1990): 360–1.

durables for the middle classes.[71] Even the encouragement of some consumer goods, such as refrigerators and convenience foods, was to benefit rearmament. Refrigerators and new forms of packaging like foil and cellophane saved food, thus suppressing the demand for imports. Ironically, given Hitler's complaint that the German economy had been too heavily weighted toward export, the manufacture of luxury items for foreign markets, such as silverware, tapestries, and porcelain generated much-needed hard currency that the Reich government reinvested in armaments production.[72]

Curtailing demand and encouraging consumers to dampen their "materialistic" desires became especially evident after 1936 when the Four-Year Plan instituted stricter economic controls and the accelerated production of materials that could be derived from domestic resources. Through measures such as capping wage increases, however difficult that remained in practice, redirecting labor to armaments-related industries, and increasing taxation to limit disposable income, the Third Reich ensured that consumer production and real earnings failed to achieve the levels of 1929. Workers bore the brunt of the regime's crackdown on consumption, even though the destruction of the left could not prevent labor shortages that rearmament created from modestly enhancing their bargaining position. If the incomes of workers, especially male skilled workers in industries crucial to rearmament, fared better during the Third Reich compared to the wage levels of the Depression, they resulted more from longer work days to meet production goals than from wage hikes. Poor housing, usually a cramped two-room flat or a small space as a border in the flat of another, as well as the rising cost and declining variety of food and clothing, constrained working-class lives. Import restrictions and inflated prices for domestic agricultural commodities, the "synchronization" of consumer cooperatives, and housing shortages that the regime but minimally addressed resulted in higher living costs despite the controls that the

---

71 Richard Overy, "Guns or Butter? Living Standards, Finance, and Labour in Germany, 1939–1942," in *War and Economy*, ed. Overy, 262–5; Hans–Dietrich Schäfer, *Das gespaltene Bewußtsein: Über deutsche Kultur und Lebenswirklichkeit 1933–1945* (Munich, Vienna: Carl Hanser Verlag, 1981), 117; Schneider, *Unterm Hakenkreuz*, 591–638. Among other evidence, the Reich's discrimination against consumer production constitutes a major stumbling block to the recent claim of Werner Abelshauser in his "Kriegswirtschaft und Wirtschaftswunder: Deutschlands wirtschaftliche Mobilisierung für den Zweiten Weltkrieg und die Folgen für die Nachkriegszeit, *Vierteljahrshefte für Zeitgeschichte* 47 (1999): 503–38, that the standard of living steadily improved. See the rebuttal by Christoph Buchheim, "Die Wirtschaftsentwicklung im Dritten Reich – Mehr Desaster als Wunder: Eine Erwiderung auf Werner Abelshauser," in the same journal, vol. 49, no. 4 (2001): 653–64.

72 Loehlin, *Rugs to Riches*, 28; Paul Betts, "The *Nierentisch* Nemesis: Organic Design as West German Pop Culture," *German History* 19, no. 2 (2001): 197.

regime placed on rents.[73] The degree to which Nazi Germany remained a low-wage, low-consumption economy became evident in the proportion of the gross national product that the Reich devoted to rearmament. Until 1939, Germany's outlays for armaments amounted to nearly double the proportion of the GNP that the British spent, and ten times the proportion that the United States consumed.[74]

The privileging of rearmament did not fail to influence Robert Ley, who succeeded Gregor Strasser as Reich organization leader, and who after 1933 as leader of the German Labor Front pushed for a "high" standard of living to assure workers of the regime's desire to meet their needs. Ley would insist that wage increases accomplished only an upward, self-defeating, spiral of costs and inflated desires that could never be satisfied. Yet he also claimed that the regime would improve the status of workers by providing them access to the "cultural property" of the German nation, once the preserve of the middle and upper classes. Although deprived of goods, access to previously unattainable cultural practices would allow workers to overcome their collective "inferiority complex" and welcome their integration as members of the racial community. The elimination of the invidious distinctions between workers of the "head" and "fist" would thus be complete.

The greed of Nazi party leaders after 1933 contrasted starkly with their disdain toward the unfettered consumption implied in Americanism, the detritus of international, "Jewish," capitalism. Nazi leaders proved susceptible to the lure of materialism even before taking power, having profited from the generosity of the party's well-heeled backers.[75] The conspicuous consumption of Nazi paladins grew more evident after 1933, fueled by party patronage and the opportunities that power offered, and by the regime's racially charged definition of merit as achievement by the fittest. Many engaged in the sort of hedonism that once prompted their scorn: purchasing large mansions and furnishing them with style, and accumulating wine cellars and works of art by old masters (often stolen from Jews or purloined from the occupied territories). Those commodities in turn cemented patronage and fealty among them while elevating them to the status of aristocrats by race instead of by birth.[76] Rather than

---

73 For working-class living standards, see Schneider, *Unterm Hakenkreuz*, 591–638.

74 Mark Mazower, *Dark Continent: Europe's Twentieth Century* (New York: Alfred A. Knopf, 1998), 128.

75 See Kershaw, *Hubris*, 343, 359; and Jeremy Noakes, "Nazism and High Society," in *Confronting the Nazi Past: New Debates on Modern German History*, ed. Michael Burleigh (New York: St. Martin's Press, 1996): 51–65.

76 See Michael Burleigh, *The Third Reich: A New History* (New York: Hill and Wang, 2000), 219–77; and Jonathan Petropoulos, *Art as Politics in the Third Reich* (Chapel Hill, London: University of North Carolina Press, 1996). Corruption and its connection to genocide has emerged as a powerful theme in recent scholarship on the Third

adhere to "German" or "Aryan" fashion, as suggested by Nazi women's magazines, the wives of Nazi leaders, most prominently Magda Goebbels, eschewed dirndls in favor of elegance and chic.[77] Few leaders, except for Hermann Göring, exceeded the opulent lifestyle of the Labor Front leader, Ley. Ley's self-proclaimed advocacy of workers' interests deterred him neither from compensating for the painful childhood experiences of his father's financial ruin nor from satiating his upwardly mobile ambitions to the tune of four cavernous villas and a fleet of expensive cars. The German Labor Front became a cesspool of graft, fueled by the dues of its enormous membership.[78] Having destroyed the republic and disabled all organized opposition with at least tacit popular consent and the collusion of most of Germany's elites, Nazi leaders confronted few obstacles to the private appropriation of public resources.

Nevertheless, the widespread approval that greeted the Nazi dictatorship's installation could not have endured in the face of such corruption if the regime had not attended to popular demands for a better life. Seared by the experience of World War I, when inflation and chronic shortages of basic necessities brought defeatism, revolution, and the hated Weimar Republic, the Nazi leadership's long-term and immediate solutions to the consumption problem evolved from the Third Reich's major priorities and internal rivalries. The long-term solution, territorial enlargement, was to be sure the most important. Only living space would permanently satisfy expectations for a higher material standard of living. Drawing from his understanding of the sources of American prosperity, Hitler maintained that a decent standard of living, defined in this case as the possession of economic goods, would ascend from sufficient territory and the resources derived from it to match the size of its population. The acquisition of empire, however, depended on realizing mutually reinforcing goals that the führer and his party shared. They included the elimination of social divisions and the creation of "community," the willingness to sacrifice for the attainment of future reward, racial purification and achievement through natural selection, and finally, the eagerness to assume the bearing of a "master race" (*Herrenvolk*), which the Jewish inventions of liberal democracy and socialism had sapped. Unless the nation assented to the moral commitments flowing from their inborn racial superiority, claimed Hitler in a speech in Erlangen in June 1931, they would have "no right to a

---

Reich, as evidenced by Frank Bajohr's *Parvenüs und Profiteure: Korruption in der NS-Zeit* (Frankfurt am Main: Fischer, 2001), which argues that it was central to the Nazi regime's destructiveness.

77 Historisches Museum Frankfurt, *Frankfurt Macht Mode 1933–1945* (Frankfurt: Jonas Verlag, 1999), 13.

78 Smelser, *Robert Ley*, 108–16; Bajohr, *Parvenüs und Profiteure*, 55–8, 71.

life of material luxury and ease" (*ein materielles Herrenleben*) appropriate to a dominant race.

> That life of luxury then is only morally justified when it has its deepest roots in a moral conception of lordship (*einem moralischen Herren-Sinne*), and it must fall upon a young movement, which can pull a people such as the Germans back again from their despondency and inner despair, and above all put together a political organization that is at least as effective as an economic one; indeed one that can in part be looked upon as even more effective.[79]

Until war could be waged and living space secured, however, the Nazi regime's ability to retain the support of its disparate constituencies depended on an interim solution that would assuage popular needs. Strength through Joy emerged as that solution; a genuinely "national socialist" one. It represented Nazism's management of consumption as the Third Reich strove to temper mass desires without class conflict and without unleashing a putatively hedonistic, individualistic, and Americanized materialism that ideologically and functionally clashed with Nazi goals. Strength through Joy embodied the Third Reich's concern to "raise" popular living standards without jeopardizing rearmament or capitulating to "materialism," while simultaneously providing respite to encourage the higher productivity that war preparations required. By claiming the inseparability of work and leisure and instituting programs that linked the two spheres, KdF hoped to lure workers away from the left's class-based road to a better life and the full-throttle consumer individualism of American capitalism.

---

79 See Kershaw, *Hubris*, 245–50. Hitler's longer speeches on the road to power reveal the seamless connections among antisemitism, living space, and the standard of living. See in particular, *RSA*, vol. I, 239–63; vol. II, part 1, 165–79; vol. II, part 1, 193–219; and vol. IV, part 1, 413–31. The quotation is found in *RSA* vol. IV, part I, 426. The degree to which Nazism's "socialism" was grounded in the principle of natural selection can be seen in Hitler's monologue to Otto Wagener in *Hitler – Memoirs of a Confidant*, ed. Henry Ashby Turner, Jr. and trans. Ruth Hein (New Haven and London: Yale University Press, 1978): 39–48. For a rebuttal to Rainer Zitelmann's argument as to the regime's modernism, see Philipp Gassert, *Amerika im Dritten Reich: Ideologie, Propaganda und Volksmeinung 1933–1945* (Stuttgart: Franz Steiner Verlag, 1997), 87–103.

2

"A Volk *Strong in Nerve*": Strength through Joy's Place in the Third Reich

On November 27, 1933, ten months after the Nazi takeover, the German Labor Front leader, Robert Ley, announced the formation of Strength through Joy in a speech before the upper house of the Prussian parliament.[1] Strength through Joy was to become a subsidiary of the Labor Front, which the führer had decreed into existence the previous May just days after the SA and SS dissolved the Social Democratic trade unions. Consistent with the DAF's mission to transform workplaces from sites of class conflict to "plant communities" (*Betriebsgemeinschaften*) that harmonized the interests of management and labor, Ley assigned KdF the "special historical task" of making visible the "ideal value" of work over and above its mere "material" or "technical–mechanical" worth. Yet as an organization devoted to leisure unlike other divisions of the Labor Front, KdF strove to organize its "after work" activities "in the closest connection" to the workday itself.

Stressing what would become KdF's *Leitmotif* – that work and leisure were complementary and mutually reinforcing aspects of life – KdF's charter claimed that "after work" activities amounted not to the escape from work but its affirmation.[2] Because it addressed a fear that had become common in the industrialized world, that leisure meant the unhealthy separation from work and a flight into unregulated spare time, Strength through Joy became the Labor Front's most wide-ranging agency. By using leisure programs and shop floor improvements to prod workers into abandoning their putative roles as agents of class conflict to become full-fledged members of the racial community, KdF's programs sought to reconnect the spheres of work and free time.[3]

1 "Die Gründung der NS-Gemeinschaft "Kraft durch Freude," in Ley, *Durchbruch der sozialen Ehre* (Berlin: Mehden Verlag, 1935), 23–44.
2 Der Reichsorganisationsleiter der NSDAP, *Organisationsbuch der NSDAP* (Munich: Franz Eher Verlag, 1943), 210.
3 On the "problem of worker leisure," see Victoria de Grazia, *The Culture of Consent: Mass Organization of Leisure in Fascist Italy* (Cambridge: Cambridge University Press, 1981), 238–9, and Gary Cross, *Time and Money: The Making of Consumer Culture* (London and New York: Routledge, 1993).

In his inaugural address, Ley justified KdF's existence by placing it in a broader context: the problem of work in an era in which America had emerged as the dominant economic power and pioneer in mass production. Because of the increased productivity inherent in mechanization and rationalization, American entrepreneurs established the forty-eight hour week and eight-hour workday for workers as compensation for the dramatic acceleration in the tempo of work. Ley admitted that no alternative to assembly lines and stopwatches existed. Germany's failure to rationalize, he acknowledged, would undermine its competitiveness and reduce its workers to the status of Chinese and Japanese "coolies." Nevertheless, the "Marxists" who created the Weimar Republic had grown so enamored of the eight-hour day that they hastily introduced it after the revolution without alleviating its negative consequence, the acceleration of production. As a consequence, they neglected to structure free time for workers that would have allowed them to recover from their exhaustion. Citing the International Labour Office (ILO) in Geneva in his support,[4] Ley termed that failure "one of the capital crimes of our former Marxists power holders." Not only had German workers succumbed to the deprecating effects of mechanization, they also, or so Ley implied, suffered from an "inferiority complex" stemming from the manner in which their work had become deskilled, degraded, and routinized. Borrowing from the Belgian socialist Hendrik de Man, whose 1927 essay *Joy in Work* advocated an ethic of labor which emphasized work as a "debt to the community."[5] Ley argued that leisure would develop workers' "personalities" and increase their self-respect. Thus, KdF would provide a solution that presupposed, indeed underscored, the inseparability of labor and leisure. Organized recreation would cultivate character while relaxing body and soul, and as a result, workers would derive satisfaction from their work, abandon their inferiority complexes, and become more productive.

The Labor Front leader's references to de Man and the ILO betrayed the extent to which, for all its autarky, Nazism joined the international discussion on labor relations during the interwar period. Although insisting that mass leisure activities should emerge from the collective enthusiasm of the

4 See "Gründung," 27–9. Ley quoted the ILO to the effect that workers needed time for relaxation if the eight-hour day was to be effective.
5 "Joy in work," in *A Documentary Study of Hendrik de Man, Socialist Critic of Marx,* ed. and trans. Peter Dodge (Princeton: Princeton University Press, 1979): 195. See also Alf Lüdtke, "The 'Honor of Labor': Industrial Workers and the Power of Symbols under National Socialism," in *Nazism and German Society 1933–1945,* ed. David Crew, (London and New York, 1993): 83–4. On de Man's variant of socialism, which was more radical or less depending on one's perspective, see Gerd-Rainer Horn, *European Socialists Respond to Fascism: Ideology, Activism and Contingency in the 1930s* (New York and Oxford: Oxford University Press, 1996), 74–95; and Stanley Pierson, *Leaving Marxism: Studies in the Dissolution of an Ideology* (Stanford: Stanford University Press, 2001), 31–75.

nation, rather than being imposed and directed by class-based political
parties and the trade unions, Ley expressed the distrust of autonomous
working-class leisure shared by economists, social scientists, and political leaders across the industrialized world. Many rejected the proposal
of trade unionists, socialists, and other reformers to shorten the workday, which would have allowed workers extended free time.[6] Workers
should not be left to their own devices, Ley maintained, for the boredom,
lassitude, and subversion that would result would compromise the state
and the racial community. A questionnaire that the DAF circulated with
the company's permission in early 1934 to the Berlin-based employees of
Siemens, the huge electrical engineering concern, lent support to the "necessity" of a comprehensive, well-supervised, leisure organization. Left on
their own, the survey suggested, workers showed low rates of visitation
to museums, concerts, and even the cinema. Although half regularly read
a newspaper, most purchased no more than two books per year.[7]

Nevertheless, if Ley shared many of the prevailing international assumptions regarding leisure, he took pains to stress Strength through Joy's
superiority to other organized leisure programs and especially its distinctiveness as a National Socialist solution to the leisure "problem." KdF
would not simply structure and monitor workers' time after hours. Rather,
as Ley saw it and as KdF's constitution ultimately stated it, KdF would
embrace the totality of workers' "creative" (*schaffende*) lives on and off
the job. It would elide the accustomed boundaries between workplace
and home and public and private by arranging activities on and off the
shop floor with equal ease. Strength through Joy would not only improve
the physical conditions of workers' labor, it would also enable workers
to pursue spiritually and culturally uplifting activities, such as art, music, the theater, sport, and tourism. Unlike the leisure programs of the left,
which presupposed workers' segregation from the nation, the DAF and its
subsidiary would eliminate the barriers between workers and employers,
the workday and free time. To illustrate KdF's uniqueness, Ley contrasted
its goals with the feckless efforts of trade unions in Britain and France
to provide their members with culturally enriching respite. The evening,
Sunday, and summer schools of trade unions in England reached only a
few workers, while in France, workers were subjected to tedious preach-
ing filled with class hatred. In the Soviet Union, furthermore, "after work"
programs took on the additional burden of concealing or explaining

6   See Cross, *Time and Money*, 3–75.
7   *Siemens-Mitteilungen* no. 147 (February 1934): 19, found in the Siemens-Archiv (hereinafter cited as SA), Munich. See also Carola Sachse, *Siemens, der Nationalsozialismus
   und die moderne Familie: Eine Untersuchung zur sozialen Rationalisierung in Deutschland im 20. Jahrhundert* (Hamburg: Rasch and Röhring Verlag, 1990), 200. The questionnaire went to 80,000 employees.

away the unfulfilled promises of Bolshevik five-year plans. Insisted Ley, the journalists of the Communist party paper, *Izvestia*, produced the most boring lectures that workers had ever experienced.[8]

KdF's claim to be "more" than a leisure-time organization did not cease with Ley's inaugural address. KdF's publicists continued to deploy that theme to define their enterprise against the organized recreation of the German Socialists and Communists, as well as the European left as a whole. They reiterated their claims with even greater vehemence after the victory of the Popular Front in France in 1936, which introduced the two-week paid vacation as an entitlement for all salaried employees and wage earners. The Popular Front program according to KdF literature presupposed the artificial distinction between work and leisure, for the beneficiaries of the latter pursued leisure solely for personal enjoyment without regard for its value as edification or spiritual and physical regeneration. By contrast, National Socialist social policy, as expressed in Strength through Joy, cultivated the whole person, starting with the workplace where the ethical meaning of work took shape.[9] Although seeking to outdo Marxism by recognizing the dignity of labor, the Nazi version of cultivating individuality derived from its antisemitism: because the "Judaization" of German culture pitted workers against employers, so too had manual labor become degraded.[10]

Indeed, KdF's full name, the "National Socialist Community Strength through Joy," articulated the intentions implicit in its assertion as to the seamlessness of work and leisure. Citing Hitler's pronouncement that only a nation strong in nerve could accomplish the tasks before it, Ley maintained that "strength" would arise from the increased productivity of workers who took pride in their creativity, refreshed by the "joy" of character-enriching cultural pursuits, a healthful work environment, and vacation trips.[11] Ley's emphasis on character building and cultural access could not conceal the insidious purpose behind Strength through Joy that the führer's remark betrayed: raising the productivity of wage earners so that the Reich could rapidly rearm. For KdF's founding to have occurred simultaneously with the regime's withdrawal from international

---

8 Ley, "Gründung," 28–9.
9 Anatol von Hübbenet, *Die NS-Gemeinschaft "Kraft durch Freude." Aufbau und Arbeit* (Berlin: Junker und Dünnhaupt Verlag, 1939), 2–28; "Der Sinn der Freizeitgestaltung: Zum Dritten Weltkongress, 'Arbeit und Freude,'" clipping from unidentified newspaper, July 1, 1938, Niedersächsisches Hauptstaatsarchiv, Hannover (hereinafter cited as NHH), VVP 15, no. 2455. For Popular Front leisure-time policy, see Ellen Furlough, "Making Mass Vacations: Tourism and Consumer Culture in France, 1930s to 1970s," *Comparative Studies in Society and History* 40, no. 2 (April 1998): 253–60.
10 Adolf Hitler, *Mein Kampf*, trans. Ralph Manheim (Boston: Houghton Mifflin, 1971), 318.
11 Ley, "Gründung," 29–44.

disarmament negotiations was no mere coincidence.[12] As leisure and work comprised a partnership, so too did Nazism's short- and long-term solutions to the consumption problem. Ley concluded his address at KdF's inauguration by reiterating the regime's anti-Marxism. The DAF's and KdF's goal of generating higher productivity abetted not just the regime's promotion of economic recovery, it also rectified the "Marxist" errors of the Weimar state. "The previous power holders believed that they could make the *Volk* happy with full stomachs and abdomens alone. Material demands and material wishes made up the content of their entire statecraft."[13] By contrast, KdF defined the standard of living more expansively than just the possession of material goods to include "spiritual" pursuits, which demonstrated the "honor" that the regime bestowed on wage earners.

Filling the Available Space: Strength through Joy's Empire

The Italian Fascist leisure organization "After Work" (Dopolavoro) inspired Strength through Joy's creation owing to the appeal that the Fascists' authoritarian approach to labor relations had for German conservatives before 1933. Ley's proposal for a Nazi counterpart suggested little more than an After Work copy, so much so that ten days after his address to the Prussian parliament, KdF's official name remained identical to that of its Fascist counterpart.[14] Ley had visited Italy in 1932, then as a Nazi delegate to the Prussian legislature, and came away impressed with the Fascist regime's "achievements," especially in the management of leisure. Following his return, he proposed that the party establish a similar institution in Germany after it claimed power. With the support of the propaganda minister, Joseph Goebbels, who urged the Labor Front to create a cultural division, Ley laid the groundwork for a German "After Work" in the summer following the Nazi takeover. Strength through Joy's first director, the stage and theater producer Horst Dressler-Andress, had

---

12 Daniela Liebscher, "Mit KdF 'die Welt erschließen': Der Beitrag der KdF-Reisen zur Außenpolitik der Deutschen Arbeitsfront 1934–1939," *1999: Zeitschrift für Sozialgeschichte des 20. und 21. Jahrhunderts* 12, no. 1 (March 1999): 47.

13 Ley, "Gründung," 33.

14 For the maelstrom surrounding the founding of KdF, see Ronald Smelser, *Robert Ley: Hitler's Labor Front Leader* (Oxford, New York, Hamburg: Berg, 1989), 201–2; Hasso Spode, "Arbeiterurlaub im Dritten Reich," in *Angst, Belohnung, Zucht und Ordnung: Herrschaftsmechanismen im Nationalsozialismus*, ed. Carola Sachse et al. (Opladen: Westdeutscher Verlag, 1982), 288–94; and Hermann Weiß, "Ideologie der Freizeit im Dritten Reich: Die NS-Gemeinschaft 'Kraft durch Freude'," *Archiv für Sozialgeschichte* 33 (1993): 292–4.

been an ally of Goebbels since the late twenties.[15] The DAF's negotiations with Siemens in the fall of 1933 toward the questionnaire that would circulate among the firm's employees was intended to strengthen the case for the Nazi "After Work" organization.

Despite Ley's positive assessment of After Work in the wake of his trip to Italy, the limitations of the Italian model did not take long to appear. The DAF's goal of "restoring" the "joy" of work and KdF's own rationale to reconnect the spheres of work and leisure caused Ley to minimize the productivism implicit in the Fascist agency. Although superior to other nations in its management of workers' free time, Ley and other DAF spokesmen believed that After Work managed workers' time only off the shop floor. Leisure unconnected with work would result in mindless entertainment rather than the "elevation of personality."[16] In addition, KdF followed the Labor Front in embracing all "creative" Germans as individuals, thus forging a "community" undivided by class or occupation, unlike After Work, which was subdivided into vocational corporations. Finally, unlike After Work which excluded them, employers were to join Strength through Joy along with workers, shopkeepers, white-collar workers and others, just as they were required to join the Labor Front itself. The Third Reich's inheritance of long-standing conceptions of "German" work,[17] and its more intense integral nationalism when compared with Fascist Italy, necessitated a different structure for the implementation of its leisure policy.

Ley's assessment of After Work attested to foreign policy clashes between Italy and the Third Reich and especially to the Nazi regime's internal social Darwinian conflicts.[18] Having emerged after the dissolution of the trade unions in the spring of 1933, the DAF raised the suspicions of industrialists, whose indispensable role in economic recovery and rearmament meant that Hitler could ill afford to alienate them. Because the Labor

---

15 Interview mit Herrn Horst Dressler-Andress am 5./6. 10.1966 im Institut für Zeitgeschichte, Munich. Archiv, Institut für Zeitgeschichte, Munich (hereinafter cited as IfZ).

16 Ley, "Gründung," 29; and Willy Müller, *Das soziale Leben im neuen Deutschland unter besonderer Berücksichtigung der Deutschen Arbeitsfront* (Berlin: Verlag E.S. Mittler & Sohn, 1938), 175–6. Ley's claim was misleading. Although Dopolavoro did not have a counterpart to Schönheit der Arbeit, its intentions were thoroughly productivist. See de Grazia, *Culture of Consent*, 35–6, 72–3.

17 For further elaboration, see Joan Campbell, *Joy in Work, German Work: The National Debate, 1800–1945* (Princeton: Princeton University Press, 1989), 312–36, especially, 334.

18 Nazi agitation in Austria and German economic expansion in the Danube region, which offended the Italians, contributed to Ley's change of heart. See Daniela Liebscher, "Organisierte Freizeit als Sozialpolitik: Die faschistische *Opera Nazionale Dopolavoro* und die NS-Gemeinschaft *Kraft durch Freude* 1925–1939," in *Faschismus und Gesellschaft in Italien: Staat-Wirtschaft-Kultur*, ed. Jens Petersen and Wolfgang Schieder (Cologne: SH Verlag, 1998): 78–81.

Front sought the exclusive right to negotiate wage agreements, business feared that it would prove as costly as any wage proposal that the Social Democrats and the trade unions ever put forth. Moreover, because the DAF incorporated numerous members of the party's factory agitation and recruitment troops, the National Socialist Factory Cell Organization (Nationalsozialistische Betriebszellenorganisation or NSBO), employers feared the imposition of NSBO proposals in their domains, among them the right of workers to strike, the corporativist representation of economic interests including labor, and activist shop floor "cells" that would represent the interests of workers against management.[19]

By November, however, the employers had prevailed. The DAF assumed the shape of a mass organization structured from the top down according to the Nazi leader principle. Its membership became mandatory for all employers and employees in commerce and industry. It consisted of individuals joining simply as "creative Germans of the head and fist" rather than as members of a corporation. That implicitly excluded Jews, for according to the party, Jews were culture "destroyers," not culture "creators." On the very day that Ley officially announced the creation of Strength through Joy, the DAF ceded the right to negotiate on behalf of workers in wage matters in an accord concluded with representatives of industry, the labor minister Franz Seldte, the economics minister Kurt Schmitt, and Hitler's commissioner for economic affairs, Wilhelm Keppler. Finally, the National Labor Law (Gesetz zur Ordnung der nationalen Arbeit or AOG) adopted in January 1934 formalized the boundaries erected against the DAF. It asserted the complete hegemony of employers, officially termed "leaders," over their employees, now called the "retinue" (*Gefolgschaft*). After having celebrated the destruction of the trade unions and the suppression of the NSBO, industrialists were not about to negotiate with Ley's sprawling megaunion, regardless of the DAF's intention to eliminate class conflict. Although the DAF secured the right to oversee the political education of workers, which allowed it representation on the shop floor, Ley had not achieved his primary goal.

Apart from the political realities of the Third Reich, which curtailed Ley's ambitions for the DAF, Ley's background and unquestioning loyalty to Hitler constrained his ability to protest. After serving on the western front during World War I and returning home with a head injury

19 On the development of the DAF, see Smelser, *Robert Ley*, 117–48; Tim Mason, *Social Policy in the Third Reich: The Working Class and the 'National Community,'* ed. Jane Caplan and trans. John Broadwin (Providence and Oxford: Berg, 1993), passim; Tilla Siegel, *Leistung und Lohn in der nationalsozialistischen "Ordnung der Arbeit"* (Opladen: Westdeutscher Verlag, 1989), 62–124; and Michael Schneider, *Unterm Hakenkreuz: Arbeiter und Arbeiterbewegung 1933 bis 1939* (Bonn: J.H.W. Dietz Nachf., 1999), 168–82.

that never fully healed, Ley earned a doctorate in chemistry. He subsequently took a position with Bayer at Leverkusen, then a division of the chemical conglomerate IG-Farben, a leader in company-sponsored vocational training and recreation. During his tenure, Ley became familiar with the approaches of the German Institute for Technical Labor Training (Deutsches Institut für technische Arbeitsschulung) or Dinta, a right-wing vocational program founded in 1925 by Karl Arnhold. On top of teaching technical skills to young workers, Dinta sought to instill the virtues of military discipline, personal productivity and achievement, reward on the basis of performance, and obedience to employers.[20] Combined with his experience at IG-Farben, Ley's bitter anti-Marxism, antisemitism, and "front generation" inspired "socialism" produced a labor "advocate" more interested in "caring" for workers than empowering them. Although IG-Farben dismissed him for his antisemitic attack on one of its directors, Ley received financial compensation in return for not hiring on with a competitor.[21] Despite his personal liabilities, arrogance, alcohol abuse and a messy personal life, Ley owed his rise through the ranks of the Nazi party from gauleiter of Rhineland-South to Reich Organization Leader to his willingness to follow Hitler with nary a murmur of dissent. Ley assumed the latter position in late 1932 following Gregor Strasser's defection from the party, Hitler having chosen him because Ley's führer worship and vaulting ambition ruled out the independence that characterized his predecessor. Even at Nuremberg during his interrogation before trial as a war criminal, Ley refused to abandon his veneration of Hitler. Until he committed suicide while awaiting his day in court, he remained unyielding as to the positive legacies of Nazi social policy.[22]

The staff that Ley appointed to head Strength through Joy's divisions personified the outcome of the jockeying between the Nazi party and business, the confirmation of corporate power and the defeat of a labor movement independent of the regime. KdF's leadership drew a few "old fighters" (*alte Kämpfer*), such as the aristocratic head of its sports department, Hans von Tschammer und Osten from Dresden, who joined the

---

20 Schneider, *Unterm Hakenkreuz*, 565. My discussion of Ley draws from Smelser, *Robert Ley*, 70–97, as well as his shorter biographical sketch of Ley, "Robert Ley: The Brown Collectivist," in *The Nazi Elite*, ed. Ronald Smelser and Rainer Zitelmann, trans. Mary Fischer (New York: New York University Press, 1993): 144–54. Smelser's characterization of Ley as "patron" (*Betreuer*) is particularly apt. On Ley's relationship to Dinta, see John Gillingham, "The 'Deproletarianization' of German Society: Vocational Training in the Third Reich," *Journal of Social History* 19 (1986): 423–32, especially 425.

21 Peter Hayes, *Industry and Ideology: IG Farben in the Nazi Era* (Cambridge: Cambridge University Press, 1987), 65–6. On Ley's understanding of himself as the *Betreuer* of workers, see Smelser, *Robert Ley*, passim.

22 Richard Overy, *Interrogations: The Nazi Elite in Allied Hands, 1945* (New York: Viking, 2001), 166–7, 546.

Nazi party in 1922 in opposition to the leftist government in Saxony.[23] Yet it also attracted young technocrats, who conformed to Ley's vision that workers would be cared for rather than allowed to determine their own destiny. The appointment of Bodo Lafferentz, the jurist employed by the United German Employers Association, as the head of the KdF office of Travel, Hiking, and Vacations typified a leadership that defined workers' interests for them rather than permitting them self-representation.[24] So too did the accession of Hitler's architect, Albert Speer, and Speer's successor, the architect and engineer Herbert Steinwarz, to KdF's office, the Beauty of Labor. Although their desire to rid the shop floor of class conflict meant to reconstruct the nation, rather than to boost the profits of employers (which provoked the concerns of employers that their autonomy might be compromised), Strength through Joy's leaders pursued the sort of interventionism in workers' lives that characterized corporate social policy in the twenties.[25]

Strength through Joy's structure, as Ley outlined it, conformed to its stated intentions, for it immediately allotted a bureau each for cultural events, "self-help and support," vacations, instruction and education, travel and hiking, sports, and finally the Beauty of Labor. The last office, emblematic of KdF's desire to integrate work and leisure, assumed the task of persuading employers to initiate aesthetic and hygienic improvements in their enterprises, which would boost the self-respect of workers and improve productivity. According to Speer, its first director, Ley came away impressed by mines conspicuous for their cleanliness and the gardens that surrounded them during a trip to the Netherlands, which inspired him to undertake the renovation of the workplace at home.[26] By 1936, following several reorganizations, KdF had been streamlined to six offices, including the Beauty of Labor, sports, and adult education (Volksbildungswerk). Travel, hiking, and vacations were joined into one with Lafferentz remaining as head, while new branches emerged to deal with after-work activities (Amt Feierabend), the Volkswagen, and the entertainment of troops (Amt Wehrmachtheime), the last arising from an agreement between KdF and the armed forces. Another office for the work brigades (Amt Werkscharen), which Ley organized to inject the

23 Laurence Van Zandt Moyer, "The *Kraft durch Freude* Movement in Nazi Germany: 1933–1939" (Dis: Northwestern University, 1967), 82.

24 Hans Mommsen with Manfred Grieger, *Das Volkswagenwerk und seine Arbeiter im Dritten Reich* (Düsseldorf: Econ. Verlag, 1997), 142–44.

25 The paragon of this trend was Siemens. See Sachse, *Siemens*, passim. On the intervention implicit in the social engineering of interwar Europe in general, see Charles S. Maier, "Society as Factory," in Maier, *In Search of Stability: Explorations in Historical Political Economy* (Cambridge: Cambridge University Press, 1987): 19–69.

26 Albert Speer, *Inside the Third Reich: Memoirs*, trans. Richard and Clara Winston (New York: Macmillan, 1970), 67.

military spirit that Dinta saw as essential to the shop floor, was transferred to the Labor Front's Education Office.

As a division of the Labor Front, KdF's structure mirrored that of the NSDAP, which originally conformed to Weimar election districts. Following the leader principle, it flowed from the top down from the district (Gau), to the county (Kreis), and to the local (Ort) levels. At each stage, DAF officials and KdF "wardens" (Warte) reported to the party leader, yet as was customary in the Third Reich, the practice of multiple feudalities often rendered nugatory formal chains of command. Like the DAF, which was itself linked to the Reich party organization in the person of Ley, the offices of party leader and DAF leader were often joined, while DAF leaders often assumed responsibility for KdF matters.[27] Revealing the goal of creating "plant communities," as well as the Labor Front's not-to-be-denied place on the shop floor, the DAF and KdF structure extended as well to business. The DAF plant representative (Obmann) in each workplace designated a KdF warden with the approval of management. Wardens were appointed for each KdF division in firms with more than twenty employees. In firms with more than two hundred employees, the KdF sport warden supervised one or two subordinates, who oversaw physical education and sport competitions.[28] By 1935, KdF's personnel on the shop floor alone encompassed nearly 57,000 volunteer plant wardens, who organized KdF events in cooperation with their employers. Combined with the over fifteen thousand local groups (Ortsgruppen) and local wardens (Ortsgruppenwarten) KdF's staff numbered in the neighborhood of 75,000 functionaries, most of them volunteers.[29] By 1939, KdF engaged over 7,000 paid employees and over 135,000 volunteers.[30] (see Figure 2.1.)

Intentionally or otherwise, Strength through Joy amounted to a consolation prize, compensation to the Labor Front for having lost its battle to direct wage negotiations, which remained the prerogative of the Trustees of Labor, whom Seldte's ministry appointed. If Hitler backed the DAF's

---

27 Smelser, *Robert Ley*, 154–5; *Organisationsbuch der NSDAP*, 214–17.

28 *Organisationsbuch der NSDAP*, 206 a-e. The KdF office for the entertainment of the Wehrmacht operated at the Reich level only.

29 "Tätigkeitsbericht über die Leistungen der NS Gemeinschaft Kraft durch Freude von Dr. Robert Ley, 26 November 1935," Bundesarchiv, Berlin-Lichtenberg (hereinafter cited as BAL), NS 22/781.

30 For the evolution of KdF's organization, see Ley, "Gründung," 36–7; and Weiß, "Ideologie der Freizeit im Dritten Reich": 295–6. At one point, KdF included eleven offices before being reconfigured, according to the *Organisation der deutschen Arbeitsfront und der N.S. Gemeinschaft Kraft durch Freude*, undated, Stiftung Westfälisches Wirtschaftsarchiv, Dortmund (hereinafter cited as WWA), A1285 S6/776. For a summary of previous corporate policy, focusing especially on Siemens, see Carola Sachse, "Freizeit zwischen Betrieb und Volksgemeinschaft: Betriebliche Freizeitpolitik im Nationalsozialismus," *Archiv für Sozialgeschichte* 33 (1993): 305–28.

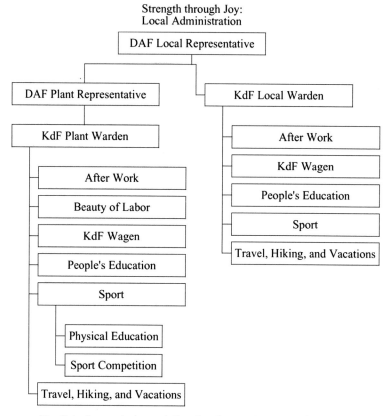

Fig. 2.1. Strength through Joy: local organization. Adapted from Reichsorganisationsleiter der NSDAP, *Organisationsbuch der NSDAP* (Munich: Franz Eher Verlag, 1943). Unlike KdF's plant structure, which obviously necessitated a Beauty of Labor division, the local organization contained no such office.

subsequent intrusions in the workplace and made an occasional public relations appearance on a KdF cruise ship, his immediate priorities left little space for KdF in his considerations.[31] Ley's bombast, his well publicized extramarital affairs, and his chronic alcohol abuse made him the target of ridicule. Moreover, Ley found himself embroiled in turf wars because of his ambition to direct the regime's entire social and economic policy. Throughout his tenure, Ley conducted running feuds with the Minister of Labor Seldte over wage policy, social insurance, and the mediation of

---

31 See Albert Speer's remarks in *Inside the Third Reich*, 67; Schneider, *Unterm Hakenkreuz*, 82–4; and Spode, "Arbeiterurlaub": 288–9.

shop floor disputes, as well as the economics minister Hjalmar Schacht over vocational training and the installation of DAF-dominated labor committees in plant management. He quarreled with powerful members of Hitler's inner circle, notably the führer's deputies Rudolf Hess and Martin Bormann, who neither shared Ley's passion for mass mobilization and spectacle, nor appreciated Ley's attempts to free the DAF from the direct supervision of the führer's lieutenants.[32] Ley's interventions in agricultural labor relations and wage policy, as well as the DAF's effort to extend its jurisdiction to housing and settlement policy, ran afoul of Walter Darré, the minister of agriculture.[33] His relationship with propaganda minister Goebbels, although less acrimonious than that with others, was nonetheless punctuated by competition, so much so that the formation of Goebbel's pet project, the Reich Chamber of Culture, blocked the Labor Front's pressure on artistic associations to join it.[34]

Finally, despite his initial cooperation with Alfred Rosenberg in staging theatrical and musical performances, Ley waged a bitter battle with the self-proclaimed party ideologist over which would dominate the popular dissemination of the fine and performing arts, KdF or Rosenberg's National Socialist Cultural Community (NS Kulturgemeinschaft), the successor to the Combat League. Although Ley concluded an agreement with Rosenberg's group within a year of KdF's founding,[35] the competition between them, inflamed by Ley's appointment of the ambitious Goebbels ally Horst Dressler-Andress without having consulted Rosenberg, did not end until 1937 when Ley's improved relationship with Goebbels brought more formal and mutually beneficial ties between the Chamber of Culture and KdF. To be sure, Dressler-Andress, whom Rosenberg considered a dangerous competitor and "cultural Bolshevik" for subordinating "cultural heritage" to the exhibition of modern art and art produced by workers, lost his job to the competent but less overtly ambitious leader of the office for Travel, Hiking, and Vacations, Bodo Lafferentz. Yet not only had Ley sacrificed little, having already grown disenchanted

---

32 See Mason, *Social Policy*, 151–78; Siegel, *Leistung und Lohn*, 65–85; Smelser, *Robert Ley*, 80–297; and Dietrich Orlow, *The History of the Nazi Party 1933–1945* (Pittsburgh: University of Pittsburgh Press, 1973), 207–8.

33 Gustavo Corni, *Hitler and the Peasants: Agrarian Policy of the Third Reich, 1930–1939*, trans. David Kerr (New York, Oxford, and Munich: Berg, 1990), 79–80; and Dan P. Silverman, *Hitler's Economy: Nazi Work Creation Programs, 1933–1936* (Cambridge, Massachusetts and London: Harvard University Press, 1998), 103–4.

34 Alan Steinweis, *Art, Ideology, and Economics in Nazi Germany: The Reich Chambers of Music, Theater, and the Visual Arts* (Chapel Hill and London: University of North Carolina Press, 1993), 38–44.

35 Die Deutsche Arbeitsfront Zentralbüro an die NS.-Kulturgemeinde in der NS.-Gemeinschaft "Kraft durch Freude," 18 December 1934, *Akten der Partei-Kanzlei der NSDAP* (hereinafter cited as *APK*), ed. Institut für Zeitgeschichte (Munich and New York: Saur, 1983), no. 126 00794.

with Dressler-Andress, Rosenberg's cultural community subsequently dissolved for want of Ley's financial contribution.[36]

For all the ferocity of Ley's rivalries and the ridicule that he endured, Ley's battles were hardly unusual in the Third Reich. Social Darwinian conflicts that reflected Hitler's "divide and rule" tendencies and the turf building of upwardly mobile men routinely characterized government under Nazism. And even if countervailing interests prevented Ley from obtaining everything he wanted, the DAF's supremacy in wage negotiations being the prime example, Strength through Joy metamorphosized into a vast empire, in which the workplace emerged a major site of its operations.[37] Nazi party leaders with the potential to challenge Ley in the delivery of leisure-time services either capitulated, such as Rosenberg, or accommodated him such as Goebbels. No rival agency or person could compete with Strength through Joy in reaching mass audiences with low-cost offerings, particularly the program that generated the most income, mass tourism.

The Nazi regime's suppression of the left, which it accomplished by the summer of 1933, proved crucial to Strength through Joy's structural and financial viability and the viability of the Labor Front as well. The dissolution of the trade unions brought in its wake the confiscation of their bank, subsequently renamed the Bank of German Labor (Bank der deutschen Arbeit or BdA), to which the DAF ultimately laid claim. The dragnet against the left, furthermore, destroyed a formidable rival in organized recreation and leisure. Social Democracy's prewar status as the pariah of the imperial state had necessitated a dense web of educational and recreational associations that partially deviated and partially borrowed from the dominant culture.[38] The Social Democrats, who organized museum visits and concert outings, as well as tourism, oversaw an extensive network of libraries and leisure clubs devoted to activities from gymnastics to boating, soccer, chess, bicycling, Esperanto, and choruses. Until the late twenties, when rising unemployment and bitter conflicts between the

---

36 Dressler-Andress interview, 5–6 October 1966, IfZ, F 104, 5. See also Reinhard Bollmus, *Das Amt Rosenberg und seine Gegner. Zum Machtkampf im nationalsozialistische Herrschaftssystem* (Stuttgart: Deutsche Verlags-Anstalt, 1970), 61–103, as well as Steinweis, *Art, Ideology and Economics*, 69–72; Jonathan Petropoulos, *Art as Politics in the Third Reich* (Chapel Hill and London: University of North Carolina Press, 1996), 64–5; Michael Kater, *The Twisted Muse: Musicians and Their Music in the Third Reich* (New York and Oxford: Oxford University Press, 1997), 16–17; Spode, "Arbeiterurlaub": 294, and Wolfhard Buchholz, "Die Nationalsozialistische Gemeinschaft 'Kraft durch Freude': Freizeitgestaltung und Arbeiterschaft im Dritten Reich" (Diss: Munich, 1976), 14 ff., 248 ff. Goebbels reported on Ley's decision to dispense with Dressler-Andress in his diary entry for 24 September 1937, *Die Tagebücher von Joseph Goebbels* (hereinafter cited as *Tagebücher*), ed. Elke Fröhlich, part 1, vol. 1 (Munich: K.G. Saur, 2000), 325.
37 This is similar to Sachse's own view of the DAF. See *Siemens*, 61 ff.
38 See Vernon L. Lidtke, *The Alternative Culture: Socialist Labor in Imperial Germany* (New York and Oxford: Oxford University Press), 1985.

parties of the left terminated the practice, the clubs included both Social-ists and Communists because the associational life of the latter remained underdeveloped. That lingering cultural unity on the left encouraged the expansion of Socialist sporting and cultural associations that persisted during the Weimar Republic in the face of the increasing popularity of commercialized leisure.[39] Thus the elimination of working-class institu-tions brought to KdF substantial material resources. By itself, the vacation and hiking group the "Friends of Nature" (Naturfreunde), which main-tained an informal but conflict-ridden relationship with the Social Demo-cratic national leadership, maintained 230 hiking and vacation hostels, 1,000 local chapters, and 100,000 members.[40]

To be sure, the forcible incorporation of the left's subsidiary associ-ations was not an unmixed blessing for the regime, for unless arrested or driven into hiding, members with leftist sympathies did not simply disappear. Indeed, the process of synchronization often consisted of dis-solving a club, only to resubscribe its members in a Nazi version with the same recreational or educational purpose.[41] Nonetheless, the incor-poration of the left's associational network provided Strength through Joy with ready-made lodgings and equipment for vacations, hikers, and sports enthusiasts. For KdF to have set up shop in the same building in Berlin that had once housed the Social Democratic newspaper *Vorwärts* testifies to the connection between the elimination of the left and the prospering of Nazi organizations that replaced it.[42]

To add to the nest egg, which the Labor Front secured from the trade unions, came the dues, deducted by employers, that accrued to the DAF from its rapidly increasing membership, which grew from fourteen million in 1934 to twenty-two million by 1939. The BdA also deposited the in-come generated from various party welfare initiatives, such as the Winter Relief (Winterhilfswerk). The mushrooming assets of the Bank of German

39 Wickham, "Working-Class Movement": 338–9; Heinrich-August Winkler, *Der Schein der Normälitat: Arbeiter und Arbeiterbewegung in der Weimarer Republik, 1924 bis 1930* (Berlin/Bonn: J.H.W. Dietz Nachf., 1988), 120–34; Hasso Spode, "'Der deutsche Arbeiter reist': Massentourismus im Dritten Reich," in *Sozialgeschichte der Freizeit: Untersuchungen zum Wandel der Alltagskultur in Deutschland*, ed. Gerhard Huck (Wupperthal; Peter Hammer Verlag, 1980): 285–7.

40 "Der Touristenverein 'Die Naturefreunde' und sein Wirken für Volk und Staat," BAL, R58, no. 782, 103–18; Nick Hopwood, "Producing a Socialist Popular Science in the Weimar Republic," *History Workshop Journal* 41 (Spring 1996): 123. The Friends of Nature were themselves divided into Socialist and Communist wings. See Hartmann Wunderer, "Naturfreundebewegung," in *Die Arbeiter: Lebensformen, Alltag und Kul-tur von der Frühindustrialisierung bis zum "Wirtschaftswunder,"* ed. Wolfgang Ruppert (Munich: C.H. Beck Verlag, 1986): 343. For workers' travel before and after World War I, see Frommann, "Reisen im Dienste politischer Zielsetzungen: Arbeiter-Reisen und 'Kroft durch Freude'-Fahrten," (Diss: Stuttgart, 1993), 21–104.

41 To wit: the case of leftist folk-dancing clubs that KdF subsequently took over, which the Gestapo feared would merely perpetuate the left's influence, BAL R58, no. 316.

42 Smelser, *Robert Ley*, 211.

Labor constituted one of the main bones of contention between Ley and Hjalmar Schacht, the economics minister. Schacht complained bitterly that the BdA's pressure on party officials to support it with deposits discriminated against the Deutsche Bank, Schacht's one-time employer.[43] The monies given over to the BdA underwrote the Labor Front's hydra-headed business ventures that ranged from job creation programs to insurance companies, consumer retailing, publishing, and finally KdF itself, one's membership in which became automatic upon joining the DAF. The Labor Front's subsidies to KdF increased dramatically from eight million RM in 1934 to nearly twenty-nine million RM in 1937, to almost thirty-three million in 1939, dipping slightly in 1940 before increasing once more to thirty-three million RM in 1942.[44]

The subsidies that the DAF provided covered KdF's administrative costs, especially those of the office for Travel, Hiking, and Vacations that consumed most of the overhead even as it generated most of KdF's income. KdF's financial dependence on the DAF allowed it to keep the cost to participants of its programs, including tourism, relatively low. It also meant KdF's continuing ability to operate despite receiving minimal state support – the result of the opposition of the finance minister, Lutz Schwerin von Krösigk, and the unforgiving budgets of local governments. Strength through Joy was not entirely dependent on the Labor Front, however, for it developed its own sources of revenue. KdF's savings programs, which allowed members to put money aside on a weekly basis for a vacation, or after 1937 a Volkswagen, were administered through the BdA, as was the income that KdF generated from selling its tour packages. Local KdF volunteers appropriated the interest earned from savings accounts, which in turn paid the travel costs of low-income participants. KdF's officials at the Reich level were not loath to publicize contributions to economic recovery either, claiming that in 1934 alone Strength through Joy tourism brought 52 million Reichsmarks into circulation. By the following year, the amount increased to nearly seventy million Reichsmarks.[45]

Strength through Joy's zeal in advertising its impact and thus generating further growth brought forth incessant, numbingly voluminous, and (possibly) inflated statistics to document the number of participants in its

43 Ibid., 161–70.
44 Buchholz, "Nationalsozialistische Gemeinschaft 'Kraft durch Freude'," 214.
45 Deutsches Konsulat, Liverpool an das Auswärtige Amt, 27 May 1936, Auswärtiges Amt, Politisches Archiv, Bonn (hereinafter cited as AA-PA), R48527 18–19. For the details of KdF's finances, see Buchholz, "Nationalsozialistische Gemeinschaft," 213–25; Bruno Frommann, "Reisen mit 'Kraft durch Freude': Eine Darstellung der KdF-Reisen unter besonderer Berücksichtigung der Auslandsfahrten" (MA thesis: Karlsruhe, 1977), 21–36, and "Reisen im Dienste politischer Zielsetzungen," 115–29; and David Schoenbaum, *Hitler's Social Revolution: Class and Status in Nazi Germany 1933–1939* (Garden City, New York: Doubleday, 1967), 104n.

programs. Nevertheless, little reason exists for doubting KdF's influence in light of the destruction of the left, its principal competition for the mass leisure market, and the proliferation of KdF functionaries in and outside of the workplace. KdF's sport program alone, which offered instruction in pastimes from tennis to sailing, grew from 8,500 offerings in 1933/4 to 48,500 in 1934/5, according to its evidence. Its physical education and gymnastics evenings skyrocketed to 190,000 in 1934/5 from 55,000 the previous year. The total number of participants increased from 450,000 in 1933/4 to over three million in 1934/5.[46]

By 1936, Strength through Joy had evolved into the largest single tourism promoter in Germany with roughly 9.5 million overnight stays to its credit, over 11 percent of all overnight stays in German hotels and pensions.[47] Despite the announcement of the Four-Year Plan that same year, which accelerated the pace of rearmament, KdF tourism remained robust, even as the regime found ways to suppress the manufacture and sale of other kinds of consumer goods. In 1938 alone, roughly 8.5 million took part in its trips, many of them repeat travelers, while between 1934 and 1939 approximately forty-three million Germans availed themselves of KdF trips. The majority of the tours consisted of excursions of up to three days. Yet the participation in the longer, two- and three-week vacation trips and cruises was by no means negligible, amounting to approximately 690,000 million vacationers by the outbreak of war.[48] KdF's mammoth resort on the Baltic, Prora, the construction for which began in May 1936, was only the flagship for an additional four such leisure sites then on the drawing boards. By the outbreak of war the following year, the DAF owned or leased twelve cruise ships for KdF, including two, the *Wilhelm Gustloff* and *Robert Ley*, that it commissioned itself. The Volkswagen, which KdF believed would enhance tourism, also fared well. Following the launch of the Volkswagen project in 1937, well over 300,000 Germans enrolled in its savings plan, through which subscribers put aside five marks per week.[49]

Likewise, according to Ley, KdF's claim to straddle the customary boundaries between work and leisure found the appropriate statistical

46 Robert Ley, "Zwei Jahre 'Kraft durch Freude,'" in Ley, *Durchbruch der sozialen Ehre*, 79.
47 Spode, "Arbeiterurlaub": 299.
48 See Spode's, figures in "'Der deutsche Arbeiter reist,'": 295. Spode's data does not include tourists from the territories annexed to Germany. For further data on the volume of tourism, see Chapter 4, pp. 120–21, and 135. Contrary to Hartmut Berghoff, "Enticement and Deprivation: The Regulation of Consumption in Pre-War Nazi Germany," in *The Politics of Consumption: Material Culture and Citizenship in Europe and America*, ed. Martin Daunton and Matthew Hilton (Oxford and New York: Berg, 2001): 173–5, who argues that KdF tourism amounted to "virtual reality of imagined consumption," KdF did in fact sell a consumer good, albeit a cut-rate and less tangible variety.
49 Smelser, *Robert Ley*, 171, 215.

support. Beginning with a staff of five, the Beauty of Labor supposedly persuaded 17,000 businesses and plants to undertake various improvements by 1935, including recreation rooms and canteens, green spaces, and swimming pools.[50] By 1939, the Beauty of Labor had overseen the creation of over 13,000 green spaces, as well as the construction of over 15,000 canteens and recreation rooms, over 20,000 workrooms, over 20,000 washing and changing rooms, over 2,000 "comradeship homes" and vacation spots, not to mention the two thousand plus sport facilities in plants.[51] By 1938, KdF managed over 300 adult education centers and thirty music schools throughout Germany, including many that the Socialists had operated under the republic.[52]

KdF's program in the performing and visual arts served as a prime indicator of its expanding empire, for its participants numbered in the millions. In Berlin alone, KdF ticket holders occupied over 50 percent of the available theater seats.[53] In most cases, KdF purchased blocks of tickets, securing low prices through the volume it could generate, and distributed them through its numerous local and plant functionaries, an indication of why Rosenberg's Culture Community fared poorly in comparison.[54] Yet KdF went well beyond a reliance on the existing network of state supported museums and performing arts venues. Apart from the exhibits and concerts that it staged in factories,[55] KdF expanded the seating capacity for cultural events outside the workplace and thus the exposure of "creative Germans" to the arts. In large cities, it built and managed "people's theaters," while reaching small towns and villages without cultural resources through open-air theaters, traveling stages, and troupes of artists. It organized a Reich and several regional orchestras that toured workplaces and communities to supplement those already in existence.[56] Although making accessible the "cultural property" of the nation, KdF's offerings catered to different tastes and audiences. Its desire to spare workers from "mindless" leisure did not in practice exclude popular entertainment, even as it sought to educate workers in the products of high culture.

---

50 Ibid., 91.
51 Anatol von Huebbenet, *Die NS-Gemeinschaft "Kraft durch Freude": Aufbau und Arbeit* (Berlin: Junker and Dünnhaupt Verlag, 1939), 28.
52 Otto Marrenbach, *Fundamente des Sieges: Die Gesamtarbeit der Deutschen Arbeitsfront von 1933 bis 1940* (Berlin: Verlag der Deutschen Arbeitsfront, 1940), 343. The Socialists ran 215 urban *Volkshochschulen* by 1929. See Dieter Langewiesche, "Freizeit und 'Massenbildung': Zur Ideologie und Praxis der Volksbildung in der Weimarer Republik," in *Sozialgeschichte der Freizeit*, ed. Huck: 223–47, especially 228.
53 Günther Adam, "Practical Activities of the National-Socialist Fellowship *Kraft durch Freude,*" *German Addresses for Committee I, World Congress "Work and Joy,"* Rome 1938 (Berlin: Buchdruckwerkstätte, 1938), 19.
54 Bollmus, *Amt Rosenberg*, 62.   55 See Chapter 3, 215–18.
56 See Adam, "Practical Activities," 17–21; Ludwig Klemme, "The Cultural Use of Leisure in Nazi Germany," *German Address for Committee VII, World Congress "Work and Joy,"* Rome 1938, 7–9; and Marrenbach, *Fundamente des Sieges*, 331–5.

Thus, it counterbalanced its performances of Beethoven and Wagner with cabarets and so-called "light evenings" (*Bunte Abende*), the latter being revues staged in beer halls, in which a band or comedian provided the entertainment. (See Table 2.1.)[57]

If varying degrees of commitment characterize the functionaries of most organizations, Strength through Joy operated with the apparent enthusiasm of the many who administered its programs. Like many Nazi organizations, KdF offered employment, a good example being the rapidly growing number of sport teachers and trainers, whom KdF could place within its ambitious mass sport program.[58] Yet the huge number of volunteers suggests by itself that "idealistic" reasons intervened as well. Without understating the corruption that often accrued to party "bosses" at all levels, the postwar justifications of many KdF employees and volunteers, as evidenced by the denazification files of Lower Saxony, underscored the appeal of the Nazis' mythic racial community and the durability of the party's discourse against "materialism."

One functionary, a locksmith and former Socialist and union member who joined the Nazis in 1932, became a KdF district operative and closed his career as a DAF county representative. He changed his political allegiance because he believed the Nazi party would better the social condition of the working class. Another, who also joined the party out of similar motivation, worked for the Beauty of Labor at the county level, having desired to improve social and hygienic conditions in the workplace. He was happy to be of service to the workers, he averred. Also charged with organizing concerts, theater visits, and tours for KdF, he enjoyed good enough relations with his constituency to win the nickname, "Uncle Herbert," despite his subsequent removal from office because of "differences in his cash balance." And yet another, a café singer who served the Beauty of Labor, committed himself to the Nazis because the party, in his view, wanted to raise the "standard of living" of the working class.[59] Despite the suspicions that such files raise because of the exculpatory motives of the accused, their claims are convincing, for the best evidence on Nazism's rise to power reveals similar yearnings behind voter choices. The caliber of KdF's organization from top to bottom contributed significantly to the appointment of Bodo Lafferentz to the board of the Volkswagen project. Not only had Lafferentz earned a reputation as an effective and compliant administrator, having overseen the office of Travel, Hiking, and

---

57 Cabarets usually offered more extensive entertainment and took place in more intimate settings than the *Bunte Abende*. See Peter Jelavich, *Berlin Cabaret* (Cambridge, Massachusetts and London: Harvard University Press, 1993), 2; and Moyer, "*Kraft durch Freude* Movement," 92–3.
58 Hajo Bernett, "Nationalsozialistischer Volkssport bei 'Kraft durch Freude,'" *Stadion. Zeitschrift für Geschichte des Sports und der Körperkultur* 5 (1979): 102–3.
59 NHH, Nds. 171 Hannover, nos. 19069, 38435, and 20483.

Table 2.1. *Strength through Joy Cultural Events*

	1934		1935		1936		1937		1938	
	N	P	N	P	N	P	N	P	N	P
Concerts	1,020	576,594	3,020	1,406,404	3,102	1,635,597	4,216	2,087,741	5,291	2,515,598
Folk performances	725	285,037	6,042	959,378	2,943	601,293	2,029	331,263	54,813	13,666,015
Operas, operettas	959	540,841	2,190	1,458,747	3,665	2,342,470	3,421	2,902,429	12,407	6,639,067
Theater	2,839	1,581,573	8,425	3,653,040	9,700	4,060,670	14,265	5,982,987	19,523	7,478,633
Variety, cabaret	1,315	481,855	5,155	2,394,942	7,146	2,576,800	6,184	2,551,507	7,921	3,518,833
Light evenings	3,189	1,228,457	14,506	4,884,761	13,848	6,396,313	10,954	4,206,172	10,989	4,462,140
Films	3,372	316,968	7,435	1,760,274	5,850	1,467,862	4,419	989,273	3,586	857,402
Exhibits	72	237,632	383	1,318,297	584	832,198	380	1,160,296	555	1,595,516
Guided tours	1,528	90,242	8,124	585,584	16,043	951,049	26,947	1,279,126	676	58,472
Other	9,653	3,772,464	11,811	5,107,327	23,500	10,333,383	37,695	16,064,510	15,084	11,118,636
Autobahn entertainment			2,044	214,462	4,942	598,566	6,484	880,359	13,589	2,658,115
Total	24,672	9,111,663	69,135	23,745,116	91,323	31,796,702	116,994	38,435,663	144,434	54,568,467

N = Number of performances.
P = Number of participants.
Source: Otto Marrenbach, *Fundamente des Sieges: Die Gesamtarbeit der Deutschen Arbeitsfront von 1933 bis 1940* (Berlin: Verlag der Deutschen Arbeitsfront, 1940), 334–5.

Vacations and then replacing Dressler-Andress as KdF's director. KdF's network also provided well-oiled channels for the advertisement and sale of the "KdF-Wagen."[60]

Strength through Joy's breadth and depth, especially in its management of leisure activities, were unmatched by similar endeavors elsewhere. Despite the extensive cooperation that emerged between KdF and After Work, particularly in the exchange of tourists, KdF's leadership and publicists bragged that the size of its membership, conferred automatically upon joining the DAF, dwarfed that of the Italian Fascist agency, some thirty-five million by 1936 compared to the mere two million in After Work.[61] Boasting aside, the numerical comparisons between memberships actually understate the degree to which the scale and penetration of KdF outdid After Work.[62] Unlike KdF, which counted on the generous subsidies of the German Labor Front, After Work received only modest state and party endowments, remaining exclusively dependent on fees, dues, and private donations. No Italian counterpart existed to the Beauty of Labor. Because of the relatively low standard of living in Italy, mass tourism remained underdeveloped despite Mussolini's attempts to impress the population with launching ocean voyages for their consumption, vicarious or otherwise.[63]

Having synthesized the information that it received from its informants inside the Reich, the situation reports of the Social Democratic Party in Exile (Sopade) – the SPD executive body that decamped to Prague after the Nazi assault against the left, acknowledged KdF's formidable growth and octopus-like reach, even as it remained critical of KdF's claims to popularity. As Sopade agents observed in late 1935, KdF intended that "no space remain for individual recreation, physical fitness, and cultural activity, nor should room remain for free association and independent initiative, from which it could develop." Of all Nazi organizations, Kraft durch Freude had experienced the greatest growth as its radius "expanded extraordinarily," incorporating not just tourism, despite its propagandistic prominence, but the countless cultural, educational, and athletic events

---

60 Mommsen and Grieger, *Volkswagenwerk und seine Arbeiter*, 141.
61 See for example Gerhard Starke, "Kraft durch Freude hebt den Lebensstandard unseres Volkes. Der sozialpolitische Sinn der KdF-Gemeinschaft," *Arbeitertum: Blätter für Theorie und Praxis der Nationalsozialistische Betriebszellen Organisation. Amtliches Organ der Deutschen Arbeitsfront* (hereinafter cited as *Arbeitertum*) 5, no. 22 (15 February 1936): 3–4; "Dopolavoro und Kraft durch Freude," *Arbeitertum* 5, no. 21 (1 February 1936): 17.
62 de Grazia, *Culture of Consent*, 73, 181.
63 Ibid., 73, 75, 181. The return of the liner *Rex* illustrates how spectacle intruded in everyday life under Fascism, as captured by Frederico Fellini's cinematic memoir, *Amarcord*, released in 1974.

that it staged.[64] A report from a Sopade agent in Saxony from the following summer recognized, although certainly not without regret, that for workers, no other leisure option remained. "The fact that one can still hardly get around KdF if one wants to take part in sports or take a trip is pretty generally known (*ziemlich allgemein*)."[65]

The Discreet Charm of Appeasement: KdF's International Impact

Strength through Joy's rapid growth garnered foreign admirers. During the interwar period, authoritarian and fascist regimes acquired considerable prestige internationally for their leisure-time programs, distinguishing themselves less in their suspicion of the unsupervised free time of workers, which was common in the liberal democracies as well, but in their conviction that the intervention of the state or ruling party would solve the leisure "problem."[66] Yet among the authoritarian leisure-time agencies, KdF occupied a class by itself, recognized by other states as a model worthy of emulation, particularly for its tourism. To be sure, because of Germany's withdrawal from the League of Nations shortly after the Nazi takeover, relations between the DAF and the International Labour Office were hardly harmonious. They worsened when Ley failed to win the ILO's recognition as the legitimate representative of German labor. Nonetheless, even the ILO acknowledged that KdF cruises represented "the most extensive official experiment" to date in providing travel.[67] KdF's efforts in mass sport earned it two trophies from the International Olympic Committee, the first of them in recognition of its contribution to the 1936 Olympiad in Berlin. Its architectural design for its resort at Prora won a grand prize at the Paris Exhibition the following year.[68] KdF even won the attention of the Roosevelt administration. Although recognizing Strength through Joy's distinctly Nazi character, its compensation for low wages, its authoritarian structure, and its exclusion of Jews, the

---

64 *Deutschland-Berichte der Sozialdemokratischen Partei Deutschlands 1934–1940* (hereinafter cited as *Sopade*) (Frankfurt am Main: Petra Nettelbeck Verlag, 1980), December 1935, 1455.

65 Ibid., 3 July 1936, 884.   66 de Grazia, *Culture of Consent*, 239.

67 International Labour Office, Studies and Reports, Series G (Housing and Welfare), no. 5, *Facilities for the Use of Workers' Leisure during Holidays* (Geneva: International Labour Office, 1939), 44.

68 Frohmann, "Reisen mit 'Kraft durch Freude'," 204; *The International Olympic Committee – One Hundred Years. The Idea – The Presidents – The Achievements*, vol. 1. *The Presidency of Henri de Baillet-Latour (1925–1942)* (Lausanne: International Olympic Committee, 1994), 216; "Die Deutsche Arbeitsfront erhielt den Olympischen Pokal," *Brauschweiger Neueste Nachrichten*, 3 May 1938, NHH, VVP 17, no. 2455.

administration acknowledged similarities between KdF's cultural programs and those of the Works Progress Administration (WPA).[69]

The favorable response to fascist leisure testifies to the appeal that fascist social programs, with their anti-Marxist premises, enjoyed in conservative circles internationally. In Britain, the presumed benefits of Nazi social policy contributed to the support for appeasement and account for why an industrialist and local conservative party leader in York, Sir Benjamin Dawson, would have arranged for the hand delivery of his admiring letter to Hitler. Convinced of the führer's desire for peace and the justice of his claims against the Versailles settlement, Dawson averred that Hitler's "highest aim is to better the way of life (*Lebensform*) of the great mass of the people." On those grounds, he naively proposed that Hitler support an international agreement to reduce the workweek, for he believed that it would earn the gratitude of workers around the globe.[70] For many conservatives, the Third Reich's claims to have improved the standard of living of its citizens rang true.

Strength through Joy sought to enhance its reputation by advertising and self-promotion. It invited foreign guests to its annual conventions, affairs that occasioned the usual barrage of impressive statistics, lavishly entertaining attendees with tourist extravaganzas. At its third annual meeting in 1937, KdF treated guests to a cruise through the Norwegian fjords, as well as guided tours within Germany. Drawn from an international coterie of political, social, and economic leaders, the guest list favored invitees from the Scandinavian countries, in addition to representatives from eastern and southeastern Europe. Yet it also included a sizeable contingent from France, then governed by the Popular Front.[71] Another cruise to Norway in 1939 on the brand new Strength through Joy liner the *Robert Ley* impressed its foreign passengers, most of them engineers and their wives, with the Reich's technological prowess. To make its point, Fritz Todt, the general inspector of the autobahn project and the plenipotentiary for construction under the Four-Year Plan, hosted that event.[72] The combination of technological glitz and creature comfort did not fail to impress, as indicated by the report of an Irish

---

69 In August 1938, the American Ambassador to Germany, Hugh R. Wilson, submitted a report on Strength through Joy to Roosevelt. At Roosevelt's request, the WPA prepared a response by Aubrey Williams, Deputy Administrator, Works Progress Administration, to Roosevelt, 18 October 1938. The report and Williams' letter are found on the Web, courtesy of the Franklin D. Roosevelt Library and Digital Archives. See http://www.fdrlibrary.marist.edu/psf/box32/afolo301.html.

70 Benjamin Dawson an den Kanzler und Führer des Deutschen Reiches, 24 June 1935; Deutsche Botschaft, London an das Auswärtige Amt Berlin, 25 July 1935, BAL R 43II/546a.

71 Vorläufige Liste der Ehrengäste aus europäischen Ländern und der III Reichstagung der NS-Gemeinschaft 'Kraft durch Freude'," 10–13 June, 1937, BAL, Bibliothek.

72 "Norwegenfahrt der Deutsche Technik," 10–16 May 1939, BAL, Bibliothek.

delegate to the World Congress for Leisure Time and Recreation in 1938, which convened first in Hamburg before moving on to Rome. No other industrialized nation had anything like Strength through Joy, he noted. Foreign representatives were housed "in one of those vast liners," the newest KdF ship, the *Wilhelm Gustloff*, "which surpassed anything it is possible to imagine for comfort and luxury."[73] Nor did KdF limit its self-promotion to tourism. The Beauty of Labor's depiction of German workers as nonalienated craftsmen, whose creative force gave life to their products, assumed a prominent place in the German pavilion at the 1937 Paris Exposition.[74] In 1938, Ley accompanied the Duke and Duchess of Windsor, high profile representatives of appeasement despite the scandal surrounding the Duke's abdication from the British throne, on a tour of German factories modernized by the Beauty of Labor. Ley's ability to ingratiate himself with the Duke, coupled with the Duke's admiration for the Reich's social policy, prompted the tour.[75]

In part, KdF's public relations emerged as a way to avoid isolation and in the process distinguish itself among other authoritarian and fascist leisure programs, especially the Italian Fascist agency, After Work. Thus, the International Labour Office's recognition of After Work in 1935, following Italy's invasion of Ethiopia, prompted Ley to convene the World Congress for Leisure Time and Recreation in Hamburg that was to overlap with the eleventh Olympiad in Berlin. Modeled on the American National Recreation Association, the founding of which dovetailed with the 1932 Olympics in Los Angeles, this congress would, as Ley planned it, showcase the premier authoritarian alternative in organized leisure. In addition to staging "folk festivals" in several German cities, culminating in a folk music and dance extravaganza at the closing ceremony of the Olympics, it proposed tours organized by KdF to various sites, including the autobahn.[76] Only a subsequent congress, which convened sequentially in

73   "Kraft durch Freude:" Report of a visit made by the Director of Recreation and Welfare, Civic Institute of Ireland, to Hamburg, September 1938; AA-PA, R49245.
74   Karen A. Fiss, "In Hitler's Salon: The German Pavilion at the 1937 Paris Exposition Internationale," in *Art, Culture, and Media under the Third Reich*, ed. Richard A. Etlin (Chicago and London: University of Chicago Press, 2002): 330–3.
75   William D. Bayles, *Caesars in Goosestep* (New York and London: Harper and Brothers Publishers, 1940), 190. See also Goebbel's diary entry for 12 October 1937, *Tagebücher*, vol. 1, part 1, 356–7. Despite his irritation at the vulgar tea, with which Ley feted the duke on a previous visit to Germany, Goebbels himself gushed that the duke was "wonderful" and "a pleasure to talk with" because of his grasp for "modern life and the social question." "We talked about a thousand things: parliamentarianism, social and workers' problems, national and international questions. It's a shame he's no longer king."
76   Auswärtiges Amt an alle diplomatischen und konsularischen Vertretungen im Ausland, 30 December 1935, AA-PA, R49242; Weltkongress für Freizeit und Erholung: Deutschland, Hamburg 23–30 Juli 1936, AA-PA, R49237; Auswärtiges Amt an die in der Anlage ausgegebenen Anschriften: Betr.: Weltkongress für Freizeit und

Hamburg and Rome during the summer of 1938, gave a nod to Italy's achievements. Reflecting the emergence of the Italian–German axis after Mussolini's distancing from Britain and France, KdF arranged for the German delegation and invited foreign guests to sail to Rome on the *Wilhelm Gustloff.* The trip included excursions to the duce's model towns, Aprilia and Sabaudia, which emerged out of his ambitious program to reclaim marshlands.[77]

Following the 1936 congress, Ley created a permanent mechanism for assuring Germany's prominence as a leisure promoter, the Berlin-based International Central Bureau for Joy and Work. Although Ley included prominent and sympathetic British and American representatives in its deliberations, the bureau's promotion of organic communities of interest between workers and employers against the "collectivism" of the left found its greatest resonance among authoritarian states.[78] Intended to rival the ILO, it further promoted Strength through Joy's accomplishments by distributing its magazine *Joy and Work* abroad, inviting foreigners to Germany and incorporating them on its board. The bureau also organized traveling exhibits that documented the evolution of leisure, while stressing the KdF mantra, the harmony of leisure and work. One exhibit, which consisted of photomontages, artifacts, models of Strength through Joy ships and resorts, and examples of Beauty of Labor furnishings, toured Yugoslavia, Bulgaria, Romania, and Greece, where Germany wished to expand its influence. On opening night in Athens, King George and the dictator, Ioannis Metaxas, who sympathized with Nazism and incorporated fascist elements in his government, greeted Ley in person.[79] Although the bureau, initially proposed by Horst Dressler-Andress, had been a source of tension between Strength through Joy and Rosenberg, as well between

---

Erholung in Hamburg 1936, 7 May 1936, AA-PA, R49237. See as well Liebscher, "Mit KdF 'die Welt erschließen'": 53–5, for Ley's reaction to the ILO's recognition of Dopolavoro.

77 Ibid.: 56–8; *Unter dem Sonnenrad. Ein Buch von Kraft durch Freude,* ed. Reichsamtsleitung Kraft durch Freude (Berlin: Verlag der Deutschen Arbeitsfront, 1938), 54–5.

78 Abschrift (Auswärtiges Amt) mit Beziehung auf den Runderlaß vom 7. Mai v. J- v. 6426 betreffend den "Weltkongreß für Freizeit und Erholung in Hamburg 1939," AA-PA R49233; Franz Mende, "The Movement 'Work and Joy' in Connection with Working Life and Beyond It," *German Addresses for Committee II, World Congress, "Work and Joy," Rome 1938,* 7. The American G. T. Kirby, the president of the National Recreation Association, served as president of the World Congress in 1937. Interest from the British, however, was more hesitant, according to a series of reports from 1939, "Freude und Arbeit" im Ausland, Betrifft: Länder-Informationen aus dem Quellenmaterial des I.Z.B, AA-PA R99029. On the Central Bureau as anti-Geneva bloc building, see Liebscher, "Mit KdF 'die Welt erschließen'," 57–8.

79 "Die Wanderausstellung 'Freude und Arbeit'," AA-PA, R49234; Arthur A. Manthey, "Das Internationale Zentralbüro 'Freude und Arbeit,'" 7 September 1938, AA-PA, R49234; Mark Mazower, *Inside Hitler's Greece: The Experience of Occupation 1941–1944* (New Haven and London: Yale University Press, 1995, 13–14.

KdF and the foreign ministry, its emergence testified to KdF's international recognition and its effectiveness as an instrument of the Reich's foreign policy.[80]

Nevertheless, KdF's campaign amounted to more than an escape from diplomatic isolation. Rather, in the company of the regime it served, it sought to demonstrate the high standard of living in the "new" Germany. Of all the Nazi spectacles, the 1936 Olympics in Berlin stand out as the regime's most egregious attempt to propagandize the good deeds of the Hitler government and win plaudits from abroad. As an enterprise that disproportionately favored the industrialized nations – the only ones that could afford to send large contingents of athletes – the Olympic Games assumed special significance in the Reich's efforts to broadcast its achievements. Following on the heels of the 1932 Olympics in Los Angeles, whose proximity to Hollywood could not have eluded Nazi organizers, the Berlin Olympics became the stuff of cinema through Leni Riefenstahl's feature-length film, *Olympiade*. They also became the first televised games, for the organizers placed large-screen televisions strategically near the grounds, and authorized the transmission of over three thousand radio programs worldwide.[81] Challenged by the Soviet Union's boycott and the rival Socialist games in Barcelona as the Spanish Civil War raged, the polarization of sport magnified the Reich's accomplishments among European and American conservatives. Faced with a population uneasy over the prospect of war and chafing at shortages in basic foodstuffs, the regime intended the Olympics as a demonstration of Germany's peacefulness and its triumph over the hardships and class conflict of Weimar.[82]

The International Olympic Committee's decision to stage the 1936 games in Berlin against a boycott movement, which protested the German organizers' discrimination against non-Aryan athletes who sought places on the German Olympic team looked past the troubling evidence that the protesters offered. Confident that the boycott amounted to little more than the proposal of Jews and Marxists, the Belgian, virulently anticommunist president of the IOC, Henri de Balliet-Latour, proceeded with the spectacle. As a reward, the Olympiad's German hosts lavishly entertained IOC committee members with exhibits of ancient Greek sculpture, concerts, and opulent gatherings, including an elegant reception that Goebbels hosted on Peacock Island (*Pflaueninsel*) west of Berlin, and a luncheon at Göring's estate, Karinhall, which displayed his collection of Frederick

---

80 Protokoll der Gespräche mit Herrn Dressler-Andress am 22. Juli 1944 in Berlin-Karlshorst, IfZ, F104.

81 Reinard Rürup, ed., *Die Olympischen Spiele und der Nationalsozialismus 1939: Eine Dokumentation* (Berlin: Argon Verlag, 1996), 121–2. On the success of the games, see Ian Kershaw, *Hitler 1936–1945: Nemesis* (New York: W.W. Norton, 2000), 5–9.

82 For commentaries on the nervousness at home, see *Sopade*, particularly for July and August 1936.

the Great's porcelain.[83] The pro-German president of the United States Olympic Committee, Avery Brundage, who defeated an American-led boycott of the games and won a seat on the IOC for his efforts, complained that Jews "with communistic and socialistic antecedents have been particularly active, and the result is that the same sort of class hatred which exists in Germany and which every sane man deplores is being aroused in the United States."[84]

Strength through Joy's presence at the games was considerable, and it contributed to the IOC's ensuing decision to award it its trophy. Its contributions began at the top with the ardent Nazi and SA man, Hans von Tschammer und Osten, who in addition to heading KdF's sport office and the National Socialist Reich League for Physical Education served as president of the German Olympic Committee. Tschammer obtained the latter position as a result of a compromise between the regime and the IOC, which spared the non-Aryan chair of the local Olympic organizing committee, Theodor Lewald, from being removed on racial grounds.[85] As president of the German committee, Tschammer reassured Baillet-Latour that his committee had invited non-Aryan athletes to try out for the German Olympic team, although few in his estimation were of the caliber necessary to winning a spot on the team.[86] Moreover, KdF occupied a prominent place in commemorative guides for foreigners, which lavished attention on Nazism's achievements, its defeat of the "Marxists," and its ability to raise the standard of living of ordinary Germans. "Life is worth living again," claimed one such book, now that unemployment and civil war have ceased. Savings accounts, meat consumption, and radio usage had increased, attractive new housing had been built, and now ordinary workers had the opportunity to take vacation trips, attend the theater,

83 Of the works on the Berlin Olympics, the best is Rürup, ed., *Die Olympischen Spiele und der Nationalsozialismus*. See also Richard P. Mandell, *The Nazi Olympics* (London, 1972), and Allen Guttmann's biography of Avery Brundage, *The Games Must Go On: Avery Brundage and the Olympic Movement* (New York: Columbia University Press, 1984). Brundage ultimately became IOC president. The Swedish member of the IOC, Sigfrid Edström, wrote a note to his wife about the provenance of Göring's porcelain collection on the back of his engraved luncheon menu, Berlin 1936/Invitations, IOC Olympic Studies Center, Lausanne (hereinafter cited as OSC).
84 Avery Brundage to Sigfrid Edström, August 29, 1935, OSC, Berlin 1936/Correspondance 1932–6, President avec Membres Pour L'Allemagne.
85 *The International Olympic Committee: Presidency of Henri de Baillet-Latour*, 257–71.
86 Hans von Tschammer und Osten to Henri de Baillet Latour, 24 September 1935, and Baron Coupertin to William May Garland, H. Sherrill, and Commodore Ernest Lee Jahncke, 5 October 1935, OSC, Berlin 1936: Correspondance 1932–6, President avec Membres Pour L'Allemagne. As the correspondence indicates, Coubertin, the founder of the modern Olympics, became involved in the controversy. Satisfied that Tschammer had kept his promise that Jewish athletes were being invited to try out for the German team, and noting as well that Germany had invited Palestine to field a team, Coubertin remarked that Germany could raise similar objections regarding the exclusion of African–Americans from sports clubs in the United States.

and because of the Beauty of Labor, toil in clean, aesthetically pleasing workplaces.[87]

Indeed, the Olympics became a tourist site, a prime venue for attesting to KdF's "success" in eroding the barriers of class privilege. To feed, house, and entertain the expected thirty thousand German tourists, who would be brought to the games by train, KdF built a temporary "city" comparable to that erected in Garmisch-Partenkirchen, the site of the Winter Olympics in February. Located near the Olympic Stadium, Werner March's monumental renovation of a preexisting modernist structure that Speer had approved to satisfy the führer, the "KdF City" bespoke a populist, motif.[88] Consisting of five large wooden, rustic halls decorated with peasant or otherwise populist figures and scenes, the KdF city merged rusticity and regional "folk" styles to express the regime's nationalizing of regionalism and its democratization of tourism. Although dismantled afterwards for re-use at party rallies in Nuremberg, the city claimed its own S-Bahn station, newly constructed to accommodate the expected legions of visitors.[89] Yet Olympic ticket prices exceeded the reach of the workers whom KdF had hoped to attract. Although tourists received bus tours of Berlin and were treated to musical and dance performances in KdF City's five halls, relatively few of them attended athletic events.[90] The disparity between intention and practice underscored KdF's most serious weakness.

The Racial Community Writ Small? KdF's Social Constituencies

Despite the acclaim it garnered as the Third Reich's answer to the "leisure problem," Strength through Joy's replication of bourgeois leisure practices remained qualified, defying the adamant claims of its promoters. KdF's impact in agriculture, which accounted for the livelihood of nearly one-third of the population, was limited, even though its tourism occasionally caused a stir in the countryside. According to the recollection of Christian von Krockow, the scion of a prominent Pomeranian landowning family, "vacations were still unknown," and "a trip on a KdF ship" was "nearly unheard of, a sensation and more accurately a decoration." During the Third Reich, estimated Krockow, only three of the approximately eight

---

87 *Germany: The Olympic Year 1936* (Berlin: Volk und Reich Verlag, 1936).
88 On *völkisch* motifs in Nazi architecture, which competed with neoclassicism and modernist functionalism, see Barbara Miller Lane, *Architecture and Politics in Germany, 1918–1945* (Cambridge and London: Harvard University Press, 1985), 197–200. On Speer's role in the design of the stadium, see his memoirs, *Inside the Third Reich*, trans. Richard and Clara Winston (New York: Macmillan, 1970), 95.
89 "KdF-Stadt Berlin: XI. Olympiade 1936," OSC, Berlin 1936/Sites Olympiques.
90 See Rürup, ed., *Olympischen Spiele*, 119.

hundred villagers attached to his family's estates traveled with KdF.[91] As a movement that targeted industrial workers, KdF was slow to extend its programs to rural areas until the demands of rearmament and the need for foreign exchange brought renewed attention. The Olympics in Garmisch-Partenkirchen and Berlin provided such an occasion, for although projections went unrealized, the regime expected that the games would draw thousands of foreign visitors. Thus, it initiated a campaign subsumed under the Beauty of Labor office, the "beautiful village" (*das schöne Dorf*). Designed to improve the appearance of towns along major travel routes, it would persuade the anticipated horde of foreign tourists that the regime was improving the lives of its citizens.[92] Thereafter, to do its part to stem the "flight from the land" (*Landflucht*), the outward migration from the countryside that rearmament exacerbated, KdF initiated "village evenings" to spawn comradeship and the preservation of collective memory through the compilation of village histories. Its film trucks and mobile stages delivered entertainment to rural dwellers. Regardless, KdF's sports program remained anchored in the cities where it originated, broadening its focus to industry by 1936.[93] Its most spectacular program, tourism, had little practical effect in agriculture where the vacation as the extended respite from industrial time discipline remained a foreign concept.[94]

Second, Strength through Joy's ambition to make bourgeois privileges accessible to nonagricultural wage earners amounted to something less than a smashing success. To be sure, by giving its own statistics the benefit of the doubt, KdF might well have attracted more workers than the working-class travel clubs of Weimar.[95] Moreover, paid vacations were gradually extended to cover a broader range of occupational categories and the duration of vacations increased, even though the Labor Front did not achieve Ley's goal of securing a legally codified, three- to four-week paid vacation as an entitlement for all workers regardless of age, skill level, or industry. If the most generous vacations remained concentrated in trade, commerce, and the civil service, as had been the case during the twenties, and fewer than 25 percent of workers governed by wage

---

91 Christian Graf von Krockow, *Die Reise nach Pommern. Bericht aus einem verschwiegenen Land* (Stuttgart: Deutsche Verlags-Anstalt, 1985), 84.

92 Ebenhahn, Gaureferent des Amtes Schönheit der Arbeit an samtliche Herrn Landräte im Gau Magdeburg-Anhalt, 12 May 1936, Landeshauptarchiv Magdeburg (hereinafter cited as LHAM), Oberpräsidium des Provinz Sachsen-Magedeburg XXV, no. 68.

93 Bernett, "Nationalsozialistischer Volkssport," 102.

94 See Theresia Bauer, *Nationalsozialistische Agrarpolitik und bäuerliches Verhalten im Zweiten Weltkrieg: Eine Regionalstudie zur ländlichen Gesellschaft in Bayern* (Frankfurt am Main: Peter Lang, 1996), 194.

95 Keitz, *Reisen als Leitbild*, 252–3. According to Keitz, KdF's figures suggest that it mobilized twenty times more workers than the workers' travel of the twenties. Nevertheless, because of the lack of data from Weimar that could be used to measure KdF's claim as to the social composition of its trips, arriving at a precise number is futile.

agreements received a vacation of over twelve days, the notion of a vacation as an entitlement won greater acceptance. Once more, the ILO singled out Germany for special recognition, for in its view Germany was the only industrialized nation to have followed its recommendations for regularizing paid vacations.[96] Nevertheless, leaving aside the one-day hikes and weekend trips, workers were usually underrepresented on the two- to three-week vacations relative to other occupational groups.

On the passenger lists of Strength through Joy cruises, which reified KdF's claim to democratize a previously unaffordable luxury, salaried employees emerged as the dominant contingent, consistent with the recreational travel patterns of the twenties. The participation of women, particularly female salaried employees and unmarried women "without occupation," proved remarkably high; so high in fact that had the number of working-class women approached that of male workers, the female participation rate would have approached fifty percent. Indeed on the domestic trips, women often outnumbered men. The workers whose names did appear on tour rosters, furthermore, were generally single, male, and skilled with sufficiently high aspirations and disposable income to devote to such an undertaking, or workers whose employers had subsidized their trips. Workers with children were rare.[97] Thus, the observation of the Swiss poet Jakob Schaffner, who celebrated the presence aboard a KdF cruise ship of occupationally diverse "little people," and whose sympathy for National Socialist social policy offers yet another example of Strength through Joy's international éclat, distinguished itself more for its impressionism than for its validity.[98]

The underrepresentation of workers proved sufficiently transparent to contemporaries that spokesmen for the Labor Front and KdF both took pains to refute the claim that KdF tours remained a middle-class preserve. Presenting statistics from the tour manifests of four districts, Ley asserted that industrial workers constituted half the travelers, while he and other KdF publicists challenged the putatively superficial observations of critics: they assumed that the well-dressed vacationers that they saw were middle class, when in reality the tourists were workers dressed

96 For vacation policy in the Third Reich, see Spode, "Arbeiterurlaub": 277–88; and Keitz, *Reisen als Leitbild*, 219–23. Spode sees the Third Reich as having been more successful than does Keitz in extending vacations as an entitlement.

97 The surveillance reports of SD agents found in BAL, R58, files 943–950 contain breakdowns according to age, income, and occupation, and the existing literature on Strength through Joy has resorted to them extensively. See Buchholz, "Kraft durch Freude," 356–73; Spode, "Arbeiterurlaub:" 296–305; and Keitz, *Reisen als Leitbild*, 248–54, 331, 332. My investigation of those files largely confirms this conclusion.

98 *Volk zu Schiff: Zwei Seefahrten mit der "KdF"Hochseefahrten* (Hamburg: Hanseatische Verlagsanstalt, 1936), 13. Schaffner's "little people" lumped together workers, salaried employees, civil servants, shop girls, artisans, typists, and stenographers without indicating which occupational categories predominated.

in their Sunday best.[99] Based on the reported incomes of participants in forty trips, a local study from Lower Saxony maintained that over sixty percent earned monthly incomes of 150 marks or less, followed by another twenty percent with monthly incomes that ranged between 150 and 200 marks.[100] Yet another report, a "random" analysis of eighteen vacation trips (excluding weekend outings and factory excursions) from Berlin in 1937 claimed that thirty-nine percent of the holiday makers were "hand workers," without distinguishing between independent artisans and wage earners.[101] Defensive self-defenses notwithstanding, the number of complaints from commercial travel agencies, which grumbled that KdF tourism siphoned off clients who would have otherwise used their services, confirm the limitations of Strength through Joy's social reach.[102] To counter the accusations that Strength through Joy's tourism did not live up to its populist promise, KdF functionaries created loopholes that they believed would enhance KdF's social diversity and assuage the agency's collective conscience. A "child rich" family or serious illness could win a potential participant an exemption from KdF's increasingly fluid income limits, as could the willingness of a financially comfortable traveler to sponsor the trip of a participant, who could not otherwise have afforded a vacation trip.[103]

Low working-class wages – the average wage being as low as twenty-five marks per week[104] – raised an obvious barrier to KdF's attempts at inclusion, which the Nazi regime's restrictive wage policy exacerbated. Because improving working-class family incomes derived from longer workdays, they curtailed, rather than enabled, leisure especially for working-class women who bore the double burden of paid work and homemaking.

99 Tätigkeitsbericht über die Leistungen der NS Gemeinschaft Kraft durch Fraude von Dr. Robert Ley, 26 November, 1935, BAL, NS 22/781, 5–6; Buchholz, "Kraft durch Freude," 364.

100 "'KdF'-Urlauber und ihre Berufe," *Peine Zeitung*, 16 April, 1936, NHH, VVP 17, no. 2456.

101 Adam, "Practical Activities," 21. Adam's address to the World Congress of Joy and Work in 1938, which was distributed in English translation, appears to anglicize *Handwerker*. By contrast, KdF's and the Gestapo's own surveys of the passenger lists for the cruises routinely distinguished between *Arbeiter* and *Handwerker*.

102 "Lebensfragen des deutschen Reisebürogewerbes," *Das Fremdenverkehr*, no. 50 (11 December, 1937), Bayerisches Hauptstaatsarchiv (hereinafter cited as BHA), no. 2754.

103 Der Reichs und Preussische Minister des Innern an den Oberpräsidenten der Provinz Hannover, 14 August 1937, NHH, Hann. 122a, no. 577, 227: "Teilnehmerbedingungen für KdF.-Reisen," N.S.-Gemeinschaft, "Kraft durch Freude," Gau Tirol-Voralberg, *Frohe Fahrt mit KdF: Urlaubsfahrten 1939* (Berlin: Verlag der Deutschen Arbeitsfront, 1939), unpaginated.

104 Mommsen and Grieger, *Volkswagenwerk*, 201. Schneider, *Unterm Hakenkreuz*, 602. Hasso Spode, "Arbeiterurlaub," 303, gives a higher figure of 180 RM per month or roughly 45 RM per week. Nevertheless he acknowledges that even at this higher income, vacation trips remained beyond the means of most workers.

And, even assuming that a worker could cover the cost of a trip out of his or her own resources, the inability to purchase appropriate vacation attire, a matter of course for middle- and upper-class travelers, constituted an additional obstacle.[105] The cultural horizons of workers provided another barrier still. For many, vacations appeared as luxuries, a lower priority than securing food, clothing, and shelter, earning a higher wage, and improving the conditions of one's labor. Beyond the "materialism" implicit in such expectations lay identities still defined by the workplace.[106] Not surprisingly, many workers deemed KdF tourism as more show than substance, as revealed in the ditty that circulated among Ruhr miners: "Honor, says Dr. Ley, is the most beautiful wage of the miner, who although has nothing to eat, honor will now satiate."[107]

Nevertheless, Strength through Joy's inability to secure state, and not simply party subsidies to supplement the income that it received from the Labor Front, proved equally constraining. Without the resources to offer a more extensive subsidizing of working-class travel, KdF could chip away at, but not undermine, the class-defined roadblocks to a middle-class privilege. The strategies that KdF did employ – encouraging individuals to save toward their vacations through weekly paycheck deductions and lobbying business for voluntary contributions in the name of building the "plant community" – confirmed the autonomy and initiative that business preserved during the Third Reich. Thus, employers negotiated the terms of their contribution, offering intermittent rather than routine financial support toward the purchase of trips, including additional vacation days sufficient to the length of the trip that was proposed. The employers who did incorporate KdF trips into their annual budgets limited them to a set number of employees, whom they chose outright or selected randomly by lottery. The steel conglomerate Krupp refused to accede to across-the-board subventions, instead singling out those it deemed deserving. In 1938, it granted KdF-trips and extra paid vacation days to seventeen workers, all of them men, who had been with the firm for fifty years or more. Merit and length of service also defined the vacation trip policy of Anchor Works (Anker-Werke), an export dependent Bielefeld firm that manufactured sewing machines and bicycles.[108] Like a number

---

105   Claudia Koonz, *Mothers in the Fatherland: Women, the Family and Nazi Politics* (London: Jonathan Cape, 1987), 198–9. The Gestapo in the Ruhr reported that the lack of proper clothing presented a problem for miners who wanted to take trips, according to Klaus Wisotzky, *Der Ruhrbergbau im Dritten Reich: Studien zur Sozialpolitik im Ruhrgebau und zum sozialen Verhalten der Bergleute in den Jahren 1933 bis 1939* (Düsseldorf: Schwann, 1983), 102.

106   Keitz, *Reisen als Leitbild*, 253.

107   "Die Ehre spricht Dr. Ley, der schönste Lohn des Bergmanns sei, wer also nichts zu fressen hat, der wird jetzt von der Ehre satt.," Wisotzky, *Ruhrbergbau*, 103.

108   Historisches Archiv Krupp, Essen (hereinafter cited as HA Krupp), WA 41/6–41 contains correspondence regarding selection procedures for KdF trips; Geschäfts-Bericht der Anker-Werke A.G. zu den ordentlichen Generalversammlung, 11 May 1937,

of other firms, the small Westphalian textile firm, the Bleaching, Dyeing, and Starching Works (Bleicherei, Färberei und Appreturanstalt), with 183 employees resorted to lottery to pick its winners. From 1936 to the outbreak of war, it sent twenty-five employees selected by an annual lottery on an all-expenses-paid, one-week trip.[109] Finally, a commitment to the Nazi party weighed heavily in the selections, not least because the KdF warden, the DAF overseer, and the Councils of Trust (Vertrauensräte) established by the National Labor Law to ensure nonconfrontational management–labor relations recommended to employers only those employees who combined political and occupational reliability.[110]

Yet however small their numbers relative to those of other social groups, the presence of workers, even on Strength through Joy's longer tours, created mixed classed constituencies that differed from the working-class and white-collar tourism of the Weimar era, not to mention the travel of the educated middle classes. Despite the limits that employers imposed on it, their sponsorship was appreciable. In 1938/39 alone, 27,610 companies paid at least some of the travel expenses of 463,800 employees. Owing to the resistance of the Reich finance ministry, subventions for the trips of workers and salaried employees in the public sector could not approach those given by private corporations, a subject of extended discussion, and frustration, at the local level.[111] In some firms, the number of employees who traveled on sponsored vacations was impressive. The Waltrop mine in the Ruhr, for example, conducted a lottery in 1939 that yielded one hundred winners, the resources for which came from a KdF fund that had drawn in regular employee contributions, matched by the employer's donation. Other major Ruhr concerns, such as Hoesch and the Rhine Steel Works (Rheinische Stahlwerke), annually sent several hundred of their employees on KdF trips.[112]

To be sure, much of the travel that employers were willing to support focused on company outings, rather than on KdF trips, which were

WWA F42, no. 2, 35–7. For company practice in the Ruhr in general, see Matthias Frese, *Betriebspolitik im "Dritten Reich": Deutsche Arbeitsfront, Unternehmer und Staatsbürokratie in der westdeutschen Großindustrie, 1933–1939* (Paderborn: Ferdinand Schöningh, 1991), 374–83.

109 "Leistungskampf der Bleicherei, Färberei und Appreturanstalt Uhringen A.G.", Wirtschaftsarchiv Baden-Württemberg, Stuttgart (hereinafter cited as WABW), B26, no. 119. Lotteries held at Christmas were relatively frequent; Bericht: KdF-Italienfahrt mit dem Dampfer "Oceana" vom 31.12.37 bis 11.1.38, BAL R58, no. 949.

110 Even the Nazi-sympathizing Jakob Schaffner, *Volk zu Schiff*, 47–8, admitted the relevance of such considerations in the selection criteria that employers used to choose worthy vacationers.

111 Frommann, "Reisen mit 'Kraft durch Freude,'" 21 ff. The files of the Deutscher Gemeindetag, R36, nos. 455 and 456, BAL, contain the lengthy discussion over vacation policy and subventions of KdF trips.

112 Verlosung von K.d.F.-Urlaubsfahrten der K.d.F. Kasse der Zeche Waltrop, 8 April, 1939, Bergbau Archiv Bochum (hereinafter cited as BAB), Bestand 72, no. 495. Cf. Wisotzky, *Ruhrbergbau*, 101.

to instill comraderie and employee loyalty. Large firms with numerous subsidiaries spread throughout the country, such as Siemens, relied on Strength through Joy only to provide low-cost travel for employees who visited the company's headquarters in Berlin, while Siemens picked up most of the remaining expenses.[113] Moreover, although it is impossible to establish with certainty the exact numbers in each category, employee groups included salaried personnel as well as workers. Nevertheless, the number of wage earners at times achieved a size sufficient to rival salaried employees on the regular trips. This was especially true in the off-season, or when slow ticket sales encouraged local recruiters to lobby businesses to fill the tours, or when tour groups were recruited from largely industrial regions. Thus, a cruise in January 1938 to various ports in Italy that originated from the Gau Halle-Merseburg consisted of a high percentage of skilled workers from the Leuna chemical concern. Their employer took advantage of the lower prices to subsidize them. Nearly three quarters of the passengers on a cruise to Norway that June, which originated in the industrialized region, the Niederlausitz, were workers.[114] Company-sponsored travel thus created discernible cohorts, whose identification as workers influenced the social dynamics of many vacation trips. The mixed composition of KdF tours, which bore a rough resemblance to the Nazi electoral constituency itself, exposed class tensions and shaped KdF's choices as to destinations. It also laid bare the paradoxes of KdF tourism, as well as the pressure that the consumption problem placed on the Nazi regime. On the one hand, KdF promoted a spartan variety of travel, while insisting that tourists should be disciplined and obedient in keeping with the regime's martial spirit. Yet on the other, it increasingly promised comfort along with relaxation and personal pleasure.[115]

The circumstances that accompanied Strength through Joy's emergence and development – rearmament and polycratic infighting – fashioned its identity as the Nazi regime's answer to mass consumption. If at times the Nazi regime described its contributions to raising German living standards in material terms, as its brochure for the Berlin Olympics indicated,[116] KdF preferred to distinguish between consumption with its evident "materialist" connotations and a "high" standard of living, which enhanced the "creative" lives of workers in all their totality. In February 1934, three months after KdF's founding, Ley addressed a reception in the foreign ministry, in which he cast the regime's promised benefits for labor in terms of the "honor" that workers would receive. Proclaiming

---

113 KdF-Stoffsammlung; KdF-Fahrten 1939, SA 14 Lr 583.
114 Bericht über die K.d.F.-Reise Rund-um-Italien mit dem Dampfer "Der Deutsche," 19.11.-29.11.38," BAL R58, no. 950, 311–12; Bericht über 104. Urlaubsfahrt KdF 5.-11.6.38 mit "Der Deutsche" nach Norwegen, BAL R58, no. 948, 94.
115 See Chapters 4 and 5 for further detail.
116 *Germany: The Olympic Year 1936* (Berlin: Volk und Reich Verlag, 1936).

that in their eagerness to foment class conflict and the disintegration of the nation, the Socialists reduced workers to the status of "proletarians" and "slaves," leaving them with an "inferiority complex," "rootless" and "homeless" in their own land. Rather than delivering what workers really yearned for, comradeship with their countrymen and the respect that their labor deserved, the trade unions and the left stirred up class hatred, while prattling on about higher wages and a shorter workday as the only true way to improve the lives of wage earners. Evoking the "socialism" of the World War I battlefields, where comradeship transcended class divisions, Ley pointed to KdF as representing the essence of the National Socialist "revolution." Instead of the materialism, individualism, and class conflict of the past, community, courage, and obedience had become the watchwords of the present.[117] As a Sopade informants sarcastically remarked: "wages in the Third Reich are lowered (*gekürzt*), but the 'total position' of the worker is to be elevated," KdF having become the means to that end.[118]

Other Strength through Joy leaders and publicists emphasized higher productivity on the job and equal access to the "cultural property" of the nation in their criteria for a "high" standard of living. Thus, Bodo Lafferentz stipulated that attending the well being of workers would bring "contentment and joy in living" that would become "the greatest incentive to high achievement."[119] In a lecture to a British audience, the German consul to Liverpool stressed the indivisibility of social and economic policy in the Third Reich, stating that the new social order valued not "money and possessions" but "performance and achievement." Strength through Joy, he suggested, stood for the principle that workers deserved more than just material advantages. Rather they should be elevated by spiritual values, especially those of the racial community. KdF aimed "at extending and deepening the life of the soul of the working people." It extended beyond the goal of recuperation for recuperation's sake to transform work into a vocation, and overcome the division between work and private life.[120] Similarly, the DAF functionary, Theo Hupfauer, argued that the "standard of life" was measured not merely in the number of material goods that one possessed but also by the extent to which workers shared in the total creative product of the community.[121] For the Labor Front publicist Gerhard Starke, finally, a raised standard living meant in the first

117 "Nicht um Lohn – um die Ehre!," *Durchbruch der Sozialen Ehre*, 88–103.
118 *Sopade*, December 1935, 1455–6.
119 Bodo Lafferentz, "Exchange Visits as a Means toward Understanding among the Nations," *Plenary Session, World Congress "Work and Joy,"* Rome 1938, 3.
120 Deutsches Konsulat, Liverpool, an das Auswärtige Amt, 27 May 1936, AA-PA, R 48527.
121 Theo Hupfauer, "The Standard of Life of the Individual Depends on the Creative Efforts, the Joy in Work, and the Achievement of the Community," *German Addresses for Committee X, World Congress "Work and Joy,"* Rome, 1938, 3–10.

place having a job, in contrast to the past, and improved access to hitherto inaccessible pleasures, such as travel and tourism. The social position of "creative" Germans, he argued, could not be measured according to whether wages were increased or decreased. Rather, returning to the theme of "honor," it would be measured according to the position that workers occupied in the racial community. The Third Reich was committed, he said, to maintaining a balance between prices and wages in order to avoid the never-ending spiral of price increases that followed wage hikes. Yet if the regime could not raise wages, KdF at least enabled workers to get more for their money than ever before, for in Adolf Hitler's Germany, ordinary Germans could now afford the finer pastimes in life.[122]

Strength through Joy's position in the Third Reich resembled a stream flowing down a mountainside, picking up speed and force during a moderate rainfall, but unlikely to engulf the boundaries that nature set for it. The permanent solution for a high material standard of living – a land empire – necessitated rearmament and war, neither of which would tolerate rising wages or an inflated consumer demand. Thus, KdF's commitment to "honoring" labor entailed a different standard for measuring improvements in working-class lives. Neither Robert Ley nor Strength through Joy's leadership quarreled with the Nazi regime's primary goal, even if the Labor Front did not realize its ambitious economic aims. And in the space that it was allowed to occupy, KdF sought to lessen the tension between promises of a better life in the future and the present sacrifices. Aestheticizing the workplace and providing access at low cost to the "cultural property" of the nation would not only increase productivity and celebrate "performance," but also convincingly demonstrate the regime's willingness to accommodate popular expectations. Yet the unity of work and leisure that KdF spokesmen promoted in order to highlight Nazi social achievements became less important to the audiences of KdF programs than leisure alone. Although designed to improve the status and self-image of employees, Strength through Joy's campaign to beautify the shop floor through its Beauty of Labor project revealed the Third Reich's coercive face in a way that allowed little room for imagining Nazism's "positive" social achievements.

---

122 "Kraft durch Freude hebt den Lebensstandard," *Die Deutsche Arbeitsfront. Eine Darstellung über Zweck, Leistungen und Ziele* (Berlin: Verlag für Sozialpolitik, Wirtschaft und Statistik, 1940), 142–3.

3

The Beauty of Labor: "Plant Community" and Coercion

The workplace was central to Strength through Joy's ambitions to increase productivity, restore the ethical meaning of labor, and purge workers of "Marxism." By addressing the standard of living at the point of production as well as consumption, KdF proposed to offer workers a higher status that neither replicated American "materialism" nor succumbed to the class "egoism" of the left. Labor Front and KdF leaders believed that the shop floor served as the primary site of class conflict before the Nazi takeover, the product of Germany's social divisions and the workers' councils that the Weimar Republic mandated to increase the bargaining power of the labor movement. If the discord between employers and employers persisted, they feared, the regime's goals of economic recovery, national cohesion, and rearmament would be jeopardized.

Consistent with their conception of work and leisure as mutually reinforcing spheres, KdF's leaders maintained that eradicating political divisions on the shop floor required environmental improvements in the factory, as well as the supervision of the recreational choices and personal habits of workers. They intended to transform the workplace from a venue of management–labor hostility to the replication of the well-ordered racial community. If they succeeded, they would triumph over the corrosion of mass culture, the discouragement of work discipline, and the individual pleasure seeking promoted by mass consumption. To achieve its goals, Strength through Joy combined racism, especially the equation of "performance" (*Leistung*) and biological fitness, with a collage of contemporary academic and business practices. The latter merged scientific management techniques suitably modified to fit German needs, the pacifying and efficiency-building approaches of industrial psychology, and a well-developed tradition of company sponsored leisure activities that had existed well before 1933.[1] Strength through Joy's ambitions,

---

1 Even the "plant community" was not a new idea, but one that business leaders commonly held after World War I. See Paul Erker's introduction in Paul Erker and Toni Pierenkemper, *Deutsche Unternehmer zwischen Kriegswirtschaft und Wiederaufbau:*

however, did not stop at eliminating class conflict in the workplace or abolishing the visible signs of commercial sale and exchange.[2] Rather, KdF imagined an even more fundamental and far-reaching outcome: the conversion of workers from loyalty to their class to fealty to a racialized nation. Improving the aesthetics and physical environment of plants, instituting sports programs and company outings, as well as staging art exhibits and concerts as respites during the workday, would affirm the regime's elimination of the "Jewified" distinction between workers of the "head and fist." It would impart to wage earners a new appreciation of themselves as members of the German "master race."

To be sure, like those of the DAF itself, KdF's shop floor programs carried out by scores of company "wardens" and Beauty of Labor "consultants" (Referenten) signified from the business point of view an ominous degree of state intervention. Ley's gigantomania and dual feudalities as leader of the DAF and the Reich party organization threatened to become the elephant in the living room. Strength through Joy's role in the workplace intensified after 1936 as the regime's stepped up rearmament program, encapsulated in the Four-Year Plan, pressured business to accelerate production, improve the allocation of essential raw materials, and increase the efficiency of labor. Nevertheless, KdF's interventions proved less onerous to employers, who within limits tolerated them, than for workers, whose relative legal and institutional powerlessness subjected them more completely to the regime's agencies. That subjection likely did not render workers as compliant and free of resentment as the regime would have wished, but it nailed the coffin shut on class-based organization and political activism.

As the KdF office responsible for recasting the shop floor, the Beauty of Labor (Schönheit der Arbeit, or SdA) became Strength through Joy's self-described "cornerstone,"[3] the refutation of the perception that KdF's leaders most feared, that Strength through Joy was "only" a leisure-time organization. The Beauty of Labor's charge included overseeing the quality, efficiency, and healthfulness of plant design and construction, monitoring the length of the workday and working conditions, such as lighting, ventilation, sanitation, noise and temperature levels, improving the functionality of work stations, and designing furniture and artifacts for recreation rooms and canteens. Its duties eventually encompassed the provision of cultural activities during midday breaks. With the acceleration of rearmament after the Four-Year Plan, SdA supported a new KdF project,

---

Studien zur Erfahrungsbildung von Industrie-Eliten (Munich: R. Oldenbourg Verlag, 1999), 1–18.

2   See Anson Rabinbach, "The Aesthetics of Production in the Third Reich," in *International Fascism: New Thoughts and New Approaches*, ed. George L. Mosse (London and Beverly Hills: Sage Publications, 1979): 189–222.

3   "Leistungen sprechen," *Schönheit der Arbeit* 3, no. 5 (September 1938): 223–6.

"sport in the plants," which linked increased productivity with physical and racial fitness.[4] Despite the Nazi regime's aversion to the paid employment of women, the number of working-class women who needed to earn a living and the regime's own pressing need for labor after 1936 encouraged the Beauty of Labor to advocate the extension of on-site kindergartens and day care facilities where they had not existed before.[5] SdA intruded in non-industrial settings as well. In addition to overseeing a rural beautification program, it assured the quality control of accommodations for foreign tourists, the cleanliness, comfort, and friendliness of which were to advertise Germany's high standard of living and attract much needed foreign currency.[6] The Beauty of Labor received little formal legal authority to buttress the responsibilities that it claimed. Still it energetically pursued a goal, which the unions and the parties of the left had largely ignored, of bettering the conditions of work in the private economy. Thus like Strength through Joy itself, it filled the space that the regime's priorities allotted to it while accommodating the desire of employers to minimize the regime's intervention.

Germanizing the Shop Floor: Aesthetics and "Community"

Although emblematic of the harmony of work and leisure that Strength through Joy envisioned, one of the Beauty of Labor's first undertakings testified to the personal ties that existed between the führer and its director, Albert Speer. As Hitler's architect and confidant, who shared his mentor's passion for monumental architecture, Speer's connections landed his agency the assignment to construct model barracks for construction workers on Hitler's pet project, the autobahn, after private contractors proved unable to house the number of workers that the undertaking expected to employ. The DAF underwrote the project to the tune of two million Reichsmarks.[7] Designed to modernize the countryside through an efficient network of highways, the autobahns were to revitalize Germany's automobile industry, motorize the masses, reconnect the ties

4 Wolfhard Buchholz, "Die Nationalsozialistische Gemeinschaft 'Kraft durch Freude:' Freizeitgestaltung und Arbeiterschaft im Dritten Reich" (Diss: Munich, 1976), 70.
5 "Wie sollen unsere Kindergärten eingerichtet sein?" *Schönheit der Arbeit* 3, no. 5 (September 1938): 227–9.
6 Hermann Esser, "Gastgewerbe und Fremdverkehr," *Schönheit der Arbeit*, 3, no. 9 (January 1939): 377–8; Richtlinien für die Besichtigung und Überprüfung der Gaststätten im Landesfremdenverkehrsverband Niedersachsen-Weserbergland, Niedersächsisches Hauptstaatsarchiv, Hannover (hereinafter cited as NHH) Hann. 122 a, VIII, no. 577, 365–9.
7 Willy Müller, *Das soziale Leben im neuen Deutschland unter besonderer Berücksichtigung der Deutschen Arbeitsfront* (Berlin: Verlag E.S. Mittler & Son, 1938), 189.

between the nation and nature, bring in revenue from foreign tourists, and demonstrate the high living standard that befited a great nation. Aside from believing that the Beauty of Labor's contribution to the autobahn would become a fitting monument to the führer's social conscience, Speer adhered to the view of the autobahn's general inspector, Fritz Todt, who sought accommodations that would provide homelike settings for autobahn workers.[8]

Launched in early 1934 shortly after Speer assumed his position, the barracks contained kitchens, laundry rooms, reading rooms, and semi-private sleeping quarters. Flower beds and green spaces surrounded their exteriors. The inclusion of recreation rooms underscored the place of relaxation in the Beauty of Labor's scheme of things such that by December 1934, the first model camp had already been the site of numerous KdF recreational programs, including films, art exhibits, and concerts.[9] Speer imagined that hygienic and rationally structured autobahn camps would inspire German industry to imitate them, although ultimately the low wages of autobahn workers and the dismal working conditions they endured testified to the failure of the Labor Front to improve their lot.[10] Speer's responsibilities as Hitler's architect required that he increasingly delegate his duties to subordinates, among them the Labor Front ideologue, Karl Kretschmar. In 1936, accompanying the acceleration of rearmament, Herbert Steinwarz, an industrial architect experienced in the design and engineering of factories, assumed the Reich directorship with Speer remaining as titular head.[11] In addition to his service to Hitler, Speer's career, which took him from the directorship of the Beauty of Labor office to the position of armaments minister, did not merely personify the Beauty of Labor's cordial relations with business.[12] It also revealed

---

8   Gitta Sereny, *Albert Speer: His Battle with Truth* (New York: Alfred A. Knopf, 1995), 108. On the autobahn, see James Shand, "The *Reichsautobahn*: Symbol for the Third Reich," *Journal of Contemporary History* 19, no. 2 (1984): 189–200; and Thomas Zeller, "'The Landscape's Crown': Landscape, Perception and the Modernizing Effect of the German Autobahn System, 1933–1941," in *Technologies of Landscape: Reaping to Recycling*, ed. David Nye (Amherst, Massachusetts: University of Massachusetts Press, 1999): 218–40. Contrary to the still widespread perception, the autobahn had little military value. See especially Franz Seidler, *Fritz Todt: Baumeister des Dritten Reiches* (Munich and Berlin: Hebrig, 1986), 136–43.

9   Erhard Schütz and Eckhard Gruber, *Mythos Reichsautobahn: Bau und Inszenierung der 'Straßen des Führers' 1933–1941* (Berlin: Ch. Links Verlag, 1996), 76–7.

10 For the labor practices employed on the autobahn, see Dan P. Silverman, *Hitler's Economy: Nazi Work Creation Programs, 1933–1936* (Cambridge and London: Harvard University Press, 1998), 171–3. His description of working conditions differs from the impressionistic suggestions of Shand, "*Reichsautobahn*."

11 Rabinbach, "Aesthetics of Production": 191.

12 Rüdiger Hachtmann, *Industriearbeit im "Dritten Reich": Untersuchungen zu den Lohn-und Arbeitsbedingungen in Deutschland 1933–1945* (Göttingen: Vandenhoeck and Ruprecht, 1989): 298.

Strength through Joy's conformity to the regime's martial and imperial priorities.

Although meeting the needs of the Nazi regime, the Beauty of Labor's lineage was nonetheless of long duration, for it borrowed from proposals to aestheticize production in place for over a century. By making the work environment attractive and healthful, and reawakening workers' identification with their products, the utopian planning of Saint Simon, Fourier and the British "Garden Cities" movement sought to overcome the alienation of labor arising from industrialization. The introduction of open spaces, light, and fresh air, they believed, would restore pride in craftsmanship and render workers amenable to the bourgeois values of self-discipline, sobriety, cleanliness, and order.[13]

As the German experience came to reveal, however, concerns regarding the alienation inherent in mechanization proved compatible with modern functionalist architecture and design. Thus in the decade before World War I, industrial psychologists and architects, among them Hugo Müsterberg and Speer's teacher, Heinrich Tessenow, a prominent member of the German Werkbund, pioneered in the design of everyday artifacts and championed the modernization of workplaces. They aimed to re-infuse work with moral value and elevate workers to the status of "creators," whose products carried moral integrity. Clean-lined plant architecture, better lighting, ergonomically constructed workstations, temperature control, and background aesthetics, all attributes of the Werkbund, would honor labor and mitigate the estrangement between workers and their products that spawned conflict between employers and employees. The management–labor strife that the Depression exacerbated, crumbling physical plants, and a level of factory hygiene that government factory inspectors complained was lamentable provided the immediate context for the Beauty of Labor's emergence, as did the evolving political sensibilities of the Werkbund's modernist designers and architects. Those who during the twenties had celebrated social reform, urban planning, and internationalism moved to National Socialism as the antidote to economic hardship. In addition, the rightward drift of industrial psychologists and engineers incorporated a desire to emphasize the spiritual and moral value of work, and with it the

13 See Rabinbach, "Aesthetics of Production": 198–201," and *The Human Motor: Energy, Fatigue, and the Origins of Modernity* (New York, Basic Books, 1990), 280–88; Sabine Weißler, "Interview mit Albert Speer am 16.11.1978 in München," in *Die Zwanziger Jahre des Deutschen Werkbunds*, ed. Deutscher Werkbund (Giessen/Lahn: Ababas-Verlag, 1983): 292–312; Peter Reichel, *Der schöne Schein des Dritten Reiches: Faszination und Gewalt des Faschismus* (Frankfurt am Main: Fischer Taschenbuch Verlag, 1996), 239; and the forthcoming book by Paul Betts, *The Authority of Everyday Objects: A Cultural History of West German Industrial Design, 1930–1965* (Berkeley and Los Angeles: University of California Press, 2004), Ch. 1.

furtherance of obedience to firm hierarchies and loyalty to the workplace "community."[14]

The Beauty of Labor's initiatives, called "campaigns" in a manner that accorded with National Socialism's populist militarism, confronted a range of issues arising from the increased mechanization of production, which modernizing plant designers, architects, and psychologists throughout the industrialized world had themselves addressed. As such, the campaigns departed from the comprehensive plant inspections that the bureau undertook during its first year in the hope that the now more focused projects would yield more visible improvements.[15] Beginning in the spring of 1935, SdA proposed reductions in plant noise levels and the creation of on-site green spaces, following that up with the "Good Light–Good Work" project. Together those "actions" composed an effort to increase the "joy" and efficiency of work by providing quieter and brighter workplaces, along with spots of nature for workers to enjoy during breaks. (See Figure 3.1.) By 1937, SdA was calling for the construction or renovation of washing and changing facilities, as well as the institution of better ventilation through its project, "Clean People in Clean Plants." In the following year, it broadened its reach still further by advocating proper nutrition in company canteens. Recalling the increase in the number of canteens during World War I, SdA's "Hot Food in the Plant" project reinforced the practice of providing on-site meals and addressed the requirements of production in service of rearmament.[16] While insisting on the health benefits of hot, nutritional meals, and the renovation and decoration of company canteens to improve the dining experience of the "retinue," the Beauty of Labor emphasized that meals with little meat and few fats should be served. Both commodities had to be imported at the expense of the Reich's currency reserves.[17] All told, SdA's various

14   See Tilla Siegel, *Leistung und Lohn in der nationalsozialistischen "Ordnung der Arbeit"* (Opladen: Westdeutscher Verlag, 1989), 107, for the perceptions of factory inspectors before 1933; and Thomas von Freyberg, *Industrielle Rationalisierung in der Weimarer Republik: Untersucht an Beispielen aus dem Maschinenbau und der Elektroindustrie* (Frankfurt, New York: Campus, 1989), 321–84; Jeffrey Herf, *Reactionary Modernism: Technology, Culture, and Politics in Weimar and the Third Reich* (Cambridge: Cambridge University Press, 1984), 153–88; and Mary Nolan, *Visions of Modernity: American Business and the Modernization of Germany* (New York and Oxford: Oxford University Press, 1994), 179–205, who discuss Weimar attempts to improve the skills, subordination and discipline of workers. On the self-*Gleichschaltung* of the Werkbund, see Joan Campbell, *The German Werkbund: The Politics of Reform in the Applied Arts* (Princeton: Princeton University Press, 1978), 243–87.

15   Chup Friemert, *Schönheit der Arbeit: Produktionsaesthetik im Faschismus* (Munich: Damnitz Verlag, 1980), 118.

16   Belinda Davis, *Home Fires Burning: Food, Politics, and Everyday Life in World War I Berlin* (Chapel Hill and London: University of North Carolina Press, 2000), 152–8.

17   "Warmes Essen im Betrieb," NSG Kraft durch Freude, Gau Weser-Ems, *Kraft durch Freude* (April 1938): 8–9. For SdA's "actions," see Buchholz, "Nationalsozialistische Gemeinschaft," 84–5.

Fig. 3.1. A model shop floor, according to the Beauty of Labor. The
caption reads "Let Spring in the Factory." The model reflects the
Beauty of Labor's belief that space, light, and cleanliness would
improve worker morale and efficiency.
Source: Schönheit der Arbeit, undated issue. Author's collection.

undertakings progressively widened their original focus. Instead of pushing for improvements in the work environment alone, albeit improvements with consequences for the health and well being of the "retinue," SdA's campaigns after 1936 used plant betterment to target directly the bodily appearance and health of workers.

Although the Beauty of Labor projects took note of international trends, the Nazi regime's priorities and the inclinations of the SdA staff shaped its German character and mission. If German industrialists rejected American mass-produced commodities for their "inferiority," the Beauty of Labor perpetuated the mythical and symbolic edifice of "German quality work." In a regime that increasingly denigrated American production methods in order to highlight its Germanness,[18] so too did the Beauty of Labor claim the superiority of its accomplishments over plant renovations in the United States. Thus, although Speer's successor Herbert Steinwarz acknowledged the contributions of scientific management to raising the technical, productive, and hygienic standards of the American workplace, he argued that plant modernization in Germany contained an element that American industrialists ignored. Steinwarz asserted that rather than having simply confined itself to technocratic betterment, the Beauty of Labor engineered the rediscovery of the "soul" of companies, thus making possible the emergence of a "new human type."[19] At the core of the Beauty of Labor's conception of its task stood the nonalienated, "creative" (*schaffende*) worker; one who was no mere cog in a machine, but one who infused the product of his endeavor with moral content.[20] Echoed Anatol von Hübbenet, the Beauty of Labor transcended rationalization and external aestheticization to recreate the experience of work as the expression of its ethical meaning.[21] Redefining the experience of individual workers, furthermore, contained a larger purpose consistent with Nazism's assignment of racial superiority to the creators of culture. Belying his postwar reinvention of himself as an apolitical technocrat with no direct responsibility for Nazism's war crimes, Speer alluded to the Beauty of Labor's contribution to the Nazi regime's goals: "The company is, according to us, the living space of a community of men, a living cell in the construction of the racial community, which for this task is every bit as important as the other cell: the community of the family."[22]

18 Philipp Gassert, *Amerika im Dritten Reich: Ideologie, Propaganda und Volksmeinung 1933–1945* (Stuttgart: Franz Steiner Verlag, 1997), 148–63.
19 Herbert Steinwarz, *Wesen, Aufgaben, Ziele des Amtes Schönheit der Arbeit*, Institut für Zeitgeschichte, Munich (hereinafter cited as IfZ), Archiv, Db 72, 16, 6.
20 "Reichstagung des Amtes 'Schönheit der Arbeit' in Düsseldorf," *Schönheit der Arbeit*, 2, no. 7 (November 1937): 298–302.
21 Anatol von Hübbenet, *Die NS-Gemeinschaft "Kraft durch Freude" Aufbau und Arbeit* (Berlin: Junker und Dünnhaupt Verlag, 1939), 23.
22 *8. Reichstagung Schönheit der Arbeit 1.-3. Oktober 1937 in Düsseldorf*, 9. For Speer's postwar assessment of himself, see Sereny, *Albert Speer*; Richard Overy, *Interrogations:*

Navigating between the Scylla of Marxism and the Charybdis of Americanism, the Beauty of Labor embodied Strength through Joy's belief that bettering the conditions of production would raise the standard of living. By restoring the honor and integrity of labor – indeed infusing workers' products with transcendental meaning instead of reducing them to their material value[23] – the Beauty of Labor attacked the left's class egoism and American commercialism. In so doing, SdA deployed the "German" capitalism that right-wing intellectuals and the Nazi party enunciated during the twenties, reinforcing the hierarchy of employer over employee enshrined in the National Labor Law. At the same time, the Beauty of Labor sought to enhance the status of workers according to a "socialism" that rendered will and commitment to the racial community rather than the transformation in the mode of production as the catalyst of social change. Well-kept grounds complete with flowers and generous green spaces, good lighting, clean and modern changing rooms, civilized dining rooms that facilitated pleasant conversation among the "retinue," and uplifting lunchtime recreation would promote a degree of personal and collective well being that the hungering after material goods could not satisfy.

Because America was the most advanced consumer culture, the Beauty of Labor took pains to contrast the honor that it accorded workers with the presumed lack of it in the United States. Across the Atlantic, SdA claimed, workers were forced to wolf down their lunches at their workstations, while German workers received service from attractive waitresses, whose good health was medically certified. Workers dined, or would dine, in simply furnished but tasteful canteens, perhaps decorated with window boxes and flowers on each table. They would use silverware and glassware designed according to SdA standards for its aesthetic appeal.[24] (See Figure 3.2.) Moreover, the once common practice of separate lunchrooms for workers and salaried employees would be eliminated in the name of the classless "community."[25] To make its point, the Beauty of Labor's periodical by the same name, *Schönheit der Arbeit*, composed by the former editor of the Werkbund's journal, Wilhelm Lotz, published photos that depicted American workers at the Rockefeller Center construction site balanced precariously on a beam high above the New York skyline, struggling to eat their midday meals. French workers, the journal claimed, suffered in similarly degrading conditions, belying France's reputedly fine

The Nazi Elite in Allied Hands, 1945 (New York: Viking, 2001), 132–40, as well as Speer's memoir, *Inside the Third Reich.*

23 Betts, *Authority of Everyday Objects*, Ch. 1, manuscript p. 73.

24 Herbert Steinwarz, *Speiseräume und Küchen in gewerblichen Betrieben* (Berlin: Verlag der Deutschen Arbeitsfront, 1942).

25 NSG Kraft durch Freude, Gau Sachsen, *Monatsprogramm* (January/February 1936): 13–15.

Saubere Tische, bequeme Stühle, ein freundlicher Wandanstrich, einige Bilder und Blumen, – man kann schon mit bescheidenen Mitteln einen Frühstücks- und Aufenthaltsraum schaffen, der die Würde des arbeitenden Menschen wahrt.

Das Ergebnis ist: frohe Gesichter, ein froher, kameradschaftlicher Geist im Betrieb!

Fig. 3.2. The ideal lunchroom, according to the Beauty of Labor. Civilized dining reinforced the "honor" accorded to labor. *Source: Schönheit der Arbeit*, undated issue. Author's collection.

cuisine and the civility of its mealtimes.[26] The Beauty of Labor's proposal to aestheticize on-site mealtimes, asserted Herbert Steinwarz, directly affected "the practical life of the creative German and shows him the way to raising his own standard of living."[27]

In line with its anti-Marxism and anti-Americanism, the Beauty of Labor waged war against commercial advertising in the workplace. Although impossible to confirm, SdA's own estimates claimed the near total removal of advertisements from plants by 1938, thus removing inducements to unrestrained consumption.[28] In keeping with the regime's predilections, however, SdA deemed advertising acceptable if it evoked German customs and a mythologized view of German history, and if it employed human figures with appropriately Nordic features. "Jewish–Marxist" images of sexy film stars and American-style cartoons that appealed to the simple minded did not qualify.[29] SdA's ban on commercial advertising extended not only to large firms, but especially to the thousands of artisanal operations, in which American "kitsch" and crass advertisements undermined the transcendental significance of the products that Germans created and the skills they used to create them.[30] It also extended to the autobahns in opposition to the trend in America to use highways as commercial space.[31] The Beauty of Labor assured the consumers of advertisements that the regime cared about their well being. Yet its proscriptions against advertising more closely conformed to the regime's need to meet its most pressing economic objectives, suppressing the demand for foreign goods and images, and encouraging the savers' mentality necessary for rearmament.[32]

The Beauty of Labor further distinguished its "Germanness" and that of Strength through Joy through its charge to bring cultural productions to the workplace. KdF's arts program, a mélange of high and popular

---

26 "Essen und Essen ist Zweierlei," *Schönheit der Arbeit* 2, no. 1 (March 1938): 446–50.

27 Steinwarz, *Wesen, Aufgaben, Ziele des Amtes Schönheit der Arbeit*, ed. NSG Kraft durch Freude, Veröffentlichung des Amtes Schönheit der Arbeit, 1934/37, 10.

28 Anatole von Hübbenet, ed., *Das Taschenbuch Schönheit der Arbeit* (Berlin, 1938): 46–7.

29 Hartmut Berghoff, "Von der 'Reklame' zur Verbrauchslenkung: Werbung im nationalsozialistischen Deutschland," in *Konsumpolitik: Die Regulierung des privaten Verbrauchs im 20. Jahrhundert*, ed. Hartmut Berghoff (Göttingen: Vandenhoeck und Ruprecht, 1999), especially 92–7.

30 The journal *Schönheit der Arbeit* regularly featured "model" small enterprises, including automobile repair shops that SdA rewarded for their neatness, cleanliness, good lighting, and lack of objectionable ads. See for example "Autowerkstatt-vorbildlich," *Schönheit der Arbeit*, 3, no. 4 (August 1938): 176–7.

31 Zeller, "'The Landscape's Crown.'"

32 Berghoff, "'Reklame' zur Verbrauchslenkung": 77–112, especially 98–106. For the Nazi regime's management of a quintessentially modern commercial enterprise, fashion, see Historisches Museum Frankfurt, *Frankfurt macht Mode 1933–1945* (Frankfurt am Main: Jonas Verlag, 1999), especially 28.

culture ranging from the operas of Richard Wagner and plays of Friedrich Schiller to acrobatic and animal acts, was primarily the responsibility of its district, county, and local wardens, who acquired blocks of tickets and sold them by subscription to those attracted by the announcements in each district's monthly periodicals. Outside the cities and larger towns, where few opera houses and theaters existed, KdF's trains and trucks brought entertainment to its audiences. Nevertheless, arranging cultural events on the shop floor became essential to demonstrating the "joy" of work. By joining the "creativity" embedded in industrial production with the creativity of cultural production, culture in the workplace became visual and aural evidence of the compatibility between work and leisure. The infusions of German culture tempered the harshness of industrial civilization.[33]

In 1936, the Beauty of Labor concluded an agreement with the Reich Chamber for the Visual Arts, which enabled employers to hire artists and craftsmen to paint murals, design office furniture, and contribute to on-site art exhibits where they could sell their work, and where workers could gain an appreciation for aesthetics during their breaks. Portable equipment allowed art exhibits to be transported from one site to another, usually in two-week intervals. In 1935 alone, some 144 exhibits took place featuring in most cases original works by living German artists.[34] Noontime concerts by chamber and symphony orchestras were arranged as well, in which the ensembles consisted variously of employees, regional symphonies, the National Socialist Reich Symphony Orchestra, and on occasion major musicians and conductors. The electrical engineering concern, Siemens, organized one of the most extensive cultural programs, which by late 1936 had included the distribution of over 413,000 theater and concert tickets and nearly 25,000 KdF trips, most of them short excursions. It staged a huge concert involving employee musicians and performers in the Berlin Sports Palace in 1939, while the company's on-site concerts included the appearance of Wilhelm Fürtwangler, who conducted a widely publicized wartime concert on the shop floor.[35]

33 See Betts' insightful remarks on the Beauty of Labor's marriage of aesthetics and labor, *Authority of Everyday Objects*, manuscript pp. 67–8.
34 See Alan Steinweis, *Art, Ideology, and Economics in Nazi Germany: The Reich Chambers of Music, Theater, and the Visual Arts* (Chapel Hill and London: University of North Carolina Press, 1993), 77; and the "Arbeitsabkommen zwischen dem Amt Schönheit der Arbeit und der Reichskammer der bildenen Kunst," *Schönheit der Arbeit* 2, no. 13 (11 April 1936): 83–4. Further details of cultural programs in the plants are found in Otto Marrenbach, *Fundamente des Sieges: Die Gesamtarbeit der Deutschen Arbeitsfront von 1933 bis 1940* (Berlin: Verlag der Deutschen Arbeitsfront, 1940), 333; and Ludwig Klemme, "The Cultural Use of Leisure in Germany," *German Addresses for Committee VII, World Congress "Work and Joy,"* Rome, 1938 (Berlin: Buchdruckwerkstätte, 1938): 9.
35 "3 Jahre KdF-Leistungen in den Berliner Siemenswerken," *Siemens-Mitteilungen* no. 179 (November 1936), Siemens-Archiv Munich (hereinafter cited as SA); "Das

The endeavor to bring cultural productions directly to workers, especially the "classics" of German high culture, sought to eliminate class particularism and harmonize the interests of leaders and retinue. To begin with, the introduction of the visual and performing arts on the shop floor elided invidious distinctions between art and artisanship. The Beauty of Labor's periodical, *Schönheit der Arbeit*, equated the creativity of the artists who displayed their work on the shop floor with the that of employees, who decorated the "community rooms" of their plants.[36] The effort to raise the artistic and cultural awareness of workers was not limited to the workday, however. As the Siemens program testified, Strength through Joy persuaded employers to underwrite at least part of the cost of tickets that it procured for concerts, plays, and the opera as a gesture to the plant community.[37] Company-sponsored outings, which KdF plant functionaries facilitated by providing tickets and transportation, served yet another purpose, highlighting Germany's heritage, technological achievements, and attainments in the arts. Company field trips visited major cultural sites, be they the Pergamon Museum in Berlin and San Souci palace in Potsdam or the German Museum in Munich, combining those visits with meals at well-known eateries and beer halls in order to cement the comraderie between leaders and followers.[38]

Clean Bodies, Clean Minds

The Beauty of Labor's attention to the bodies of workers became its most distinctive characteristic. Its obsession with the public and private selves of company "retinues," and especially their physical appearance, spoke to its task of building "communities" where racial hierarchies assumed pride of place and class loyalties evaporated. From its inception the Beauty of Labor counterpoised the cleanliness of the work environment with its

Grosskonzert im Sportpalast," *Siemens-Mitteilungen*, no. 207 (July/August 1939): 131–4, SA. Material on the Fürtwängler concert is in SA, file L. 583.

36   "Kunst im Betrieb," *Schönheit der Arbeit* 4, no. 2 (June 1939): 50–9.

37   See Matthias Frese, *Betriebspolitik im "Dritten Reich:" Deutsche Arbeitsfront, Unternehmer und Staatsburokratie in der westdeutschen Großindustrie, 1933–1939* (Paderborn: Ferdinand Schöningh, 1991), 387–95; "Der deutsche Arbeiter in Bayreuth: 7,000 Gäste besuchen die Festspiel in Bayreuth," *Arbeitertum: Blätter für Theorie und Praxis der Nationalsozialistische Betriebszellen Organisation: Amtliches Organ der Deutschen Arbeitsfront*, (hereinafter cited as *Arbeitertum*) 9, no. 11 (1 September 1939): 7. On the regime's efforts to popularize the "classics," see Adelheid von Saldern, "'Art for the People': From Cultural Conservatism to Nazi Cultural Policies," in von Saldern, *The Challenge of Modernity: German Social and Cultural Studies, 1890–1960*, trans. Bruce Little (Ann Arbor: University of Michigan Press, 2002): 322–29.

38   *Siemens-Mitteilungen*, no. 175 (August 1936): 142, SA; NSG KdF Kreisdienstelle Göppingen an die Gaudienststelle Stuttgart, Abt. Reisen, Wandern, und Urlaub, 10 September 1937, Wirtschaftsarchiv Baden-Württemberg (hereinafter cited as WABW), 10, no. 292.

stark alternatives. Its numerous pamphlets, instructional manuals, and posters grouped related virtues or vices and opposed them in manichaean fashion. The desired outcomes of spotlessness, spaciousness, health, fresh air, brightness, and green spaces would triumph over their opposites; grime, darkness, cramped and unhealthy work spaces, and dankness by vigorous acts of will.[39] (See Figure 3.3). With the introduction of the "Clean People, Clean Plants" project, SdA focused increasingly on the rigid spatial separation of daily routines and bodily functions so that order and tidiness would transcend disorder, squalor, and the threat of disease. Thus, changing rooms with their lockers for each worker, according to SdA manuals, were to stand conveniently adjacent to washrooms, but remain sufficiently partitioned to keep the workday's grime in its proper place. As workers moved from the showers and washbasins to changing rooms, they would perform a ritualistic leap across a perceptible divide.[40] Other preventive measures, such as the use of sunlamps to warm the bodies of apprentices and insulate them against disease, would conquer what soap, water, and spacial segregation could not dissolve. (See Figure 3.4.)

The photographs of workplaces and workers in Beauty of Labor literature justified SdA's oft-used mantra, "squeaky clean" or "scrupulously clean" (*peinliche Sauberkeit*), that it used with numbing frequency to describe its sanitary expectations. They reveal page after page of tidy workplaces and workers without so much as a speck of grime on their clothing or bodies. The most direct and, from the perspective of middle-class sensibilities, repugnant signs of class distinction were nowhere to be seen, having been eliminated by dint of commitment and effort. "The floor of the great machine shop (*Machinenhalle*) is as clean as a dinner plate" remarked *Schönheit der Arbeit* as it praised conditions at the Rhineland-Westphalia Electric Works (Rheinisch-Westfälische Elektrizitätswerk). That description typified its regular coverage of "model" firms, in which more than any other criterion – be it noise levels of recreational facilities – cleanliness ranked first in distinguishing the models from the antimodels.[41] To tie cleanliness with the "joy" of work and the "honor" accorded to workers, smiling "retinues" were photographed in the act of scrubbing away the day's grime with the aid of up-to-date washbasins. (See Figure 3.5.) Even mining, which obviously presented formidable challenges to achieving "squeaky cleanliness," did not deter SdA's agents, who lobbied the industry to construct modern

39 Deutsche Arbeitsfront, NS-Gemeinschaft "Kraft durch Freude," Schönheit der Arbeit, *Schönheit der Arbeit*, 1934.
40 Herbert Steinwarz, *Das Kamaradschaftshaus im Betrieb* I. Teil (Berlin: Verlag der Deutschen Arbeitsfront, 1939), 3–5.
41 "Rheinisch-Westfälische Elektrizitätswerk A.G.," *Schönheit der Arbeit* 3, no. 2 (June 1938): 48–9.

Fig. 3.3. The "before" picture of a changing room, according to the Beauty of Labor. The filthy conditions, it suggests, degrade the workers in this plant and it urges employers to "honor" their employees with clean facilities.
Source: Schönheit der Arbeit, undated issue. Author's collection.

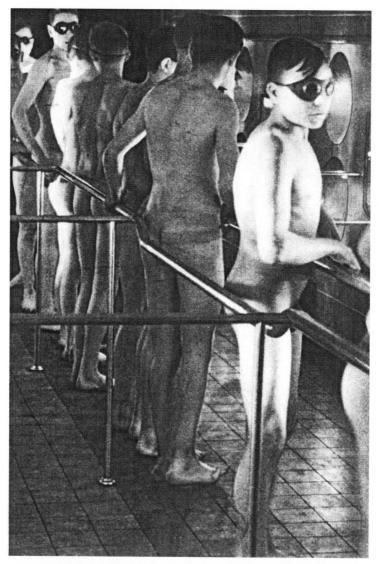

Fig. 3.4. Apprentices receiving sunlamp treatment as a disease prevention measure. Such a practice testified to the Beauty of Labor's attentions to the bodies of workers and not just to the work environment.

Source: Heinrich Schulz, *Sozialpolitik im neuen Deutschland* (Berlin, 1941). Reproduced by courtesy of the Department of Special Collections, General Library System, University of Wisconsin-Madison.

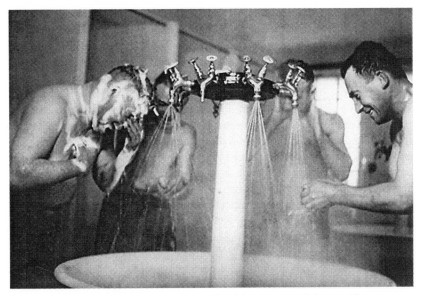

Fig. 3.5. "Washing with hot and cold water – and then we'll put on clean clothes." Workers in a washroom modernized according to Beauty of Labor standards.
Source: Reichsamtsleitung Kraft durch Freude, *Unter dem Sonnenrad: Ein Buch von Kraft durch Freude* (Berlin: Verlag der Deutsche Arbeitsfront, 1938), 63. Courtesy of the Center for Research Libraries, Chicago.

washrooms and institute aesthetic improvements in areas external to the mineshaft. The Beauty of Labor doggedly pushed the mining industry, an industry long reputed for its appalling washing and changing facilities, for renovations which would permit the strict segregation of tasks that it deemed essential to improving the self-esteem of workers and recovering the "joy" of work.[42]

The Beauty of Labor's passion for cleanliness was to eradicate the "inferiority complex" that filth induced, which discouraged workers from seeing their work as the source of creativity and "joy."[43] As such, it aesthetically complemented the arrests, emergency decrees, and concentration camps that destroyed the Socialist and Communist movements. A

42 Die Deutsche Arbeitsfront, Amt für Schönheit der Arbeit der NSG. Kraft durch Freude, *Schönheit der Arbeit im Bergbau*, 1938; *"Schönheit der Arbeit" besucht Bergbaubetriebe*, NSG Kraft durch Freude, Gau Württemberg-Hohenzollern, *Kraft durch Freude* (1937): 35–7. See also Klaus Wisotzky, *Der Ruhrbergbau im Dritten Reich: Studien zur Sozialpolitik im Ruhrgebau und zum sozialen Verhalten der Bergleute in den Jahren 1933 bis 1939* (Düsseldorf: Schwann, 1983), 182–3.
43 Friemert, *Schönheit der Arbeit*, 125.

clean body dispelled all visible signs of manual labor, the most observable badge of class differentiation and conflict. According to SdA's literature, leftist agitators in the past ridiculed efforts of socially responsible employers to provide their workers with shower and changing facilities as nothing more than a capitalist trick to distract workers from pursuing their real interests. Initially Strength through Joy's literature accepted the appearance of dirt to the extent that it photographed workers who greeted Robert Ley in their grime during a plant visit while the Labor Front leader heartily and fearlessly shook hands with them. What did dirt matter if the hearts of workers remained pure and loyal to the nation over class? Like the dreck on their bodies, the dreck of Marxism was but skin deep.[44] But given the growing importance of "squeaky cleanliness" to the Beauty of Labor, photographs of workers came to eschew even the barest acknowledgment of dirt. The clean bodies of workers signified not only the common purpose that emerged from the hierarchy of employer–leader over worker–follower – their joint desire to produce for the racial community – they also indicated decontamination; the eradication of the plague of class conflict from the social body. Thus a clean and ordered body like a clean and ordered shop floor would incline individual dispositions toward a comradeship that would dissipate the potential for "Marxist" disorder and upheaval.[45] The "dirty" worker, insisted one KdF periodical, "should according to Marxist theory not become clean and well-dressed. Rather he should remain, so to speak, a walking advertisement for the infamous lie of the class struggle."[46]

Arising in the nineteenth century as a signifier of bourgeois culture and a badge of respectability that denigrated and effaced manual labor, cleanliness distinguished the proper and upstanding male citizen from the unkempt and unclean lower classes, a perception that grew more marked in the wake of urbanization and the technological improvements in sanitation. Yet cleanliness also elevated Europeans over colonized peoples of color. The tangible products of European consumer culture, soap among them, became the means of transmitting through advertising social Darwinian assumptions of racially defined white superiority.[47] The Beauty

44 Robert Ley, *Schaffendes Volk: Sitten deutscher Arbeit in 83 Bildern* (Berlin: Verlag der Deutsche Arbeitsfront, 1934), 14.

45 "Sauberkeit im Betrieb ist eine Notwendigkeit," NSG Kraft durch Freude, Gau Hessen-Nassau, *Kraft durch Freude* 4, no. 4 (April 1937): 10–12.

46 "Sauberkeit und Ehre gehören zusammen," NSG Kraft durch Freude, Gau München Oberbayern, *Kraft durch Freude*, (April 1937): 14.

47 See in particular Timothy Burke, *Lifebuoy Men, Lux Women: Commodification, Consumption, and Cleanliness in Modern Zimbabwe* (Durham: Duke University Press, 1996), 17–62; Anne McClintock, *Imperial Leather: Race, Gender and Sexuality in the Colonial Contest* (New York and London: Routledge, 1995), 207–31; and Thomas Richards, *The Commodity Culture of Victorian England: Advertising and Spectacle, 1851–1914* (Stanford: Stanford University Press, 1990), 119–67.

of Labor's campaign for "squeaky cleanliness" not only borrowed from the ideological baggage of empire, it also deployed the racism of cleanliness in the regime's campaign for racial segregation and purification at home before Nazism's own war for empire began. Cleanliness separated those spared the racial "hygiene" that the regime introduced from its inception, including workers whom bourgeois notions of cleanliness once denigrated, from Nazism's victims, whose "asocial" slovenliness merited forced sterilization, social exclusion, and death.[48]

Moreover, the Beauty of Labor associated dirt not just with "Marxism" but with "Jewish Marxism," for the "class hatred" preached by socialism amounted to the detritus of "an alien race."[49] Evoking the distinction, which the party appropriated during the Weimar period between "Jewish" and "German" capitalism, the "Jewish model company" became the mirror image of the purification and renovation that German business was supposed to realize. Before "Aryanization" in November 1938, which resulted in the confiscation of Jewish assets and the final dissolution of Jewish-owned businesses, Jewish-owned firms stood out in the negative publicity that SdA meted out in periodicals and newspapers against companies that had not met its standards.[50] Envisioned in Strength through Joy's literature as a place of filth, poor ventilation, gloomy and dank darkness, and conditions ruinous to workers' health, the "Jewish" company spawned ceaseless conflict between employer and workers. By contrast, the German model company stood for a healthful and sanitized workplace, aesthetically pleasing surroundings, civilized mealtimes with attractive china and flatware, and the employer's fatherly concern for the well being of his workers where the community of interest between leader and followers reigned supreme.[51] Even when racism and antisemitism appeared less overt and seemingly removed from the messages being conveyed in the Beauty of Labor's publications, Strength through Joy's oft-recited description of workers as "creators" (Schaffende), who deserved pristine surroundings befitting the moral and transcendental value of their work, rested on a racial categorization crucial to National Socialism. That was the division between culture-creating, culture-bearing, and culture-destroying races in Hitler's Mein Kampf that permeated Nazi ideology and the Nazi regime's racial "hygiene."

---

48 The literature on Nazi racial policy has grown to gargantuan proportions in the last two decades. For a summary statement by an historian who has contributed significantly to the discussion on Nazi racism, see Michael Burleigh, The Third Reich: A New History (New York: Hill and Wang, 2000), Chs. 4 and 5.

49 Robert Ley, Die deutsche Arbeitsfront: Ihr Werden und Aufgaben (Munich: Franz Eher Verlag, 1934), 5.

50 See Friemert, Schönheit der Arbeit, 95–6.

51 "Ein jüdischer 'Musterbetrieb,'" Nationalsozialistische Gemeinschaft Kraft durch Freude, Gau Sachsen, Monatsprogramm (March 1936): 25–7.

Rejecting the compartmentalization of life between the workday and after work, the Beauty of Labor applied the standards of the shop floor to workers' private lives in keeping with its role in the Labor Front's ambitious housing program. According to Ley, whose empire included an agency devoted to the construction of housing for workers, which would supplant working-class ghettos, the task of creating a healthy, clean, and aesthetically pleasing shop floor would encourage workers to create an aesthetically pleasing, immaculate home.[52] To be sure, rearmament forestalled Ley's plans, yet their existence testified to the depth of the desire to reshape the lives of workers as crucial to reshaping their identities. Speer's successor Herbert Steinwarz followed with the suggestion that merely attending to the workplace alone would not suffice. The necessity of building more housing for workers lay in the fear that a clean workplace by itself would only dramatize the misery of working-class living conditions if the Beauty of Labor did not attend to the private sphere as well.[53] In an explicit attack on Marxism he argued "An ordered economy in the business enterprise will bring an ordered economy to one's private life." In turn, orderly and clean working conditions would have a similar impact in the home. Overcoming the divide between public and private would mitigate the inclination of industrialists to push productivity at all costs at the expense of their workers' well being, and attack the nonsense of equality and brotherhood, which "the emissaries of Moscow" preached on the streets.[54]

The Beauty of Labor's proposed intrusions resembled the household rationalization movement of the twenties and the company social programs of the interwar period, which sought to simplify the interior design of living quarters to render workers, especially working-class women, more efficient and content.[55] Yet, while stressing home management skills, self-discipline, the elimination of kitsch and clutter, and cleanliness with a vengeance, SdA softened its rationalization with elements of "traditional" working-class German domesticity.[56] Thus, SdA's accommodations to the

---

52 "Tätigkeitsbericht über die Leistungen der NS Gemeinschaft Kraft durch Freude von Dr. Robert Ley, 26 November 1935," Bundesarchiv Berlin-Lichterfelde (hereinafter cited as BAL), NS 22/781, 22. On the prewar DAF housing program, see Smelser, *Robert Ley*, 199–201.

53 "Eine nachdenkliche Geschichte," *Schönheit der Arbeit* 2, no. 7 (November 1937), 277–82.

54 "Sauberkeit und Ordnung: Grundlagen für die Schönheit der Arbeit," 9 March 1937, BAL, NS 22/554.

55 See especially Carola Sachse, *Siemens, der Nationalsozialismus und die moderne Familie: Eine Untersuchung zur sozialen Rationalisierung in Deutschland im 20. Jahrhundert* (Hamburg: Rasch and Röhring Verlag, 1990); and Mary Nolan, *Visions of Modernity: American Business and the Modernization of Germany* (New York and Oxford: Oxford University Press, 1994), 178–226.

56 Betts, *Authority*, Ch. 1, argues similarly.

needs of employed women cast them as mothers first, who in its view worked only out of economic necessity rather than from the desire for independence. SdA depicted plant kindergartens decorated with puppets and toys, signifying a worthy substitute during the workday for the nurturing of the family. Unlike the kindergartens in the Soviet Union, German kindergartens would not alienate mothers from their children.[57] As for the "private" space of workers and their families, the Beauty of Labor's architects and designers envisioned modest and functional living spaces decorated with appropriately German furnishings, while providing a sufficient number of bedrooms to allow separate quarters for the parents and each child. SdA departed, however, from the plans of the progressive architects and designers of Weimar workers' flats. Rejecting the smaller, streamlined "Frankfurt kitchen" of the twenties, it opted for the "live-in kitchen" (*Wohnküche*), which had long occupied the center of cramped working-class living quarters, and which reformers of the twenties had condemned as unhygienic.[58] That preference for "tradition" bespoke the Beauty of Labor's desire to create spaces that would restore the imagined hierarchical nuclear family that the Great War, revolution, and class conflict had threatened to destroy, and in addition, transfer the communal hierarchy of plant "leaders" over the "retinue" to the home. Consistent with the Labor Front housing plans, which emphasized rural settlements or small planned communities away from urban neighborhoods, SdA would dissipate class consciousness through the implementation of its interior designs.[59]

Despite its modifications of domestic space, the Beauty of Labor rivaled household reformers and business efficiency experts in its desire to discipline consumption, accepting the long established practice of feminizing consumption as the sphere of irrational, uncontrolled materialistic excess.[60] To counter the influences of consumerism, the Beauty of Labor urged simplicity and subdued tastefulness in the furnishings, attire, and personal bearing, particularly of working women. A drawer for a toothbrush in the bathroom would do, intoned *Schönheit der Arbeit*, for a dressing table would only encourage frivolity, which was incompatible

57 "Wie sollen unsere Kindergarten eingerichtet sein?", *Schönheit der Arbeit* 3, no. 5 (September 1938): 227–9. Cf. Siegel, *Leistung und Lohn*, 98–106, on the explicitly anti-Marxist assumptions behind the DAF's interventions on behalf of employed women.

58 See Adelheid von Saldern, "Neues Wohnen: Wohnverhältnisse und Wohnverhalten in Großwohnanlagen der 20er Jahre," in *Massenwohnung und Eigenheim: Wohnungsbau und Wohnung in der Großstadt seit dem Ersten Weltkrieg* (Frankfurt, New York: Campus Verlag, 1988): 208.

59 Smelser, *Robert Ley*, 200. For contemporary summaries of the DAF's housing program, see Marrenbach, *Fundamente des Sieges*, 377–80; and Müller, *soziale Leben*, 192–5.

60 See Victoria de Grazia's introduction in *The Sex of Things: Gender and Consumption in Historical Perspective*, ed. Victoria de Grazia and Ellen Furlough (Berkeley, Los Angeles, London: University of California Press, 1996): 14–15.

with the responsibilities that working women managed. If the Beauty of Labor deemed the status of German workers superior to that of their American counterparts, that came not from the satisfaction of unlimited consumer desires that Hollywood films engendered. The flats to which workers would return home would be clean, uncluttered, furnished attractively but inexpensively, and unburdened by the necessity of catering to the false expectations generated by "film people."[61] SdA's model housing envisioned not only a disciplined, Spartan consumption in keeping with German values, but, like the workplace itself, a "scrupulous cleanliness" that separated the racially fit from the "asocials."[62]

Strength through Joy's sports program reinforced the Beauty of Labor's aestheticizing of workers and work environments. Its shift in emphasis from after-work activities to fitness in the workplace complemented SdA's emphasis on bodily health. Since it was founded, KdF offered sports courses to men, women, and children at low cost, having recognized the potential of athletics as a means of indoctrination and as a way to strengthen the racial quality of the nation. In addition, the popularity of sport among workers, many of whom had joined Socialist or Communist sport clubs during the Weimar era, provided an additional incentive to outdo "Marxism" in the delivery of mass leisure.[63] Yet, belying the KdF mantra as to the unity of work and leisure time, the KdF sport bureau, led by Tschammer und Osten, who doubled as director of the National Socialist Physical Education League, confined itself at first to organizing programs off the shop floor, targeting especially the cities and larger towns where it could reach substantial numbers. Despite the inclination to expand sport courses to the workplace, which the Reich interior ministry urged as early as 1934, the sport office adhered to that original focus.[64] Offering "open" courses that accommodated personal convenience and catered to a wide range of skill, KdF promoted a variety of sports ranging from those relevant to military needs, such as boxing, shooting, and the martial arts, to the popular pastimes among the upper classes, tennis, golf, horseback riding, and sailing. It promoted "sport holidays" in "sport hostels" where, depending on the location, vacationers could ski, take a canoe trip, or sail. Rather than promote individual competition among the athletically talented, Strength through Joy

61 "Eine nachdenkliche Geschichte," *Schönheit der Arbeit* 2, no. 7 (November 1937): 277–82.
62 For a discussion of how the regime used housing to determine racial fitness, see Lisa Pine, *Nazi Family Policy 1933–1945* (Oxford and New York: Berg, 1997), 88–146.
63 Reichel, *schöne Schein*, 255–8.
64 "Niederschrift über die Zusammenkunft der Gefolgschaftsführer, der Abteilungsvorsteher, der Vertrauensrats, ihrer Stellvertreter und der Hilfsvertrauensmänner, 26 July 1936," 14–17; Historisches Archiv Krupp, Essen (hereinafter cited as HA-Krupp), 41/6–217.

advocated sports as a means of relaxation, personal enjoyment, increased fitness, and especially comradeship.[65] Expressing pride in the delivery of sport to all ages and across gender lines, sport courses were nonetheless scaled according to what Strength through Joy deemed appropriate. Thus although the participants in many KdF sport courses were women, they were concentrated in the putatively less physically taxing activities.[66]

In 1936, however, the sport office expanded its reach, spearheading its new campaign "Sport in the Plants." Although partly the consequence of the Labor Front's stepped-up effort to deepen its role in the economy and its attempt to offload the spiraling costs of the KdF sport program onto business, external pressures proved decisive. The Winter and Summer Olympic Games in Germany, which heightened national interest in athletic competition, the worsening international climate following the remilitarization of the Rhineland, and the Four-Year Plan, demanded a more formal, indeed a more concentrated, effort to fortify the bodies of "retinues." Their reinvigoration would boost their performance on the job and ready them for war. Moving beyond its modest goal of relaxation that had emphasized individual fulfillment in addition to comradeship, the sport office now required the participation of employees and the pursuit of team competition, utilizing precise standards graded according to gender and age group. The "industrial brigades" (Werkscharen) – the military-like troops composed of Labor Service volunteers that the DAF created in 1935 to indoctrinate managers and workers with the values of the "plant community"[67] – became models for the appropriate deployment of sport on the shop floor. Female employees were not simply invited, but expected to participate in calesthenics, gymnastics, and other regimens appropriate to their limited physical abilities as long as those over thirty received a doctor's certification.[68]

By 1938, an agreement between Ley and Baldur von Schirach, the leader of the Hitler Youth, mandated a minimum of two hours per week of sports

65   Karl Lorch, "Aims and Importance of Works Sports," *German Addresses for Committee V, World Congress, "Work and Joy,"* Rome, 1938: 4–5; Marrenbach, *Fundamente des Sieges*, 344–6; "Der Reichssportführer von Tschammer und Osten in Siemensstadt," *Siemens-Mitteilungen* no. 159 (March 1935): 43–4, SA; Hajo Bernett, "Nationalsozialistischer Volkssport bei 'Kraft durch Freude,'" *Stadion: Zeitschrift für Geschichte des Sports und der Körperkultur* 5 (1979): 89–146; *Dienstanweisung des Sportamtes der NSG "Kraft durch Freude"* (Berlin: Verlag der Deutschen Arbeitsfront, 1937), 8–11.
66   Frauamt der Deutsche Arbeitsfront, *Tagewerk und Feierabend der schaffenden deutschen Frau* (Leipzig and Berlin: Verlag Otto Beyer, 1936), 98.
67   Tim Mason, *Social Policy in the Third Reich: The working Class and the "National Community"* trans. John Broadwin, ed. Jane Caplan (Providence and Oxford: Berg, 1993), 165.
68   Die Deutsche Arbeitsfront, NSG "Kraft durch Freude," Sportamt, *Sportappell der Betriebe 1939*, 8.

for young workers.[69] To complement the "Sport in the Plants" campaign, the Beauty of Labor found a new category of physical improvements to advocate, the renovation or construction of sports facilities on company grounds. The aestheticized workplace would mean not only less noise and good lighting, but also football fields, gymnasiums, and swimming pools, the presence of which testified to their relevance to workers' performance and thus their fitness as members of the future master race. By the same year, the Labor Front claimed, business and other enterprises had constructed three thousand sport facilities, including football fields, swimming pools, and gymnasiums.[70]

No aestheticization project could rival the plans for the huge Volkswagen plant and its neighboring planned community, "the KdF-Wagen City," near Fallersleben in Lower Saxony, the construction for which began in the spring of 1938. Unlike the improvements asked of existing plants, the Volkswagen project began from scratch, thus becoming a showcase for Nazism's fusion of productivism and disciplined consumption. Resorting to superlatives for the benefit of domestic and foreign audiences, the DAF claimed the Volkswagen plant would become the "most modern and beautiful factory in the entire world." At the same time, the city was to become "the most beautiful and most exemplary in the Reich."[71] In one sweep the Volkswagen project would beat the Americans at their own game of mass production, while "honoring" workers with living quarters that neither the Marxist nor American degradation of labor could produce. As the dream of Ferdinand Porsche, who could not persuade German automakers to manufacture the car, the Volkswagen depended on the support of the führer and financing from the Labor Front. Thus, the Volkswagen undertaking gave the Beauty of Labor more latitude than privately owned firms permitted it. In addition to the involvement of Beauty of Labor architects in the design of the plant, the architect for the city, Peter Koller, enjoyed the favor of Speer, who now combined his titular leadership of SdA with the position of general inspector for the reconstruction of Berlin. The plans for the factory incorporated a post office, a hospital, sport facilities, a center for various kinds of staged entertainment, and state-of-the-art showers and washrooms.[72]

If the architectural specifications for the city amounted to an uneasy compromise between the monumental axis that Speer envisioned for the capital and the antiurban motifs embedded in the Labor Front's rural and small town settlement proposals, they nonetheless conformed to the DAF's

---

69 Lorch, "Aims and Importance of Works Sports," 8.
70 Marrenbach, *Fundamente des Sieges*, 325.   71 Ibid., 364.
72 "Der Bau des Volkswagenwerks," *Schönheit der Arbeit* 3, no. 8 (December 1938): 336–9. For the paradoxes of Volkswagen, see Hans Mommsen and Manfred Grieger, *Das Volkswagenwerk und seine Arbeiter* (Düsseldorf: Econ, 1997), 250–82.

and the Beauty of Labor's recommendations for workers' housing in one important respect. Their conceptions of size and allocation of space would encourage the appropriate behavior.[73] Flats were to be bright, airy, and practically designed to promote cleanliness. Consistent with SdA's proposals for the housing of industrial workers, the housing for the Volkswagen project envisioned separate bedrooms for parents and bedrooms for each child over the age of twelve. Rooms designated for other purposes, most obviously the kitchen, were not to be used as sleeping quarters. Nor were animals other than house pets permitted inside, an implicit remedy for the common practice of sheltering farm animals, especially in rural areas. Although the plans allowed for the continuation of the working-class practice of renting out space to boarders, access to boarders' rooms was to bypass the bedrooms of the family. Imagined as housing suitable for "creative" Germans workers as full-fledged members of the master race, the plans implicitly privileged marriage as central to a healthy national community, giving generous space to children befiting their status as Germany's future. Dirt, grime, and darkness, the evidence of class conflict and racial degeneration, would disappear.[74]

From the Plant to Rural Community: The Beauty of Labor in the Countryside

The 1936 Olympics and the acceleration of rearmament encouraged the Beauty of Labor to reassess its function of eradicating the ugliness and alienating effects of the industrial workplace. Thus SdA attended to the countryside through its project, "the Beautiful Village" (das schöne Dorf). The following year, peasant holdings and agricultural latifundia, such as the Pennekow estate of the Belows, one of Pomerania's largest land-owning families, had received the designation of "model enterprise," which the Beauty of Labor bestowed on firms that met its criteria for a productive, efficiently designed, and clean workplace.[75] By 1938, SdA

---

73 For details as to the city's layout, see ibid., 268–70; and Erhard Forndran, *Die Stadt- und Industriegründungen Wolfsburg und Salzgitter: Entscheidungsprozesse im nationalsozialistischen Herrschaftssystem* (Frankfurt, New York: Campus Verlag, 1984), 72–6. On antiurbanism in the Third Reich as applied to housing, see Elke-Paul Weber and Dirk Schubert, "Die Volksgemeinschaft unter dem Steilen Dach? Ein ideologiekritischer Beitrag zum Wohnungs- und Städtebau der Zeit zwischen 1933 und 1945 in Hamburg," in Schildt and Sywottek, eds., *Massenwohnung und Eigenheim*, especially 307–11.

74 Sonder-Beilage zum Stück 45 des Regierungs-Amtsblatts, 11 November 1939. Polizeiverordnung (Wohnungsordnung für die Stadt des KdF.-Wagens), NHH Hann. 80, Luneburg III, XXXIV, no. 325.

75 *Schönheit der Arbeit* 2, no. 2 (June 1937): 108–9.

had mapped out a three-year rural beautification program that focused in the first year on generalized cleanup and the improvement of drainage. Structural modifications that included the construction of common buildings, as well as the renovation of peasant and laborer living quarters, were to follow.[76]

Intended to overcome the cultural and economic divide between the city and countryside, which had contributed to Nazism's electoral advances before 1933, and which from the Nazi regime's perspective impeded the racial community,[77] this new Beauty of Labor campaign, like the introduction of sport in the workplace, addressed the challenges arising from Germany's resurgence on the continent. Aestheticization, the bureau hoped, would stem a long festering problem, the "flight from the land" (*Landflucht*), the emigration of agricultural labor, especially young workers and peasants. Less the consequence of mechanization, which because of rearmament's claim on essential raw materials amounted to less than the regime had promoted, than of rural poor wages and living conditions, the depopulation of the countryside jeopardized food production and rendered Germany vulnerable to an enemy blockade, threatening a repeat of the experience of World War I.[78] Consistent with the Beauty of Labor's expectations of industrial plants, however, villages and rural enterprises would have to pay for improvements themselves. They received due assurances that the expected ameliorations would neither be expensive, nor bereft of volunteers, especially the women who belonged to the National Socialist Women's League, who were encouraged to volunteer their time.[79] Equally in accord with SdA's role on the shop floor, SdA's campaign in the countryside addressed structural issues through the institution of aesthetic improvements that would transform attitudes and raise morale.

76 DAF NSG.KdF, Amt Schönheit der Arbeit, Gauarbeitsgemeinschoft "Das schöne Dorf," Arbeitsplan 1938–40, NHH Hann. 122 a, no. 577, 334.

77 On the rise of Nazism in the countryside, see Robert G. Moeller, *German Peasants and Agrarian Politics, 1914–1924: The Rhineland and Westphalia* (Chapel Hill: University of North Carolina Press, 1986); Jonathan Osmond, *Rural Protest in the Weimar Republic: The Free Peasantry in the Rhineland and Bavaria* (New York, 1993); Wolfram Pyta, *Dorfgemeinschaft und Parteipolitik 1918–1933: Die Verschränkung von Milieu und Parteien in den protestantischen Landgebieten Deutschlands in der Weimarer Republik* (Düsseldorf: Droste Verlag, 1996), and my *The Sanctity of Rural Life: Nobility, Protestantism, and Nazism in Weimar Prussia* (New York and Oxford: Oxford University Press, 1995).

78 For an analysis of Nazi policy toward agriculture, see Gustavo Corni, *Hitler and the Peasants: Agrarian Policy of the Third Reich, 1930–1939*, trans. David Kerr (New York, Oxford, Munich: Berg, 1990).

79 Gauwart, NSG.KdF, Gau Süd-Hannover-Braunschweig an den Oberpräsidenten der Provinz Hannover, Staatsrat Lutze (12 March 1936), NHH, Hann. 122a, VIII, no. 577, 91–7.

The "Beautiful Village" served yet another purpose, a demonstration of the Third Reich's commitment to improving the lives of the its citizens. Delegates to the World Congress on Leisure and Recreation and the hard-currency bearing visitors to the Olympic Games, who traveled through the German countryside en route to their destinations, would see with their own eyes that the new regime had liberated Germany from Weimar's decay. Following the desire of KdF's office of Travel, Vacations, and Hiking to encourage economic development through tourism, the commitment of villagers to the beautification of their surroundings would improve the income of rural villages by attracting KdF tourists. Warned the Strength through Joy warden for the Gau South Hannover-Brunswick: "We cannot expect our KdF vacationers to feel comfortable in a village in which the inhabitants themselves neither feel comfortable nor find true recreation there."[80] KdF encouraged employers to form partnerships between their firms and nearby villages as a way to strengthen urban–rural ties and develop hamlets as vacation sites for their workers. Such undertakings would provide recreation for employees and achieve economic benefits for economically weak rural areas.[81]

Detailed guidelines for the "Beautiful Village" project specified "cleanliness and order" even in work buildings, and consistency in architectural style, landscape and furnishings so as to reify villages as "typically" German. The touristic purposes became evident as well in the argument that village entrances should be made more attractive, like "calling cards" extended to visitors. The village cemetery would be the German cultural site par excellence, for it was to eschew foreign vegetation such as cypress trees, in accordance with the dominant trend in landscape design during the Third Reich.[82] Tombstones were to conform to the general tenor of the graveyard as a whole. Peasant living quarters and work buildings should avoid garish colors and styles, abstain from the use of urban building materials, such as concrete retaining blocks, and strive instead for a subdued coherence in keeping with their natural surroundings. Whitewashed houses complete with window boxes and climbing roses, trimmed shrubbery, and mended and painted fences would lift rural spirits and heighten the commitment of locals to maintaining the soil as an honorable calling. (See Figures 3.6 and 3.7.) The Beauty of Labor's putatively successful crusade to eliminate advertising from industrial plants encouraged an equally

---

80   Ibid.
81   Bruno Malitz, "Das Problem der Werkdorfkameradschaft: Schönheit des Dorfes-Freizeitstätten und Sportplätze," *Arbeitertum* 8, no. 15 (1 November 1938), 9.
82   Joachim Wolsche-Bulmahn and Gert Gröning, "The National Socialist Garden and Landscape Ideal," in *Art, Culture, and Media under the Third Reich*, ed. Richard A. Etlin (Chicago and London: University of Chicago Press, 2002): 79.

Fig. 3.6. How rural housing should not look, according to the Beauty of Labor. Note the use of concrete blocks in the structure on the bottom.

Source: Deutsche Arbeitsfront Amt "Das Schöne Dorf." *Der Mensch in Dorf* (Berlin: Verlag der Deutschen Arbeitsfront, 1939?), 13. Courtesy of General Research Division. The New York Public Library. Astor, Lenox and Tilden Foundations.

Fig. 3.7. The model village (top) and its mirror image (bottom).
Source: Deutsche Arbeitsfront Amt "Das schöne Dorf." *Der Mensch in Dorf* (Berlin: Verlag der Deutschen Arbeitsfront, 1939?), 7. Courtesy of General Research Division, The New York Public Library, Astor, Lenox and Tilden Foundations.

persistent effort to remove it from the countryside, where advertising had become sufficiently pervasive as to turn up in cemeteries.[83] Villages could permit "good, healthy" advertising, by which was meant advertising that did not contribute to the "urbanization" (*Verstädtlichung*) of the soil. Like the exteriors of homes and work buildings, rural advertising was to shun loud colors and remain understated in size, proportion, and frequency of appearance. It should be devoid of "foreign" images, and represent the sensibilities of local artists and craftsmen, who best understood rural values. No advertisements were to be posted on doors, trees, or bridges, and only modest ads were allowed on the outside walls of shops.[84]

For large estates, the Beauty of Labor's guidelines urged the upgrading of the living quarters of agricultural laborers, long acknowledged as appalling. Comparable to its guidelines for housing for industrial workers, rural housing was to include a roomy live-in kitchen, abundant light, a separate cellar for storage, indoor plumbing where practicable, stalls for animals kept separate from the home, and above all, separate sleeping quarters for parents and children, a durable mantra of urban reformers repelled by the suspected sexual permissiveness of the "backward" countryside. (See Figures 3.8 and 3.9.) The Beauty of Labor devoted much attention to educating rural women in the art of creating and maintaining a nice home, assuring healthful ventilation and cleanliness, and avoiding citified styles in furniture. In addition, local volunteers were asked to train rural women in infant care, personal hygiene, exercise techniques, and proper nutrition – the latter an attempt in how to plan meals with few fats and little meat, imported commodities that conflicted with the regime's goal of agricultural self-sufficiency. To that end, the Beauty of Labor exhorted homemakers to use cellophane to preserve food and volunteers to staff kindergartens, especially during the planting and harvesting seasons.[85]

As it planned for the urban or industrial workplace, the "Beautiful Village" embraced the totality of "creative" lives, recognizing the seamless bond between work and leisure. The Beauty of Labor pushed for the construction of sport facilities and swimming pools in the countryside to provide rural people with recreation and equalize living standards between city and country.[86] In 1937, following the absorption of

83 NSG.KdF Kreiswart, Kreis Hannover an alle Orts- und Betriebeswarte der NSG. "Kraft durch Freude," 2 December 1936, NHH Hann. 122a, VIII, no. 577, 180.
84 "Die Werbung im Dorf," Landeshauptarchiv Koblenz (hereinafter cited as LK), Bestand 714, no. 5406.
85 Richtlinien Zur Dorfverschönerungsaktion, 1937, NHH, Hann. 122a, VIII, no. 577, 240–56, Deutsche Arbeitsfront, Amt "Das schöne Dorf," *Der Mensch in Dorf* (Berlin: Verlag der Deutschen Arbeitsfront, 1939).
86 Richtlinten, NHH, Hann. 122a, VIII, no. 577, 252; *Mensch in Dorf*, 9.

Fig. 3.8. A model "live-in" kitchen for the countryside.
Source: Deutsche Arbeitsfront Amt "Das schöne Dorf." *Der Mensch in Dorf* (Berlin: Verlag der Deutschen Arbeitsfront, 1939?), 21. Courtesy of General Research Division, The New York Public Library, Astor, Lenox and Tilden Foundations.

Fig. 3.9. Model dwellings for agricultural workers.
Source: Deutsche Arbeitsfront Amt "Das schöne Dorf." *Der Mensch in Dorf* (Berlin: Verlag der Deutschen Arbeitsfront, 1939?), 11. Courtesy of General Research Division, The New York Public Library. Astor, Lenox and Tilden Foundations.

Rosenberg's agency, Strength through Joy assumed responsibility for organizing after-work recreation, particularly in the countryside. A joint com-
muniqué in mid-June from Ley and Walter Darré, the leader of the Reich
Food Estate, charged each KdF district office with organizing entertainment in rural areas, with the support of the Food Estate's peasant leader
(Landesbauernführer). The so-called "village evenings" emphasized activities that resonated with the peasant ethos. They entailed the revitalization
of peasant customs and the expulsion of the urban influences of "nigger"
or "Jewish" jazz and swing. Poetry readings, chamber music, folk music
and dance, amateur theater, marionette shows, and paintings of agrarian
scenes constituted appropriate folk pastimes and reawakened an appreciation for the values of land and soil among youth so that they would not
"flee" from the land.[87]

Those recreational agendas did not simply target rural people, however. Other after-work activities sought to deepen urban dwellers' appreciation for Germany's agrarian roots by exposing them to folk customs. Be they Christmas tree candles and Christmas cookies, folk attire
(*Trachten*), or "plant community evenings" where local choruses praised
the virtues of land and nature, after-work activities were to rescue "community" (*Gemeinschaft*) from its destruction by a soulless, mechanistic
"society" (*Gesellschaft*), protect authenticity from commercialism, and
promote racial integrity against its pollution by "racially alien," urban
elements.[88] Like "German" capitalism, which tamed industrialization
with the national spirit, the Beauty of Labor's "beautiful village" project
was to Germanize the city with the seemingly timeless values and customs of the countryside. Thus, the community of interest between city
and country would overcome one of Germany's most persistent sources
of division, the urban–rural divide. Notwithstanding that ambition, the
Labor Front's own statistics betrayed the extent to which the Beauty of
Labor remained anchored in industry. While by 1938, the DAF could
claim that nearly 34,000 plants had been improved in response to SdA
visitations, only 708 villages had been so affected. The rural migration to
the cities, which rearmament accelerated, left behind deserted, not "beautiful," villages.[89]

87 "Die Betreuung des Dorfes durch die Nationalsozialistische Gemeinschaft 'Kraft durch
    Freude,' 13 June 1937," NHH Hann. 122a, VIII, no. 577, 199–212.
88 *Vorweihnachtliche Feier*, ed. NSG.-"Kraft durch Freude," Amt Feierabend (Berlin:
    Verlag der Deutschen Arbeitsfront, ca. 1938); Heinz Hecker, *Trachten unserer Zeit*,
    IfZ, no. 72.01; *Die Betreuung des Dorfes*, IfZ, no. 72.01; *Volkstumsarbeit im
    Betrieb: Grundsätze und Arbeitsmittel der Abteilung Volkstum/Brauchtum im Amt
    "Feierabend" der NSG "Kraft durch Freude"* (Berlin: Verlag der Deutschen Arbeits-
    front, 1939).
89 Marrenbach, *Fundamente des Sieges*, 325; Corni, *Hitler and the Peasants*, 220–44.

A Small Price to Pay: The Beauty of Labor and Employers

Employers shared with the Beauty of Labor the desire to "honor" wage earners and defuse class conflict. Yet the autonomy that the National Labor Law granted to business and the Beauty of Labor's lack of legal authority presented obstacles to SdA's ambitions. It could not compel companies to follow the requirements of its "consultants," despite its regional advisory centers that provided technical and scientific assistance, its distribution of instructional films, traveling exhibits and slide shows, and its own glossy publication, *Schönheit der Arbeit*, which touted the benefits of an aestheticized workplace. To compensate for its shallow legal footing, SdA implored the regular government factory inspection network to identify firms that needed improvements, urging inspectors to support its directives. Those appeals, however, took pains to reassure employers that compliance was voluntary. Nevertheless, despite the initial competition between government inspectors and SdA consultants, the agencies forged a high level of cooperation by the social Darwinian standards of the Third Reich. At the local and plant levels, the Labor Front's oversight encouraged the mutually reinforcing need of SdA and government inspectors to extend their influence in the workplace.[90] Ironically, greater conflict ensued between SdA consultants and Dinta, the right-wing industrial think tank that the Labor Front had appropriated to coordinate vocational counseling and testing. Dinta's engineer–founder, Karl Arnhold, disparaged the Beauty of Labor's nonconfrontational approach to employers and its emphasis on transforming attitudes through aesthetics instead of overt indoctrination. In the end, the Beauty of Labor's more sophisticated and less heavy-handed approach to ending class conflict likely achieved greater influence.[91]

The lack of financial resources to underwrite projects, however, created a more serious problem. Financial assistance from state ministries could not be had because economic recovery and rearmament assumed priority, leaving the Beauty of Labor to advocate improvements while pleading austerity, a recourse that coexisted uncomfortably with Strength through Joy's drive to "raise" the living standards of workers in nonmaterial and noncommercial ways. SdA proposed to solve its problem by appealing to the Nazi version of altruism: Employers who made improvements at

90 Der Preussische Minister für Wirtschaft und Arbeit an die Herren Regierungspräsidenten und den Herrn Polizeipräsidenten in Berlin, 5 June 1934, NHH, Hann. 122a, VIII, no. 557, 15. For SdA's limited authority, see Friemert, *Schönheit der Arbeit*, 87–110: and for its relationship to the regular factory inspection network, see Frese, *Betriebspolitik*, 334–51.
91 Rabinbach, *Human Motor*, 286–7.

their own expense would improve the dedication of their "retinues" by demonstrating their willingness to sacrifice for the sake of the plant "community. Yet Speer's intercession on behalf of employers provided a more practical, and likely more effective, incentive, tax abatements. Although the regulations were unclear and inconsistently applied because of the finance ministry's reluctance to award tax breaks for improvements, which increased a company's assessed value, the prospect of relief offered more incentive than exhortations.[92]

Nevertheless, although the cost of SdA projects determined the extent to which small companies participated, usually the largest firms or firms with sufficient capital could commit themselves to the improvements that SdA advocated.[93] Thus, companies such as Siemens and IG Farben, whose modern design and facilities minimized the costs of remodeling, had little difficulty meeting SdA standards,[94] but even older heavy industries such as Krupp invested in infrastructure. The firm believed that doing so would ease worker resentment over the longer workdays and stagnant wages, especially after 1936, when the competition for workers in war-related industries markedly increased.[95] The 1934/35 annual report of the huge United Steelworks (Vereinigte Stahlwerk) in Düsseldorf proudly described its extensive social spending, which included not only the construction of a swimming pool and sulphur baths, but also recreation and wash rooms, all of which it linked to the conglomerate's long tradition of employee welfare.[96] The improvement in the economy by 1936 contributed as well. It encouraged employers to be more generous in their allocations to nonmandatory spending, a good example being the Anchor Works (Anker-Werke) in Bielefeld that planned to construct sports facilities in light of its increased profits.[97] Firms that profited handsomely from the rearmament boom, such as a machine tools and munitions factory on

92 Weißler, "Interview mit Albert Speer," 304. On the tax implications of Beauty of Labor improvements, see Friemert, *Schönheit der Arbeit*, 109–10.
93 Annegret Walesch, "Das Amt 'Schönheit der Arbeit' in der NS-Organisation 'Kraft durch Freude' 1933–1939," (Technische Universität Hannover: Hausarbeit für die fachwissenschaftliche Prüfung für das Lehramt an Realschulen, 1975), 4. As Friemert points out in *Schönheit der Arbeit*, 201, installing better lighting was cheaper than improving ventilation systems.
94 "Schönheit der Arbeit," *Siemens-Mitteilungen* no. 163 (July 1935): 113, SA.
95 On the willingness of older firms to invest in plant improvements, see Frese, *Betriebspolitik*, 343–4, who challenges Wolfgang Zollitsch's suggestions to the contrary in, *Arbeiter zwischen Weltwirtschaftskrise und Nationalsozialismus* (Göttingen: Vandenhoeck and Ruprecht, 1990), 133–34.
96 Geschäftsjahr 1934/35, Bergbau-Archiv Bochum (hereinafter cited as BAB), Bestand 55 (Vereinigte Stahlwerk Aktiengesellschaft Düsseldorf), no. 526, 24–6.
97 Anker-Werke Aktiengesellschaft Bielefeld, Geschäftsbericht 1937, Stiftung Westfälisches Wirtschaftsarchiv, Dortmund (hereinafter cited as WWA) F42, no. 2. For company social spending by branch, see Hachtmann, *Industriearbeit im Dritten Reich*, 258–68.

the outskirts of Berlin, could appear downright "progressive" in their investments in plant hygiene. In addition to the well-lit, well-ventilated machine shops, attractive canteen, tennis courts, and nicely manicured green spaces, the factory contained "luxurious" washrooms, including one for the war wounded.[98]

The Beauty of Labor's statistics failed to distinguish between small, medium, and larger firms, much less differentiate between major and minor renovations. Neverthless, Strength through Joy's national and local publications spouted the usual reams of statistics to underscore its achievements in keeping with its disposition to hyper documentation. By the end of 1935, 12,000 companies, it claimed, had cleared away debris, constructed recreation areas, painted and decorated recreation rooms, and repaired or built sanitation facilities. By 1938, the Beauty of Labor asserted that the annual expenditure by German employers on SdA recommended projects exceeded 200 million Reichsmarks: projects that included not only improvements at work stations, but also sport facilities and gardens for midday breaks. The expenditures also incorporated funds set aside for the construction or renovation of resort homes that workers and salaried employees could retreat to during their vacation time.[99] Moreover, SdA tracked a sharply rising number of "improved" companies until the outbreak of war; from 2,037 in 1934, to 33,756 in 1938.[100]

The Beauty of Labor found other means besides tax incentives to encourage business to create plant communities, especially the DAF-initiated "plant performance battle" (*Leistungskampf im Betriebe*), a competition that awarded "model enterprise" certificates and a series of lesser designations that testified to corporate success. Unlike the findings of the state factory inspectors, the recommendations of which remained confidential, the publicity surrounding the awards gave the DAF and SdA additional leverage, for praise or condemnation of a firm in the media including *Schönheit der Arbeit* could influence potential markets.[101] Introduced in August 1936, the "performance battle" testified to the accelerated production of the Four-Year Plan. It rewarded company social policies that improved surroundings, granted respite, and bettered personal health and hygiene that taken together raised productivity and increased the nation's readiness.[102] The criteria for the awards included the quality of

---

98   Report on Strength through Joy, August 1938, submitted by Hugh R. Wilson to Franklin D. Roosevelt, http://www.fdrlibrary.marist.edu/psf/box32/a301i01.html, 49–51.
99   Rabinbach, "Aesthetics of Production,"192–3.
100   Walesch, "Amt 'Schönheit der Arbeit,'" 86.
101   Friemert, *Schönheit der Arbeit*, 94.
102   Marrenbach, *Fundamente des Sieges*, 326.

training, skill development and performance of apprentices, the extent of plant health, safety, and sanitation measures, the quality and availability of workers' housing, and finally the company's willingness to sponsor Strength through Joy's recreational programs.[103] All told, the criteria gave proof of an employer's attentiveness to "raising" the standard of living of their "retinue."[104] Firms that achieved the status of a "model enterprise" received generous space in the Beauty of Labor's monthly, which regularly contrasted the bright "scrupulously clean" facilities of the winners with firms that had failed to modernize. The conspicuous absence of criteria related to wages aside from Christmas bonuses, consistent with the regime's having clamped down on wage increases, encouraged companies to participate. The number of competitors rose significantly from the 81,000 firms that participated in 1937/38 when the first "battle" took place, to the some quarter million companies that took part in 1939/40. Although embracing workplaces of widely varying size and number of employees, the participation of prestigious large firms, the auto manufacturer Daimler-Benz for example, contributed to the growth of the competition. By 1939, 202 enterprises had received "model firm" certificates signed by the führer.[105]

The biggest incentive for business to cooperate, however, resided in the Nazi regime's destruction of organized labor, which removed a major obstacle to profitability. Improvements in physical plants and workers' bodies, furthermore, accorded with long-standing traditions of paternalistic social policy, which companies modernized after World War I with infusions of psychology, education, and the rationalized emphasis on the "joy" inherent in craftsmanship.[106] The favor that firm newspapers bestowed on the Nazi regime's labor policy, many of them published by Dinta, attested to employers' appreciation for the greatest benefit that they had received from the Third Reich. However intrusive the Labor Front and its daughter agencies may have appeared, they never seriously challenged managerial control or corporate profitabiltity. Like the United Steelworks, many firms placed their relationship with the Beauty of Labor in a broader context, as complementary to their own relatively long-standing efforts to improve the aesthetics and efficiency of their enterprises. Admittedly,

103 BAB Bestand 13 (Zechenverband, Bergbau-Verein, Bezirksgruppe Ruhr der Fachgruppe Steinkohlenbergbau/Wirtschaftsgruppe Bergbau), no. 1680. This folder includes the criteria for model companies, as spelled out by Robert Ley in May 1937. See also, Sachse, *Siemens*, 70–1.

104 BAB Bestand 10 (Schachtanlage Friedrich der Grosse, Herne), no. 526. The folder includes an application and questionnaire that firms were required to fill out in order to participate in the competition.

105 Siegel, *Leistung und Lohn*, 113; Sachse, *Siemens*, 71; Neil Gregor, *Daimler-Benz in the Third Reich* (New Haven and London: Yale University Press, 1998), 163–4.

106 Nolan, *Visions of Modernity*, 181.

noted the Westphalian textile firm, the Bleaching, Dyeing, and Starching Works (Bleicherei, Färberei und Appreturanstalt), SdA's lobbying encouraged it to build a new gate house, plant flower beds on its grounds, and repaint its buildings, but the installation of good lighting and new windows had begun in the midtwenties.[107] The family-owned paper company Kübler and Niethammer of Saxony described an even longer lineage for its projects, which included a kindergarten begun in 1879, a housing construction program initiated in 1881, and baths which the firm completed in 1928.[108] The labor shortages after 1936 reinforced the attentiveness to plant improvements, at least until the outbreak of war forced their curtailment. Like Krupp, employers saw them as a way to keep workers from seeking positions with better working conditions and under-the-table bonuses, the few options that workers could exercise to compensate for wage freezes.

To be sure, despite relatively smooth relationships between employers and the Beauty of Labor, and the positive attitude of employers toward National Socialism in general, employers rarely let down their guard against the intrusions of party agencies. The "performance battle" drew the vehement protests of Ruhr industrialists for having contradicted the Leipzig agreement of March 1935, which along with the autonomy promised to business in the National Labor Law subordinated the Labor Front's economic activities to "economic chambers" (Wirtschaftskammer) in Schacht's ministry. If some Ruhr industries joined the "performance battle," Hoesch among them, most refused to participate.[109] Thus, companies insisted that KdF and SdA plant officials had to enjoy the confidence of employees and especially of managers. In the end the Labor Front and KdF conceded the point, recruiting their operatives from each firm rather than imposing them from outside.[110]

Of all the KdF initiatives, the campaign "Sport in the Plants" aroused the greatest worry, for it not only signified a degree of indoctrination that threatened corporate independence, it also required that

107   "Leistungskampf der Bleicherei, Färberei und Appreturanstalt Uhringen A.G.," undated WABW Bestand B 26, no. 119, 9–30.
108   Nachlass Niethammer v. 31.3, Materialien Sozialbericht, Statistiken, 1936–1937, 401/2, Sächsisches Wirtschaftsarchiv (hereinafter cited as SWA), Leipzig.
109   The Ruhr mining industry devoted a good deal of attention to this, as summarized in Abschrift Ernst Buskühl, Leiter der Bezirksgruppe Ruhr der Fachgruppe Steinkohlenbergbau an Gottfried Dierig, Leiter der Reichsgruppe Industrie, 24 July 1937, BAB Bestand 13, no. 1680. Cf. Wisotzky, *Ruhrbergbau*, 208–10.
110   "Die Organisation der NSG 'Kraft durch Freude' in den Siemenswerken, Gau Groß-Berlin," *Siemens-Mitteilungen*, no. 163 (July 1935):112, SA; Frese *Betriebspolitik*, 342; Günther Adam, "Practical Activities of the National-Socialist Fellowship *Kraft durch Freude*," *German Address for Committee I, World Congress "Work and Joy,"* Rome, 1938: 16.

company-sponsored sport clubs be incorporated in plant "sport communities" subsumed under Strength through Joy.[111] The concern subsided, however, once employers found that they could domesticate the "sport in the plants" project and the subsequent numerous company team competitions (*Betriebsappell*). As was true for other KdF and SdA shop floor operatives, employers usually leveraged a trusted employee with a pipeline to the plant leadership into supervisory control over the "sport communities" to such a degree that few resisted the "synchronization" of company clubs.[112] And, however forcefully the Beauty of Labor lobbied for football fields and sports equipment, company budgets determined the pace and extent of funding. The voluntarism of SdA improvements and the Beauty of Labor's lack of resources guaranteed that business retained the initiative. A report from the American ambassador to Germany in 1938 to President Roosevelt spelled out some of the consequences. Germany's record of accident prevention, putatively one of the Beauty of Labor's responsibilities, compared unfavorably to the American, for workers had no access to courts or juries with the power to award large judgments against employers, nor to a state apparatus that could adequately protect them.[113]

Certainly workers retained some means of expressing their dissatisfaction with their employers, however much the Nazi regime enhanced the authority of employers. The Councils of Trust (Vertrauensräte), which the National Labor Law established, although hardly equal to Weimar factory councils in their power to remedy grievances, did transmit employees' complaints to management on pragmatic grounds. Good morale was essential to sustaining or increasing production. Moreover, those complaints at times revealed the extent to which workers shared the Beauty of Labor's objectives of cleanliness and the division of function to achieve it, proving their susceptibility to the regime's claims to raise their status by recovering the "joy" involved in "quality" work.[114] The demand of some Krupp

---

111 Kohler to Ernst Buskühl, 27 October, 1937, BAB Bestand 13, no. 1694.
112 Vereinbarung zwischen dem Sportamt der NS-Gemeinschaft "Kraft durch Freude" der Deutschen Arbeitsfront und der Vereinigte Stahlwerk A.G., 26 November 1937, BAB Bestand 13, no. 1694.
113 Report on Strength through Joy, August 1938, Submitted by Hugh R. Wilson to Franklin D. Roosevelt, http://www.fdrlibrary.marist.edu/psf/box32/a301t09.html, 52.
114 Alf Lüdtke discusses the Nazi regime's success in appropriating the symbolic universe of workers. See especially, "'Ehre der Arbeit': Industriearbeiter und Macht der Symbole: Zur Reichsweite symbolischer Orientierung im Nationalsozialismus," in *Arbeiter im 20. Jahrhundert*, ed. Klaus Tenfelde (Stuttgart: Klett-Cotta Verlag, 1991). An abridged version in English, "The 'Honor of Labor': Industrial Workers and the Power of Symbols under National Socialism," can be found in *Nazism and German Society 1933–1945*, ed. David Crew (London and New York: Routledge, 1994): 67–109.

workers, for example, that the company provide a breakfast room so that they would not have to eat their meals at their workstations suggests the popular acceptance of bourgeois values, as well as the limits of company cleanliness.[115] Many workers participated enthusiastically in the "performance battles" and sports competitions, adhering to goals that they and their colleagues held in common. The sports competitions alone involved 2.3 million men in 1937.[116] In registering its disappointment that it did not win a "Gau diploma" (*Gaudiplom*), the award second only to the "model enterprise" certificate, the paper firm, Kübler and Niethammer, complained that the decision came as a shock to its employees who confidently believed that they would succeed.[117] Indeed, their disappointment implies that the praise with which the Beauty of Labor bestowed on retinues dedicated to improving their workplaces[118] was less empty than it might retrospectively appear.

Nevertheless, the Beauty of Labor's appeals to volunteerism on behalf of the "plant community" often depended on coercion, subtle or otherwise, to be efficacious. Despite the Labor Front's claims to represent their interests, "retinues" possessed less room to maneuver than their "leaders," for they lacked even the rudiments of autonomous organization. Employers made it clear that for all their willingness to invest in physical and aesthetic improvements, their employees bore the primary responsibility for ensuring the "plant community's" realization. The remarks of Rolf Boehringer, who led his family's machine-tools firm, Boehringer Brothers (Gebrüder Boehringer) at a morning roll call were typical of company expectations. Boehringer could say in good conscience that his company had established all the necessary preconditions for a pleasant and comradely workplace. Its physical plant met all the Beauty of Labor's standards. The physical plant, however, could not by itself maintain the spirit of common endeavor, which depended on employees putting their hearts and souls into it. In a way that suggested the pressure of commitments held in common, the commitment to pride in an aesthetically pleasing workplace, Boehringer resorted to shaming. Unless his employees derived satisfaction from slovenly surroundings, they should decorate the plant with flowers

---

115   Auszug aus dem Stimmungsbericht vom Juni 1940, HA Krupp 41/6–10.
116   Reichsamtsleitung Kraft durch Freude, *Unter dem Sonnenrad: Ein Buch von Kraft durch Freude* (Berlin: Verlag der Deutsche Arbeitsfront, 1938), 172. Company sports continued to do well thereafter. See Vierteljahresbericht 1939 des Sicherheitshauptamtes in *Meldungen aus dem Reich, 1938–1945: die geheimen Lageberichte des Sicherheitsdienstes der SS*, ed. Heinz Boberach (Herrsching: Pavlak, 1984), vol. 2, 286.
117   Döbeln, Kübler and Niethammer an die Deutsche Arbeitsfront, 29 July 1938, SWA 130/176
118   Such as the commendation in *Schönheit der Arbeit* 2, no. 2 (October 1937), 237–9 given to workers in a Düsseldorf plant for renovating a deteriorating work building.

from their gardens and keep recreation and changing areas clean.[119] Although at times difficult to enforce, particularly in plants close to rural areas where employees tended agricultural plots on the side, employers supported the directive of KdF sport wardens in making participation in sport appeals mandatory, save for a compelling excuse.[120]

Beyond shaming and the streams of directives, workers endured financial exactions and the pressure to accede to the demands placed on them. As revealed in the situation reports of Sopade agents and those of the left socialist underground organization, "New Beginning" (Neu Beginnen), firms regularly expected their workers to "volunteer" their time after hours on SdA projects without additional compensation, planting flowers, cleaning workrooms, installing washrooms, and painting recreation rooms. If workers showed an understandable skepticism in the face of claims that spruced up facilities would uplift them spiritually or physically, and wished for higher wages and a shorter workday as alternatives, they were in no position to resist. Employers passed the costs of improvements onto their employees in lost wages. In one reported case, the expected annual bonus to workers and salaried employees was sacrificed to the construction of a dining and recreation room.[121] An egregious example of covering costs from the wallets of workers arose in a Saxon cardboard factory, where the Council of Trust and the plant managers decided that employees would give up an hour and a half's wages each to pay for a radio purchased at the suggestion of the Beauty of Labor. The council's assertion that the employees themselves had requested the radio left the retinue "speechless." The workers would have preferred peace and quiet during the midday pause as a break from the noise of machinery. Those who refused to sign the payment agreement that the council circulated ultimately relented under the pressure of their peers, who feared the consequences of noncompliance.[122]

Frequently the pressure to perform "voluntary" labor came packaged with threats of firing and further punishment for political subversion, including a stint in a concentration camp. According to one Sopade situation report, a manager of a Saxon factory asked a worker why he always left for home promptly at 6 p.m. when his colleagues remained behind to

119 Ansprache des Herrn Rolf Boehringer beim Betriebsappell am 14.8.37 (copy of original), WABW, Bestand 10, no. 292, 3–4.
120 "Betriebssport," 11 July 1939, WABW Bestand 30 (A. Stolz AG Maschinenfabrik), no. 510.
121 *Sopade*, July 1936, 886–7; Situation report no. 9, August/September 1934, *Berichte über die Lage in Deutschland: Die Meldungen der Gruppe Neu Beginnen aus dem Dritten Reich 1933–1936*, ed. Bernd Stöver (Bonn: Verlag J.H.W. Dietz Nachfolger, 1996): 259.
122 *Sopade*, July 1936, 887. *Neu Beginnen* organized a common front between Socialists and Communists.

do what was required. When the worker pointed to his grimy attire, the testimony of an already eleven-hour workday, he was accused of harboring communist sympathies. "If you continue that way," the worker was warned, "you'll soon see what will become of you."[123] Despite their limited room to negotiate, workers showed their displeasure by boycotting recreation rooms, gardens, and football fields ostensibly constructed for their benefit, refusing the offer of theater tickets that their employers subsidized, and avoiding the organized "comradeship evenings" that KdF organized and employers usually underwrote. Even that passive aggressive behavior became sufficiently worrisome for the DAF to issue warnings to employers to relax their pressure. Regardless, until the war determined that other demands took priority over SdA plant beautification projects, employers continued to accommodate the Beauty of Labor on the backs of their "retinue."[124]

The elimination of class conflict on the shop floor and the retraining of workers to realize their calling as members of the Nazi racial community were to emerge in the aesthetics of the Taylorized plant, on-site education in bourgeois values, comradely if competitive sport, and an appreciation of the fine arts as a respite from toil. The reward to employers for bearing the cost of such projects was a police state that protected them from a powerful labor movement. The ostensible reward for workers was an end to their social debasement and the appreciation of themselves as "creators," the nonalienated producers of quality German goods. As Anatol von Hübbenet proclaimed in 1939, the term "company" now had a new meaning. No longer was it merely a "functional association" (*Zweckverband*), or a site of worker–employer strife. Instead, it had become a "community" dedicated to the principle of "common use" (*Gemeinnutz*), a "spiritual and performance-oriented community."[125] Nonetheless, although many employees cooperated with SdA's initiatives and employers' appeals to them on behalf of "community," plant improvements did not compensate for longer hours, frozen wages, harsh work discipline, the oxymoron of coerced "volunteerism," and SdA's limited impact in the countryside.[126] Thus, despite Strength through Joy's

---

123 *Sopade*, 5 February 1938, 174–5.
124 Frese, *Betriebspolitik*, 348. Krupp directors grew impatient with KdF's pressure on the firm to purchase tickets for their employees, when the demand was often lacking. Die Deutsche Arbeitsfront, NS-Gemeinschaft Kraft durch Freude, Gau and Kreis Essen, 11 November 1937 an Direktor/Krupp, HA Krupp, WA 41/73–125.
125 Hübbenet, NS-Gemeinschaft "Kraft durch Freude," 54–5.
126 This is clear in oral histories. See Michael Zimmermann, "Ausbruchshoffnungen: Junge Bergleute in den dreißiger Jahren," in *"Die Jahre weiß man nicht, wo man die heute hinsetzen soll:" Faschismuserfahrungen im Ruhrgebiet*, vol. 1, *Lebensgeschichte und Sozialkultur im Ruhrgebiet 1939 bis 1960*, ed. Lutz Niethammer (Berlin and Bonn: J.H.W. Dietz Nachf., 1983): 113–19.

commitment to the harmony of work and "after work" as the way to achieve a high standard of living, KdF made a stronger case by cultivating the realm of leisure. To be sure, KdF continued to promote "performance" on the job, which would propel the regime's drive for empire. Yet its after-work programs, tourism especially, contributed more to the legitimacy of the Third Reich, so much so that they expanded to meet demand as rearmament and war preparations proceeded apace.

4

Mass Tourism, the Cohesive Nation, and Visions of Empire

The use of tourism to foster nationalism did not begin with the National Socialists, however extreme their chauvinism. During the nineteenth century, bourgeois tourists and vacationers displayed their patriotism and aspirations to national leadership in their preoccupations with personal discovery, health, responsible consumption, and self-improvement. As the activism of the lower middle and working classes forced governments to assume responsibilities beyond their obligations of law, policing, and defense, nation–states promoted tourism to achieve complementary ends. In addition to marking tourist sites that would forge the common bonds of citizenship, governments used tourism to stimulate economic development by attracting revenue from abroad and improving regional economies within their own borders.[1] Moreover, tourism contributed to European imperialism, for it reinforced the infrastructures of colonial domination and the racial hierarchies that lay at the foundations of empire. It reconceived popular concepts of the nation by encouraging travel between metropoles and colonial possessions.[2]

---

1 See Rudy Koshar, *German Travel Cultures* (Oxford and New York: Berg, 2000), 19–64; Douglas Peter Mackaman, *Leisure Settings: Bourgeois Culture, Medicine, and the Spa in Modern France* (Chicago and London: University of Chicago Press, 1998); Cindy Aron, *Working at Play: A History of Vacations in the United States* (New York and Oxford: Oxford University Press, 1999); and the introduction in Shelley Baranowski and Ellen Furlough, *Being Elsewhere: Tourism, Consumer Culture, and Identity in Modern Europe and North America* (Ann Arbor and London: University of Michigan Press, 2001), 11–17.

2 The relationship between tourism and empire is finally attracting the attention of historians. Scholars in literary criticism and comparative literature have been influential in this respect. See Mary Louise Pratt, *Imperial Eyes: Travel Writing and Transculturation* (London: Routledge, 1992). For recent historical studies of colonial tourism, see Barbara Ramusack, "Tourism and Icons: The Packaging of the Princely Estates of Rajasthan," in *Perceptions of South Asia's Visual Past* (New Delhi: American Institute of Indian Studies and Swadharma Swarajya Sangha, 1994); Angela Woollacott, "'All This Is the Empire I Told Myself': Australian Women's Voyages 'Home' and the Articulation of Colonial Whiteness," *American Historical Review* 103, no. 4(1997): 1003–29; and Ellen Furlough, "*Une leçon des Choses*: Tourism, Empire, and the Nation Interwar France," *French Historical Studies* 35, no. 3 (Summer 2002): 441–73.

Nazi tourism, however, represented an unusually ambitious and conflicted project. To fashion the racial community, Strength through Joy strove to make accessible a middle- and upper-class practice to deepen ethnic identification and popular support for the regime. Yet as a consumer good, its costs could not threaten economic recovery and rearmament. Its potential to do just that provoked anxiety among those in the Reich government most responsible for the war preparations, notably Colonel Georg Thomas, the head of the War Economy Staff (Wehrwirtschaftsstab), whose office spearheaded the military's war preparations. In November 1936, after nearly three years of sustained growth in KdF's tourism, Thomas warned Ley that KdF should confine itself to the strengthening the *Volk* in soul and body, but "under no circumstances" should it "mushroom into an organized pleasure system" (*zu organisierten Vergnügungsmaßnahmen auswachsen dürfen*) that threatened the regime's first priority.[3] Thus to maintain its position as a key pillar of the regime's social policy, Strength through Joy promoted its noncommercial consumption while simultaneously marketing its tourism as a desirable consumer good. The final product, an array of low-cost domestic package tours, overseas cruises, and resorts under construction and in the planning stages, supported Nazism's claims to have improved the quality of life for ordinary Germans. At the same time, KdF's inexpensive package tourism, like nineteenth-century bourgeois values, stressed self-improvement, thrift, personal edification, and Nazism's version of nationalism against the hedonism that Nazi leaders associated with market-based consumption. Improving family incomes and the restlessness over the shortages of consumer goods, however, forced KdF to promise personal pleasure and comfort, thus complicating its tidy solution to the dilemma that rearmament presented.

Racial Community, Economic Development, and Vested Interests: Strength through Joy's Domestic Tourism

On 17 February 1934, barely three months after Strength through Joy's founding, KdF's first package tours commenced. Beginning with its homeland tourism, trainloads of tourists, each carrying between eight hundred

3 Wortprotokoll der 5. Tagung der Reichsarbeitskammer am 24. November 1936 in Berlin, in Timothy W. Mason, *Arbeiterklasse und Volksgemeinschaft: Dokumente u. Materialien zur deutschen Arbeiterpolitik 1936–1939* (Opladen: Westdeutscher Verlag, 1975): 182. This document occupied a key place in Mason's work. See *Social Policy in the Third Reich: The Working Class and the 'National Community'*, trans. John Broadwin, ed. Jane Caplan (Providence, Oxford: Berg, 1993), 19–40.

and one thousand persons, left stations in Berlin, Dresden, Altona and Hamburg, Königsberg, Essen, Dortmund, and Hannover. Their destinations included the upper Bavarian, Harz, Rhone, and Silesian mountains, as well as the Bavarian and Thuringian forests. Tours departing from Nuremberg, Munich, Stuttgart, Cologne, and Aachen began on the days immediately following.[4] In keeping with the wartime front and postwar paramilitary experiences of KdF propagandists, subsequent trips adhered to the populist and militarist elements that the inaugural trips introduced.[5] Launched with pomp and circumstance, delegations of party officials, uniformed formations, and boisterous band music accompanied the departure of KdF trains. When the trains arrived at their destinations, mayors, local KdF wardens, and more bands greeted the vacationers, who then collectively marched to the center of town.[6] In pursuing Nazism's assault against the left by other means, KdF's publications and pronouncements differentiated between KdF and earlier attempts at mass tourism. Unlike the previous government that promised workers the opportunity to travel but failed to deliver, National Socialism brought to fruition the "socialism of deed."

The itineraries of the "participants" (*Teilnehmer*), as Strength through Joy called its tourists, testified to KdF's solidarist agenda. Sending tour groups from one region to another would erode the local and religious particularism that undermined "community," for tourists would recognize their kinship with their hosts. Thus, the Berlin workers who toured Munich and Berchtesgaden, site of the führer's Obersalzburg retreat, would become emissaries, who would strengthen the bonds between north and south. Again establishing a practice that KdF tours would religiously follow, the Berliners attended several get-togethers with locals during their stay, including a final "comradeship evening" before their departure, which included singing, dancing, and beer. KdF required local officials as well as the proprieters who fed and housed vacationers to host the events, which ranged from displays of local customs and costumes to hikes.[7]

Strength through Joy's domestic destinations underscored one of its most distinctive contributions to the German tourism industry: KdF's use of tourism as a stimulus to economic development in depressed areas,

---

4   Werner Kahl, *Der deutsche Arbeiter reist!* (Berlin: Deutscher Verlag, 1940), 7–8.
5   Daniela Liebscher, "Mit KdF 'die Welt erschließen': Der Beitrag der KdF-Reisen zur Außenpolitik der Deutschen Arbeitsfront 1934–1939," *1999: Zeitschrift für Sozialgeschichte des 20. und 21. Jahrhunderts* 14, no. 1 (March 1999): 46.
6   For the mechanics of KdF's domestic tours, see Bruno Frommann, "Reisen im Dienste politischer Zielsetzungen: Arbeiter-Reisen und 'Kraft durch Freude'-Fahrten" (Diss: Stuttgart, 1993), 143–54.
7   Siemens workers from Berlin experienced a similar welcome on their trip to Bavaria, as described in "Mit 'Kraft durch Freude' nach Oberbayern," *Siemens-Mitteilungen* no. 148 (April 1934): 49–50, Siemen-Archiv, Munich (hereinafter cited as SA). See also Frommann, "Reisen im Dienste," 152.

especially along Germany's borders.[8] How better to build a common commitment to "Germanness" (*Deutschtum*) than to provide cheap package tours that mobilized hundreds of tourists, whose friendly presence and impact on local economies would integrate their neglected and culturally threatened countrymen? The number and scale of Strength through Joy trips distinguished it from the package tourism of white-collar workers and the social tourism of the left that became popular during the twenties. In an insidious choice of words that spoke to the memory of the industrially mobilized mass armies of World War I, Strength through Joy's organizers and tour leaders referred to their trains as "transports," a term used to refer to the movement of troops that would later be applied to the trains that deported Jews to death camps in the east.

Nevertheless, KdF's promise of democratized tourism belied the selectivity that produced the recipients of the vacation trips. Although determined to extend privileges to workers, KdF district, county, local, and shop floor wardens insisted just as strongly on discrimination. They sought "deserving" comrades, who by virtue of their stability, outstanding work performance, and long years of service to their employers, had earned their trips, and who upon their return would rave about the achievements of National Socialism. In addition, the bias toward Nazi party members, especially those who had suffered during the economic crisis, asserted itself.[9] The corruption and patronage that typified the Third Reich by no means bypassed Strength through Joy's tourism as party membership emerged as a conspicuous criterion for selection. Nor, of course, did the Third Reich's antisemitism and racism. Because participants had to belong to the Labor Front, which also included membership in KdF, Jews were excluded. Reward for "performance," a key component in the Reich's attempts to build racial superiority, figured prominently in KdF's guidelines for the selection of tourists.

Advertised in periodicals that KdF published for every district and organized locally by KdF local and company operatives, KdF's domestic tourism mushroomed in the prewar years, crisscrossing Germany with its trains and busses full of travelers. Strength through Joy's inland vacations, which lasted from three to fifteen days, encompassed 400,000 tourists in 1934 and over double that number in the year following. Achieving their maximum catchment of 1.4 million tourists in 1937, the number of

8 Domestic tourism grew in the thirties, partly because of the Reich's strict regulations against taking marks out of the country. See Rudy Koshar, *German Travel Cultures* (Oxford and New York, 2000), 126–7.

9 Liebscher, "Mit KdF 'die Welt erschließen'": 45; NSG Kraft durch Freude an die Gaureferenten des Amts für Reisen, Wandern u. Urlaub der NS-Gemeinschaft "Kraft durch Freude." Betr. Arbeiterurlaubszüge im Monat Februar, 23 January 1934 and "Zwolf Sonderzüge nach Oberbayern: Die ersten Reisen der Freizeitorganisation," Auszug aus der *Rhein-Westfälischen Zeitung*, no. 34 (19 January 1934), Bergbau-Archiv Bochum (hereinafter cited as BAB), Bestand 13, no. 1693.

participants in the longer domestic tours declined during the last two pre-war years due to the competition for transport from the military. Yet it never dropped below one million. The weekend excursions to local sites of interest experienced an even more dramatic increase, rising from 1.8 million in 1934 to 4.8 million persons in 1935, reaching their high water mark in 1937 with 6.8 participants. Thereafter, they declined to slightly above five million by 1939, similar to the pattern of organized hiking, a separate category of outing. Involving 100,000 hikers in 1934, the number expanded to 1.6 million in 1937, sliding back to 1.1 million in 1939.[10] The list of vacation trips that each district offered annually became extensive. By 1939, to give but one example, Gau South Hannover-Brunswick organized 172 trips, a list that included neither the short excursions or hikes, nor cruises.[11]

Strength through Joy's large clientele and the revenue intake from its trips, amounting to nearly 80 percent of its total income, made the office for Travel, Hiking, and Vacations its most significant arm.[12] Compared to the prices of commercial tourism and those of the organized working-class tourism of the twenties, the cost of KdF excursions remained remarkably low. The volume that Strength through Joy could promise, the Depression's downward pressure on prices, and KdF's willingness to settle for third- and fourth-class train compartments translated into a 75 percent reduction in rail fares. Room and board rates for KdF tourists amounted to half the normal cost of staying at a low-end pension. Subsidies from the Labor Front and KdF's largely volunteer staff ensured that its overhead would not undermine its goal of providing cheap travel.[13] Thus, an eight-day cruise to Norway from Gau Swabia in 1935 cost 61.50 RM, including transportation to and from the point of disembarkation. In 1939, a two-week vacation trip from the same district to the Pomeranian seacoast, which included travel, room and board, and a steamer trip on the Baltic, cost a mere 60 RM. In the same year, a week's trip from the Gau Tirol-Voralberg to the Mosel Valley cost 37.40.[14] A ten-day cruise to San Remo in the Italian Rivera from the Austrian Gau of Upper Danube cost only RM 73.50, inclusive. A nine-day cruise from the same Gau to Norway,

10 For a complete table, see Hasso Spode, "Arbeiterurlaub im Dritten Reich," in *Angst, Belohnung, Zucht und Ordnung: Herrschaftsmechanismen im Nationalsozialismus*, ed. Carola Sachse, Tilla Siegel, Hasso Spode, and Wolfgang Spohn (Opladen: Westdeutscher Verlag, 1982): 298.

11 NSG Kraft durch Freude, Gau Süd-Hannover-Braunschweig, *KdF-Monatsheft*, April 1939.

12 Spode, "Arbeiterurlaub": 295.   13 Keitz, *Reisen als Leitbild*, 239–41.

14 NSG Kraft durch Freude, Gau Schwaben, *Jahres-Urlaubsprogram 1935* (Berlin, 1935): 37; NSG Kraft durch Freude, Gau Schwaben, *Dein Urlaub 1939* (Berlin, 1939): unpaginated; Deutsche Arbeitsfront, N.S.- Gemeinschaft "Kraft durch Freude," Gau Tirol-Voralberg, *Frohe Fahrt mit KdF: Urlaubsfahrten 1939*: unpaginated.

which disembarked from Linz to Kiel cost RM 95.[15] By contrast, even the organized working-class travel of the twenties exceeded the prices of KdF tours. A sixteen-day trip from Frankfurt to Tunis arranged by the Reich Committee for Socialist Educational Work (Reichsausschuss für sozialistische Bildungsarbeit) cost 400 marks compared to 150 RM for KdF's thirteen-day deluxe "around Italy" cruise which included a visit to Tripoli.[16] An eight-day Rhine River trip with KdF cost 39.50 marks compared to a similar trip organized by workers' organizations in Leipzig, which was double the price.[17]

Strength through Joy's selection of domestic tourist sites exploited the Romantic awe of nature that contributed enormously to the emergence of tourism as a "modern" practice, even as it downplayed the perils of nature that the Romantics had found so captivating. Like modern tourism generally, KdF tourism exposed its participants to the sublime and novel while minimizing inconvenience and danger.[18] Juxtaposing panoramic vistas of mountains, valleys, lakes, rivers, seas with picturesque, quaint villages and half-timbered edifices, as well as villagers in vernacular costume, KdF's tour brochures promoted a restorative escape from urban hustle-and-bustle and the contemplation of a profound, but nonetheless unthreatening, sublime (See Figure 4.1.) Whether they steamed down Rhine River, gazed at the Bavarian Alps or Harz Mountains, hiked through the Black Forest, or sunned themselves on the Baltic seacoast, participants would come away enchanted and calmed by their idyllic surroundings (See Figure 4.2.)[19] Consistent with broader developments in tourism, the putatively vast and unspoiled vistas that KdF advertised took for granted

---

15 NSG Kraft durch Freude, Gau Oberdonau, *Dein Urlaub 1939 mit Kraft durch Freude* (Berlin: Verlag der Deutschen Arbeitsfront, 1939): unpaginated.

16 See Keitz, *Reisen als Leitbild*, 142.

17 For further data on KdF's low cost, see Ibid and Spode. "Arbeiterurlaub": 317–19. It is worth pointing out again, however (see Chapter 2, 169), that even these low purchase prices would have been difficult for workers to afford, given low average weekly wages.

18 For the impact of Romanticism on tourism, see Alain Corbin, *The Lure of the Sea: The Discovery of the Seaside 1750–1840*, trans. Jocelyn Phelps (London: Penguin Books, 1994); Orvar Löfgren, *On Holiday: A History of Vacationing* (Berkeley and London: University of California Press, 1999), 13–40; Eric Purchase, *Out of Nowhere: Disaster and Tourism in the White Mountains* (Baltimore and London: Johns Hopkins University Press, 1999); and Lynne Withey, *Grand Tours and Cook's Tours: A History of Leisure Travel 1750–1915* (New York: William Morrow and Company, 1997), 32–57.

19 Such as NSG Kraft durch Freude, Gau Halle-Merseburg, *Urlaubsfahrten im Jahre 1939*; NSG Kraft durch Freude, Gau Schleswig-Holstein, *KdF-Urlaub 1939*; NSG Kraft durch Freude, Gau Sachsen, *Mit Kraft durch Freude in Deutschlands Gaue: Die Urlaubsfahrten der Gauen Sachsen 1935, 1936, 1937, 1938*, and *1939*; and NS.-Gemeinschaft "Kraft durch Freude," Deutsche Arbeitsfront, Gau Hamburg, *Urlaubsreisen 1938* (January 1938).

Fig. 4.1. Young women in folk dress. Such scenes were typical in KdF tour brochures.
Source: NS-Gemeinschaft "Kraft durch Freude," Deutsche Arbeitsfront, Gau Hamburg, *Urlaubsreisen 1938* (January 1938), 22. Courtesy of Randall Bytwerk, Calvin College, Grand Rapids. Michigan.

Fig. 4.2. A tourist gazing at the Rhine River.
Source: Die Deutsche Arbeitsfront, NS-Gemeinschaft "Kraft durch Freude" Gau Sachsen, *Urlaubsfahrten 1939*, 43. Author's collection.

the uniquely modern ways of seeing that derived from technological improvements in transportation and visualization.[20] Thus, Strength through Joy periodicals sponsored snapshot contests, the winners of which depicted the favorite themes of panorama, quaintness, or joy in nature through the skilled manipulation of their instruments.[21] The modernism of KdF tourism, furthermore, emerged as well in its inclusion of technology, speed, and excitement as important subthemes of KdF travel. Trips to Berlin, which ranged from the exploration of the city's landmarks to those that stressed a specific purpose, such as the 1936 Olympics or the International Automobile and Motorcycle Exhibition in 1938, underscored Germany's industrial and technological sophistication.[22] Even panoramic photos of the Rhine in all its glory featured barges heading down river, thus acknowledging the commercial and industrial nearly as prominently as the natural.[23] Like KdF's art exhibits in the factories, KdF's approach to the beauty of the nation's natural endowments claimed a specifically German, as opposed to international, version of modernity.

Nevertheless, Nazified nationalism emerged as the most consistent message of Strength through Joy tourism, providing the narrative that stitched together the diversity in destinations. The specific history of National Socialism surfaced not merely in the trips that took in sites explicitly important to the Nazi party such as Munich, which traced Nazism's beginnings, and Nuremberg, the site of the party's spectacular rallies. They also incorporated destinations that the nationalist right had constructed since German unification, among them the huge statue of Arminius the Cheruscan (also known as Hermann), who in 9 C.E. defeated the Roman legions in the Teutoburger Forest near Detmold. Directed against Germany's enemy, the French, the Hermann monument commemorated the origins of the German struggle for liberation from foreign influence.[24]

20 For the emergence of the "panoramic" view, see Wolfgang Schivelbusch, *The Railway Journey: The Industrialization of Time and Space in the 19th Century* (Berkeley and Los Angeles: University of California Press, 1986), 52–69.

21 "Der KdF Photowettbewerb 1937 – ein betrachtliches Erlebnis," NSG Kraft durch Freude, Gau Sachsen, *Monatsprogramm* (December 1938): 2–6.

22 Tours to Berlin especially emphasized its modernity, an example being the ad in NSG Kraft durch Freude, Gau Essen, *Urlaubsfahrten 1939*: 39.

23 NSG Kraft durch Freude, Gau Tirol-Voralberg, *Frohe Fahrt mit KdF: Urlaubsfahrten 1939* (Berlin: Verlag der Deutschen Arbeitsfront, 1939): unpaginated.

24 NSG Kraft durch Freude, Gau Westfalen-Sud, *Mit Kraft durch Freude in den Urlaub 1938*; NSG Kraft durch Freude, Gau Berlin, *Urlaubsreisen 1937* (Berlin: Verlag der Deutschen Arbeitsfront, 1937): 76–7. For the Hermann monument, see Rudy J. Koshar, *From Monuments to Traces: Artifacts of German Memory, 1870–1990* (Berkeley, Los Angeles, London: University of California Press, 2000), 35–40; Charlotte Tacke, *Denkmal im sozialen Raum: Nationale Symbole in Deutschland und Frankreich im 19. Jahrhundert* (Göttingen: Vandenhoeck und Ruprecht, 1995), 201–88; and Simon Schama, *Landscape and Memory* (New York: Alfred A. Knopf, 1995), 75–120.

Or, sites included "authentically" German towns such as Rothenburg. KdF marketed the Franconian town's half-timbered medieval architecture as emblematic of German rootedness and civic communitarianism.[25] KdF tourism never ceased to assert the goal of its domestic travel program: Germans, workers especially, would come to appreciate the German past and feel the common ethnic bond with their countrymen. Argued Ley, workers whose nationalism could not help but be awakened by touring with Strength through Joy would abandon Marxist internationalism and no longer yearn for Moscow.[26]

KdF tourism underscored for its participants the legitimacy of the Nazi regime's revisionist claims against the Entente. Those claims asserted, implicitly or otherwise, Germany's cultural, technological, and racial superiority over its neighbors. Consistent with its claim to democratize tourism, Strength through Joy periodicals disparaged the "Baedecker trips" of the cultivated middle classes with their fixation on palaces and churches taken in at "the pace of a hunt." Regardless, KdF offered Baedecker-like "cultural trips" that highlighted German achievements, especially the monuments, churches, museums, and fortresses of the border regions of the German east, Franconia, Silesia, and Upper Bavaria.[27] KdF's tours to Danzig and East Prussia, separated from Germany by the Polish Corridor, recounted in its brochures the history of ethnic German accomplishment that transcended the transitory borders imposed by the Entente. The architecture and ethos of East Prussia signified the "civilizing" of the Slavic lands during the Middle Ages and to the injustice of Germany's post–World War I boundaries.[28] As if to recognize the natural place of German culture east of the Reich's borders, a KdF trip to the Polish spa at Zopot included a performance of Wagner's *Lohengrin*.[29] The trips of

25 Joshua Hagen, "The Most German of Towns: Creating the Ideal Nazi Community in Rothenburg ob der Tauber," *Annals of the Association of American Geographers*, 94, no. 1(2004) forthcoming.

26 "'Kraft durch Freude:' Leistungen des Deutschen Sozialismus," *Siemens-Mitteilungen*, no. 156 (December 1934): 254–5, SA.

27 NSG Kraft durch Freude, Gau Schwaben, *Dein Urlaub 1939* (Berlin, 1939): 29; "Die Kultur-Fahrten," NSG Kraft durch Freude, Gau Sachsen, *Urlaubsfahrten 1939*: 56–7.

28 Kraft durch Freude, Gau Halle-Merseburg, *Jahresfahrtenbuch 1939*: unpaginated. KdF tapped into the then well-established academic celebration of the Teutonic Knights and the German colonization of the east. See Michael Burleigh, *Germany Turns Eastwards: A Study of Ostforschung in the Third Reich* (Cambridge: Cambridge University Press, 1988); and Robert Jan van Pelt, "Bearers of Culture, Harbingers of Destruction: The *Mythos* of the Germans in the East," in *Art, Culture, and Media under the Third Reich*, ed. Richard A. Etlin (Chicago and London: University of Chicago Press, 2002): 98–135.

29 "KdF Urlaub im internationalen Weltbad: Die ersten 1400 KdF-Urlauber in Zoppot," *Arbeitertum: Blätter für Theorie und Praxis der Nationalsozialistische Betriebszellen Organisation. Amtlichte Organ der Deutschen Arbeitsfront* (hereinafter cited as *Arbeitertum*) 8, no. 10 (15 August 1938): 16–17.

Danzigers to the homeland included visits to Hamburg, a port city that spoke to the commercial colonialism of the Hanseatic League.[30] After Germany annexed Austria in the spring of 1938 and the Sudenten region of Czechoslovakia the following fall, Strength through Joy quickly organized trips to the territories that the führer had triumphantly "brought home," while simultaneously introducing Austrians and Sudenten Germans to their *Volk* comrades to the north.[31]

Beyond KdF's revisionism, which addressed the injustices of the recent past, its tourism embraced Germany's coming resurgence under Nazism. The Reich's imaginings of Germany as the dominant power on the globe found expression in KdF's tours to Hamburg, the "door to the world," and to Berlin, the site of Speer's architectural plan to transform the city into a "world capital."[32] Tours to the border city of Constance that involved side trips to Switzerland anticipated KdF's propaganda value as an advertisement of Nazism's social policy. If the Swiss harbored suspicions as to the Potemkin village-like character of the Reich's achievements, or so German Security Service (SD) agents feared, the visits of German workers would disabuse them.[33] Ironically, despite the centrality of the World War I "front experience" to National Socialism, battlefield tourism remained conspicuously absent from KdF's itineraries, aside from visits to the East Prussian memorial that commemorated Germany's greatest victory, the battle of Tannenberg. With the exception of the occasional tour that affirmed KdF's racial messages, the Reich's restrictions against exporting marks and the overvaluation of the franc, and KdF's likely desire to avoid the symbols of Germany's defeat excluded France from most KdF and private itineraries.[34]

30 NSG Kraft durch Freude, Gau Danzig, *Dein Urlaub 1938 mit KdF* (Danzig: A.W. Kasemann, 1938): unpaginated.

31 "Die Tiroler Berge rufen!," NSG Kraft durch Freude, Gau Essen, *Urlaub mit Kraft durch Freude 1939*: unpaginated; "Acht Tage in den jüngsten deutschen Gau Sudetenland," NSG Kraft durch Freude, Gau Oberdonau, *Dein Urlaub 1939 mit Kraft durch Freude*: unpaginated; "Sudetenland," NSG Kraft durch Freude, Gau Halle-Merseburg, *Jahresfahrtenbuch 1939* (Berlin: Verlag der Deutschen Arbeitsfront, 1939): unpaginated. KdF's use of Alpine images to advertise its tours to stress commonalities among Germans drew from images that Habsburg tourism promoters introduced before World War I. See Jill Steward, "Tourism in Late Imperial Austria: The Development of Tourist Cultures and Their Associated Images of Place," in Baranowski and Furlough, *Being Elsewhere*, 108–34.

32 NSG Kraft durch Freude, Gau Danzig, *KdF-Urlaubsfahrten 1939* (Danzig: A.W. Kasemann, 1939): 30–1.

33 Sicherheitsdienst RFSS Oberabschnitt Süd-West an Sicherheitshauptamt Zentralabteilung Berlin, 25 January 1938, Bundesarchiv Lichterfelde (hereinafter cited as BAL) R58, no. 943, 103.

34 "Ostpreussen," Die Deutsche Arbeitsfront, Gau Sudetenland, *KdF-Urlaub 1939*: 14. On postwar battlefield tourism, see David Lloyd, *Battlefield Tourism: Pilgrimage and Commemoration of the Great War in Britain, Australia and Canada* (Oxford and New York: Berg, 1998); Thomas Laqueur, "Memory and Naming in the Great War,"

Although less prestigious and often consigned to the back of its brochures, KdF's weekend excursions and hikes pursued the regime's political and racial messages with equal fervor. Because these attracted the majority of KdF tourists, they provided in numerical terms the better opportunity for indoctrination. Unlike the tours with trainloads of participants, many short trips and particularly the hikes were limited to fifteen to twenty people, who enjoyed an intimate encounter with nature and the experience of true comradeship. Exploring the *Heimat*, an untranslatable term to which the English words "home" or "homeland" do not do justice, was billed as crucial means of understanding the economy, history, and culture of a locality. Participants would appreciate each local *Heimat* as a piece of the greater national *Heimat*. The strangers with whom they set forth would in short order become compatriots in a shared endeavor.[35] Photos in brochures depicted smiling trekkers with their arms around each other, marching and singing in casual unison, and signified the racial community in the making.[36] In addition to enjoying one's spiritual bonds with the natural world, participants were to appreciate the insights that nature offered into the core of National Socialist ideology. "The plant and animal worlds show us," stated one KdF periodical, "how they stand fast in the struggle for existence." Entire species of plants "reciprocally nourish and maintain themselves" while they "mercilessly exterminate everything that is alien within their areas of existence . . . intolerant of sinners against their species and race."[37] The shorter trips were not limited, however, to the great outdoors, or to palaces and factories. They also included sites that blatantly featured antisemitism, the most notorious of which

in *Commemorations: The Politics of National Identity*, ed. John R. Gillis (Princeton and London: Princeton University Press, 1994): 150–67; "War, Memory, and the Modern: Pilgrimage and Tourism to the Western Front," in *World War I and the Cultures of Modernity*, ed. Douglas Mackaman and Michael Mays (Jackson: University of Mississippi Press, 2000): 151–60; and Stephen L. Harp, *Marketing Michelin: Advertising and Cultural Identity in Twentieth-Century France* (Baltimore and London: Johns Hopkins University Press, 2001), 89–125. On the relative paucity of German tourists to France, see A. J. Norval, *The Tourist Industry: A National and International Survey* (London: Sir Isaac Pitman & Sons, 1936), 64–5. An eight-day trip to France pointed out the disparities in wealth, as well as putatively casual French attitudes towards interracial couples: "Frankreich in 8 Tagen erlebt," *Arbeitertum* 7, no. 13 (1 October 1937): 6–10.

35 "Wir erwandern uns Deutschland," NSG Kraft durch Freude, Gau Düsseldorf, *KdF-Urlaub 1939, Die Jahresfahrtenbuch des Gaues Düsseldorf*: unpaginated; NSG Kraft durch Freude, Gau Sachsen, *Monatsprogramm*, (August 1937): 22–4; "Wir wandern, warum wandern . . .?", NSG Kraft durch Freude, Gau Mecklenburg-Lübeck, *Kraft durch Freude*, no. 7 (July 1935): 36–8.

36 "Wandern, wandern mit KdF," NSG Kraft durch Freude, Gau Oberdonau, *Dein Urlaub 1939 mit KdF*: unpaginated.

37 "Scheinbare oder echte Ferienerholung? Eine Betrachtung zur Urlaubsgestaltung, wie sie war und wie sie sein soll?" NSG Kraft durch Freude, Gau Mainfranken, *Kraft durch Freude*, no. 5 (May 1941): 3–4.

were the 1937 exhibits on "degenerate art" and "The Eternal Jew," which "documented" the "Jew's" destruction culture and "his" sponsorship of Bolshevism.[38]

Although reinforcing the trend among Germans to confine their travel to the homeland, albeit one that expanded after 1938 to include Austria and the Sudetenland, KdF's domestic tourism carved out its own niche in the German travel industry, ferreting out new vacation spots and tourist sites. Local governments and civic associations certainly looked to tourism before 1933 as a route to economic recovery,[39] yet as a party agency Strength through Joy could launch a more systematic effort from the top down. Thus, the introduction to the tour brochure for Gau Westphalia South focused on the impoverished Rhenish Eifel region, a previously untouched and unspoiled mountainous area now "discovered" by KdF, which trumpeted its magnificent panoramas and bracing air.[40] Not only would the national interest be served by economically and culturally buttressing regions such as the Eifel, the low cost of touring there guaranteed the accessibility appropriate to Strength through Joy's projected clientele. For the tourism year 1934/1935, some three million of KdF's 5.5 million tourists traveled to economically depressed sites, particularly along Germany's borders.[41] The prospect of improved incomes for those areas, where road construction and rearmament had not had an impact, became a means by which KdF would demonstrate the Third Reich's achievements against the hapless republic that preceded it.

The economic outcome of KdF tourism underscored its value for hard-pressed districts. The Black Forest alone, according to one source, contained "four million people locked in the misery of unemployment, and the struggle against this horrific legacy of a period of incompetence yielded [through KdF tourism] the first signs of success."[42] The mountainous regions of Silesia painted a similar picture. In 1938, the district of Hirschberg took in five thousand vacationers in one week, a figure that included neither the numbers generated by weekend travel nor the company outings that KdF encouraged.[43] To keep the price of its package tours low, KdF

---

38 NSG Kraft durch Freude, Gau München-Oberbayern, *Kraft durch Freude* (December 1937): 24.

39 Rudy J. Koshar, *Germany's Transient Pasts: Preservation and National Memory in the Twentieth Century* (Chapel Hill and London: University of North Carolina Press, 1998), 145.

40 NSG Kraft durch Freude, Gau Westfalen-Sud, *Mit KdF in den Urlaub, 1938*: 40.

41 "Jeder zweite Deutsche von der KdF-Gemeinschaft erfaßt," *Arbeitertum* 5, no. 18 (15 December 1935): 3–11; Frommann, "Reisen im Dienste," 263; Tätigkeitsbericht der NS Gemeinschaft Kraft durch Freude von Dr. Robert Ley, November 26, 1935, BAL, NS 22/781, 3.

42 Kahl, *deutsche Arbeiter reist*, (Berlin: Deutscher Verlag, 1940): 8. See also Kristin Semmens, "Domestic Tourism in the Third Reich" (Diss: University of Cambridge, 2002), 206–7.

43 DAF, NSG Kraft durch Freude, *5 Jahre Kraft durch Freude, Gau Schlesien* (1938): 9.

eschewed large establishments for small hotels or rooms in private homes or peasant quarters, which in turn generated second incomes for local people. Strength through Joy tourists could be a godsend for many pension owners, a good example being the wood carver Josef Schauer of Oberammergau, the site of the famous passion play. The local tourism office deemed Schauer's modest and poorly situated accommodations unsuitable to foreign tourists traveling with Thomas Cook, an ironic judgment given Cook's long-standing reputation as the purveyor of tourism for the masses. Citing his need for extra income, Schauer received the assurance that he would be registered with KdF in addition to earning money as a baggage handler for Cook.[44] So-called "emergency regions" (*Notstandsgebiete*), appealing on grounds of economic and cultural necessity, lobbied regularly for "transports" of KdF guests.[45] Refusing to allow the assignment of KdF guests to hoteliers, as was the punishment meted out to Alfons Schneider, attested to the economic pressure that mayors imposed to ensure political conformity. Schneider, an innkeeper on the Bavarian Schliersee, whose parents had been arrested and who himself had been accused of withholding tax revenue, was blacklisted until an SA man interceded for him.[46]

Overall, KdF's economic weight was impressive, particularly in regions that it targeted for development through tourism. In 1934, KdF's inaugural year, KdF tourism brought in an estimated 5.5 million Reichsmarks and 175,000 vacationers to southern Bavaria alone.[47] In the following year, the number of KdF vacationers traveling to the Gau Munich–Upper Bavaria was over three times larger than the number of its residents who traveled to other destinations in the Reich.[48] Between April 1937 and April 1938, when KdF tourism achieved its high water mark, its tourism generated for the same district 2,126,000 overnights, 3,253,000 meals, and 17 million Reichsmarks, quite apart from the side trips and outings that its vacation trips to that region incorporated. Even less explored southern Bavarian districts such as the Salzachgau and Schongau did well. Altogether, KdF travel accounted for 756,000 tourists, fifty thousand of

44 Verkehrsamt Oberammergau an Bayerisches Staatsministerium für Wirtschaft, Abteilung für Handel, Industrie und Gewerbe, 14 August 1935; Staatsministerium an Josef Schauer, 20 August 1935, Bayerisches Hauptstaatsarchiv, Munich (hereinafter cited as BHA), no. 2784.

45 Abdruck: Bürgermeister Grenzstadt Fürth im Wald an Staatsminister Esser, 11. August 1934, BHA, no. 2784.

46 Rechsanwälte Lorenz Roder, Ludwig Roder, Sachdarstellung, 8 June 1934, BHA, no. 2680.

47 24. Sitzung der Landes-Fremdenverkehrsrates für Bayern am 28. November 1934, BHA, no. 2715, 3.

48 "Zwei Jahre Kraft durch Freude im Gau München-Oberbayern," NSG Kraft durch Freude, Gau München-Oberbayern, *Kraft durch Freude* (December 1935): unpaginated.

them during the off-season on ski trips that its sport office organized.[49] Its tourists produced a strong ripple effect, moreover, generating income for industries involved in the production of tangible memories, such as photographs, and postcards.[50] Hard-pressed areas within Germany's pre-1938 borders were not alone in profiting from KdF tourism. Following the Anschluss in April 1938, Austria experienced a boom in tourism despite the sharp drop in the number of foreign visitors. Whereas prior to annexation, the Reich's rule against taking more than ten marks out of the country might have discouraged German tourists from traveling there, the restriction no longer applied following Austria's absorption.[51]

The intervention of and containment by commercial interests, however, defined Strength through Joy's special mission as much as its ethnic nationalism. Commercial tourism establishments, among them travel agencies, hotels, restaurants, and spas, complained continuously of KdF's negative impact on their profitability. The exemption of KdF tourists from certain resort taxes, KdF's "price dumping" and its inroads into the customer base of the tourist industry, and the implicit threat that KdF vacationers presented to the social tone of traditionally upper-class destinations became the stuff of trade association meetings.[52] By late 1934, the Reich Tourism Association, formed in mid-1933 under the propaganda ministry to centralize national and state commercial tourism interests, insisted that KdF should identify its own tourist locales and not compete with commercial promoters. If KdF proposed to open tourism to working-class Germans, argued Hermann Esser, the association's rabidly Nazi chairman, then it should send its vacationers and hikers to less traveled locales and seek lodging in private quarters or with peasants so as to be closer to the *Volk*. Except for the off season when the revenue from KdF vacationers would be welcome, KdF should avoid the established resorts and spas, especially those that drew an international clientele. Otherwise, KdF's presence compromised the right of hotels, restaurants, and casinos that catered to an upscale market to charge enough to remain viable. In an implicit nod to the desire of upper-class resorts to maintain their social

49   Landesfremdenverkehrsverband München und Südbayern, e.V., Geschäftsbericht für die Zeit vom 1 April 1937 bis 31 März 1938, BHA, no. 2719, 11–18. These figures did not distinguish between short outings and the longer vacations.

50   Die Deutsche Arbeitsfront, NS-Gemeinschaft "Kraft durch Freude," Reichsamt Reisen, Wandern und Urlaub, *Das Werk der KdF-Urlaubsreisen*: 8.

51   Evan Bukey, *Hitler's Austria: Popular Sentiment in the Nazi Era 1938–1945* (Chapel Hill and London: University of North Carolina Press, 2000), 124. The American tourist William Van Til believed that the rule was designed to squeeze Austria economically. See his *The Danube Flows through Fascism: Nine Hundred Miles in a Fold-Boat* (New York: Charles Scribner's Sons, 1938), 99–100. A. J. Norval, *Tourist Industry*, 58–60, drew a similar conclusion.

52   See Keitz, *Reisen als Leitbild*, 234, 238; and especially Semmens, "Domestic Tourism," 208–28.

character, Esser maintained that KdF and commercial tourism should observe the strict separation of function in their search for clienteles. KdF's formal incorporation in the Reich Tourism Association by October 1935 undoubtedly stemmed from Esser's largely successful desire to delimit its mandate. Despite its wish to extend a bourgeois privilege to workers, KdF was forced to steer its tours away from the prestigious spas and vacation spots. Whereas at the beginning 60 percent of KdF's tours went to the established spas and natural wonders, only 5 percent went to them by the outbreak of war.[53]

To be sure, the German Labor Front, as well as the Beauty of Labor, strove to assume oversight of commercial tourism establishments. The Beauty of Labor saw high standards of cleanliness, training, and guest accommodations as essential to attracting the foreign tourist, who brought in the foreign currency that aided the Reich's first priority.[54] Nevertheless, although Bodo Lafferentz won a seat on the executive committee of the Reich Tourism Association and KdF functionaries were represented in state and local tourism associations,[55] their presence was to ensure Strength through Joy's containment. The positive value that the association assigned to KdF tourism could not conceal its concern that Strength through Joy threatened vested interests, which in turn anchored KdF's status as a quintessentially Nazi project. Rather than advocating wage hikes that would have afforded its clientele access to established tourist sites in high season, KdF's low-cost tourism, the product of its mediation between its clientele and commercial tourism providers, presupposed low-wage participants and down-market destinations.[56] Ironically, the opposition of German resorts to KdF tourists contributed to the popularity of KdF's urban tourism. Strength through Joy's most popular tours, aside

53 24. Sitzung der Landes-Fremdenverkehrsrates für Bayern am 28. November 1934, BHA, no. 2715, 6. On the incorporation of KdF in the Reich Association, see Semmens, "Domestic Tourism, Ch. 2. On the redirection of KdF tourism, see Hasso Spode, "Ein Seebad für zwanzigtausend Volksgenossen: Zur Grammatik und Geschichte des fordistischen Urlaubs," in *Reisekultur in Deutschland: Von der Weimarer Republik zum "Dritten Reich,"* ed. Peter J. Brenner (Tübingen: Max Niemeyer Verlag, 1997): 30; and Spode again, "The 'Seaside Resort of the 20,000': Fordism, Mass Tourism and the Third Reich," paper given at the XIII Economic History Congress, Buenos Aires, July 2002, 7.

54 "Zur Hebung der Gaststättenkultur," Ausschnitt der *Fremdenverkehr* 15 (August 27, 1938), BHA, no. 2680.

55 Arbeitstagung des Reichsfremdenverkehrsverbandes in Heidelberg am 4. November 1935, BHA, no. 2715; 25. See Semmens, "Domestic Tourism," 216–17.

56 Landesfremdenverkehrsverband München und Südbayern, e.V., Geschäftsbericht für die Zeit vom 1. April 1937 bis 31. März 1938, BHA, no. 2719, 19, 24. Sitzung der Landes-Fremdenverkehrsverbandes für Bayern am 28. November 1934, BHA, no. 2715, 6; Ausschnitt der *Fremdenverkehr* Nr. 16 vom 16. April 1938, BHA, no. 2784; "Lebensfragen des deutschen Reisebürogewerbes," *Der Fremdenverkehr* 50 (11. December 1937), BHA, no. 2754.

from those to the less-visited natural wonders, journeyed to the cities. Munich, Karlsruhe, Frankfurt, Koblenz, and Berlin each drew over a million KdF tourists, with Hamburg drawing over 775,000, not including the tourists who traveled there to embark on cruises. The exception resided in the KdF trips to cities, such as Danzig and the East Prussian capital of Königsberg, which drew only 26,000 and 56,000 respectively. Being endangered by the proximity of Slavs did not provide sufficient incentive for tourists to travel there. [57]

Imagining Empire: KdF Cruises and the Master Race-to-Be

Strength through Joy's land vacations and especially its one- and two-day outings attracted the vast majority of its "participants." Nevertheless, its cruises occupied a prominent place in its monthly periodicals and tour brochures, emblematic of KdF's claim that by making the pleasures of the prosperous available to workers at low cost, a high standard of living could be achieved without ruinous wage increases. That cruises should have been attractive testified not simply to Germany's formidable steamship lines, Hamburg-South America and North German Lloyd Bremen, or to the growing popularity of sea travel in the twenties. They also spoke to the Nazi regime's own, if still inchoate, imaginings of a future German world empire beyond the acquisition of living space in Europe, which would reawaken the popularity of prewar "global politics" (*Weltpolitik*).[58] The link between tourism and global hegemony had already been well established during the age of high imperialism. Before the war when Britain served as the primary rival to German ambitions, the wealthy tourists whom the British travel agency Thomas Cook deposited at foreign ports and major colonial outposts personified British naval,

---

57 Reichsamtsleitung Kraft durch Freude, *Unter dem Sonnenrad: Ein Buch von Kraft durch Freude* (Berlin: Verlag der Deutschen Arbeitsfront, 1938), 196.

58 On the popularity of cruises in the twenties and thirties see Lorraine Coons and Alexander Varias, *Tourist Third Cabin: Steamship Travel in the Interwar Years* (New York: Palgrave MacMillan, 2003.) Visions of *Weltpolitik*, which saturated prewar imperial German politics, were articulated with special force by the Navy League. See Geoff Eley, *Reshaping the German Right: Radical Nationalism and Political Change after Bismarck* (New Haven and London: Yale University Press, 1980). On Nazi *Weltpolitik*, see Jost Düffler, *Weimar, Hitler, und die Marine: Reichspolitik und Flottenbau 1920–1939* (Düsseldorf: Droste, 1973); Jochen Thies, *Architekt der Weltherrschaft: Die "Endziele" Hitlers* (Düsseldorf: Droste, 1980); and Woodruff Smith's placement of Nazi ambitions in the broader context of German ambitions since the 1870s, *The Ideological Origins of Nazi Imperialism* (New York and Oxford: Oxford University Press, 1986), Ch. 10.

commercial, and imperial supremacy.[59] Strength through Joy's cruises would not only challenge the Entente's control of the high seas as a weapon in the Reich's "anti-Geneva" foreign policy arsenal,[60] it would also legitimate a future German "global politics" by opening sea voyages to workers.

The number of participants who signed onto the cruises, which ranged from approximately 60,000 in 1934 to as many as 140,000 in 1939, never approached that of the homeland vacations nor that of the shorter excursions. Yet aside from a dip in 1938, the number of vacationers taking sea voyages steadily increased until the outbreak of war.[61] In May 1934 as soon as weather permitted, KdF initiated its cruise program by sending the steamships *Dresden* and *Monte Olivia* from Bremerhaven to the North Sea island of Helgoland. The ships, filled with well-dressed and allegedly awestruck workers at sea for the first time in their lives, sailed through the Straits of Dover to the English Channel and Isle of Wight before returning to their port of disembarkation. At a time when Hitler sought an alliance with Great Britain that would have allowed Germany command of the continent, the ships also demonstrated the success of Nazi social policy and Germany's determination to enlarge its navy.[62] Like the flourish that characterized the domestic tours, KdF staged its cruises according to the principle of rapid proliferation, dispatching them in flotillas of three or four.[63] By the summer, KdF had seven ships at its disposal and an expanded repertoire of tours, especially through the Norwegian fjords. The cruise program received a big boost when in October 1934 the DAF formally assumed control of confiscated trade union assets.[64]

---

59 In the last quarter of the nineteenth century, Cook voyages brought wealthy tourists to Egypt and the Middle East, followed by around-the-world cruises. See Withey, *Grand Tours and Cook's Tours*, 223–93.

60 This is Daniela Liebscher's argument in "Mit KdF 'die Welt erschliessen.'" Despite Hitler's admiration for the British empire and his desire to forge an alliance with Great Britain, as expressed in his "second book" of 1926, translated as *Hitler's Secret Book*, ed. Telford Taylor and trans. Salvator Attanasio (New York: Grove Press, 1961), 146–59, the inherent limitlessness of Nazi expansionism made a permanent arrangement impossible. See Norman J. W. Goda in *Tomorrow the World: Hitler, Northwest Africa, and the Path toward America* (College Station, Texas: Texas A&M University Press, 1998), Introduction.

61 Spode, "Arbeiterurlaub:" 298. Despite Spode's understandable skepticism as to the reliability of KdF data and his efforts to compensate for it, his figures disagree modestly with those of the DAF publicist Otto Marrenbach, *Fundamente des Sieges*, 355. Marrenbach's data, however, do not include 1939.

62 *Arbeitertum* 4, no. 5 (1 June 1934): 5–11. On the führer's plans for an alliance with the British, see Jost Düffler, *Nazi Germany 1933–1945: Faith and Annihilation* (London: Edward Arnold, 1996), 63–5.

63 Hans Biallas, *Der Sonne entgegen! Deutsche Arbeiter fahren nach Madeira* (Berlin: Freiheitsverlag, 1936), 82.

64 Heinz Schön, *Die KdF Schiffe und Ihr Schichsal: Eine Dokumentation* (Stuttgart: Motorbuch Verlag, 1987), 21.

By agreement with the authoritarian, Nazi-sympathizing regime of Antonio Salazar, KdF further expanded its cruise program in spring 1935 to include voyages to Lisbon and the Portuguese island of Madeira. Two years later, the conclusion of an accord with the officials of another authoritarian regime, this one between Robert Ley and Tullio Cianetti, the leader of the Italian Fascist Confederation of Industrial Workers, allowed After Work–sponsored Italian workers to travel to Germany. Trainloads of German workers crossed the Alps in the other direction. By that fall, the collaboration between KdF and After Work enabled KdF voyages to the Italian ports of Genoa, Naples, and Palermo. Some of the trips combined visits to the Italian peninsula with cruises to Yugoslavia, Greece, and especially Italy's North African colony, Libya, where the Fascist government had finally succeeded in suppressing a long-standing anti-colonial rebellion. Additional sea voyages took in ports of call in the Baltic states and Finland, the Balkans, Bulgaria, and the Black Sea region, while simultaneously following in Cook's footsteps to the major sites of the Middle East: Alexandria and Cairo, Istanbul, and Jerusalem.[65]

By the outbreak of war, Strength through Joy's fleet consisted of twelve ships, two of them, the *Monte Olivia* and *Dresden*, chartered from the Hamburg-South America and North German Lloyd Bremen lines respectively, and eight purchased outright.[66] Having demonstrated the popularity of its cruises, which Germans experienced directly or (most often) vicariously, KdF commissioned the construction of two liners of its own, the *Wilhelm Gustloff* launched in the spring of 1938, and the *Robert Ley*, which first set sail in the spring of 1939. The maiden voyage of the *Robert Ley* included the führer among its passengers. He shook hands with the crew, conversed with passengers, posed for his picture flanked by two young and attractive women clad in dirndls, and granted another the experience of a lifetime by dining next to her.[67] KdF's ports of call, which ranged from the fjords beloved by Kaiser Wilhelm II to the sunny climates that had enticed the titled and wealthy since the eighteenth century, announced that sea voyages were now available to modest earners. Consistent with his penchant for gigantism, Ley promised not only cruises to more destinations, including by 1940 Tokyo, Sweden, Finland and the Canary Islands, but also the construction of an additional eight ships.[68]

65   Frommann, "Reisen mit 'Kraft durch Freude:' Eine Darstellung der KdF-Reisen unter besonderer Berücksichtigung der Auslandsfahrten" (MA thesis: Karlsruhe, 1977), 144–6. On the Fascists in Libya, see John Wright, *Libya: A Modern History* (Baltimore: Johns Hopkins University Press, 1981), 31–6.

66   Kahl, *deutsche Arbeiter reist!*, 46.

67   *Arbeitertum* 9, no. 3 (1 May 1939): 12–17; NSG Kraft durch Freude, Gau Köln-Aachen, *Kraft durch Freude* 4, no. 5 (May 1939): 4–6.

68   "Erholungsurlaub für 14 millionen deutsche Arbeiter: Das ist das Ziel von 'Kraft durch Freude,'" (name of newspaper indecipherable), March 26, 1934, Niedersächsisches

"The German *Volk* has once again become a nation of seafarers," exclaimed one KdF periodical, referring not only to KdF's pleasure cruises but also implicitly to the Reich's goal of extending its naval power. "Today there isn't a single firm, in which at least one member among the retinue hasn't gone on a high seas trip with KdF."[69] Cartoons in KdF publications drummed home the contrast in the status of workers between the Weimar Republic and the Third Reich. Under the former, strikes, demonstrations, and unemployment reigned. Under Nazism, neatly attired workers garbed in ties stood ready, suitcases in hand, to sail with KdF to Madeira.[70]

Like its domestic tourism, which inserted KdF's unsubtle political messages into the seeming goodwill that bound Germans from different regions, the political purposes entwined in Strength through Joy's cruises made every claim to transparency. The "classless" accessibility to privilege resonated in all aspects of KdF tours, from the structure of its ships to the politicization that accompanied dockings in foreign ports, and to the quasi militarization of its tours, which was to forge the racial community in minature. Thus, KdF claimed to adhere scrupulously to its maxim of one-class sea travel by not filling its ships to capacity. No passengers, it asserted, would occupy the least desirable interior cabins below deck. Apart from the evidence from tourists that contradicted its assertions, namely KdF's maximization of the number of passengers to pay charter fees, KdF's need to live up to its standard forced it to purchase and redesign some of the ships it had originally leased.[71] KdF's newest ships, the *Wilhelm Gustloff* and *Robert Ley*, however, presented fewer problems, for in common with the growing practice of steamship companies during the interwar period to appeal to a broader social constituency, their design eschewed the demarcations of first, second, and steerage class. That social distinctions did emerge in the assignment of cabins did not discourage KdF periodicals from claiming the opposite: after all, its very intention to alter the past practice of segregated classes, even if requiring time to institute, indicated the Nazi regime's seriousness of purpose.[72]

Hauptstaatsarchiv, Hannover (hereinafter cited as NHH), VVP 17, no. 2455; "Zum 5. Jahrestag der Gemeinschaft 'Kraft durch Freude: Hochseefahrten – eine Bilanz," *Hannoverscher Wechruf* (November 1, 1939), NHH, VVP 17, no. 2456; Der Bau von zwanzig KdF-Schiffen geplant: Vier grosse KdF.-Bäder an der Ostsee – 1940 mit KdF. nach Tokio/Eine Unterredung mit Dr. Ley," *Hannoverscher Anzeiger*, 27 March 1938, NHH, VVP, no. 2456.

69 Die Deutsche Arbeitsfront, NS-Gemeinschaft "Kraft durch Freude," Reichsamt Reisen, Wandern und Urlaub, *Das Werk der KdF-Urlaubsreisen*, 6.

70 "Einst und jetzt!," Kraft durch Freude, Deutsche Arbeitsfront, Gau Mittelfranken, *Kraft durch Freude* (June 1935): 5.

71 On KdF's claims, see Schön, *KdF-Schiffe und Ihr Schicksal*, 14–15. For the reality, see Spode, "'Der deutsche Arbeiter reist'": 298.

72 See Coons and Varias, *Tourist Third Cabin*, 25–64 on the reconfiguration of passenger accommodations to attract a broader spectrum of the middle class.

KdF periodicals frequently resorted to humor to attack privilege; specifically the elevation of personal needs or social station over the good of the racial community, the "Ten Commandments for KdF Vacation Travelers" being a good example. Highlighting unacceptable behavior through satire, the commandments included such "virtues" as ignoring the directions of tour guides, reserving eight places for oneself on the train, and insisting on first-class hotel accommodations while other tourists gamely accepted the standard accommodations in private residences. Complaining that all was superior at home instead of opening oneself to new experiences and unfamiliar places, flaunting one's money, and refusing to pay for a side excursion for a less well-off comrade completed the list of offenses.[73] Periodicals poked fun at putative snobs, who looked down their noses at the "organized poverty" of Strength through Joy, while flaunting their superior cultural attainment and expensive finery.[74] Such un-*völkisch*, class-defined behavior, warned KdF periodicals, guaranteed one's exclusion from future KdF trips.

In practice, KdF could not deny individual choice, self-determination, or private experience. Yet its emphasis on discipline, edification, and the interests of the "community" over the whims of individuals continued in its self-representation. Sacrifice on behalf of "community," after all, was a prime marker of racial superiority that KdF sought to cultivate. Evoking the "front experience" of World War I, KdF's communitarianism called for the regimentation of tourists, who were warned unceasingly to observe punctuality, obey their tour leaders, attend to their assigned places on trains and at inns, and eschew self-centeredness, especially of the sort that would aggravate class distinctions. Mornings on board ship began with a blast of the trumpet from a cabin steward at 6:30 or 7 a.m., followed by calisthenics on deck until breakfast at 7:30, followed then by a flag parade led by the ship's orchestra playing the national anthem, numerous "sieg heils," and the singing of KdF's own anthem, ironically entitled, "Enjoy Life" ("*Freut Euch des Lebens*"). Only afterwards could passengers pick and choose among the planned shipboard activities.[75] The insistence on discipline could temper human weakness in times of crisis, as indicated by its retrospective report on the sinking of the *Dresden* off the coast of Norway in June 1934, the result of the ship's having struck a rocky cliff. According to the ship's captain, the orderliness and common purpose

---

73 "Zehn Gebote für KdF-Urlaubsfahrer," *Kraft durch Freude in der Deutschen Arbeitsfront, Gau München Oberbayern* (August 1935): xii–xv, Stiftung Westfälisches Wirtschaftsarchiv (hereinafter cited as WWA), A236/568, 01/384.
74 NSG Kraft durch Freude, Gau Sachsen, *Monatsprogramm* (November 1935): 15–16.
75 "Mit 'Kraft durch Freude' auf dem Dampfer 'Oceana' nach England," *Krupp: Zeitschrift der Kruppschen Werksgemeinschaft* 26, no. 19 (1 July 1935): 373, HA Krupp. See also Frommann, "Reisen im Dienste," 243.

that the passengers demonstrated, which unexpectedly enough included the women among them, triumphed over the injuries and loss of life that they suffered.[76]

Not surprisingly Strength through Joy's revisionism was as pronounced at sea as it was on land. The addition of overseas destinations, notably in Portugal, Italy, and Tripoli, dovetailed with major foreign policy initiatives, the regime's withdrawal from the League of Nations and the International Labour Office in 1933, its negotiation of the Anglo–German Naval Treaty in 1935, and the emerging alliance with Italy after its annexation of Ethiopia during the same year.[77] Italian receptions for arriving KdF passengers became expressions of fascist solidarity, periodic welcomes by the Duce, and the solemn commemoration of fallen Fascists amidst tours to the ruins of the Colosseum in Rome, visits to the opera in Florence, or gondola rides in Venice. Cruises to Lisbon and Madeira allowed German tourists to sing the national anthem, the *Deutschlandlied*, and the Nazi party tune, the "Horst Wessel Song" accompanied by Portuguese bands, as they solidified the ties between KdF and Portugal's leisure-time organization modeled on KdF, "Joy in Work."[78] Receptions aboard ship in the Greek port of Piraeus included the Greek minister of labor and representatives from labor organizations loyal to the Metaxas dictatorship.[79] Demonstrations of German sea power by the cruisers and destroyers of the Reich's navy became a staple of passenger entertainment while en route, the impressive impact of which first-person accounts of the cruises unfailingly reported. After the victory of Franco's nationalist forces in the Spanish Civil War, four KdF ships, the *Robert Ley, Wilhelm Gustloff, Stuttgart,* and *Der Deutsche,* transported members of the Condor division to Germany: troops that had been crucial to the final victory of the Spanish nationalist forces. German camera crews filmed the cocktail parties that took place on board ship to honor dignitaries from both nations including Ley and high-ranking Spanish government officials.[80]

---

76   *Unter dem Sonnenrad*, 39.
77   Leibscher, "Mit KdF 'die Welt erschließen'": 51–60.
78   "Wegbereiter einer großen Freundschaft: Mit Kraft durch Freude nach Italien," *Arbeitertum* 7, no. 15 (1 November 1937): 6–9; NSG Kraft durch Freude, Gau Pommern, *Monatsprogramm* (March 1939): 1–4; Deutsches Generalkonsulat Genua an Deutsche Botschaft, Rome, 16. November 1937, Auswärtiges Amt/Politisches Archiv, Bonn (hereinafter cited as AA-PA), no. 1306, Soz. 3b; Frommann, "Reisen mit 'Kraft durch Freude,'" 94–5.
79   Bericht des SS-Untersturmführers Prieb über die Teilnahme an der KdF-Auslands fahrt nach Dalmatien, Griechenland mit dem Dampfer "Oceana" vem 6, bis 18. November 1938, BAL R58, no. 950, 284.
80   Entziffertes Telegram 4.17 1939 an Deutsche Botschaft San Sebastian, Einladung zum 3. Mai (Bilbao. "Robert Ley"), Deutsche Botschaft San Sebastian an Ministerio de Asuntos Exteriores, Burgos, 4. Mai 1939, all located in AA-PA 436 22-5/1. See as well Frommann, "Reisen im Dienste," 247–50.

Madeira's prominence among Strength through Joy's cruise destinations, which became clear in the regularity of the island's appearance in its periodicals and promotional literature, illustrated Strength through Joy's fusion of populism and global politics. A long-standing target for British sugar, wine, and real estate interests, as well as its strategic importance owing to Portugal's allowance of the stationing of British naval squadrons, Madeira also earned a reputation among the British upper classes by the mid-nineteenth century as a recuperation spot. Because of its mild climate, reputedly healthful air, and its distance from the unification conflicts of Italy where the British elite usually traveled, Madeira drew British tuberculosis patients in large numbers. Although the island's reputation for curing TB declined after 1880, Madeira evolved thereafter into a British holiday resort. Significantly, the island emerged as a bone of contention in the Anglo–German rivalry before World War I, for in addition to stocking coal to fuel German ships, German business interests acquired gambling rights and established a consortium of sanatoria. The avatar of German commerce on the island, Prince Friedrich Karl Hohenlohe-Oehringen, a friend of both the queen of Portugal and the German Kaiser, convinced the British that the German presence was but a front for their global ambitions.[81] As a symbol of British power and of the British elites who availed themselves of the island's resources, Madeira became an irresistible stage for KdF's dual demonstrations of German ascendancy and the democratization of privilege.

The German diplomatic corps and German "colonies" living in Strength through Joy's ports of call contributed to the politicization of overseas tourism and to the imperial longings embedded within it. German legations in KdF ports of call greeted the German vacationers personally, facilitated the landing rights of KdF ships, traveling in their flotillas to demonstrate Germany's power to maximum effect, and finalizing security arrangements – particularly necessary in Portugal due to its proximity to Spain and its civil war. Moreover, they organized onshore tours for the passengers, acquiring tickets for side trips from their hosts that would otherwise have been impossible in light of the Reich's restrictions against the exporting of currency. In some cases, they negotiated free passage to major tourist attractions, such as admission to the Akropolis in Athens bestowed on the passengers of the liner *Oceana*.[82] The diplomatic

---

81   See Desmond Gregory, *The Beneficent Usurpers: A History of the British in Madeira* (Rutherford, Madison, Teaneck: Fairleigh Dickenson University Press, 1988), especially 112–24, and Benedita Câmara, "The Image and Tourism Industry of Madeira (1850–1914)," unpublished paper presented to the meeting of the XIII Economic History Congress, Buenos Aires, July, 2002.

82   Deutsche Gesandtschaft Athens an das Auswärtige Amt, 15 November 1938, AA-PA, R49245.

corps arranged on-board entertainment for local dignitaries and German expatriates (*Auslandsdeutsche*) to strengthen the Reich's ties to the host nations and the bonds between racial compatriots abroad and the German homeland. Germans who resided locally served as tour guides and educated their countrymen as to local social conditions.[83] The deployment of Germans as tour guides for KdF vacationers posed few problems for states closely allied with the Reich, with the exception of the Baltic nations. Confronted by the restiveness of resident Germans, for example, the authoritarian government of Latvia under Karlis Ulmanis, which was beset by a thoroughly nazified German minority, made it clear that Latvian tour leaders should direct the tours on land, not local German volunteers.[84] Yet KdF's exploitation of Germans living abroad visibly supported the Nazi regime's larger effort to challenge Germany's postwar borders. It would reassert Germany's imperial claims, which the postwar settlements had temporarily undermined, by awakening the nationalism of expatriates. In return for their volunteering to aid KdF tourists, KdF organized trips for expatriates to Japan, China, Palestine, and South West Africa, among other places, also giving them vacations in Germany at one-half the already low KdF price.[85]

Resurrecting the Wilhelmine desire for a colonial "place in the sun," KdF envisioned its ships as the touristic harbinger of the coming global empire, a connection that KdF at its admirers often made. Argued Helmut Böttcher in the Siemens firm newspaper, Germans had always demonstrated their need to travel by, among other things, the colonization of the east and southeast during the Middle Ages.[86] While reporting on the maiden voyage of the *Robert Ley* with Hitler on board, the DAF's house newspaper, *Arbeitertum* proclaimed that the opposition of the democracies to Germany's legitimate global stature resulted from the lurking hostility of international Jewry.[87] Moreover, KdF understood travel abroad as a perfect opportunity for teaching racism. As Robert Ley himself

83 Zentralbüro NS-Gemeinschaft Kraft durch Freude, Amt Reisen Wandern und Urlaub an die Deutsche Gesandtschaft Riga, 21 June 1939, AA-PA, no. 473, S7; Deutsche Gesandtschaft in Lissabon an das Auswärtige Amt, 14 June 1938, AA-PA, R49245; Deutsche Gesandtschaft Lissabon an das Auswärtige Amt, 16 October 1937, AA-PA, R49244; Deutsche Gesandtschaft Lissabon an das Auswärtige Amt, 29 July 1937, AA-PA, R49244; Deutsche Konsulat Palermo an die Deutsche Botschaft, Rome, 5 February 1938, AA-PA no. 1306, Soz. 3b; Deutsche Konsulat Neapel an die Deutsche Botschaft, Rome, 2 April 1938, AA-PA, 1306, Soz. 3b.
84 Zentralbüro NS-Gemeinschaft Kraft durch Freude, Amt Reisen, Wandern und Urlaub an die Deutsche Gesandtschaft Riga, 21 June 1939, AA-PA, no. 473, S7.
85 *Unter dem Sonnenrad*, 191–6.
86 "Deutsche Arbeitskameraden ziehn mit 'Kraft durch Freude' in die Welt," *Siemens-Mitteilungen*, no. 172 (April 1936): 72–3, SA.
87 "Der Führer fuhr mit dem Flaggschiff 'Robert Ley,'" *Arbeitertum* 9, no. 31 (1 May 1939): 12.

expected, workers would come to appreciate racial differences once they broadened their horizons on a mediterranean cruise.[88] At least, "worker comrades would be convinced that National Socialism [had] created a matchless level of care unequalled anywhere else in the world for the working people among our *Volk* by observing the living conditions of other peoples."[89] Tours of Greece were to demonstrate the importance of national unity as the bedrock of greatness. A visit to Mount Parnassus, the site of the Delphic oracle, awed German workers, who listened with rapt attention, when told of the "modern rebirth of [Greece's] national unity, for which Delphi had already stood for more than two thousand years as its immortal symbol." Workers were to come away impressed not simply by the architecture of the temple of Apollo. Rather, they were to appreciate the Greek "spirit," which embodied the triumph of solidarity over division, a prime virtue of culture-creating races, and recognize its lessons for the present.[90]

Luxurious Spartanism: KdF Tourism and Consumption

The regime's ability to mitigate the conflict between consumption and rearmament, however, became more fundamental to its legitimacy than the opportunities that KdF tourism presented for inculcating racial bonding. Without convincing its population that it would satisfy its desires, Nazism could not win the consent necessary to achieve its larger goals. Building the racial community depended on defusing the tension between the popular demand for consumer goods and the regime's need to restrain consumption. Although more covert than its propagandistic bombast and its deployment of travel toward imperialist ends, KdF's status as the mediator between consumption and rearmament, and between its clientele and the leisure market, became essential to the marketing and operation of its tourist program. Partly a reflection of Strength through Joy's diverse social bases and partly a mirror of the Nazi regime's priorities, KdF's tour programs straddled the boundaries between Spartanism and luxury, materialism and antimaterialism, combining its appeals to self-sacrifice with its willing capitulation to the hedonistic purchase and consumption of pleasure.

88   Rede des Reichsorganisationsleiter Pg. Dr. Ley am 11.7.1938 auf dem Schiff "Wilhelm Gustloff," BAL R 58, no. 944, 195.
89   Der Deutsche Arbeitsfront, Gau Westfalen-Süd, NS.-Gemeinschaft 'Kraft durch Freude,' *Dein Urlaub 1939*: 44.
90   "Hellas offenbart sich deutschen Arbeitern: Mit KdF. nach Griechenland," *Göttinger Tageblatt*, 24 November 1938, NHH VVP 17, no. 2426.

Monthly programs and tour brochures bespoke a straightforward rejection of materialism, borrowing from the language of tourism to transmit Strength through Joy's redefinition of the "standard of living" in noncommercial and nonmaterial terms to correspond to the regime's ethic of sacrifice and deferred gratification. It insisted that its tourism opposed mere pleasure seeking, consonant with the regime's repeated calls for self-restraint and the individual's obligation to the racial community. That in general, tourism and tourism promoters stressed the serious purposes and deep meaning of their enterprise precisely to efface the development of tourism as a commercial enterprise, helped KdF's case considerably. "Our vacation trips are not commercial undertakings," one KdF monthly bulletin intoned in the context of a discussion of KdF rules, "but an occasion [sic] for the highest idealism."[91] Vacation trips were to provide recreation, discipline, and a sense of "community," insisted Robert Ley, and not become an opportunity for hedonistic "orgies."[92] Consistent with the edification and spiritual uplift embedded in the classical Greek and imperial Roman ruins that KdF favored as sightseeing destinations, KdF eschewed the "materialist" quest for personal pleasure. Instead, one was to contemplate the sublime, cultivate comradeship with one's fellow tourists, improve one's education by studying ancient art and architecture, regain one's equilibrium in preparation for the return to work, kindle one's historical consciousness, and broaden one's horizons by leaving one's village or region to visit exotic locales. The language that KdF employed confirms the recent and trenchant observation that tourism expresses dreams, fantasies, and the imagination acted out in "reality;" that is, the aesthetic experiences that render tourism a less tangible, if entirely purchasable, commodity than other kinds of consumer goods.[93] The KdF trip was, according to its periodicals, "magical," "like a dream" or a "long-buried childhood dream," a "fantasy" that had now come true, a "dream come true," or a "fairy tale." Taken together, KdF trips were "unforgettable experiences" that encouraged tourists to transcend the everyday world. They provided opportunities to observe an alien culture, experience the exotic, and elevate oneself above the daily routine.[94]

---

91   This statement appeared in description of KdF's rules. NSG Kraft durch Freude, Gau Pommern, *Monatsprogramm* no. 1 (1 December 1934): 5–9.

92   Rede des Reichorganisationsleiter Pg. Dr. Ley am 11.7.1938 auf dem Schiff "Wilhelm Gustloff," BAL R58, no. 944, 192.

93   See Christoph Hennig, *Reiselust: Touristen, Tourismus und Urlaubskultur* (Frankfurt am Main: Suhrkamp Taschenbuch, 1999).

94   Good examples of such language can be found in the NSG Kraft durch Freude, Gau Pommern, *Monatsprogramm* from 1934 and 1935; "Spar für Deinen Urlaub," NSG Kraft durch Freude, Gau Schwaben, *Jahres-Urlaubsprogramm 1935* (Berlin: Verlag des Deutschen Arbeitsfront, 1935); and G. Müller-Gaisberg, *Volk nach der Arbeit* (Berlin: Verlag Richard Carl Schmidt, 1936), 294–300.

In addition to metaphors of dreams, KdF periodicals underscored the serious purposes of its tourism through photographs and story telling. Tour brochures opened with a full-page photo of Hitler gazing at the Bavarian Alps from his Berchtesgaden hideaway; determined, resolute, with eyes squarely facing the future. At the bottom of the page, resting beneath the Nazi eagle, appeared a quotation from the führer that reminded readers as to the expected outcome of leisure. Vacations would fortify the nerves of workers to prepare them for the "great politics" demanded of them.[95] The stories of tourists that appeared frequently in KdF magazines transmuted potentially risky and uncontrollable emotions, such as love, into the desirable results of travel. Thus the tale, "Love in Africa: A True KdF experience," which related the story of Schorsch who fell in love with Claire on their cruise to Madeira and Tripoli, became a lesson in how travel matured a previously confirmed bachelor rather than a means of acquiring a real knowledge and understanding of exotic locales, or the empathetic interaction with local people. Schorsch had never given much thought to marriage despite being thirty-two. Yet under the stars that glittered "like a thousand diamonds" as the KdF ship docked in Madeira's port city Funchal, he met the woman who would change his life. Later, in an oasis near Tripoli, surrounded by Arabs and "Sudanese Negroes," Claire put a silver ring on Schorsch's finger, which she had purchased from an Arab silversmith. Alas, the two had to part in Genoa and return to their respective districts in separate trains, he to the Rhineland, she to Berlin, but Schorsch could not get Claire out of his mind. Suddenly, a gift appeared in the mail, a photo album from Claire that brought back the "beautiful hours" that he had spent with her on his cruise. Overcome with emotion, he rushed to Berlin to propose to her, surprising his friends with his seemingly impulsive decision. What he and Claire found together "in Africa, the darkest part of the earth," they would never forget.[96] The sanctity of marriage and coincidently its relevance to increasing the quantity and quality of the racial community triumphed over a shallow and solitary existence.

The enthusiastic testimonials that tourists contributed to plant newspapers, or submitted as entries in contests sponsored by Strength through Joy periodicals, hammered home the aesthetic and communitarian purposes of its tourism, informing readers of the experiences that they could expect if they were fortunate enough to travel with KdF. Written by travelers, whom the periodicals solicited to convey the wonder of their adventures, the reports conjoined feelings of comradeship with an appreciation

95   NSG Kraft durch Freude, Gau Sudetenland, *KdF-Urlaub 1939*.
96   "Liebe in Afrika. Ein wahres KdF Erlebnis erzählt von Heinz Magka," NSG Kraft durch Freude, Gau Köln-Aachen, *Kraft durch Freude 1939* 4, no. 3 (March 1939): 4–6.

for the exotic and ritualistic thanks to the führer for broadening their horizons. Even when tourists let slip their awe at their "luxurious" accommodations, the higher purposes of travel preoccupied them, for the potential of tourism sites to encourage social mingling allowed KdF vacationers to affirm the regime's success in creating a "community."[97] Thus for Maria Forster, occupation unidentified, a cruise around the Italian peninsula fulfilled a long-time yearning to travel and the triumph over social barriers. "It is strange how quickly every mistrust fell," she exclaimed, "for it lasted only a few hours, and then what emerged was a great and trusting comradeship. . . . Here sits the factory worker next to the young office employee, the country woman next to the city woman. There are no differences."[98] The upending of normal social distinctions overwhelmed Else Dirks: the solicitude that her ship's captain and crew showed toward her, although she was neither a government minister nor the famous movie star, Greta Garbo, left her rapturous. Her enthusiasm for the royal treatment extended to her and to other passengers of equally modest background glided smoothly into expressions of national pride. "Nowhere does a German need to be ashamed any longer to be German. We have our freedom. We once again have our honor."[99]

For a Krupp ironworker, a cruise on the steamer *Oceana* also fulfilled a lifelong desire that he finally realized under National Socialism. From the departure of his train from Essen to his return to the same station, vacationers behaved more like a family than a collection of strangers, dancing together and sharing their food and drink. He praised the accommodations and food on board ship, noting that the allocation of the former encouraged a welcome democratization. He, after all, shared a cabin with a champion sprinter. The cruise allowed him to see sights that deepened his love for Germany and his faith in the current regime. Observing the yacht of an "American millionaire" in the Hamburg harbor, which he was told had a crew of 120 for six people, caused him to ask, "Will this woman with all her money be happier than we who are on this marvelous trip? I hardly think so." As for the English Channel and the Isle of Wight, he commented that "almighty Albion" was certainly beautiful,

97 "Mein größtes Erlebnis: Wer siegte im Berichtwettbewerb," NSG Kraft durch Freude, Gau Sachsen, *Monatsprogramm* (October 1936): 10–11, recorded the winners of such a contest. Of 600 entries, the "greatest experience" recorded by the majority of articles occurred during KdF trips. The social mixing that tourism has promoted, even if class boundaries are not overturned, is a prominent theme in the collection of essays, *Water, Leisure, and Culture: European Historical Perspectives*, eds. Susan C. Anderson and Bruce H. Tabb (Oxford and New York: Berg, 2002).

98 "Kameraden erleben Italien: Eine KdF.-Seefahrt "Rund um Italien" von Maria Forster, NSG Kraft durch Freude, Gau Mainfranken, *Kraft durch Freude*, no. 1 (January 1939): 1.

99 "obwohl ich kein Minister und keine Greta Garbo bin!", *Das grosse Urlauberschiff*, ed. Otto Paust (Berlin/Dresden: Wilhelm Lempert Verlag, 1936): 12–15.

but no place was as captivating and orderly as Germany. Lying in a deck chair, the ironworker recalled the words of the Social Democratic party "boss" and the first chancellor of the Weimar Republic, Philipp Scheidemann, who once promised workers tourism and automobiles. Yet only Hitler had come through.[100]

The Siemens worker, Maria Hohensee, one of nine Siemens employees from Berlin chosen for a three-week cruise to Lisbon and Madeira at company expense, found the exoticism of the sites she visited as central to the quality of vacationers' experience and to their perceptions of German distinctiveness. Visiting a foreign land strengthened the common identity among the ship's passengers; indeed so much so that regardless of what part of Germany they hailed from, passengers collectively experienced a national pride. When returning to the workplace, her account of her travels encouraged her coworkers to raise questions that reaffirmed the "otherness" of Portugal. "Did you toss coconuts to the apes?" her coworkers asked. "You're so brown," one probed as if to suggest that Maria herself had "gone native." If the bond with other passengers strengthened her Germanness, however, her gender sharpened her perceptions of difference. During a side tour on Madeira, one led by Ley and the German consul, who introduced the vacationers to local customs, Hohensee was amazed that unmarried women were not allowed on the streets unless accompanied by their mothers. In her eyes the Third Reich was not a repressive dictatorship; rather, it combined individual freedom and community.[101] For another Siemens worker, Herta Politz, who sailed to the same sites several years later, her ship the *Saint Louis* appeared to be a "floating hotel" with comfortable accommodations and fine food. Yet more than that, the ship's concerts, films, dances, poetry readings, and chess playing forged a genuine comradeship, which meeting German expatriates in Lisbon only strengthened.[102]

For those who averted their attention from the "real" purposes of KdF tourism – that is, those who wanted little more than amusement (a category of tourist that KdF tour organizers presumed existed) – KdF monthly programs settled for straightforward proscriptions that elevated collective regimentation over individual desires. Tourists were not to dress as though they were models in a fashion show, ridicule the customs and dress of others (especially other Germans), drink to excess, or disregard the

100 M. Christiansen, "Mit 'Kraft durch Freude' auf dem Dampfer 'Oceana' nach England," *Krupp: Zeitschrift der Kruppschen Werksgemeinschaft* 26, no. 19 (1 July 1935): 373, HA Krupp.

101 Maria Hohensee, "Erlebnisse auf den Madeira-fahrt," *Siemens-Mitteilungen*, no. 160 (April 1935): 68, SA.

102 "Was wir auf unserer Madeirafahrt beobachten und erleben konnten: zwei Siemens-Kameradinnen schildern ihre Eindruck auf dem Schiff in Lissabon und auf Madeira," *Siemens-Mitteilungen*, no. 172 (April 1936): 73–5, SA.

strict schedules of tour directors. "Attention work comrades" (*Arbeits-kameraden*) exhorted a voucher for a nine-day inland vacation. "Uncon-ditional obedience to the directions of the tour leader is required. He is responsible for the smooth functioning of the trip. Support him during the trip through discipline and comradeship." Those who failed in that task would be sent home immediately.[103] The inclination of some "partic-ipants" to purchase kitschy souvenirs, defined as objects constructed from artificial materials not native to the tourist site, received steady chastise-ment in monthly programs. While expecting tourists to put money aside for their vacations, especially spending money, they urged them to pur-chase worthwhile remembrances.[104] KdF tour organizers and police spies proved chronically suspicious of the behavior of young women, whom they repeatedly scrutinized for breaches in deportment, particularly in sex-ual conduct. Tourism, as KdF practiced it, thus conformed to the regime's modest and disciplined form of consumption in accord with its ethic of self-sacrifice and common purpose; one that repressed the sexual adven-turism that travel tended to unleash, especially travel to the warm, exotic climates of the south.[105] KdF's ability to keep the cost of tour packages low compared to commercial tourism by arranging lodging in private, or otherwise inexpensive, accommodations and negotiating low rail and bus fares conveniently dovetailed with the insistence of its spokesmen that workers did not need higher wages to enjoy an improved standard of living. Wage increases were unnecessary because workers could avail themselves of the "cultural property" of the nation and enjoy the sun, surf, and cruises at bargain rates.[106]

Nevertheless, for all its claims to seriousness and its opposition to com-mercialism, Strength through Joy monthly programs and tour brochures undermined or at least qualified them. Although at times containing ex-plicitly proscriptive messages against selfishness and social snobbery, such as the "Ten Commandments for KdF Vacation Travelers," other fea-tures softened them. Frequently published cartoons conveyed the fun that tourists would enjoy on their trips, which would lift the gloom of everyday life. Thus, the fictional "Müllers" intrepidly set out on their

---

103 Teilnehmerkarte für UF 82/39, NSG Kraft durch Freude, Gau Magdeburg-Anhalt, Abeteilung Reisen, Wandern und Urlaub.

104 Gauwart Max Klippel, "Kitsch!" NSG Kraft durch Freude, Gau Westfalen Nord, *Kraft durch Freude* 2, no. 6 (1939): 4.

105 On this subject, see Ian Littlewood, *Sultry Climates: Travel and Sex since the Grand Tour* (London: John Murray, 2001).

106 "Recht zur Freude: Deutsche Arbeiter fahren zur See," *Arbeitertum* 4, no. 5 (June 1934): 5–11; Gerhard Starcke, "Kraft durch Freude hebt den Lebensstandard unseres Volkes," *Arbeitertum* 5, no. 22 (15 February 1936): 3–4; "Der Weg zur Gemein-schaft," NSG Kraft durch Freude, Gau Mecklenburg-Lübeck, *Kraft durch Freude* 4 (April 1935): 5–6.

KdF ski trip, bundled to excess in their ski clothing, rather than staying home and complaining about the cold weather.[107] Much of the cartoon "fun" came at the expense of imaginary "hosts," whose exoticism encouraged caricature, satire, distortion, and blatant racism. Thus in one cartoon a "native" African chieftain, "Wahatupa," naked except for his loincloth, armed with a spear, and carrying a human bone addressed his tribe with a warning as a snake lay coiled in the background: "No one eats a KdF vacationer on my watch. We too have to show that we're cultured." Or, cartoons conveyed the exotic by reference to dangerous beasts, tamed by naïve, if intrepid, KdF tourists. "But Freddie," protested a wife to her horrified husband as she swung contentedly on a huge python draped over a tree bough, "you told me that giant snakes aren't poisonous!"[108]

KdF's advertisements proved equally dedicated to imparting the prospect of "fun" to its prospective clientele. Content initially to promote travel through small panoramic photos and extensive textual descriptions of what vacationers would see,[109] KdF periodicals increasingly resorted to the images propagated by commercial tourism to entice vacationers. Despite being mobilized for a government that promoted cultural and economic autarky, the techniques of mass advertising proved remarkably alluring and indicative of the power of transnational iconic images. Half- and full-page scenic panoramas, advertisements of young and healthy sun worshippers frolicking on the beach (see Figure 4.3) or shots of happy, well-groomed, and prosperous couples on the ski slopes, joyful and insouciant shuffleboard players aboard ship, and announcements of snapshot contests promised modern comforts and a break from daily routine, even as photos of workers on the shop floor beforehand conveyed the regime's emphasis on leisure as a means of raising productivity. Rising incomes brought about by economic recovery contributed to KdF's sophisticated sales pitches to an audience, whose expectations it gleaned partially from the customer satisfaction surveys that it distributed to tour participants.[110] Yet KdF's use of commercial advertising techniques revealed another irresistible benefit. Its choice of models for its brochures conformed to the regime's visions of what racially pure should look like.

---

107 "Was machen Müllers im Winter . . .?," NSG Kraft durch Freude, Gau Pommern, *Monatsprogramm* (January 1938): 12–13.
108 "Das Lacht der Urlauber," NSG Kraft durch Freude, Gau Süd Hannover-Braunschweig, *KdF Monatsprogramm*, June 1939.
109 NSG Kraft durch Freude, Gau Schwaben, *Jahres-Urlaubsprogramm 1935* (Berlin, 1935).
110 Report on Strength through Joy submitted by Hugh R. Wilson to Franklin Delano Roosevelt, August 1938, http://www.fdrlibrary. marist.edu/psf/box32/a301, 38. According to this report, vacationers were given postcards to return to the local KdF warden, which commented on the quality of their lodgings.

Fig. 4.3. Enjoying the Baltic beaches with KdF. Although KdF advertisements offered scenes of nature designed to induce contemplation, they increasingly depicted scenes of relaxation and pleasure.
Source: Die Deutsche Arbeitsfront. NS-Gemeinschaft "Kraft durch Freude," Gau Sachsen, *Urlaubsfahrten 1939*, 20. Author's collection.

The often flawless complexions, symmetrical and handsomely chiseled faces, and well-proportioned physiques of models were not the only striking feature of Strength through Joy's tour brochures.[111] The prominence of young, attractive, and apparently single women testified to KdF's attraction of and dependence on an important constituency, notwithstanding the concerns of tour directors and police as to their problematic behavior. Anything but the "Gretchen" stereotype attired in a dirndl, female models exuded the naturalness and freedom of the racially superior as they vacationed. Frequently depicted in pairs, packing for their trips, smiling from the window of their train compartments, or frolicking in the sand of the Baltic beaches, the models evidenced KdF's concession to the realities of female friendship that could thrive in the absence of male companionship. Always tastefully dressed, even when wearing bathing suits, they bespoke middle-class status in recognition of the female salaried employees who flocked to KdF tourism.[112] In keeping with the Nazi regime's artistic standards, which dictated that even nudes should avoid the suggestion of unrestrained sexuality,[113] KdF images eschewed sensuality even when revealing women in bathing suits, shorts, or short-sleeved blouses. Announcements of snapshot contests discouraged the submission of photos of human subjects, particularly women in alluring poses drawn from Hollywood films, recommending instead "natural" and unforced poses that radiated fitness, good health and controlled fecundity.[114] (See Figures 4.4 and 4.5.) In addition to demonstrating the physical characteristics of the racially acceptable, KdF's female models evoked a disciplined prosperity for a deserving nation.

On top of conveying good health, relaxation, and fun, KdF's advertisements and other promotions promised creature comforts beginning with those awaiting the production of the Volkswagen. By 1938, ads and articles encouraging workers to put money away for a "KdF Wagen" in their weekly savings plans emphasized not just the car's low cost, high gas mileage, ease of maintenance, and simplicity. They also stressed its speed and the comfort of its upholstery. One such article that depicted

---

111 A good example being a young, blond and contented couple lying in the sand, "Morgen in den Urlaub," NSG Kraft durch Freude, Gau Oberdonau (Berlin: Verlag der Deutschen Arbeitsfront, 1939), unpaginated.

112 NSG Kraft durch Freude, Gau Schwaben, *Dein Urlaub 1939* (Berlin, 1939); NSG Kraft durch Freude, Gau Essen, *Urlaub mit Kraft durch Freude 1939*; NSG Kraft durch Freude, Gau Sudetenland, *KdF-Urlaub 1939*; NSG Kraft durch Freude, Gau Süd-Hannover-Braunschweig, *KdF-Monatsheft*, August 1939. All unpaginated.

113 See George L. Mosse, "Beauty without Sensuality: The Exhibition *Entartete Kunst*," in *Degenerate Art: The Fate of the Avant-Garde in Nazi Germany* (New York: Henry N. Abrams, 1991): 25–31.

114 Such as the examples depicted in "Unsere Preisaufgabe: Wer will auf das Titelbild unserer KdF.-Monatsheft?," NSG Kraft durch Freude, Gau Düsseldorf, *KdF-Urlaub 1939: Die Jahresfahrten des Gaues Düsseldorf*: unpaginated.

Fig. 4.4. Young women set sail with KdF. Although two of the women shown here wear swimsuits, their poses avoid the suggestion of overt sexuality in keeping with the Third Reich's artistic rules.
Source: Reichamtsleitung Kraft durch Freude, *Unter dem Sonnenrad: Ein Buch von Kraft durch Freude* (Berlin: Verlag des Deutschen Arbeitsfront, 1938), 105. Courtesy of The Center for Research Libraries, Chicago.

Winterfreuden
in luftiger höhe

Fig. 4.5. On the ski slopes. KdF pioneered in arranging ski trips. In a practice that became increasingly typical for KdF, this brochure was pitched to young women.
Source: Die Deutsche Arbeitsfront. NS-Gemeinschaft "Kraft durch Freude," Gaudienststelle Bayerische Ostmark, *KdF – Urlaub 1938, 7* Author's collection.

well-dressed parents and their happy, well-adjusted children departing from their single-family home, combined comforting images of domesticity with modernity. "Papa" pulled the Volkswagen out of the garage, ready for a family outing, while his wife and children bounded out the door in eager anticipation. The second page of the article offered sequential images of a family picnic, a family admiring their car's engine, and a wholesome couple camping, their tent pitched next to their automotive prize.[115]

The advertising for Strength through Joy's new cruise ships, the *Wilhelm Gustloff* and *Robert Ley*, likewise betrayed KdF's inclination to convey luxury demonstrated by its literature's punctilious attention to detail. The *Wilhelm Gustloff*, named after the Nazi party leader in Switzerland whom a Jewish medical student assassinated in 1936, contained 2,500 square meters of deck space and featured a swimming pool, gymnasium, and a cinema. To eliminate the class delineations of other ships, the cabins of both ships were arranged along the open decks on the outside. Each contained separate sleeping quarters and living space complete with table, sofa, chair, and built-in wardrobes.[116] The *Robert Ley* possessed a two-story theater, 5,000 square meters of deck space, a gymnasium, swimming pool painted with mermaids riding atop frolicking dolphins, and cabins that at least equaled the *Wilhelm Gustloff* in comfort. Its dining room, consisting of attractively set tables for four, spoke for intimate conversation rather than mass travel.[117] Like the venerable luxury liner that catered to the wealthy, the *Ley* was to be the *Bremen* of the working class now available to "*Volk* comrades" (*Volksgenossen*) of modest means. In interviews with the press, Ley projected a fleet of twenty ships, as well as an enlarged harbor at Bremen complete with a hotel that would accommodate more than 3,000, a train station, a huge garage, and an entertainment center for tourists waiting to embark on their cruises.[118]

---

115 "Ein Traum wird Wirklichkeit mit dem KdF Wagen," NS-Gemeinschaft Kraft durch Freude, Gau Süd Hannover-Braunschweig, *KdF-Monatsheft* (July 1939), unpaginated; "Symbol einer neuen Lebenshaltung: Ein weiterer Schritt vorwärts: der KdF.-Wagen – Lebensstandard und Luxus," NS-Gemeinschaft Kraft durch Freude, Gau Halle-Merseburg *KdF-Monatsheft* (November 1938): 13.

116 "Eine Fahrt mit dem 'Gustloff:' Flaggschiff der deutschen KdF-Flotte, *Deutsche Weckruf*, 30 June, 1938; "Auf Wiedersehen im Salzkammergut: Eine unvergessliche Nordseefahrt für österreichische KdF-Fahrer," *Niedersächsiche Tageszeitung* 26/27 March 1938, both in NHH VVP 17, no. 2456; Marrenbach, *Fundamente des Sieges*, 358–60.

117 "Die Deutsche Arbeitsfront, NS-Gemeinschaft "Kraft durch Freude," Reichsamt "Reisen, Wandern und Urlaub," *KdF-Schiff "Robert Ley:" Die "Bremen" des deutschen Arbeiters*, IfZ, Db 72.12; Die Deutsche Arbeitsfront, NS-Gemeinschaft "Kraft durch Freude," Reichsamt Reisen, Wandern und Urlaub, "KdF-Schiff Robert Ley" (Berlin: Verlag der Deutschen Arbeitsfront, 1939).

118 "Der Bau von zwanzig KdF-Schiffen geplant. Vier grosse KdF-Bäder an der Ostsee-1940 mit KdF nach Tokio/Eine Unterredung mit Dr. Ley," *Hannoverscher Anzeiger*, NHH, VVP, no. 2426; Frommann, "Reisen mit Kraft durch Freude;" 193–9. The war

Fig. 4.6. An anonymous tourist's snapshots of the accommodations on the KdF ship, *Der Deutsche*. These were included in an album of a cruise to Norway. Author's collection.

The comfort fetish illustrated in such literature reflected KdF's sensitivity to the tastes of its clientele, whose photo albums often included snapshots and postcards of ship dining rooms, reading rooms, and decks, (See Figure 4.6.)[119] as did the modifications of some of the ships, notably the *Monte Olivia* and *Monte Sarmiento* that KdF had purchased from the major shipping lines. Whatever its skepticism toward "materialism" and commercialism, the Volkswagen and cruise liners testified to KdF's recognition that material comfort had become as important to KdF's clientele as "community."

> forced KdF to table the Bremen project. See Frommann again, "Reisen im Dienste," 284–9.

119   To wit the album of Erich Wagner, "Meine erste Seereise mit KdF nach Norwegen vom 29. Mai–5.Juni 1935," in possession of the author.

Fig. 4.7. The model for the KdF resort at Prora, on Rügen.
Source: Reichsamtsleitung Kraft durch Freude. *Unter dem Sonnenrad: Ein Buch von Kraft durch Freude* (Berlin: Verlag des Deutschen Arbeitsfront, 1938), 129. Courtesy of The Center for Research Libraries, Chicago.

Comfortable Functionalism and *Völkisch* Individualism: Strength through Joy's Resort at Prora

No Strength through Joy vacation project better illuminates the paradoxes that characterized Strength through Joy than its resort at Prora, the inlet between the resort towns of Sassnitz and Binz, on the Baltic island of Rügen that lay off the lower Pomeranian coast (See Figure 4.7.) Supervised by Albert Speer but promoted with near manic enthusiasm by Ley, the construction of the resort began on 3 May 1936 even before the final architectural drawings had been approved, and nearly three years to the day since the Nazi regime abolished the trade unions. Scheduled to open in the spring of 1940, the resort provided a spectacular example of Ley's resolve to surpass socialism as the true benefactor of workers. Rügen would become the best evidence yet of Nazism's "socialism of deed."[120]

The concept of Rügen, however, was not unique for its time. Capitalizing on the lure of beaches as places of relaxation, health, and spacial

---

120 The most significant works on the Rügen project are Jürgen Rostock and Franz Zadniček, *Paradiesruinen: Das KdF-Seebad der Zwanzigtausend auf Rügen* (Berlin: Ch. Links Verlag, 1995), and Hasso Spode, "Ein Seebad für Zwanzigtausend Volksgenossen: Zur Grammatik und Geschichte des Fordistischen Urlaubs," in *Reisekultur in Deutschland: Von der Weimarer Republik zum "Dritten Reich,"* ed. Peter J. Brenner (Tübingen: Max Niemeyer Verlag, 1997): 7–47. For the international context, see Löfgren, *On Holiday,* 240–59.

removal from daily routine that they had come to represent since the eighteenth century,[121] the resort conformed to a broader international trend that took hold during the interwar period: the construction of large seaside resorts that accommodated appropriately large numbers of vacationers, while offering sun, surf, and other forms of self-contained entertainment. Yet typically, Ley claimed that Rügen would not only outstrip its competition, it would also become the prototype for others. The Prora project was to be but the first of five such undertakings on the Baltic coast. KdF planned others for sites near Kiel, the upper Pomeranian town of Kolberg, the East Prussian capital of Königsberg, and the German enclave of Danzig. A replica was even discussed for the coast of Argentina, further evidence of fascism's international appeal as a solution to social conflict.[122] Moreover, Ley's resort building did not simply acknowledge the longstanding attraction of the Baltic coast as a leisure site. It also embraced the regime's assault on Versailles: that all resorts save for Kiel would arise in the culturally "endangered" German East, could not have been a mere coincidence.[123]

To be sure, the Strength through Joy resort, the epitome of vacations for the masses, bore a superficial resemblance to the popular holiday camps constructed during the same period by the colorful British amusement park entrepreneur, Billy Butlin.[124] Butlin's first camp at the Lincolnshire coastal town of Skegness opened the same year as the construction of Rügen began. The second in the Essex town of Clacton-on-Sea not far from London opened two years later to take advantage of the Holidays with Pay Act, which guaranteed a week's paid vacation for five out of six wage earners.[125] Similar to Butlin's holiday camps, the KdF resort planned to offer a weekly family vacation package for one low, all-inclusive fee. Yet if the population of Butlin's camps, which accommodated as many as ten thousand vacationers, placed his enterprise in a class by itself in the well-established British camping tradition, the Rügen project would outstrip Butlin by entertaining up to twenty thousand guests at one time. KdF and DAF publicists martialed hyperbole to highlight the uniqueness of their proposed vacation paradise: "The word 'KdF resort' has already become

121 See especially Corbin, *Lure of the Sea.*
122 "Erholungsurlaub für 14 Millionen deutsche Arbeiter: Das ist das Ziel von 'Kraft durch Freude,'" 3 March 1934, NHH, VVP 17, no. 2455. The Danzig resort was to have been smaller and less imposing, possibly because of intense local opposition: NSG Kraft durch Freude, Gau Danzig, *5 Jahre K.d.F. in Danzig, 1938:* 22.
123 In addition, KdF undertook the construction of smaller recreational "villages" along the Baltic. "Das erste KdF-Dorf ensteht," 23/24 1938, NHH, VVP 17, no. 2455.
124 See Colin Ward and Dennis Hardy, *Goodnight Campers! The History of the British Holiday Camp* (London and New York: Mansell Publishing Ltd., 1986), especially 57–68.
125 Ibid, 74; John K. Walton, *The British Seaside: Holidays and Resorts in the Twentieth Century* (Manchester and New York: Manchester University Press, 2000), 59.

a concept at home and abroad that binds the image of its construction's imposing size with the total novelty of its purpose."[126]

The enormity of the KdF resort, as well as the chauvinism behind it and the others on the drawing board, were not the only features to distinguish Ley's enterprise from Butlin's camps. Butlin and other British seaside resort entrepreneurs financed their operations with their own capital and that borrowed from commercial banks. Butlin in fact transformed his project into a public company with shareholders. The Rügen resort, on the other hand, exploited the dependable resources of the Labor Front and well-oiled party connections. Unlike Butlin, who aggressively lobbied town councils to permit the construction of his camps, overcoming fears of overtaxed infrastructures, environmental despoliation, and the suspected immorality of holiday-makers, the Labor Front purchased the land for the Prora project from a party comrade, Malte von Veltheim, Prince of Putbus. The scion of one of Pomerania's largest landowning families, the prince handed over property to Ley that had sat in a nature preserve. The transaction was so vaguely worded that the dimensions of Ley's acquisition were not clearly delineated. Nevertheless, the Putbus resources proved a timely answer to one of KdF's knottiest problems, its rivalry with commercial tourist interests and the refusal of established spas and their guests to accept Strength through Joy tour groups.[127]

Likewise, the selection of an architect conformed to party practice. Although Speer organized a competition among eleven well-known architects to arrive at a suitable design for the resort, Ley's personal and party connections ultimately took precedence. The "winner" of a competition, in which the selection was never in doubt, was Clemens Klotz of Cologne, an architect with a background in the German Werkbund. Klotz had made Ley's acquaintance during the twenties, when Ley was district leader of the Rhineland, through the mediation of an influential industrialist and former school friend. Although after 1945 Klotz claimed that his association with the Nazi party had been innocent of ideological motivation or commitment, the Rügen project was but one of many contributions to the architecture of the Third Reich. Benefiting from Ley's patronage as Reich organization leader and leader of the DAF, Klotz designed several office buildings, in addition to the Ordensburg Vogelsang in the Eifel region, one of several schools for the indoctrination of Hitler Youth and the SS modeled on the fortresses of the crusades and the German colonization of Slavic lands.[128]

126   Marrenbach, *Fundamente des Sieges*, 361.
127   Spode, "Seebad für zwanzigtausend Volksgenossen": 30–1.
128   Barbara Miller Lane, *Architecture and Politics in Germany, 1918–1945* (Cambridge, Massachusetts and London: Harvard University Press, 1985), 196–7. On Klotz's emergence, see Rostock and Zadniček, *Paradiesruinen*, 46–55.

Klotz's design for Rügen seemingly exemplified the domineering qualities of "authoritarian high modernism," now appropriated by an agency of the Nazi regime.[129] Most of the resort's structures adopted the steel and concrete functionalism that the Nazi regime employed in industrial buildings; so much so that Ley's enemy, the "blood and soil" anti-modernist ideologue Alfred Rosenberg, protested, claiming that Prora was nothing more than a soulless, urbanized "mass enterprise" (*Massenbetrieb*).[130] The placement of the project, moreover, made few concessions to the natural environment. Klotz slated the woods that occupied the space between the beach and the built environment for removal. In place of the history and distinctiveness of the local environment, he planned gardens that, however soothing and attractive, would not obstruct the panoramic views of the sea that vacationers would enjoy. The final version of the design, which Strength through Joy publicists touted as the most modern in the world, made a sufficiently favorable impression to win a grand prize at the 1937 Paris international exhibition, even though construction was still far from completion.[131] Yet the adjective "modernist" does not capture the specifically Nazi purposes behind the Rügen resort, even if "authoritarian" accompanies it. Rügen's industrial functionalism underscored specifically Nazi obsessions in a recreational site, the indivisibility of leisure and work and the use of respite to raise productivity, both of which were essential to rearmament.

As a site for raising the status of workers, Prora was to dominate the environment more completely than any grand hotel or resort for the upper crust. Its property extended nearly eight kilometers along the beach, with the physical structure occupying four and a half to five kilometers. All rooms in each six-storey residence hall faced the Baltic, while "community houses" spaced evenly between the residence halls extended down to the sea in order to break the monotony. In addition to featuring recreational facilities, the community houses contained dining rooms for regular meals and smaller cafés for light snacks. The workers and their families who comprised Rügen's target clientele would receive a week's vacation for a mere twenty marks, a price that included lodging, meals, and use of the resort's facilities. In so doing, Ley proposed to solve another of Strength through Joy's problems, the underrepresentation of workers with families. As one KdF spokesman, Werner Kahl, admitted belatedly, the Rügen

129   See James C. Scott, *Seeing Like a State: How Certain Schemes to Improve the Human Condition Have Failed* (New Haven and London: Yale University Press, 1998), especially 87–102. Although Scott focuses mainly on modernist projects that were intended to better the human condition, his apparent grounds for excluding Nazism, his analysis is to a point useful.

130   Spode, "Seebad für zwanzigtausend Volksgenossen," 32; Frommann, "Reisen im Dienste," 294.

131   Spode, "Seebad für zwanzigtausend Volksgenossen": 37.

resort and other KdF spas would "become the Eldorado of vacationing families with children, and therefore remedy a noticeable definicency in the KdF trips so far."[132] In further contrast to Butlin's holiday camps, where separate chalets provided a well-defined space for families or small groups, who were thus freed from the strict rules and nosiness of land-ladies who would otherwise have housed them, the accommodations at Prora suggested a blend of the barracks and assembly line. The small guestrooms, which had doors between them to permit access for fam-ilies occupying more than one room, were identical in size and lined, dormitory-like, along utilitarian hallways.

The focal point of the Rügen project, an enormous multipurpose hall, suggested the communitarian possibilities of seaside vacations. Located midway between the residence halls and community houses that fronted the beach, the building was designed to hold all 20,000 vacationers at once. Although envisioned as the site of art exhibits, musical and stage per-formances, the structure was to facilitate fascist-style spectacles. Parades, demonstrations, and other forms of live propaganda could be suitably accommodated. Given its explicitly political purposes, the neoclassical design of the structure, which departed from the functional architectural style of the resort as a whole, conformed to Speer's plans for the proposed reconstruction of Berlin: imperial architecture for the emerging German empire. The Rügen project thus embodied the imperial and militarized side of Strength through Joy's tourism, in which discipline and regimentation served as the organizing principles of working-class "leisure." Family va-cations for workers were not to be occasions for intimacy and privacy, or so it seemed. Rather, the resort would become a venue for creating loyal Germans, who would eagerly abjure their class identities and follow their führer without reservation.

Appearances aside, the KdF resort would not rely simply on regimenta-tion to sell itself to vacationers. Rather, the privilege of a seaside holiday would offer temporary social elevation and the experience of comfort. The island's prestige recommended itself as a prime venue for the display of Ley's ambition to break down the barriers of privilege by building on a site long associated with high social status; one that promised similar lev-els of comfort to KdF vacationers. During the first half of the nineteenth century, the Prussian monarchy contributed significantly to developing sea baths on Rügen. In addition to the well-heeled summer vacationers, who populated and made prosperous the villages beyond its dunes, the island became attractive to artists and musicians, among them Caspar David Friedrich and Johannes Brahms. The "Iron Chancellor" Otto von

---

132 Kahl, *deutsche Arbeiter reist!* (Berlin: Deutscher Verlag, 1940), 63. See also Spode, "Seebad" 30

Bismarck favored it as a vacation spot.[133] Unlike the innovative plans in the twenties for the Berlin "thermal palace" (*Thermenpalast*), which envisioned a spacious indoor beach and swimming area in the heart of the capital accessible to all at low cost, not to mention amenities such as free entertainment, a laundry, shoe repair, physiotherapy, and spa treatments, KdF's Rügen project would outdo the "Marxist" republic. It would entice workers to the beach and expose them to upper-class luxuries at little cost to themselves and their families.[134]

Matching Billy Butlin's claims as to the luxuriousness of his holiday camps, which he mobilized to counter their negative image as watering holes for the undiscerning masses,[135] KdF periodicals described Prora's unparalleled amenities, which would elevate it to the ranks of the spas of the elite.[136] Aside from the mammoth entertainment center, the resort would include a cinema, billiard rooms and bowling alleys, a parking garage for the KdF Wagens of workers, and a large panoramic restaurant sitting atop an eighty-five meter structure to support it. Rügen was to have two huge swimming pools, one of them enclosed and heated, which would allow the resort to be open from early spring to late fall. Measuring forty by one hundred meters, the indoor pool came fitted with a wave-making machine. A huge pier would permit KdF's cruise ships to dock there, while the resort's train station was constructed to handle up to three thousand workers and their families each day. Despite their modest size, each guestroom would come with hot and cold running water, built-in wardrobes, a table and chairs, and an upholstered sofa. In a still unusual practice for vacation hotels, rooms were to be centrally heated. Although Strength through Joy continued the practice that under the Weimar Republic had been the preserve of the left, constructing and operating smaller vacation hostels for workers, many of them in vernacular styles of architecture,[137] Prora vastly exceeded those getaways in scale and appointments.

The size of the project, however, forced Strength through Joy to assure its clientele that accommodating the masses still allowed room for vacationers and their families to satisfy their own recreational desires. Like

---

133 Corbin, *Lure of the Sea*, 180–1, 259; Klaus Granzow, *Pommern: Ein Bildband der Heimat mit 159 Fotografien*, 3rd ed. (Frankfurt: Verlag Weidlich, 1983), 23 and photo 141.

134 I have been unable to find any evidence that Rügen directly answered the "thermal palace," but it is unlikely that Rügen's planners were unaware of the project. See Gert Gröning and Joachim Wolschke-Bulmahn "The *Thermenpalast* (Thermal Palace): An Outstanding German Water-leisure Project from the 1920s," in *Water, Leisure, and Culture*, eds. Anderson and Tabb: 141–7.

135 Walton, *British Seaside*, 129.

136 For contemporary descriptions, see Kahl, *deutsche Arbeiter reist*, 60–3, and *Unter dem Sonnenrad*, 127–32.

137 "Das erste KdF-Dorf entsteht," 23/24 1938, NHH, VVP 17, no. 2455.

KdF's claims as to the comforts extended to tourists on its special trains,[138] its publications assured readers that they would have enough personal space. Each vacationer would claim fifteen square meters of beach to him or herself, not including space available in the woods behind the resort that stood ready for exploration or contemplation. The variety of entertainment would disperse vacationers to such a degree that no one would feel cramped or regimented.[139] Thus, far from being a straightforward example of modernism, or of a machine-like, "Fordist," mass tourism,[140] the built environment of the KdF Seebad Rügen more precisely reflected the paradoxes of the regime that sponsored it. It evoked sacrifice and abundance, personal pleasure and service to the nation, as well as the satisfaction of popular expectations and the claims of rearmament. For the Rügen project to have swallowed an initial outlay of 100 million marks and employed a construction crew to rival the autobahn project in its size vouched for Nazism's need to balance delayed with instant gratification.[141]

Strength through Joy's impressive number of tourists made it the Nazi regime's most popular social program. As KdF's nod to luxury and pleasure reveals, however, its success reflected KdF's willingess to allow its clientele to vacation on their own terms as much as on KdF's. Although not immune to its hyperventilated and militarized version of tourism, vacationers flocked to KdF because it increasingly promised comfort, individual choice, and outlets for fantasy. However paradoxical its dual messages of communitarianism and individualism, KdF reaped the dividend that it sought, the enhancement of the Third Reich's popular legitimacy. Its ability to exploit commercialism without succumbing to it finessed the regime's contradictory approach to the standard of living.

---

138 "Erfahrung mit KdF," NSG Kraft durch Freude, Gau Weser-Ems, *Kraft durch Freude* 3, no. 7 (July 1938): 20,
139 *Unter dem Sonnenrad*, 129–30.
140 This is Spode's argument in "Seebad für zwanzigtausend Volksgenossen."
141 Robert Ley, "Zwei Jahre 'Kraft durch Freude,'" in Ley, *Deutschland ist schöner geworden* (Munich: Franz Eher Verlag, 1942), 77.

5

Racial Community and Individual Desires: Tourism, the Standard of Living, and Popular Consent

Strength through Joy's endeavor to build the utopian racial community through tourism could not help but be modified in practice. Although serving a dictatorship that demanded conformity, KdF's sensitivity to public opinion acknowledged that Germany's well educated and relatively well off population, particularly in light of rising family incomes that the rearmament boom wrought, would assert its autonomy, seek opportunities for self-discovery, and expect material ease. Not surprisingly, KdF confronted less pleasant forms of tourist assertiveness, namely complaints about its services. Whether griping about the behavior of Nazi party "bosses" on tour or the quality of food, lodging, and entertainment, chafing at the regimentation to which vacationers were subjected, or consorting with members of their own class rather than joining the larger vacationing community, tourists complicated KdF's vision of collective harmony, not to mention the communalism that tourists themselves conveyed in their travelogues for KdF periodicals. Nevertheless, if implicitly a challenge to KdF's aims, the complaints of tourists did not undermine KdF's popular standing. Because KdF responded to the desires of its clientele more often than not, it deepened the Nazi regime's popular acceptance.

The staffs that promoted KdF's trips created mechanisms through which popular receptivity to the Nazi regime's larger message could be gauged and transmitted. Although a hierarchical organization that mimicked the leader principle, KdF's vitality and responsiveness depended on its volunteers at the district, county, and local levels. To construct tours that would appeal to their constituencies, KdF wardens staged photography contests and essay competitions, which although shoehorned into the discourse of the racial community, disseminated sincere and authentic observations. By 1936, however, KdF found another conduit for surveying its participants, the Gestapo and SD (Sicherheitsdienst or Security Service) agents who monitored them. Although charged with uncovering dissenters, SD and Gestapo agents, who within the expanding empire of the SS competed for the responsibility of monitoring opposition, proved at least as willing to convey the satisfaction, or lack of it, of tourists. And as participants on

KdF trips like the tourists they observed, SD and Gestapo agents acquired the most immediate access to the thoughts of vacationers, the expression of which was neither delayed nor mediated by KdF periodicals.

Mixing Business with Pleasure: Undercover Surveillance and Mediation

In March 1936, following an agreement between Ley and the Reich leader of the SS Heinrich Himmer, the DAF information office and KdF's director for Travel, Hiking, and Vacations Bodo Lafferentz requested that the SD provide undercover surveillance for KdF trips. Not only concerned by the presence of oppositional elements among the tourists, Lafferentz also feared illicit contacts in the hotels and inns along Germany's borders. He suspected that potentially dangerous exchanges could occur between workers and salaried employees from the armaments industry, and exiled leftists and foreign intelligence agents. That the KdF leadership distrusted workers reflected its fear that its incorporation of Socialist and Communist organizations after the Nazi takeover had not persuaded their members to abandon their previous commitments. Lafferentz in fact subsequently asked that informants observe the gamut of KdF leisure-time activities, not just tourism. Yet KdF's decision also paralleled the Nazi regime's radicalization during that year, which began with the reoccupation of the Rhineland, accelerated with the Spanish Civil War and Germany's rapprochement with Italy, and culminated in the institution of the Four-Year Plan.[1]

Despite the difficulties in providing agents with tour rosters in advance to insure the proper screening of dissidents before departure, the surveillance broadened in short order to include the KdF sea voyages. In addition to identifying suspect travelers in advance from tour registration lists, the Gestapo and SD agents traveled with the tours, disguising themselves as regular tourists or as assistant tour leaders. They were instructed to eavesdrop on conversations between tourists and third parties, be on guard against the distribution of illegal printed matter, and investigate the

---

1 The correspondence regarding the initiation of surveillance is found in the Bundesarchiv, Berlin-Lichterfelde (hereinafter cited as BAL), particularly in R58, nos. 943 and 944. Additional material on the monitoring of suspected communists is located in NS 5/IV, nos. 39, 53, 92, and 94, BAL. Cf. also Wolfhard Buchholz, "Die Nationalsozialistische Gemeinschaft 'Kraft durch Freude:' Freizeitgestaltung und Arbeiterschaft im Dritten Reich" (Diss.: Munich, 1976), 225–35; and Bruno Frommann, "Reisen im Dienste politischer Zielsetzungen: Arbeiter-Reisen und 'Kraft durch Freude'-Fahrten" (Diss.: Stuttgart, 1993), 250–58. On the international climate and the regime's radicalization, see Ian Kershaw, *Hitler 1936–1945: Nemesis* (New York and London: W.W. Norton, 2000), 1–60.

participation of tourists in anti-German demonstrations in foreign countries. To render their assignments manageable, agents were told not to concern themselves with the petty human weaknesses – drunkenness, illicit sex, and the like. And with good reason, for the small number of agents, at most two per trip, meant a limit to the information that they could be expected to glean from large KdF tour groups.[2]

Along with performing their professional obligations, the agents assumed another identity, that of tourists. In addition to dressing so as to blend in with other participants, which allowed them to circulate supposedly without detection, the terms of their employment combined business with pleasure. Given vacation leave to cover their time on tour, agents selected for surveillance duty possessed the requisite professional skills in the eyes of their superiors, and had proven themselves worthy of a respite by virtue of past performance. Their expenses, which included a per diem allowance for side trips and entertainment, were covered entirely. The wives of married agents were invited to accompany their husbands, all expenses paid.[3] As a consequence, the dual identities of agents unavoidably brought their regular engagement with the human frailties that they were supposed to overlook, often provoking them to assign a "political" significance to disturbances that might otherwise not have applied. Equally unavoidably, however, their reports included assessments of the quality of the trips and the degree of customer satisfaction. The surveillance reports thus reveal an acute sensitivity to the way in which the quality of accommodations, food, and side trips, the relations among the participants and their hosts, and even the weather affected KdF's goal of using tourism to realize the racial community. In addition to opening a window into the thoughts, attitudes, and behavior of KdF tourists, they also suggest that the agents in their dual roles as tourists and spies became the tourists' informal ombudsmen, who transmitted the desires of those they observed. Like the agent aboard an extended Mediterranean cruise, who reported of the "unforgettable impressions" that ancient Athens left with the passengers, the agents' observations borrowed from the discourses of tourism to discuss the impressions that KdF tourists derived from their trips.[4]

Obviously the surveillance reports exposed the exaggerations in Strength through Joy's claims to have achieved social harmony and

2 Abschrift 4 July 1936, BAL R58, no. 944,18. In order to facilitate the surveillance further, agents were assigned to trips where the risk of security breaches was greatest. See Buchholz, "Nationalsozialistische Gemeinschaft," 231–2.

3 RFSS Sicherheits-Dienst Nachrichten-Übermittlung an den SD-Führer des SS-Oberabschnitts West, Düsseldorf, 17 November, 1938, BAL R58, no. 944, 297.

4 Bericht des SS-Untersturmführers Prieb über die Teilnahme an der KdF. Auslandsfahrt nach Dalmatien, Griechenland mit dem Dampfer "Oceana" vom 6. bis 18. November 1936, BAL R58, no. 950, 284.

democratization through tourism. Although eager to describe the friendships that arose as well as the genuine appreciation for the opportunity to travel that participants often expressed, the agents described the petty tensions and disappointments that stemmed from regional conflict and social snobbery, the overweening sense of entitlement of Nazi party members, and the condescension that KdF vacationers received from commercial tourist establishments. Despite the ideological gulf that existed between the regime's agents and the left, their reports frequently agreed with the observations of the informants of Sopade and other underground leftist organizations, who surveyed KdF's impact on workers. Regardless, the comments of Gestapo and SD agents betrayed more than KdF's failures. They revealed how tourism sustained the regime's claims to have improved the quality of life.

The Quarrelsome Racial Community

The number of "participants" who joined Strength through Joy's tour groups, KdF's compensation practices, and the socially mixed character of its clientele spawned frequent conflicts between KdF tourists and commercial tourist establishments. Although KdF's share of the total number of overnight stays in German hotels generated by the German tourism industry as a whole never exceeded eleven percent, the intrusion of its tourists *en masse* in vacation sites previously unaccustomed to them seemed like an invasion of the hoi polloi. The dismay of regular vacationers, and particularly that of the businesses that catered to them, contributed to the Reich Tourism Association's campaign to confine KdF to destinations where it would not undermine established "private" leisure promoters. When KdF tourists descended on venerable resorts, the regular clientele abandoned them for quieter and more exclusive settings, voting with their feet against their perceived loss of exclusivity. Hoteliers and innkeepers were left to complain bitterly over losing their higher paying customers. That Strength through Joy tourists substituted for those who had departed satisfied them little, for KdF's rate of compensation to innkeepers and restaurants fell significantly below what such establishments could charge their "private" clientele.[5] Landlords and hoteliers, even in regions that needed the revenue from KdF tourism, refused tourists whom they found disruptive or otherwise unappealing. In the upper Bavarian town of Bernau, for example, a raft of complaints arose from tourism promoters against autobahn

5 *Deutschland-Berichte der Sozialdemokratischen Partei Deutschlands* (Frankfurt am Main: Verlag Petra Nettelbeck, 1980) (hereinafter cited as *Sopade*), September/October 1934, 526; July 1936, 883; February 1938, 166 and 169; April 1939, 472.

workers, most of them pressed into service from the ranks of the urban unemployed, whom KdF sent for recuperation.[6] Their alleged drunkenness, sexual promiscuity, propensity toward petty theft, filthy attire which according to innkeepers and pensioners soiled bedding and furniture, and their putative criminal records created dissension between landlords, local Nazi party authorities, and KdF officials.[7]

Wherever Strength through Joy and "private" tourists occupied the same facilities, grievances arising from perceived inequities in treatment poisoned the interactions between KdF "participants" and local tourism entrepreneurs. Disgruntled vacationers from Mecklenburg who visited Lake Constance carped about the disparities in the quality of food, accommodations, and hospitality that they received as opposed to that offered to the "private" guests.[8] Similarly, KdF travelers to Widmar near Ulm complained of the demeaning conduct of a waitress in a restaurant, who insulted a member of their group. When the tourist ordered wine with his meal, she sarcastically insinuated that he could not afford the sixty pfennigs that it cost. As a further affront, she demonstratively showered her attention on her "private" customers, while ignoring her KdF diners.[9]

Nor were those isolated examples. A Sopade infiltrator on a Strength through Joy trip to the Harz Mountains told of being denied fresh water for bathing on the grounds that his demand was unreasonable considering the meager price that KdF was paying. In the Bavarian Oberland an innkeeper, making clear his displeasure at being besieged by guests whom he considered unprofitable, served his "private" guests in their rooms while pouring lesser quality coffee to KdF guests.[10] A furor erupted in a small town, again in the Harz Mountains, when a restauranteur served his KdF customers a one-course dish (*Eintopfgericht*) to keep his costs in line with KdF's reimbursement for the meal. After witnessing more substantial repasts being served to the "private" guests, the KdF tourists vented their dissatisfaction. Showing the extent to which vacationers accepted the regime's communitarianism, they demanded that all "*Volk* comrades" should receive equal treatment. Yet, when the "private" guests refused to lower their standards to accommodate that sentiment, the innkeeper could

6   See Dan P. Silverman, *Hitler's Economy: Nazi Work Creation Programs, 1933–1936* (Cambridge, Massachusetts and London: Harvard University Press), 162–74, on the composition of autobahn workers.
7   Abschrift, Reichsautobahn/Oberste Bauleitung München an die Deutsche Arbeitsfront, N.S. Gemeinschaft Kraft durch Freude, 14 September 1935, Bayerisches Hauptstaatsarchiv, Munich (hereinafter cited as BHA), no. 2784; affidavit of Strafanstaltsbeamter Balleisen, 19 August 1935, BHA, no. 2784.
8   Bericht über die KdF.-Urlaubsreise des Gaues Mecklenburg vom. 30. Juli bis 7. August 1937 an den Bodensee, BAL R58, no. 609, 37.
9   Bericht über die K.d.F.-Urlaubsfahrt Nr. 32 v. 24 bis 30.7.39 nach Püssen i. Allg., BAL R58, no. 609. 179.
10   *Sopade*, February 1938, 169, 173.

find no other way to extricate himself from the row than to serve the KdF guests what they wanted.[11] Thus, if Strength through Joy intended to democratize tourism, defined as accessibility to wage earners, the conflicts between "private" tourism and KdF testify to the different status of KdF tourists compared to that of regular tourists.

In addition to the friction between commercial establishments and Strength through Joy, regional and religious tensions, whether between hosts and guests or among the tourists themselves, attracted the attention of SD and Gestapo agents. For all the plaudits in surveillance reports as to the "brotherly" or "comradely" relationships that developed among tourists from different districts, or the warmth that grew between tourists and those whom they met at their destinations,[12] police observers frequently conveyed a different story. Particularism not only threatened the putative "community" of KdF vacationers and its premise that Germans should get acquainted, it also endangered KdF's effort to integrate Germany's communities into a unified nation. Internally, religious discord emanating especially from Catholic enclaves created repeated occasions for discomfort. Although willing to commend the occasional nationalistic homily by priests from their pulpits, surveillance agents became attuned to the difficulties presented by KdF trips to Catholic regions, noting the refusal of locals to use the Hitler greeting or the preference for crucifixes and pictures of the Virgin rather than images of the führer. In 1936 and 1937, the escalation of discord between the regime and the Catholic hierarchy, including the Vatican, aggravated those concerns. The attack on primary schools that promoted religious exclusivity, the loud denunciation of the cultural power of the churches by Nazi neopagans, and the sham trials of priests for putative sexual offenses embittered Catholic populations.[13] Thus, KdF participants on trips to the Mosel region from the largely Protestant or unchurched cities of Berlin, Magedeburg, and

---

11   Bericht über die Lage in Deutschland, Nr. 16, July 1934, in *Bericht über die Lage in Deutschland: Die Meldungen der Gruppe Neu Beginnen aus dem Dritten Reich 1933– 1936*, ed. Bernd Stöver (Bonn: J.H.W. Dietz Nachfolger, 1996): 587.

12   Bericht über die von der NS-Gemeinschaft "Kraft durch Freude" Gau Sachsen vom 31. Juli bis 15. August 1939 durchgeführten Gaufahrt Nr. 290, BAL R58, no. 947, 20; Betr.: Überwachung der K.d.F.-Fahrt UF 52/39 vom 30.6.-6.7.39 im Schwarzwald, BAL R58, no. 947, 57–8.

13   Auswertungsnotiz aus beim Gestapa vorhandenen FMR-Berichten über KdF-Reisen. Zeit Frühjahr 1937 bis 10.10.1937, BAL R58, no. 943, 120; Bericht über die KdF-Reise UF 49 vom 26.2.39–12.3.39 des Gaues Berlin nach den Allgäu, BAL R58, no. 947, 6; Bericht über die Teilnahme an der KdF.-Urlauberfahrt Nr. 106 vom 19.5. bis 2.6.1939 nach Oberbayern, BAL no. 947, 203. For the conflict between the Nazi regime and the Catholic Church, see J. S. Conway, *The Nazi Persecution of the Churches* (London: Weidenfeld and Nicolson, 1968), Chs. 6 and 7; Ernst Helmreich, *The German Churches under Hitler: Background, Struggle, and Epilogue* (Detroit: Wayne State University Press, 1979), Ch. 14; and Guenther Lewy, *The Catholic Church and Nazi Germany* (New York, Toronto: McGraw Hill, 1964), Chs. 5 and 6.

Halle professed astonishment at the hostility of local Catholic residents. Catholic locals paid little attention to the closed formation of the Magdeburgers, for example, who marched into their midst from their train. Despite the appeal of the local KdF warden that the residents prominently display their swastika flags to greet their guests, few were to be seen. Whereas in many small towns, KdF visitations became the highlight of social calendars, Catholics often refused to attend the customary celebration on the evening before the tourists' departure. Appeals to the interests of the racial community resonated little among Catholics angered at the Nazi regime's ecclesiastical policies.[14]

Among KdF tourists themselves, participants frequently limited their social interactions to compatriots from their own regions, choosing the safety of the familiar over mixing with strangers. The organization of tours, in which KdF's district leaders collected vacationers referred by its subordinate offices, ironically fostered that tendency. Competition and contempt emerged as well, as indicated by the spats between tourists from the Palatinate, the Saar and Saxony on one cruise, and between Rhinelanders and Silesians on another. In the latter incident, a cruise to Italy on the steamship *Stuttgart*, tensions surfaced the very first day at sea when the Rhinelanders loudly criticized the deportment of the Silesians, escalating to the point where the two groups refused to remain in the same room with each other. The relative accord that developed between a few passengers from each district failed to dampen the antagonism of the majority.[15] A similar problem developed, also on the *Stuttgart*, during its voyage to Italy in early 1939. That little interaction occurred among passengers from different districts was troubling enough to the agent who submitted the report. Yet the confrontation between Westphalians and Silesians in the smoking salon, one not surprisingly fueled by alcohol, was more unsettling. Beginning with name-calling during which the Westphalians referred to the Silesians "Polacks" and "Polish pigs," the confrontation shifted to the Silesians' cabin, where an assault nearly took place that required the intervention of one of the ship's officers and several sailors.[16]

---

14 Auswertungsnotiz aus beim Gestapa vorhandenen VMR-Berichten über KdF-Reisen: Zeit Frühjahr 1937 bis 10.10.1937, BAL R58, no. 943, 120. On the local impact of KdF tourists, particularly in the Black Forest, see Kristin Semmens, "Domestic Tourism in the Third Reich (Dis.: University of Cambridge, 2002), 238–9.

15 Dienstreisebericht des Reisebegleiters über die KdF-Urlaubsfahrt mit Dampfer "Stuttgart" nach Italien vom 13.-25. November 1938, BAL R58, no. 950, 356; Bericht über die Rund um Italienfahrt v.1-12.12.1938 der KdF mit dem Schiff "Oceana," BAL R58, no. 950, 438.

16 KdF Frühlingsfahrt nach Italien, Tripolis und Madeira auf dem Dampfer "Stuttgart" vom 11.3 bis 30.3.39, BAL R58, no. 950, 588; Reisebericht über die Frühlingsfahrt nach Italien, Tripolis und Madeira der NS-Gemeinschaft "Kraft durch Freude" der Deutschen Arbeitsfront, 10.3.-31.3.1939, BAL R58, no. 950, 650.

Regional conflicts and misunderstandings occurred even in interactions in which the communal spirit was supposed to shine, according to KdF organizers and tour leaders. Despite KdF's attempts to capitalize on the annexation of Austria and the Sudetenland, resentments cropped up as Germans from the pre-1938 Reich (*Altreich*) and the new provinces intermingled. Sudeten Germans expressed their frustration with visiting Saxons, who took advantage of their higher wages to buy up cheap goods, get drunk on beer they considered inexpensive, and gobble up sweets that the local people themselves could not afford. In return, Sudeten Germans who visited Saxony carped endlessly about the higher prices they found in Germany, particularly in the train stations.[17] A comparable disgruntlement occurred among Austrians despite the boon to their rural economies that Strength through Joy tourists brought, similar to that enjoyed by disadvantaged localities in Germany. Revealing the ambivalence characteristic of "hosts," who deplore the disadvantages of tourism even as they recognize its benefits, Austrians complained of the increased noise and traffic and the propensity of Germans to buy up lower priced Austrian goods.[18]

The deportment of Nazi party members, already notorious for their ability to ferret out perquisites suitable to their *arriviste* status, aggravated the potential for resentment. Especially prominent on the cruises, KdF's most prestigious offerings, party members behaved in a manner that conformed seamlessly to stereotypes of the *nouveaux riches*, parading the kind of immodest consumption that the Nazi party once deplored. Not surprisingly, Sopade informants highlighted the ostentatious display, selfish appropriation of privilege, illicit sex, and alcohol abuse of party apparatchiks. All characterized a racially defined new "elite" celebrating the opportunities that the proliferating number of party offices had created unchecked by legal or political constraints. Nazi bosses, the Sopade reports insisted, occupied the best cabins on the most desirable trips, notably the Madeira cruise that was popularly referred to as the "bosses trip" (*Bonzenfahrt*). The "bosses" strode arrogantly on the promenade decks, showing off the expensive accoutrements of tourism, including Leika cameras. Their wives, when they joined their husbands, adorned themselves with fine furs and jewelry. Single or otherwise unaccompanied Nazi party officials caroused into the wee hours of the morning while availing themselves of yet another benefit of KdF cruises, the single women who sailed on them. According to one witty working-class passenger aboard the *St. Louis*, destination unknown, party officials who on

17 Bericht: Betrifft: KdF.-Fahrt Nr. 207 des Gaues Sudentenland von Aussig nach Cuxhaven in der Zeit vom 30.6. bis 10. 7. 39, BAL R58, no. 947, 127 and 130.
18 Evan Bukey, *Hitler's Austria: Popular Sentiment in the Nazi Era 1938–1945* (Chapel Hill and London: University of North Carolina Press, 2000), 124–5.

this occasion did not bring their spouses had the "welcome opportunity, beyond the reach of their wives, to relieve themselves of the stress of their difficult official duties. Each of them can bring home a little intimate experience for which he can thank the führer, who also satisfies the sexual fantasies of his faithful followers in this manner."[19]

A frequent traveler on KdF cruises, Robert Ley exceeded the already low standards of Nazi party deportment, violating his own pious admonitions that tourists should forego hedonism.[20] According to the *Time–Life* journalist, William Bayles, whom Strength through Joy invited on a cruise so that he could convey to an American audience the beneficence of Nazi social policy, Ley's raucousness, drunkenness, and debauchery undermined the message the reporter was supposed to absorb. Upon first meeting the Labor Front leader in a cabin redolent with the stench of alcohol, smoke, sweat, and wurst, Bayles found his host drunk, disheveled, and bloody from having cut his hand with a broken bottle. After sweeping glasses and bottles onto the floor to offer his guest a seat, he clumsily poured wine into Bayles' lap instead of into a glass. "Send the captain down to meet Mister Americano [sic]," bellowed Ley to a steward, hurridly atoning for his gaffe. Bayles later observed that the captain, whose demeanor betrayed a muted anguish, had to flank Ley with sailors to ensure that he did not fall overboard. Whether drunk or hung over, Ley surrounded himself with representatives from the professions and several industries, as well as a contingent of blond, blue-eyed Nordic women, employed in offices and factories, whom KdF wardens commandeered to provide "companionship." Justifying their presence, Ley informed Bayles that although workers should have the right worldview (*Weltanschauung*) and the proper National Socialist outlook, "we don't regard a bit of love as unhealthy."[21]

If less vehement in their expression than the Socialists, the misbehavior of party office holders proved objectionable enough to arouse the criticism of the Gestapo and SD agents. Paid and volunteer party workers availed themselves of the longer and more expensive trips to the point where the passenger lists of some cruises, as many agents recognized, contained 60 to 70 percent party members. To add insult to injury, those selected for such an honor traveled courtesy of drastically discounted package prices.[22] Complained one operative aboard a cruise through

---

19   The quotation is found in *Sopade*, July 1936, 882. See also *Sopade*, July 1936, 885; February 1938, 171; and April 1939, 477.

20   See Chapter 4, 143.

21   William D. Bayles, *Caesars in Goosestep* (New York and London: Harper & Brothers, 1940), 176–9.

22   Dienstreisebericht no. 5/39 des SS-Unterscharführers Hänsch: Überwachung der KdF-Fahrt "Rund um Italien," 2.1.-14.1.1939, BAL R58, no. 950, 513.

the Norwegian fjords, Labor Front functionaries in the company of an industrialist and his wife appropriated the one-time first-class cabins on the promenade deck for themselves, while older people with fewer connections were relegated to less desirable quarters.[23] The participation of Hitler's personal physician, Karl Brandt, on a cruise to Italy, Greece, and Yugoslavia in late 1938 provided an egregious example of the exercise of party privilege. Accompanied by his wife and the wife of Jakob Werlin, the director of Volkswagen, Brandt and his group separated themselves from other tourists from the first day on board. At meals, they insisted on dining at the best table, demanding priority service from waiters, and capturing the undivided attention of the captain and his crew. "Likewise one saw the captain and the officers only with this group of people," noted the agent, "so that one cannot spare the captain from reproach that he hardly bothered to attend to the well being of other vacationers." Brandt's presumption of entitlement extended as well to the trips on land where he commandeered private autos. "That this kind of preferential treatment on a KdF ship contributed nothing to elevating the mood of the vacationers is understandable," complained the reporter.[24] If Strength through Joy intended to transform tourism into an entitlement for workers, the inflation of privilege for the epigones of the dictatorship that sponsored it became one of its most visible outcomes.

Of all the sources of conflict, however, class tensions emerged in surveillance reports as the most numerous. Consistent with class-defined patterns of consumption then in place, the desire to preserve social distinction often defined the interactions among tourists despite the rapturous first-person accounts in KdF and company periodicals as to the togetherness that KdF's heterogenous constituency forged. Class discord assumed a prominent place in Sopade accounts of KdF trips for obvious reasons. Having viewed the Nazi dictatorship from the outset as the product of the *haute bourgeois* campaign to break the back of the working class, Sopade informants highlighted KdF's failures to deliver what it promised, especially the underrepresentation of workers at KdF-staged concerts and on the longer vacation trips.[25] When workers did participate, usually as members of employer-subsidized groups, Sopade informants noted the disadvantages that workers suffered, less desirable accommodations, and the inability to afford the extras that other tourists had at their disposal. According to one undercover operative, workers complained of being crammed with

23 Norwegenfahrt der NS-Gemeinschaft "Kraft durch Freude," Gau Mgd./Anh. Mit dem KdF-Dampfer "Der Deutsche" vom 2.-8.39, BAL R58, no. 948, 127–9.
24 Bericht über die KdF-Fahrt Italien, Griechenland, Jugoslawien vom 19.11. bis 29.11. 1938, BAL R58, no. 950, 314.
25 *Sopade* agents complained that the well dressed and well heeled got the better seats at concerts, plays, and operas. See for example *Sopade*, April 1939, 467–8.

eighteen others in quarters located in the bow of his ship, a cabin without a single locker for their belongings and bunks that resembled iron military cots. Another highlighted the disparities in access to a lively commerce that took place on a cruise to Denmark that involved the sale of foreign goods, including Danish butter which the ship's crew had procured while ashore. Because of price inflation, workers were excluded.[26]

Yet SD and Gestapo agents had their own reasons for finding such signs disturbing. Nazism's answer to class conflict in the racial community, they feared, could not long withstand social divisions, an indication of the regime's acute sensitivity to local identities that repression could not eradicate. Despite the appearance of equality in the masses of travelers departing on trains and ships, distinctions permeated the social behavior of tourists, be they in the expectations that vacationers expressed or in the interactions, or lack thereof, among them. Thus, regardless of the unhappiness of "lesser earning" tourists with the poor quality of service that they received, well-off travelers tended to complain more vocally than workers, a sign of their greater sense of entitlement.[27] For many workers, participating in one of KdF's cruises represented an intimidating luxury. As one agent reported, the "simple workers" who boarded the *Wilhelm Gustloff* for a cruise to Italy were so unaccustomed to the kind of furnishings that decorated the ship's numerous common rooms that they did not feel at home for the first few days at sea. "German workers simply could not imagine that all these rooms were at their disposal," explained the agent.[28] Another reporter's suggestion that workers learned to relax in their new surroundings did not apply to the older retrofitted cruise ships, notwithstanding Strength through Joy's propaganda to the contrary. The *Stuttgart*, the ship most frequently cited for passenger conflicts of various sorts, retained enough of its earlier spatial segregation by class to reproduce the occupational divisions of vacationers, which the passengers had no difficulty perceiving. Civil servants occupied the best cabins while workers found themselves lodged in the worst accommodations, which did not even have running water. White-collar workers resided in cabins previously designated as second class.[29]

The condescension toward workers, or at best distant politeness, of middle-class vacationers, bothered agents who had hoped that travel would produce a community so strong as to dissipate class inhibitions.

26 *Sopade*, December 1935, 1461; and April 1939, 475–6.
27 Bericht über die über führungsfahrt des KdF-Dampfers "Oceana" nach Italien des SS-Untersturmführers Boecker, undated, BAL R58, no. 950, 86–92.
28 Reisebericht über die Italienfahrt der Wilhelm Gustloff vom 7. bis zum 19.12.39, BAL R58, no. 950, p. 454.
29 Dienstreisebericht des Reisebegleiters über die KdF-Urlaubsfahrt mit Dampfer "Stuttgart" nach Italien vom 13.-25. November 1938, BAL, no. 950, 355.

Especially on the cruises, long days at sea, bad weather, and the prohibition against disembarkation in the evenings, and the less-than-pleasant sleeping accommodations produced "cabin fever" that increased the prospects for conflict. Even the sympathetic account of his cruise to Madeira by the Swiss poet Jakob Schaffner admitted that his ship the *St. Louis* would not rival a luxury liner for comfort.[30] Nevertheless, better conditions did not necessarily reduce the friction among tourists whose social provenance was easy to discern and reinforce. On a tour to Italy in 1937 composed of tourists from East Prussia and Danzig, comfortably situated middle-class tourists behaved so arrogantly that the "lesser earning" travelers resorted to boozing to excess and other objectionable practices.[31] Although workers donned the bourgeois attire of ties and jackets in the seemingly casual setting of a ship's deck, other signs of their class arose to give them away: their discomfort at their surroundings, the roughness of their hands, or their speech. The effort that KdF expended to "civilize" them, even lending them leather luggage and cameras, could not conceal their class origins, Ley's claims to the contrary.[32]

Converging with the observations of Sopade spies, the SD and Gestapo reports underscored the social consequences of KdF's tours, the seeming comprehensiveness of which belied the hidden costs that were not included in the package price. Especially on the cruises that entailed sightseeing trips on land and entertainment aboard ship, tourists faced numerous "extras" not included in the original purchase price. Middle-class travelers, many of them repeaters who had found it easy to save for their trips, availed themselves of side excursions and souvenirs on shore, and even better accommodations on land. One agent on a cruise to Italy in early 1938 succinctly described the limitations that confronted workers. Small groups began to take shape after the ship docked at Naples, he observed. On board ship workers increasingly retreated to the halls while other passengers congregated in the dining room. As the ship proceeded to Venice, workers did not take in the Greek coast, Dalmatia, or Corfu, opting instead for remaining behind to play skat.[33] Their employers' subsidies, the very means by which most workers who traveled with KdF could take a vacation trip, no doubt contributed to their segregation. The

30   VMR-Reisebericht über die Teilnahme des SS-Untersturmführer Blank an der 3. KdF-Italienreise mit dem Dampfer "Der Deutsche," vom 25.XI. bis 5.XII. 1937, BAL R58, no. 950, 123; Jakob Schaffner, *Volk zu Schiff: Zwei Seefahrten mit der "KdF"-Hochseeflotte* (Hamburg: Hanseatische Verlagsanstalt, 1936), 21.
31   VMR-Bericht über die KdF-Italienfahrt vom 19.-29.12.37 mit D. "Oceana" der Gaue Ostpreußen und Danzig, BAL R58, no. 950, 164.
32   "Unsere KdF-Schrank," *Schönheit der Arbeit* 3, no. 1 (May 1938): 2.
33   Bericht über die KdF-Reise v. 30.12.37–11.1.38 nach Italien, BAL R58, no. 950, 184–6; VMR-Bericht über die KdF-Italienfahrt vom 19.29.12.37 mit D. "Oceana" der Gaue Ostpreußen und Danzig, BAL R58, no. 950, 164.

company tours reinforced the tendency of employees to associate with those with whom they felt most comfortable, which classified them as the beneficiaries of the charity, and guaranteed their inferior treatment. On a trip from Cologne to the Mosel, for example, workers whom their firm had supported were lodged in a different location from the other KdF vacationers, much to the detriment of the workers' morale.[34] Similarly, on a KdF trip to the Baltic resorts, the solicitude that was accorded to the better off participants inflamed the resentment of those who lacked the means to preferential treatment. Reported the SD agent accompanying the outing, "vacationers of lesser means didn't feel at home in the better spas of Brunshaupten and Wustrow, exclaiming that this was their first and last KdF vacation trip."[35] His comment suggests that in addition to the resistance of the Reich Tourism Association, the discomfort of Strength through Joy's own clientele might well have contributed to KdF's decision to send its tourists to less frequented locales.

Concerns about class divisions colored the perceptions of agents regarding the participation of women. Despite KdF's advertisements that catered to the emancipatory desires of young women, the troublesome behavior of females threatened to destabilize the KdF "community" in official eyes. Women became the physical objects of surveillance, but also a discourse, in which official anxieties spoke to the regime's ambivalence toward consumption and its condemnations of materialism. Gendered assumptions as to the irrationality, frivolousness, and self-absorption of women yielded the view that female travelers could not grasp the real purposes of KdF tourism, especially young and single women who traveled without a husband or chaperone. The conspicuous consumption of middle-class women, who had the financial resources to break free of KdF's painfully constructed egalitarianism, drew much official attention. Among tourists in a trip to Fehmann in Schleswig-Holstein, women stood out, in the perceptions of the participating agent, among those who went out of their way to disassociate themselves from the rest of the group. They ostentatiously paid higher prices for better accommodations in order to advertise their status.[36] Moreover, female dress became a weapon in the class warfare that Strength through Joy sought to undermine, particularly on the cruises where evening dances, costume parties, and other kinds of entertainment offered opportunities for self-display for those who could afford it. "A group of female passengers showed a taste for the sort of jewelry and attire," according to an agent, "which cannot be considered

34 Auswertungsnotiz aus beim Gestapa vorhandenen VMR-Berichten über KdF-Reisen: Zeit Frühjahr 1937 bis 10.10.1937, BAL R58, no. 943, 123.
35 Bericht, KdF-Fahrt des DAF Gaues Koblenz-Trier nach den Ostseebädern, 13.8. bis 28.8, BAL R58, no. 609, 249.
36 Auswertungsnotiz aus beim Gestapa vorhandenen VMR-Berichten über KdF-Reisen: Zeit Frühjahr 1937 bis 10.10.1937, BAL R58, no. 943, 121.

appropriate for a KdF vacation trip."[37] That workers were so ill at ease on the *Wilhelm Gustloff* resulted mainly as the consequence of women who appeared at evening fests in such captivating garb that the workers did not at first dare to venture into the "community rooms."[38] The middle-class practice of designating women to display family status and social distinction through consumption competed with KdF's desire to use tourism to transcend class divisions.

The Purchase of Consent: The Standard of Living and the Perceptions of German Tourists

Despite the dissension, social divisions, and the abuses of power on Strength through Joy vacation trips, KdF enjoyed a favorable popular reception, as testified by the number of Germans who participated in its activities, tourism especially. Forbearing and even satisfaction in the face of KdF's spartan accommodations arose at least as often as griping, as a staff member in the American embassy in Berlin observed during a weekend trip to Helgoland in the summer of 1938. While commenting on the strenuousness of the adventure, especially the long train and boat trips to and from the destination and the brief time actually spent on the island, the American nonetheless concluded on the basis of his conversations with the participants that all enjoyed themselves.[39] Even the Nazi regime's detractors at home could not ignore Strength through Joy's allure, as the memoirs of the writer and journalist Bernd Englemann testify. The scion of a liberal family, Engelmann recalled Nazism's ability to complicate the political views of his elders, some of whom availed themselves of the regime's social "achievements." Thus, until informed by an acquaintance that war was on the horizon, which forced a disappointing postponement in their plans, an aunt and uncle treasured their "hard to obtain" tickets for a cruise on the *Wilhelm Gustloff*, looking forward to their trip on a "beautiful ship" in celebration of their silver wedding anniversary.[40] How specifically did such pleasure, which Engelmann's relatives were not alone

---

37 Reisebericht über die "Frühlingsfahrt nach Italien, Tripolis und Madeira" der NS-Gemeinschaft "Kraft durch Freude" der Deutschen Arbeitsfront (Reichamt für Reisen, Wandern und Urlaub) mit Dampfer Stuttgart, vom 10.3.31.3.1939, BAL R58, no. 950, 649.

38 Reisebericht über die Italienfahrt der Wilhelm Gustloff vom 7. bis 19.12.38, BAL R58, no. 950, 455.

39 Report on Strength through Joy submitted to President Franklin D. Roosevelt, August 11, 1938 by Hugh R. Wilson, Ambassador to Germany, 38–43, Germany: Hugh R. Wilson: March–November 1938, http://www.fdrlibrary.marist.edu/psf/box32/folo301.html.

40 Bernt Englemann, *In Hitler's Germany: Everyday Life in the Third Reich*, trans. Krishna Wilson (New York: Pantheon Books, 1986), 159.

in sharing and the American embassy official was not alone in discerning, encourage support for the Nazi regime? What value did KdF tourists derive from their experiences and how did they associate it with the state that governed them? What connections did they draw between Nazism's "achievements" and its terrorism against those many, who were excluded from the national community?

Strength through Joy's appeal worked in two complementary directions. First, the pleasure seeking, self-exploration, and individualism characteristic of modern consumer cultures, to which KdF trips gave expression, encouraged KdF's participants to evaluate the Third Reich as successful because it produced memorable experiences. Comparable to the organized leisure in Fascist Italy, the leisure program of the Third Reich could not force its clientele to conform, and thus the disciplined, noncommercial consumption that Strength through Joy claimed to represent coexisted with commercial imagery, more frequent promises of "luxury," and the tacit acceptance of pleasure-seeking individualism.[41] Yet the obstreperousness of KdF's consumers hardly precluded broader political judgments regarding the Nazi regime's effectiveness. The images of smiling tourists traveling to previously inaccessible places became a metaphor for the regime's "achievements" in other areas, the restoration of "order," the improved economy, and the reconstruction of German diplomatic and military stature. Together, Nazism's successes encouraged the majority of Germans, whom the regime's terror did not directly affect, to appreciate the Third Reich's "socialism of deed."[42] Building on the regime's

41 For an understanding of market-based consumer cultures in general, and the uneasy relationship between Fascism and consumption in particular, the work of Victoria de Grazia is essential. In addition to *The Culture of Consent: Mass Organization of Leisure in Fascist Italy* (Cambridge and New York, 1981), see *How Fascism Ruled Women: Italy, 1922–1945* (Berkeley, Los Angeles, Oxford: University of California Press, 1992); and *The Sex of Things: Gender and Consumption in Historical Perspective*, ed. Victoria de Grazia and Ellen Furlough (Berkeley and Los Angeles: University of California Press, 1996). The manner in which KdF exploited consumer individualism, its intentions to the contrary, challenges recent attempts to restore "totalitarianism" to discussions on Nazi Germany, especially Michael Burleigh's *The Third Reich: A New History* (New York: Hill and Wang, 2000). To be sure, KdF was intrusive as was the regime that sponsored it, but tourists' desire to have fun while resisting KdF's attempts to discipline them suggests that the regime's partial capitulation to less easily politicized popular desires contributed to its legitimacy.

42 Especially after the Wehrmacht's defeat at Stalingrad, the regime became increasingly draconian in its punishment of "defeatism." Until then, the repression was far less intrusive to most Germans than it was for Nazism's enemies. The relative lack of attention to consumption as an explanation for the regime's staying power is evident even in the most recent scholarship. See Robert Gellately's *Backing Hitler: Consent and Coercion in Nazi Germany* (Oxford: Oxford University Press, 2001), which explores the degree to which the regime's repression won widespread popular backing. For further references and an excellent discussion of the debate on popular attitudes, see Ian Kershaw, *The Nazi Dictatorship: Problems and Perspectives of Interpretation*, 4th ed. (London: Edward Arnold, 2000), Ch. 8.

conception of the racial community, the "inclusiveness" of which depended on the identification, exclusion, and elimination of outcasts, KdF's tourism and leisure-time activities reinforced the segregation between the regime's victims and racially and politically acceptable Germans.

Second, even though its participants valued the goods and services that they purchased as much as the loftier purposes of tourism, including the photos and souvenirs that freshened memories of their "unforgettable experiences," Strength through Joy convinced most that the Nazi regime had indeed improved their well being. Unlike the Weimar Republic with its hardships, the Third Reich produced economic recovery, full employment, increased purchasing power, and the belief that a more prosperous future was at hand, however much the regime acted to curtail consumer demand. Furthermore, in contrast to Weimar tourism, in which commercial travel still catered to class-specific markets, KdF's package tours gave flesh and blood to the imagined racial community by reaching across class lines for their tourist consumers. Especially Strength through Joy's cruises, which in most cases sailed to ports where the standard of living *was* lower, intensified preexisting prejudices by linking participants' conceptions of racial hierarchy with their perceptions of the standard of living in other nations. In so doing, the tensions that arose among passengers while on board ship dissipated in light of the perceptions of foreigners that tourists held in common. Thus, the entertainment that KdF provided was no mere "beautiful illusion," a Wagnerian "total work of art" (*Gesamtkunstwerk*) that the regime staged to deceive a population that wanted to be deceived.[43] Rather, its touristic spectacles encouraged its participants to see a cause-and-effect relationship between their own well being and the Nazi regime's attempts to remake Germans into the master race. Moreover, despite the small number of cruise tourists relative to the total number of KdF travelers, their experiences had a wider impact precisely because they embodied and enacted the dreams, desires, and imaginings characteristics of an incipient consumer culture.

Strength through Joy tourists exploited their opportunities for self-expression, ignoring in the process the attempts of tour directors to regiment them, much less the misgivings of surveillance agents. Conforming to the muted and explicit messages of KdF periodicals, they sought release, personal enjoyment, and fun. Despite the strict currency regulations that prohibited tourists from exporting cash reserves that were essential to rearmament – regulations that forced vacationers to purchase their tickets with Reichsmarks and then exchange their marks for local currency before disembarking – travelers smuggled goods purchased abroad and

43   See Peter Reichel, in *Der schöne Schein des Dritten Reiches: Faszination und Gewalt des Faschismus* (Frankfurt am Main: Fischer Taschenbuch Verlag, 1996).

crossed borders without authorization to buy souvenirs, send a postcard with a foreign stamp on it, or even look up a relative.[44] They reveled in trafficking goods with locals such as the tourists on shore in Genoa, who in addition to swapping cigarettes for souvenirs spent German silver coins for Italian jewelry, to the dismay of the SD agent who monitored them.[45]

The behavior that vacationers indulged in, especially aboard ships or steamers, challenged or ignored norms of conduct that otherwise prevailed. After leaving port, the ships gave free rein to behavioral transgressions that were by no means confined to Nazi "bosses." Thus, the Rhine River trip for the 1,200 employees of the Edel Steel Works in Uerdingen, in which the participants consumed alcohol to excess as they cruised down river, resulted in an orgy of destruction to the steamer, the costs for which the firm had to absorb.[46] Although transgressive behavior is at least as firmly embedded in tourism and vacationing as intellectual or personal exploration,[47] *Sopade* informants tended to understand it as typical of Strength through Joy. "Those who have not been sufficiently educated in the collectivism that is so beloved today perhaps feel themselves affected in the course of enjoying their vacation by the excessively uninhibited vitality of some of their fellow travelers, which for example occasionally leads to open sexual liaisons on deck and in the lifeboats."[48] Similarly, SD and Gestapo agents deplored the abuse of alcohol that KdF's cruises encouraged. Thus according to the critical observer of a cruise to Italy in 1937 on the steamer *Der Deutsche*, passengers resorted to drink to relieve the tedium of days at sea in close quarters, which in egregious cases resulted in assaults against the women and girls on board.[49] The same agent argued, however, that KdF's regimentation was counterproductive. Whereas travelers "hungry for experience" sought the freedom to explore

---

44   Evidence of this is scattered in the reports of a number of KdF trips included in the Auswertungsnotiz aus beim Gestapa vorhandenen VMR-Berichten über KdF-Reisen: Zeit Frühjahr 1937 bis 10.10.1937, BAL R58, no. 943, 115–25.

45   Bericht über die K.d.F.- Seereise mit Dampfer Oceana vom 24. Januar 1938 bis 5. Februar 1939 von Genua über Neapel, Palermo und Venedig mit K.d.F.-Urlaubern, BAL R58, no. 942, 26.

46   Bericht über die Lage in Deutschland, Nr. 19/20, Januar/Februar 1936, in Stöver, *Berichte*, 680–1.

47   See in particular, Ian Littlewood, *Sultry Climates: Travel and Sex since the Grand Tour* (London: John Murray, 2001); and John Walton, *The British Seaside: Holidays and Resorts in the Twentieth Century* (Manchester and New York: Manchester University Press, 2000), especially 3–6. Walton has effectively applied the anthropological concept of "liminality" to his scholarship on resorts.

48   *Sopade*, September/October 1934, 524.

49   VMR-Reisebericht über die Teilnahme des SS-U.'stuf. Blank an der 3. KdF-Italienreise mit dem Dampfer "Der Deutsche," vom 25. XI. bis 5. XII. 1937, BAL R58, no. 950, 123.

new surroundings, KdF's tour directors marched them around in military fashion from "morning to evening," pushing them from one site to another "at the same rushed tempo." Their restiveness at such treatment did not wait long to surface.[50]

The disinterest in politics proved almost as troubling to the regime's spies as breaches in deportment. Although partisans purchased available newspapers, such as the *Schwarze Korps* and the *Illustrierte Beobachter*, according to a Gestapo agent on a Norwegian cruise in July 1936, the "better situated" passengers avoided them. "Don't bother me with politics," snapped one middle-class tourist. "I don't want to have anything to do with them."[51] To be sure, engaged political discussions among tourists that encouraged criticism of the regime could be problematic. The institution of surveillance in the first place arose from the assumption that opponents of the regime would use KdF trips for their nefarious purposes. Thus on a cruise to Italy in 1938, one in which a large number of workers participated, negative comments about the "Crystal Night" (*Kristallnacht*) pogrom against the Jews surfaced, particularly from a one-time Socialist woodworker who termed it an "awful mess" (*Schweinerei*). There followed additional complaints that contrasted the grind of daily labor with the little payoff that workers received.[52] In the harbor of Palermo the following year, a passenger, who refused to remove his hat when the ship orchestra played the "Horst Wessel Song," drew a reprimand from the tour leader. Refusing to stop with that sin, however, the passenger insulted the tour leader who was also a member of the SA. The "victim" subsequently demanded that the tour direction on board ship gather personal data on the offender as the basis for a complaint.[53] On the other hand, the lack of engagement seemed equally deserving of concern. Unless the consequences of Reich policies directly confronted KdF vacationers, they ignored newspapers and radio broadcasts. Thus, although tensions between Germany and Italy dominated the conversation when a KdF train crossed through Tyrol following the annexation of Austria,[54] equally momentous, but more distant, events generated little discussion. Remarked another agent, the passengers on a cruise to Italy in November 1938, most of them party members, paid no attention to the assassination of a German diplomat in Paris, Ernst von Rath, who was shot by a Jewish

50 Ibid., 121.
51 Bericht über die 45. Urlaubsreise mit M.S. Monte Olivia nach Norwegen vom 13. bis 21. July 1936, BAL R58, no. 948, 4.
52 KDF.-Seereise "Rund um Italien" vom 19. bis 29 November 1938, BAL R58, no. 950, 420.
53 Abschrift: An Bord des Dampfer Stuttgart, den 21. 2. 39, BAL R58, no. 950, 554.
54 Überwachung der U.F. 3506 nach Gries am Brenner, BAL R58, no. 947, 180.

student infuriated by the expulsion of his parents from Germany to Poland.[55] Even some passengers complained of tourists who sacrificed edification, high culture, and political education for pure entertainment. The services of good propagandists are sorely needed, remarked an anonymous tourist following his cruise to Madeira in 1936. Passengers should be treated to poetry readings, lectures on German history and Germany's struggle in the world, and of course, performances of Wagner's music.[56]

Similar to their concern with class divisions, the attention that SD and Gestapo informants devoted to deportment focused as usual on the behavior of women. The modern, but modest, sexuality depicted in KdF periodicals bore little relationship to the shocking behavior that SD informants claimed to have observed. Whether tactlessly chatting with foreigners without regard for national security, flirting with their male hosts, or succumbing outright to sexual temptation, especially after abandoning all propriety to alcohol, the brazenness and witlessness of women endangered the racial community. One agent reported that several women on his trip to the Glatzer Bergland near the Czechoslovak border were eager to follow the suggestion of Czech police officers who had engaged the women in conversation to observe German fortifications from the Czech side of the border. The women were tempted, he explained, because one of the Czech officers was in their words, "such a handsome guy that one should marry him right away."[57] "The conduct of the female vacationers, as is consistent with earlier reports, still leaves much to be desired," noted another typical observation, this one from a cruise to Italy. "This evil must be remedied as soon as possible for the good of the whole." Perhaps argued the agent, "attached women" should be given preference on the Italian trips, "with the rest being given strict education and instruction."[58]

According to another report, the actions of some women and girls on a Mediterranean cruise were "shameless." One got drunk in the company of a Greek officer, wobbling unsteadily as she returned to her ship loaded down with the money and gifts that her short-term companion bestowed on her.[59] Still another complained, "again and again, women and

55 Bericht des SS-Oberscharführers Otto-Wilhelm Wandesleben über die vom 6. November bis 18. November 1938 stattgefundene KdF-Reise nach Italien, BAL R58, no. 950, 385.

56 Auszugsweiser Bericht eines Teilnehmers an einer Kraft durch Freude-Fahrt nach Madeira, 13. Mai 1936, BAL NS 22/781.

57 Auswertungsnotiz aus beim Gestapa vorhandenen VMR-Berichten über KdF-Reisen. Zeit Frühjahr 1937 bis 10.10.1937, BAL R58, no. 943, 115.

58 VMR-Bericht über die KdF-Urlaubsfahrt vom 19.-29.12.37 mit D. "Oceana" der Gaue Ostpreußen und Danzig, BAL R58, no. 950, no. 167.

59 Bericht über die KdF Reise Dalmatien-Griechenland mit der Reichsbahn und dem Dampfer "Oceana" vom 2.3.1939 bis 15.3.1939, BAL R58, no. 950, 626.

girls were observed making contact with Italian soldiers, sailors and also civilians in the port cities, exchanging addresses and having their pictures taken with them, arm in arm. The urgent and repeated appeals of the tour directors to show more discretion were hardly observed."[60] Remarked an agent, who might as well have been summarizing the collective opinion of his colleagues, the deportment of female vacationers during a visit to the island of Ischia off the west coast of Italy was appalling. "One is forced to assume," he declared in his best official prose (*Beamtendeutsch*), a linguistic style that revealed how the pressure of evidence deterred him from drawing the conclusion that he would have preferred, "that most of the women joined the Italian trip for erotic purposes."[61]

The racial implications of aberrant female behavior resided close to the surface in surveillance reports, not least because of the regime's obsessive fears regarding the transmission of racial impurities through sexual contact. Female travelers on the *Stuttgart's* trip to Italy, Tripoli, and Madeira in March 1939 proved to be soft touches in official eyes for souvenir sellers on land, who eagerly accepted their Reichsmarks for kitsch. They sacrificed all dignity by dealing with dark-skinned locals. When chastised for swapping their cigarettes for goods with Arabs, some women insolently responded that at least their Arab trading partners were not Jews, betraying a popular willingness to exploit Nazi racial hierarchies to achieve individual ends. Ignoring warnings that their deportment flouted that demanded of a "master race," the women cheerfully posed for snapshots with blacks against scenic backdrops, in return for a few cigarettes.[62] Despite Germany's alliance with Italy and governments in Greece and Portugal that expressed sympathy for the Third Reich, the lesser racial status of Mediterranean peoples reinforced the official distaste for the carefree dalliances of German women on tour. Coupled with the long-standing associations of dark skin and sunny climates with sexuality that suffused modern tourism, even the appearance of sexual familiarity breached more than just bourgeois values.[63] Thus, a KdF tour director criticized the actions of two German women, who on a visit to the ruins at Pompeii were observed in intimate conversation with two Italian policemen. Despite the women's claim that they been separated from the other passengers and found the policemen who came to their rescue more knowledgeable

60 VMR-Reisebericht über die Teilnahme des SS-U.'stuf. Blank an der 3. KdF-Italienreise mit dem Dampfer "Der Deutsche," vom 25.XI. bis 5.XII.1937, BAL R58, no. 950, 125.
61 Bericht über die Rund um Italienfahrt v.1.-12.1938 der KdF mit dem Schiff "Oceana," BAL R58, no. 950, 447.
62 KdF Frühlingsfahrt nach Italien, Tripolis und Madeira auf dem Dampfer "Stuttgart" vom 11.3. bis 30. 3. 1939, BAL R58, no. 950, 586.
63 Littlewood, *Sultry Climates*, 189–215.

about the sights, the tour director warned that their conduct damaged the reputation of German women abroad.[64]

Like its advertisements, the manner in which KdF tours operated in practice encouraged the assertive and individualistic behavior that KdF officially deplored. KdF's regimentation was real enough, and often attested to in the commendations (where appropriate) in surveillance reports regarding the admirable "discipline" of its vacationers. Yet KdF's willingness to advertise features other than the low cost of its tours showed its receptivity to popular expectations. Like KdF's public relations promotions of its newest ships, the *Wilhelm Gustloff* and *Robert Ley*, which lovingly described their numerous amenities to appeal to a variety of personal preferences, KdF catered to the expectations of tourists created by the images of cruises in commercial advertisements. Thus, KdF tours allowed leeway for individual choice, be it the side trips involving small groups, or free afternoons for personal sightseeing, a fact that the KdF functionary, Anatol von Hübbenet publicly, if belatedly, acknowledged.[65]

To be sure, in some cases, passengers did not disembark because of currency restrictions, the heightened concern for their safety, and the greater-than-usual danger of leftist infiltration. Ironically, Norway constituted such an example. Although German tourists who traveled there during the interwar period sailed through the fjords rather than explore on land,[66] the putatively Nordic racial characteristics of Norway's people might have encouraged more engagement between KdF tourists and Norwegians. Aside from the port town of Haugesund, however, where locals sympathized with National Socialism, other coastal or fjord towns offered unfriendly environments for German tourists. In Bergen and Odda with their sizeable Communist or Social Democratic enclaves, hostile Norwegians tossed bottles and other objects at KdF ships, while crews of fishing boats refused to wave in the customary manner.[67] Yet for most other destinations, Strength through Joy tour leaders permitted tourists to circulate on their own and gaze upon the exotic, while hoping that surveillance agents would curtail the less-than-desirable outcomes of such a practice. Indeed, coexisting with the search for release and pleasure was the sincere desire for edification, be it through attending lectures to

64 Reisebericht über die 128. KdF.-Fahrt mit Dampfer "Der Deutsche" – "Rund um Italien"- (20.2.39 bis 2.3.39), BAL R58, no. 950, 574–5.

65 Anatol von Hübbenet, *Die NS-Gemeinschaft "Kraft durch Freude": Aufbau und Arbeit* (Berlin: Junker und Dünnhaupt Verlag, 1939), 48.

66 See the table in Norval, *Tourist Industry*, 90.

67 Reisebericht Betr.: Norwegenfahrt der DAF mit K.d.F.-Dampfer "Der Deutsche" vom 17.7.1938–23.7.1938 Gau Berlin, BAL R58, no. 948, 65–6; Betr.: Nordlandreise des Gaues Sachsen vom 8.-14.6.1938 mit Dampfer "Oceana," BAL R58, no. 948, 84–5; Betr.: KdF-Fahrt nach Norwegen v. 9.-14.1939, BAL R58, no. 958, 125.

prepare for visiting a foreign culture, visits to the Akropolis in Athens, sitting atop camels outside Tripoli, or exploring indigenous vegetation and natural beauty on walking tours. In short, Strength through Joy's "mass" tourism complemented the mores of a predominantly middle-class and skilled worker or artisanal clientele already introduced to tourism through previous practice, Baedecker guides, the ethos of bourgeois self-improvement, and (as the presence of "extras" indicates) the ability to pay for their personal desires.

Because informants commented on all aspects of KdF trips, which in their view affected the overall experience, their observations extended to seemingly trivial matters that spoke to the satisfaction, or lack thereof, among vacationers. In addition to relaying complaints about lodging, food, the quality and attentiveness of the tour directors, or the accommodations for various events, the agents also passed judgment on the caliber of lectures, musical performances, and light entertainment. Because the tourists were forced to share bedrooms, remarked one agent of an inland trip that sent Württembergers to the Spessart nature preserve near Würzberg, "good comradeship" soon emerged. "After two to three days, most vacationers dispensed with *Sie*, exchanging it for the familiar *Du*. In general, the accommodations were a good thing."[68] The multiple performances of the Reich Labor Service (*Reichsarbeitsdienst*, or RAD) orchestra from Gau Westphalia South, noted another who traveled on a cruise to Italy, Tripoli, and Madeira, drew enthusiastic applause, especially for its concerts on land, which drew local people and tourists alike. Likewise, the organization of side trips and other events on land received unqualified praise. The passengers gave the recitations of the writer Kurt Christophé, however, thoroughly negative evaluations.[69] Another occurrence on the same ship reported by two agents revealed the convergence of official and popular antisemitism that could emerge in complaints as to the quality of entertainment. A dancer, Sula Falk, incurred the displeasure of vacationers when she wished to perform to a piece of music, "The Ways of the Gypsies." When the conductor of the RAD orchestra refused to play the work claiming that a Jew had composed it, Falk assured the tour director that the Reich Chamber of Culture had approved it. To save the performance, the ship's orchestra substituted for the RAD under pressure from the tour director, but the catcalls of an unidentified

---

68 Bericht über die Überwachung der Kraft durch Freude-Urlaubsfahrt 44/38 in den Spessart vom 13.-8. bis 20.8.38, BAL R58, no. 609, 202.
69 Reisebericht über die "Frühlungsfahrt nach Italien, Tripolis und Madeira" der NS-Gemeinschaft "Kraft durch Freude" der Deutschen Arbeitsfront (Reichsamt für Reisen, Wandern und Urlaub) mit Dampfer "Stuttgart," vom. 10.3.-31.3.1939, BAL R58, no. 950, 648.

Labor Service man in the audience were met with sympathy from other passengers.[70]

Of all issues giving rise to unhappiness, train travel occupied the top of the list, especially because the number of KdF tourists and the regime's other commitments rendered the problem impossible to remedy. The military's increasing need for transport and KdF's commitment to keeping costs low meant that KdF settled for uncomfortable third- and fourth-class compartments that did not fail to generate frustration. In addition to forcing KdF periodicals to claim the comfort of its trains, evidence to the contrary, passenger complaints required the intervention of KdF wardens, who with varying degrees of success appealed on the tourists' behalf.[71] Following the Ley–Cianetti agreement, which underwrote exchanges of tourists between Germany and Italy, the substandard compartments of Italian trains brought exchanges between district leaders and KdF's office of Travel, Hiking, and Vacations, such as that from Gau Halle-Merseburg. Upon hearing objections from tourists the district leadership expressed its dissatisfaction with the news of alcohol-driven parties and especially the uncomfortable and unclean trains that unsettled some participants. For its trouble, it received a response that ranged from reassurance to denial. Admittedly, the letter acknowledged, the Italian trains were poor but every effort had been taken to assure an adequate supply of soap and towels. The reports of boozy parties had been exaggerated.[72] Despite the unsatisfactory outcome of that warden's complaint, that and similar exchanges suggest a deeper significance. For those whom the Nazi regime designated as enemies, the SD, Gestapo, and party apparatchiks became the ambassadors of persecution. Without denying the political purpose that the regime's agents served on KdF trips, however, Nazism's agents adopted a different, but no less insidious, role. They reinforced the Third Reich's privileging of racially acceptable Germans as they mingled with and responded to KdF tourists, scrupulously investigating their complaints and pleasures.[73]

---

70   Ibid.; Betr.: KdF Frühlingsfahrt nach Italien, Tripolis und Madeira auf dem Dampfer "Stuttgart" vom 10.3. bis 30.3.39, BAL, no. 950, 587.

71   Bericht über die KdF-Reise UF 49 vom 26.2.39–12.3.39, BAL R58, no. 947, 7.

72   KdF Amt Reisen, Wandern und Urlaub Zentralbüro an Stableiter Pg. Simon Betr. Stimmungsberichte der Gauleitung insbesondere in Bezug auf die Durchführung unserer Italienfahrten, Winterhalbjahr 1937/38, 10. Mai 1938, BAL NS 22/781.

73   Popular consent to the regime's s repression has moved to center stage in the past decade or so, beginning with Robert Gellately's pioneering work, *The Gestapo and German Society: Enforcing Racial Policy 1933–1945* (Oxford: Oxford University Press, 1990). Yet Eric A. Johnson's recent book, *Nazi Terror: The Gestapo, Jews, and Ordinary Germans* (New York: Basic Books, 1999), seeks to reestablish the lethal power of the Third Reich's agents, especially toward Nazism's targets. See especially Chapter 1 for Johnson's historiographical review. The Nazi regime's racial and political hierarchies determined how or whether its repressive forces were experienced.

Strength through Joy's accommodations to taste, and its blend of hedonism and self-improvement, even extended to tours that exposed or came close to exposing participants to Nazism's horrors, potential and actual. The demonstrations of German naval strength to cruise passengers served as but one example, as KdF prepared the "*Volk* comrades" (*Volksgenossen*) under its purview for their future status as imperial masters. The tours to East Prussia that by crossing the Polish Corridor denied the legitimacy of Poland's independence constituted another.[74] Yet some of Strength through Joy's homeland trips, such as the short outings to the environs of Buchenwald and to the Bavarian village of Dachau, were even more remarkable. Such tours helped to put distance between the experiences of persecuted and ostracized minorities, especially Jews, from the majority of Germans, whose racial status, and from the regime's perspective blameless lives, protected them from repression. An outing for the employees of a printing firm to Dachau, according to a KdF monthly periodical, combined business with pleasure. It commenced with a visit to a local paper factory, followed by a tour of the garden of the Renaissance style palace and a museum of local folk art. Not least because the tour took place during the Oktoberfest, it concluded with food, drink, and dancing. The notorious concentration camp received no mention despite the widespread knowledge of its existence, perhaps out of deference to the fears of the town's elite that it would jeopardize revenue-generating tourism.[75] Thus, the Dachau of Strength through Joy tourists and the Dachau of the Nazi regime's political and racial victims occupied different universes. The first was the site of enjoyment, relaxation, and edification for the racially acceptable; the second a world of suffering for those whom the regime consigned to "social death."[76]

The exclusions that KdF's tourism reinforced resembled the impact of the radio, which like tourism, signified the Reich's partial adjustment to consumer desires. Opting in most cases for light entertainment over propaganda, radio programmers catered to audiences for whom the horrors of the Third Reich remained peripheral, or subjects to be minimized as exaggerations.[77] Nazism's victims on the other hand looked bitterly on the solicitude with which the regime treated the racial community while their

---

74 See Chapter 4, 127.

75 See Gellately, *Backing Hitler*, 52–3. At first Dachau's government welcomed the camp for the revenue it generated, but its notorious reputation soon produced a deleterious impact.

76 "In herbstliche Dachau mit der Betriebsgemeinschaft G. Franz'sche Buchdruckerei," NSG Kraft durch Freude, Gau München- Oberbayern, *Kraft durch Freude*, November 1935, 10–11.

77 Monika Pater, "Rundfunksangebote," in *Zuhören und Gehörtwerden I: Radio im Nationalsozialismus: Zwischen Lenkung und Ablenkung*, ed. Inge Marßolek and Adelheid von Saldern (Tübingen: Edition Diskord, 1998): 146.

lives became increasingly nightmarish. Unlike KdF tourists who recorded the pleasures of their travel – whose albums, diaries, and postcards, recounted the freedom they experienced, the "impeccable" food and accommodations, the magnificent views, and the warmth of new acquaintances[78] – the regime's enemies faced deprivation, suspicion, and isolation. In his diary entries from July 1936, Victor Klemperer, the Jewish professor of Romance languages from Dresden, contrasted his social marginalization to the experiences of Germans whom he knew, but whose racial status protected them from sharing his increasingly precarious predicament. Amidst comments regarding his and his wife's impoverishment, the result of his having lost his teaching post on racial grounds, he recorded the arrival of an Aryan acquaintance on a Strength through Joy train. The friend described to Klemperer the details of her trip that day, particularly its low package price, and included her recollection of another voyage to Norway on a KdF cruise ship. Concluded Klemperer sullenly, "at any rate, these KdF undertakings are prodigious circuses."[79]

The contrasting experiences arising from Klemperer's sadness and the joy of his acquaintance helps to explain the reactions of other KdF tourists, who ignored or trivialized Nazi terror and the regime's minacious foreign policy. According to some passengers on a cruise to southern Italy, the grime of Naples and Palermo departed sharply from German "cleanliness." Every complainer, they opined, should be forced to live in the miserable living quarters that they saw there, which were nonetheless "better than a year in a concentration camp." The exposure to Germany's military prowess on cruises occasioned not merely "the feeling of security and pride in [Germany's] sea power," but especially the contempt for Germany's enemies, as the snide remark of one vacationer reveals. To the glee of his fellow passengers on a cruise to Norway less than a month before the outbreak of war, the jokester quipped that the Polish liner *Piłsudski*, seen off in the distance, would soon be German.[80] If KdF tourists eschewed politics, preferring instead to "get away from it all," their revelry did not preclude observations with insidious political implications. In some instances, Hitler's personal popularity even suppressed political

78   Such as the anonymous diary of a springtime trip to the Frankenwald, year unspecified, and the postcard from the spa Wirsberg to Berlin, dated May 1937, both in the author's possession.

79   Victor Klemperer, *I Will Bear Witness: A Diary of the Nazi Years, 1933–1941*, trans. Martin Chalmers (New York: Random House, 1998), 178–9. On the everyday lives of Jews, particularly Jewish women, see Marion Kaplan, *Between Dignity and Despair: Jewish Life in Nazi Germany* (New York and Oxford: Oxford Univerity Press, 1998).

80   Bericht des SS-Oberscharführers Otto-Wilhelm Wandesleben über die vom 6. November bis 18. November 1938 stattgefundene KdF-Reise nach Italien, BAL R58, no. 950, 384; Bericht des SS-Hauptsturmführer Wossagk, BAL R58, no. 950, 81; Norwegenfahrt der NS-Gemeinschaft "Kraft durch Freude," Gau Mgd./Anh. mit dem KdF-Dampfer "Der Deutsche" vom 2.-8.39, BAL R58, no. 948, 129.

discussions. In the view of some tourists, there was no need to bother with politics since the führer had made things right. Participants attributed the success of the regime's social programs, particularly Strength through Joy, to him alone, following German popular opinion in general, in which the mythical figure of Hitler personified Nazism's achievements.[81]

In retrospect, the complacency of those remarks, the sort that in the postwar period encouraged Germans to distinguish disingenuously between the "positive" achievements of National Socialism from its repression and genocide, resided in no small measure in touristic assessments as to Germany's standard of living compared to that of other nations. Travel permitted German tourists to observe the lives of foreigners first hand, resulting in the unanimous agreement as to the superiority of Germany's living standards. Whether in the stray remarks picked up by SD, Gestapo, and Sopade informants, or the direct statements that appeared in tour recollections published in periodicals, the comparative well being of Germans and others provided a consistently lively topic of conversation.[82] Because KdF journeyed often to economically less well-developed European nations with large poverty-stricken regions, or as in the case of Poland traversed through them, its foreign tourism facilitated such conclusions. Portuguese soldiers begged for cigarettes, remarked surprised tourists on a Madeira trip, a phenomenon that grabbed their attention even amidst the poverty of Madeira's fishing villages.[83] A trip from Berlin to Königsberg through the Polish Corridor aroused great interest, according to an agent, for no one could help notice deteriorating train stations, unkempt and untended forests, and the impoverished misery that ended only with the train's approach to Danzig.[84]

To be sure, fewer tourists traveled abroad with Strength through Joy where the most revealing comparisons between standards of living arose, in contrast to those who traveled with it at home. Nevertheless, the number who took sea voyages was significant, having peaked at 140,000 in 1939, and such numbers almost certainly sufficed to have produced a ripple effect.[85] The dissemination of first-person travel accounts in factory newspapers and libraries and in KdF's inexpensive and widely distributed literature became obvious instruments for circulating the retrospectives of tourists. In fact, the manner in which the media popularized travel during the Weimar era, the travel accounts on the radio and the slick advertising

81 Überwachung der K.d.F.-Fahrt UF 52/39 vom 30.6.-6.7.39 im Schwarzwald, BAL R58, no. 947, 58. On the führer's standing, see Ian Kershaw, *The 'Hitler Myth': Image and Reality in the Third Reich* (Oxford: Clarendon Press, 1987).
82 Cf. Frommann, "Reisen im Dienste," 192–3 and 212–15.
83 Bericht über die KdF-Herbstfahrt nach Madeira, Tripolis und Italien vom 12. bis 31. Oktober 1938 des M.S. "Wilhelm Gustloff," BAL R58, no. 950, 293 ff.
84 Bericht über die KdF-Reise U.F. Nr. 4306, 29 June 1939, BAL R58, no. 947, 177.
85 See Chapter 4, 135.

of package tours, encouraged KdF to take the next step, asking tourists to recount their experiences.[86] The popularity of the People's Education program's foreign language courses testified to the manner in which traveling abroad captured the popular imagination.[87] Finally, the informal exchanges that occurred between returning vacationers and their acquaintances, postcards sent from vacation spots and the display of photo albums, commemorative KdF pins, and luggage labels to friends assured the even wider impact of touristic judgments. (See Figure 5.1.) "My first ocean voyage with KdF to Norway," one album was entitled, conveying its author's appreciation for how much his trip departed from everyday routine. Carefully composed snapshots depicted fun, relaxation, pleasure, and comraderie aboard ship, as well as panoramic views of the fjords that conformed to the visions of natural beauty laid out in KdF brochures. The painstaking arrangement of albums suggests their authors' intention not merely to engage in the private recollection of a special time, but also to share with others their experience of rejuvenation and well being. (See Figures 5.2 and 5.3.)

At times, the judgments and actions of KdF tourists discomfited KdF and DAF officials, who were keen not to compromise the Reich's essential alliances, especially that with Italy. On one occasion, much embarrassment ensued on an Italian trip when German women with prurient intentions, insinuated an agent, took seats next to "hot-blooded" (*rassig*) Italian men. Before the train left the station, however, the Italian officer in charge, who knew the sort of women whom he was confronting, ejected them from their seats and replaced them with men. The officer's limited command of German heightened the embarrassment of the SD agent and the KdF tour directors. In the future, recommended the agent, German women should be warned more often against behavior that subverted protocol.[88] Agents and KdF tour personnel took pains to compliment Germany's Fascist allies, whether by noting the clean appearance and efficiency of Italian policemen, who shielded German tourists from begging children, or in lectures on board ship that stressed the architectural and

86 See Christine Keitz, *Reisen als Leitbild: Die Entstehung des modernen Massentourismus in Deutschland* (Munich: Deutscher Taschenbuch Verlag, 1997), 95–111.

87 KdF spokesmen took the ripple effect for granted, as indicated in Günther Adam's speech, "Practical Activities of the National-Socialist Fellowship *Kraft durch Freude*," *German Addresses for Committee I, to the World Congress, "Work and Joy," Rome 1938*, 22. Similarly, Fritz Leutloff, in an address to the same congress, discussed the effect of KdF on the People's Education project's foreign language courses: "From the University Extension to the German Popular Education Section of the National-Socialist Fellowship *Kraft durch Freude* (Functions and Aims of National Socialist Educational Work)," *German Addresses for Committee VII, World Congress "Work and Joy," Rome 1938*, 16.

88 VMR-Bericht über die KdF-Italienfahrt vom 19.-29.12.37 mit D. "Oceana" der Gaue Ostpreußen und Danzig, BAL R58, no. 950, 166.

Fig. 5.1. A commemorative pin and luggage label, the tangible
evidence of having toured with KdF. Author's collection.

Fig. 5.2. Panoramic snapshot of the mountains of Norway by an anonymous tourist. As well as sharing in the conventions of touristic representations, photo albums became a means of disseminating memories. Author's collection.

Fig. 5.3. Mannheimers on the *Monte Olivia* with KdF in Norway. From the photo album of Erich Wagner, a member of the group. Author's collection.

social achievements of Fascism in the face of the poverty that the Mussolini government inherited.[89] Regardless, that discomfort did not seriously ruffle the racist and cultural presuppositions that underlay Strength through Joy tourism, and it certainly had little impact on travelers, who resorted to racial stereotypes of their own to ground their assessments. German passengers frequently and freely remarked on the hardship and squalor they observed. If they occasionally praised Mussolini's or Salazar's determination to improve the lives of their citizens, they persisted in comparing the putative filth and poverty that characterized local conditions to the "high" standard of living in Germany. Such comparisons strengthened their pride in being German.[90]

Furthermore, KdF's desire to respect the sensibilities of their hosts did not deter surveillance agents from revealing their own prejudices.[91] In the view of one, observing Italian slums made it clear to participants just how rapid Germany's progress had been since the regime took power. Indeed, he claimed in his report, the depth of poverty so evident in Italy had never existed in Germany, not even (presumably a reference to Weimar) during its greatest misery.[92] Concluded another, the passivity and lack of initiative of simple Italians could be explained only by recourse to climatic and racial differences.[93] Still others, who explained the Italian national character by reference to Catholicism, thereby expressing the regime's phobia of the Catholic Church, commented that the more miserable the urban neighborhood or rural village, the more numerous and splendid the churches.[94] And yet another agent on a cruise to Italy, Greece, and Yugoslavia allowed "locals" themselves to testify to Germany's achievements through him. A Serbian woman whom he met marveled at

89 Bericht über die K.d.F.-Seereise mit Dampfer "Oceana" vom 2.-12.3.1938, BAL R58, no. 949, 14; Dienstreisebericht des Reisebegleiters über die KdF-Urlaubsfahrt mit Dampfer "Stuttgart" nach Italien vom 13.-25. November 1938, BAL R58, no. 950, 352.

90 Bericht über die KdF-Seereise mit Dampfer "Oceana" vom 2.-12.3.1938, BAL R58, no. 949, 13–14; Bericht über die Teilname des SS-Hauptsturmführer Mulde, 2.-12.3.1939, BAL R58, no. 950, 71; Bericht über die Rund um Italienfahrt v. 1.-12.12. 1938 der KdF mit dem Schiff "Oceana," BAL R58, no. 950, 447–8. Cf. Liebscher, "Mit KdF 'die Welt erschließen'": 61–71.

91 As Frommann points out in "Reisen im Dienste," 170, KdF was accustomed to giving second-class treatment to Italian tourists to Germany. In contrast to German tourists to Italy, whom Fascist officials put up in first-class hotels, Italians in Germany had to settle for the usual KdF private accommodations.

92 Bericht über die KdF-Italienfahrt vom 7.-17.12.1937, R58, no. 949, 58–9.

93 Bericht über die Teilnahme des SS-Hauptsturmführer Mulde, 2.-12.3.1939, BAL R58, no. 950, 71.

94 Abschrift, KdF.-Seereise "Rund um Italien" vom 19. bis 29. November 1938, BAL R58, no. 950, 424. Richard Steigmann-Gall, *The 'Holy Reich': Nazi Conceptions of Christianity, 1919–1945* (Cambridge: Cambridge University Press, 2003) underscores the hostility of Nazi leaders toward the Catholic Church, even amidst their positive assessments of Christianity in general.

the ships that transported German workers on their vacations. She was amazed, or so the agent reported, at the bountiful meals that were served aboard ship and impressed that the ships were not divided according to class. Why, she wondered aloud, had Germany not done more to propagandize its achievements in her country? A Norwegian tourist, with whom the agent crossed paths with in Trieste, rued that his nation had nothing like Strength through Joy. The only "sour" note to arise in the Norwegian's comments, remarked the agent, was his criticism of the Reich's Jewish policy, presumably a reference to *Kristallnacht*.[95] Such official observations were not just expressed privately in surveillance reports. KdF publicists wrote stories for domestic consumption about previously skeptical foreigners becoming sold on Nazism's solution to the social question once they had seen Strength through Joy's tourism in action.[96]

The interactions between Germans and foreigners occurred through the visual consumption of the latter as KdF ships and trains arrived at their destinations, or when tourists visited local sites on foot or by car. They took place especially when German travelers acquired souvenirs, the commodified evidence of having traveled and the tangible signs of having been elsewhere. Stall keepers in bazaars, small scale peddlers, and beggars, especially children, became points of contact who sold the goods that Germans wanted, and whose poverty and grimy appearance deepened the prejudices that Germans shared.[97] Even the most strenuous efforts of Italian Fascist or Portuguese authorities to deter tourists from urban slums, rural poverty, and exchanges with the purveyors of petty commerce proved ineffective. Complained one agent: "As indicated by the hunt for begging children, there is no appreciation for the efforts of the Fascist organizations and police, which are clearly evident, to transform a begging people into a master race. The vacationers ignored the advice of train personnel and the police against having anything to do with the beggars."[98] Yet the apparent eagerness of tourists to engage with people who were foreign to

---

95 Bericht des SS-Untersturmführers Prieb über die Teilnahme an der KdF-Auslandsfahrt nach Dalmatien, Griechenland mit dem Dampfer "Oceana" vom 6. bis 18. November 1938, BAL R58, no. 950, 287.

96 For example, KdF disseminated the story of a British miner, John Smith, who after his visit to Germany that included a cruise to Norway wrote a letter to the London *Times*, in which he praised the Third's Reich's practical solution to eliminating social conflict. See Sepp Dobiasch, *Sonne-Wind und Weite: Ein Buch von Frohen Fahrten und Menschen* (Berlin: Wilhelm Limpert Verlag, 1936), 162–70.

97 In this case too, KdF revealed its ambivalence. Although disliking the hunt for "kitsch," news accounts showed photos of tourists haggling in bazaars as part of their normal promotion, for example "Mit KdF in Afrika," *Göttinger Tageblatt*, 21 October, 1938, Niedersächsisches Hauptstaatsarchiv Hannover (hereinafter cited as NHH) VVP 17, no. 2456.

98 Betr.: KdF Frühlingsfahrt nach Italien, Tripolis und Madeira auf dem Dampfer "Stuttgart" vom 11.3 bis 30.3.39, BAL R58, no. 950, 588.

them belied the inequality that governed the relationships between KdF tourists and locals in foreign "contact zones," whose presence sufficed for instrumental purposes.[99] KdF's photographs depicted the presumptions of superiority of its tourists at the same time that they conveyed its own implicit messages as to the German tourist's proper role. Placing its tourists in the center, KdF framed the "natives" who surrounded them as either taking direction, aiding the sightseeing trips, or simply gawking in wonder. Provided with the opportunity to send its tourists to Tripoli, courtesy of the Italian Fascists, such compositions became especially prevalent in KdF's publications. If Tripoli represented a determined Italian attempt at modernization and settlement,[100] Germans tourists as well would use the city to act out their anticipation of empire. (See Figure 5.4.)

The prejudices confirmed through such limited contact appear in the meticulously recorded diary of Otto Kühn, a civil servant from Stettin about his cruise to Portugal and Madeira. Kühn admitted his unfavorable impressions of the curious Portuguese, who greeted his ship in Lisbon, noting the raggedly clothed children who begged for handouts from tourists. He commented negatively as well on the racial composition of the audience. White harbor workers composed the majority, he observed, "but mixed in were half-breeds (*Bastarden*) and a few Negroes." On the second day of his sojourn, Lisbon's inhabitants partially won him over. He saw well-dressed people on a tour through the city's better neighborhoods, whose purposefulness disqualified them as examples of the usual "southern nonchalance (*Lässigkeit*)" that characterized the majority of Portuguese. Kühn closed his diary, one that came complete with well-composed snapshots, with an expression of appreciation for all that he had learned about Portugal. Nevertheless he had to confess that the voyage deepened his patriotism. Some may acclaim the attractions of Portugal, he said, but "our great northern *Heimat* with its mountains and valleys, plains, lakes, and seacoasts is on the other hand far more beautiful."[101] Surely Kühn's observations were unremarkable, for such condescension was and is the standard fare of tourism, a practice most evident among the populations of the wealthy, industrialized world. Yet in the context of the Third Reich, Kühn's assertion as to the superiority of Germany's landscapes sustained the interlocutor's deeply rooted sense of racial hierarchy and complemented the expectations of KdF tourism promoters as to the values that they hoped foreign travel would inculcate.

---

99   Mary Louise Pratt, *Imperial Eyes: Travel Writing and Transculturation* (New York and London: Routledge, 1992), 6.
100 John Wright, *Libya: A Modern History* (Baltimore: Johns Hopkins University Press, 1981), 37–41.
101 Otto Kühn, "Mit 'Kraft durch Freude' nach Madeira 1936," Institut für Zeitgeschichte, Munich (IfZ), MS 127.

Fig. 5.4. Oasis tour on North Africa. German tourists ride in autos while curious locals look on.
Source: Reichsamtsleitung Kraft durch Freude, *Unter dem Sonnenrad. Ein Buch von Kraft durch Freude* (Berlin: Verlag des Deutschen Arbeitsfront, 1938), 111. Courtesy of the Center for Research Libraries, Chicago.

The comments of German tourists are hardly surprising in light of the social constituency that populated KdF's more prestigious trips. In addition to being the primary market for tourism promoters, the middle classes constituted National Socialism's most reliable support. Yet neither were working-class tourists immune to seeing Nazism's advantages despite the fears of the office of Travel, Hiking, and Vacations that the closet "Marxists" among them would spread their poison. Workers expressed their gratitude for having received the "gift" of a trip to a foreign country, as did the workers of a Baden firm enjoying a company outing on a voyage to Italy in 1938.[102] Others proved themselves even more effusive. An older worker with nine children, reportedly a former "Marxist," was reputedly overcome with emotion when he recounted that he could never have dreamed of taking a cruise, particularly one that was free. He said that he had never sung the national anthem, the *Deutschlandlied*, with as much feeling as he had in Italy.[103] "Under Adolf Hitler we are now all kaisers," said a miner after having been told during his cruise on the *Sierra Cordoba* as he gazed at the Norwegian fjords that Kaiser Wilhelm had once enjoyed the same vistas.[104] Even amidst critical comments about shortages of food and consumer goods, as took place in 1938 among workers from Berlin, former trade unionists praised the Labor Front for having provided vacations for workers. According to the SD agent, they showed 100 percent trust in the führer.[105]

Similar to middle-class tourists, workers came away astonished by the differences in living standards between Germany and the ports of call that they visited. Having witnessed the poverty in Portugal on a cruise to Madeira with the ship *Der Deutsche*, some working-class passengers announced proudly that they would not change places with the Portuguese.[106] Indeed, commented the author of a report of his cruise to the same destination in a KdF periodical, the Portuguese with whom he and his comrades came into contact could not believe that the Germans were workers because they appeared so well dressed. Only when the tourists showed their hands to their hosts did the latter become convinced.[107]

---

102 KdF.-Seereise "Rund um Italien" vom 19. bis 29. November 1938. BAL R58, no. 950, 421. Similarly, the working-class passengers from Saxony on a Norwegian trip appreciated having gotten the "offer" of a vacation. Betr.: Nordlandreise des Gaues Sachsen vom 8.-14.1938 mit Dampfer "Oceana," BAL R58, no. 948, 87.

103 Bericht über die KdF-Italienfahrt vom 7.-17.12.1937, BAL R58, no. 949, 58–9.

104 Bericht über die KdF-Fahrt vom 2.-10.8.1938 auf dem Dampfer "Sierra Cordoba," BAL R58, no. 948, 60–1.

105 Reisebericht Betr.: Norwegenfahrt der DAF mit K.d.F.-Dampfer "Der Deutsche" vom 17.7.1938–23.7.1938 Gau Berlin, BAL R58, no. 948, 66.

106 Bericht über die Reise des K.d.F.-Schiffes "Der Deutsche" nach Madeira vom 21.4.38–7.5.38, BAL R58, no. 950, 241–2.

107 "Wir deutschen Arbeiter in Madeira," NS Gemeinschaft "Kraft durch Freude" Gau Sachsen, *Monatsprogramm*, May 1935, 2–4.

Although acknowledging the recent suffering in Germany, workers aboard a cruise to Italy expressed satisfaction with their own lives, having observed close up the low standard of living of Italian workers.[108]

The regime's agents could have grasped at evidence that compensated for the disruptions to the racial community that they observed in the course of their travels. Although under cover, tourists knew that KdF trips were under surveillance, which might well have constrained even the most casual comments to avoid falling under suspicion. The travelogues that appeared in KdF periodicals, furthermore, hardly understated KdF's achievements, for the manner of selection that often produced the workers who took KdF trips virtually guaranteed nationalistic responses. Nevertheless, even New Beginning and Sopade informants could not deny the favorable impact that KdF tourism made on workers, not least because KdF convinced them that their status and well being had been improved. A former Communist raved about his one-week-long trip to the Austrian Allgäu, the total cost of which did not exceed the normal roundtrip train fare to the same destination. For side trips and special events, tour organizers secured significant price reductions, and in any case, there was no pressure to participate in them. Tourists, he suggested, enjoyed a good deal of freedom, for the only sign of the trip's "official character" was the swastika on the locomotive and the staged receptions that greeted the KdF train on its arrival in each village along the way.[109] A Madeira trip impressed even Social Democrats of long standing, reported a Sopade operative from Bavaria. On this particular cruise, equality and comradeship really did govern relationships among the passengers, for better off tourists extended financial help without bidding to those who otherwise could not have afforded some of the extras. Robert Ley's participation added to the good feeling on board. Evincing greater decorum (and sobriety) than the American journalist, William Bayles, observed, the Labor Front leader set aside time during his day to listen to the complaints of workers, out of the earshot of employers, about conditions on the shop floors of their companies.[110]

Further convincing workers as to the regime's accomplishments on their behalf, a visit to the slums abutting Lisbon's harbor prompted some to speak of the differences between the lives of German workers and workers in other countries. Workers who had never visited a seaport before, and thus had no basis of comparison, were astonished at the terrible conditions in which the natives lived. "All working-class vacationers (*Mitfahren-den*) were very satisfied with their trip, even former Social Democrats,"

---

108   Betr.: Bericht über die Rund um Italienfahrt v. 1.-12.12.1938 der KdF mit dem Schiff "Oceana," BAL R58, no. 950, 449.
109   Bericht no. 16, July 1935, in Stöver, *Berichte über die Lage*, 586.
110   *Sopade*, July 1935, 848.

concluded the reporter.[111] Be it in the excitement of workers from Austrian factory towns and villages upon traveling to Germany, or to Italy or Norway, or in the way that workers in a Social Democratic bastion such as the Ruhr saw their KdF trips as the highlight of their lives, KdF's tourism weakened what possibilities existed for a coherent and effective opposition. In the midst of a sullen and generally pervasive hostility among workers toward Nazism in general, the regime's social policy yielded positive results.[112]

The Third Reich enjoyed a durable popular legitimacy despite intermittent and deeply felt expressions of discontent and the declining popular receptivity to ideological mobilization. Popular support resulted in part from the successes that Nazi foreign policy produced, inflating the führer's "genius." It arose as well from the Third Reich's suppression of the cultural diversity of the Weimar period and from the regime's ability to put the unemployed back to work. Yet although each contributed to the regime's public standing, which most Germans did not seriously question until well into the war years, Nazism's attentiveness to the popular quality of life became the rubric that united all of the regime's "achievements" as testimony to Germany's resurgence. Even when German tourists behaved contrary to Strength through Joy's hopes, their observations confirmed KdF's ability to present a credible alternative to Fordism and socialism. Symbolizing the democratization of bourgeois privilege, however limited in practice, KdF's working-class tourists stood atop a hierarchy defined by income, the luck of the draw, or merit, in keeping with the regime's stress on "performance" as a signifier of racial superiority and key to personal reward. KdF signified, furthermore, the attack on class solidarity through individual effort, consistent with the expectations of upward mobility of its electorate.

While meditating between its consumers and the market to keep its costs low, KdF adopted the techniques and hedonistic messages of commercial leisure more willingly, and more successfully, than had the Weimar Left, or Italian Fascism, a possible explanation for why greater opposition to fascism existed in Italy than in Germany.[113] KdF conveyed the notion that

---

111 *Sopade*, July 1935, 848–9.

112 Bukey, *Hitler's Austria*, 86; Ulrich Herbert, "'Die Guten und die schlechten Zeiten:' Überlegungen zur diachronen Analyse lebensgeschichtlicher Interviews," in *"Die Jahre weiß man nicht, wo man die heute hinsetzen soll:" Faschismus-Erfahrungen im Ruhrgebiet: Lebensgeschichte und Sozialkultur im Ruhrgebiet 1930 bis 1960*, vol. 1, ed. Lutz Niethammer (Berlin, Bonn: Verlag J.H.W. Dietz Nachf., 1983), 75, 90–1.

113 See Geoff Eley, "Cultural Socialism, the Public Sphere, and the Mass Form: Popular Culture and the Democratic Project, 1900 to 1934," in *Between Reform and Revolution: German Socialism and Communism from 1840 to 1990*, ed. David E. Barclay and Eric D. Weitz (New York and Oxford: Berghahn, 1998): 333–6; and Victoria de Grazia, "Nationalizing Women: The Competition between Fascist and Commercial Models in Mussolini's Italy," in *Sex of Things*: 355.

serving the racial community was compatible with personal pleasure. As a modest vision of the "good life" when scarcity was more evident than prosperity, and when consumer expectations were more subdued than those of the present, KdF helped to persuade the majority of Germans whom the terror did not directly affect that an improved economy, rising living standards, and the regime's commitment to social opportunity defined the Third Reich. Even the antimaterialism and anticommercialism of Strength through Joy would not necessarily have repelled Germans. As the consumption patterns of German households testified, skepticism toward the seemingly profligate mass consumption of the United States coexisted, however uneasily, with popular admiration.[114]

To be sure, the war dealt KdF's tourism a severe blow. Nevertheless, despite the abrupt end of its vacation trips, Strength through Joy continued to impact the lives of ordinary Germans by staging entertainment for troops in the field and for civilians at home. In addition, KdF participated in the regime's ambitious endeavor to Germanize occupied Europe in keeping with the culture-creating propensity of the "master race." Most important, KdF's place in popular memories of the thirties contributed significantly to the perceptions of German invaders as they confronted the conquered, aggravating their exploitation of Germany's newly acquired living space.

114   Nancy Reagin, "Comparing Apples and Oranges: Housewives and the Politics of Consumption in Interwar Germany," in *Getting and Spending: European and American Consumer Societies in the Twentieth Century*, ed. Susan Strasser, Charles McGovern and Matthias Judt (Cambridge: Cambridge University Press, 1998). 241–61, and "*Marktordnung* und Autarkic Housekeeping: Housewives and Private Consumption under the Four-Year Plan, 1936–1939," *German History* 19, no. 2(2001): 162–84. In any case, as Michael Geyer points out, Germans remained suspicious of market-based consumption until the 1950s because of their experience with hunger during World War I and the occupation after World War II. See Konrad J. Jarausch and Michael Geyer, "In Pursuit of Happiness: Consumption, Mass Culture, and Consumerism," in *Shattered Past: Reconstructing German Histories*. (Princeton and Oxford: Princeton University Press, 2003): 268–314.

6

Memories of the Past and Promises for the Future: Strength through Joy in Wartime

In 1940, Strength through Joy issued a lavishly illustrated pamphlet, "To the Happy Isle: With the KdF Flagship, 'Robert Ley,' to the colorful world of Madeira and Tenerife."[1] As a photographic retrospective of its signature cruise, the booklet's dust jacket answered its readers' likely query: "A picture book by Strength through Joy in the middle of the war? Of course! The book will recall the happy memories of many." In reality, however, the *Robert Ley* now belonged to the Wehrmacht. Its tasks included transporting the wounded home from Poland and relocating ethnic Germans (*Volksdeutsche*) from the Baltic lands. Having been launched just four months before war erupted, its career as a cruise ship had abruptly ended. Nevertheless, the pamphlet struggled to reawaken recollections of more pleasant times with visions of touristic pleasure interwoven with suggestions of racial hierarchy.

Offering an inviting photographic mélange, "To the Happy Isle" traced the *Robert Ley's* voyage from start to finish, its passengers composed of blond, clean, and mostly youthful German vacationers sunning themselves on deck or touring on land in shiny new autos. Determined to stress the lush and exotic, the pamphlet revealed beautiful tropical vistas and dark-skinned natives, who danced alluringly in folk costumes or perched in fruit trees, hands and clothes dirty, comfortable in their natural habitat. Images of early twentieth-century consumer culture, such as young women in bathing suits smoking cigarettes, followed a few pages after Bodo Lafferentz's introduction to the pamphlet, which included his assertion that KdF cruises symbolized "a new self-consciousness" among Germans. Going beyond the usual claims that KdF had democratized privilege, in this case by opening Madeira, a playground for the wealthy, to German workers, the pamphlet offered another suggestion as well. Cruises to

---

1 "Nach den Glücklichen Inseln: Mit dem KdF.-Flagschiff 'Robert Ley' nach der far-benprächtigen Welt von Madeira und Teneriffa," ed. Karl Busch with an introduction by Bodo Lafferentz (Berlin: Zeitgeschichte Verlag, 1940), found in the Landeshauptarchiv Koblenz (hereinafter cited as LK), Bestand 714, no. 3838.

warm, sunny climes were not just a thing of the past. Rather, they signified a promise of future consumerist abundance, which the Reich's inexorable territorial enlargement would soon realize. Like the practical and comfortable Volkswagen, the "cornerstone of a beautiful future," for which three hundred thousand Germans continued to save, the suspension of KdF's cruises and the suppression of the natural yearning of Nordic peoples to travel to the south would prove only temporary.[2]

At first glance, the pamphlet seems an act of desperation, a sorry attempt to rely on the diversions of memory. If few expected a protracted war at the time of the booklet's publication, given the regime's reliance on the tactics of Blitzkrieg to accomplish its objectives, the hostilities should have proven catastrophic for Strength through Joy, at least for its most popular projects like tourism. Indeed, they did. Strength through Joy sacrificed its most ambitious undertaking to the acquisition of living space, in light of its dependence on the Labor Front and business for its financial resources, not to mention the state for its access to rolling stock. Already inhibited before the war by the construction of the fortifications on Germany's western border, as well as the strain on transportation networks arising from the annexations of Austria and Czechoslovakia,[3] its civilian tourism declined precipitously as the military appropriated the trains and busses that KdF used to transport its participants. Only KdF's arrangements of vacations for soldiers on leave and their families, or tours that it organized for troops to the major attractions of occupied Europe, resembled its prewar function.[4] Like the *Robert Ley*, Strength through Joy's ships moved ethnic Germans and served as floating military hospitals.[5] At most, short trips and weekend outings, nature hikes and ski trips, and the occasional trip down the Danube to Hungary, Bulgaria, and Romania continued until the damage inflicted by Allied armies and the Reich's own crumbling alliances put a premium on survival. To extract a virtue from necessity,

2 NSG Kraft durch Freude, Gau Steiermark, *Kraft durch Freude*, no. 21 (July 1940): 16; "Erfüllte Wünsche in Volkswagen" NSG Kraft durch Freude, Gau Salzburg, *Die Feierstunde: Monatsheft der NSG Kraft durch Freude* (October 1939): 12–14.
3 The Wehrmacht high command ordered the cessation of KdF trips to the western border regions as early as July 1938. Chef des Oberkommandos der Wehrmacht an die Deutsche Arbeitsfront Reichsamt Reisen, Wandern und Urlaub, 7 July 1938, Bundesarchiv, Militärarchiv Freiburg (hereinafter cited as BA-MA), RW 6/176; Chef OKW an Ministerpräsidenten Göring – Beauftragter für den Vierjahresplan – Reichskommissar für die Preisbildung, 5 July 1938, BA-MA RW/176, 42.
4 See Bertram Gordon, "Warfare and Tourism: Paris in World War II," *Annals of Tourism Research* 25, no. 3 (1998): 616–38; and Joshua Hagen, "The Most German of Towns: Creating the Ideal Nazi Community in Rothenburg ob der Tauber" *Annals of the Association of American Geographers* 94, no. 1 (2004).
5 Heinz Schön, *Die KdF-Schiffe und Ihr Schicksal: Eine Dokumentation* (Stuttgart: Motorbuch Verlag, 1987), 201–42.

KdF periodicals claimed that vacations in nearby environs could offer respite and recreation without the noise of busses and trains.[6]

Ironically, the reductions in KdF tourism contrasted with the experience of commercial tourism, which thrived until late in the war. The regime's inability to decide whether tourism was crucial to maintaining morale or a hindrance to the war effort encouraged commercial tourist interests to circumvent the few tentative restrictions that it put into effect.[7] Tourists crammed the trains that the Wehrmacht and SS needed to move troops to the front. Consistent with past practice, single women emerged in official eyes as the primary culprits in the disruption of military priorities. In their view, women had become carelessly self-indulgent, refusing to give up their seats on trains even to injured soldiers. Baedecker and Woerl continued to produce their popular guidebooks to newly acquired sites for soldiers and civilians. They ranged from well-established destinations like Paris and Strassbourg, to Polish cities such as Posen, the origins of which Baedecker located in the superior German culture and racial stock. As in the prewar KdF outings to the village of Dachau, the extermination centers went unmentioned in guidebooks to the General Government, thus continuing to segregate experientially the privileged from the persecuted. At home, commercial tourism promoters professionalized their operations and doggedly pursued their interests to anchor their competitive position after the war ended.[8] Strength through Joy's status, however, as an idiosyncratic, party-underwritten intermediary between its clientele and the tourism market place brought it a different fate.

Having struggled to forge the partnership between work and leisure, KdF felt the war's impact especially on the shop floor. It went without saying that the vacation trips that workers won either by luck, meritorious service, or party connections could no longer take place. Even company outings declined in frequency because KdF could not provide

6 "Einschränkung des Reiseverkehrs: Erneuter Ausfall der KdF.-Fahrten," NSG Kraft durch Freude, Gau Sachsen, *Monatsprogramm* (February 1940); "Winterfahrten und Skisport im Erzgebirge," NSG Kraft durch Freude, Gau Sachsen, *Monatsprogramm* (January 1941): 21; "Urlaub im Krieg?" NSG Kraft durch Freude, Gau Süd Hannover-Braunschweig, *KdF Monatsheft*, July 1940:1. The outbreak of war brought a memo from Ley, in his capacity as Reich organization leader, to the DAF's gau leadership regarding KdF's status in wartime, particularly that of the office for Travel, Hiking, and Vacations: Der Reichsorganisationsleiter der NSDAP an die Gauobmänner der DAF, 3 October 1939, *Akten der Partei-Kanzlei* (hereinafter cited as *APK* followed by the fiche number), ed. Institut für Zeitgeschichte (Munich and New York: Saur, 1983), no. 117 00021. For a brief description of KdF's wartime tourism, which has generally received little to no attention, see Frommann, "Reisen im Dienste," 302–4.
7 I am indebted to here to Kristin Semmens' "Domestic Tourism in the Third Reich" (Dis.: University of Cambridge, 2002), Ch. 6.
8 Rudy Koshar, *German Travel Cultures* (Oxford and New York: Berg, 2000), 149–56; and especially Semmens, "Domestic Tourism," ch. 6.

transportation. The workplace rationalization and beautification projects of the Beauty of Labor suffered as well. Despite Ley's belief in the continued viability of SdA projects in wartime and SdA's ambitious plans to cater to military needs by building recreation halls for the military in the occupied territories, the commitment of employers to aestheticization waned.[9] Although some companies remained determined to acquire or retain the status of "model enterprise" and thus proudly announced the completion of projects in the face of adversity, most reduced their allocations for Beauty of Labor undertakings.[10] Modest factory beautification campaigns with the prospect of completion faced obstacles, especially the loss of workers to the Wehrmacht. Moreover, the deployment of foreign labor to replace drafted Germans required greater than normal expenditures in training and oversight to motivate a reluctant work force, and thus employers would no longer justify outlays for physical improvements.

To be sure, business social spending did not neglect other KdF projects that companies deemed as important for morale, such as sports, theater, concert, and opera performances, comradeship evenings, and adult education courses. Yet employers redirected much of their outlay to benefit employees in the military in order to maintain their loyalty. Christmas packages and other types of succor were intended to solidify the "family" relationship between "leaders" and "followers" that the distance between home front and battlefront disrupted. Encouraged by the Labor Front, company-subsidized newspapers regularly featured letters from employee soldiers, who shared the combination of fear and tedium that characterized life at the front with those left behind. The suspension of Beauty of Labor projects was not simply confined to industry. SdA's campaign in the countryside to improve the appearance, cleanliness, and charm of rural villages existed only in SdA and KdF periodicals. In light of the more pressing problems in agriculture, notably labor shortages and the continued emigration to industrial regions, the Reich's difficulties in assuring an adequate food supply for its population took precedence. Ultimately, the fertile agricultural lands of eastern and southeastern Europe would compensate for the shortfall.[11]

---

9   Ley to Gauobmänner, *APK*, 117 0021; Ley an Kommandeur der Feldpostnummer 06577; Betrifft: Urlaubsantrag für den Leutnant Herbert Steinwarz, 6 June 1941, Bundesarchiv, Berlin-Lichterfelde (hereinafter cited as BAL), NS 22/962.

10 "Nachtrag zum Leistungsbericht," Wirtschaftsarchiv Baden–Württemberg Stuttgart (hereinafter cited as WABW), B26, no. 119, 3; Kraft durch Freude Fond, Anker-Werke, Stiftung Westfälisches Wirtschaftsarchiv Dortmund (hereinafter cited as WWA), F42, no. 107, 57.

11 "Das schöne Dorf im Kriege," NSG Kraft durch Freude, Gau Steiermark, *Monatsprogramm*, nos. 33 and 34 (July, August 1941): 13, 5, 7. On the Reich's losing battle with domestic agriculture and its exploitation of the occupied territories, see Gustavo Corni, *Hitler and the Peasants* (New York, Oxford, Munich: Berg, 1990), 156–268.

Nevertheless, Strength through Joy proved adept at maintaining its position in the polycratic, hypercompetitive world of National Socialism despite the setbacks of war. It was, after all, an institution that had survived and even prospered by operating within the priorities that the party, state, and business had established. Its offerings aside from tourism and plant aestheticization gave it the wherewithal to endure. Thus, KdF concentrated its energies in non-touristic, morale sustaining, education and entertainment programs that although well established before the war, took on increased importance after 1939. Fearful, and not without reason, of becoming irrelevant, KdF's leaders exploited every opportunity to proclaim KdF's indispensability. As long as paper shortages did not inhibit their publication, Strength through Joy's periodicals spewed forth a barrage of statistics to prove that now more than ever, the racial community would not last without it. KdF's recreational programs, averred Bodo Lafferentz in 1943 after the huge military reverses in North Africa and the Soviet Union, reached not just the home front. Rather, its artists and operatives still performed heroically in the territories that remained under the Wehrmacht's control. In that year alone, he continued, KdF increased its cultural events among civilians by 128,000 over the previous year, raising the size of its audience from thirty-eight to fifty-one million participants. The number of KdF-led company competitive sports clubs, he claimed further, stood at ten thousand.[12] After all, according to the author of a ten-year retrospective of its accomplishments, KdF would have shut down altogether during the war had it been but a mere "luxury." Yet the expansion of the Reich had only made it more necessary.[13]

German Domination and the "European Community": KdF's Troop Entertainment

Emblematic of its protean development and its ability to exploit the opportunities that the regime conceded to it, Strength through Joy actually laid the foundations for its wartime status less than two years after its founding. In the summer of 1935, several months after Hitler's introduction of universal military conscription, KdF concluded an agreement with the Wehrmacht that allowed it to provide at low cost to its audiences theater performances, concerts, variety, puppet, and marionette shows, lectures,

12 "Die Gesamtleistung von KdF: Ein Rechenschaftsbericht über zehn Jahre," 28 November 1943, Niedersächsisches Hauptstaatsarchiv Hannover (hereinafter cited as NHH), VVP 17, no. 2455.
13 "KdF. Im Frieden und im Kriege. Zum zehnjährigen Bestehen am 27. November – Quelle der Sammlung und seelischen Stärkung," *Deutsche Ukraine-Zeitung*, 26 November 1943, NHH, VVP, no. 2455.

and craft lessons to enlisted men stationed in garrisons throughout the Reich. Formally known as "caring for the troops" (*Truppenbetreuung*), KdF's offerings were neither to undermine its primary function as a source of civilian recreation nor to compromise the special standing of the officer corps in the state. Thus, the Wehrmacht high command forbade officers from attending KdF performances, for in its view, KdF catered to the lower social classes.[14] KdF also opened its tours to Wehrmacht personnel with the proviso that officers and civilians earning more than 250 Reichsmarks per month, the KdF income limit, would be accommodated only on a space available basis.[15] Finally, members of the Wehrmacht high command received invitations to attend the World Congress on Work and Recreation in Hamburg in 1936. A Wehrmacht delegate served on the committee for sport and calisthenics in preparation for the same conference two years later.[16] The rapid expansion of the armed forces after 1935 well beyond the Versailles limit of 100,000 land and 15,000 naval troops and 4,000 officers convinced the Wehrmacht of the necessity of leisure programs that would maintain the morale of draftees. By the end of 1938, KdF's troop entertainment program had organized over 1.3 million events, including vacation trips and outings.[17]

With the invasion of Poland troop entertainment assumed even greater importance. In March 1940, the propaganda ministry laid the foundation for the further expansion of "caring for the troops" by creating a new office led by Hans Hinkel, the director of the Reich Chamber of Culture and a close associate of Goebbels. Apart from extending his propaganda and enlightenment empire, Goebbels believed implicitly that satisfying the recreational needs of the troops would strengthen their fighting spirit.[18] "Caring for the Troops" would also cultivate the cultural superiority appropriate to a master race, now that Germany had officially launched its bid for continental hegemony. Although Strength through Joy's troop entertainment was clearly subordinated to the propaganda ministry, KdF

---

14   Reichskriegsminister an Oberbefehlshaber des Heeres, der Kriegsmarine, und der Luftwaffe, Betr.: Beteiligung der Wehrmacht an der NS-Gemeinschaft "Kraft durch Freude," 29 July 1935, BA-MA RW6/176.

15   Der Reichs und Preussicher Minister des Innern an den Herrn Oberpräsidenten der Provinz Hannover, 14 August 1937, NHH, Hann. 122a, VIII, no. 577, 227.

16   Der Reichskriegsminister an das Reichsministerium für Volksaufklärung und Propaganda, Betr.: Weltkongress für Feierabendgestaltung, 14 July 1936, BA-MA RW 6/86, 179–80; Wehrmachtsamt an O.K.H., O.K.M., R.L.M., 6 January 1938; Betr: Weltkongress für Arbeit und Freizeit in Rom, BA-MA, RW6/86, no. 384.

17   Otto Marrenbach, *Fundamente des Sieges: Die Gesamtarbeit der Deutschen Arbeitsfront von 1933 bis 1940* (Berlin: Verlag der Deutschen Arbeitsfront, 1940), 338.

18   Reichsministerium für Volksaufklärung und Propaganda an den Herrn Präsidenten der Reichsschriftumskammer, 1 March 1940, Betr. Truppenbetreuung, BAL R56V, Michael H. Kater, *Different Drummers: Jazz in the Culture of Nazi Germany* (New York and Oxford: Oxford University Press, 1992), 117.

derived substantial benefits from Hinkel's office, not the least of which was the significant infusion of funds. Equally important, it gained access to a crucial resource, the Chamber of Culture's members, each of whom was required to devote six weeks per year to entertaining the armed forces.[19] Apart from the commissioning and delivery of most films, which the propaganda ministry and Reich Film Chamber undertook on its own, Strength through Joy was authorized to present concerts, theater performances, variety shows, poetry readings, lectures, and craft classes without cost to the troops.[20]

For entertainers, the relative ease and direction of the Wehrmacht's conquests on the continent during the first year and a half of the war brought attractive dividends. Service in Strength through Joy troupes provided stipends of up to one hundred Reichsmarks per day and travel that from a tourist's perspective appeared desirable. Aside from German-occupied Poland, the western parts of which were directly incorporated directly into the Reich as Danzig–West Prussia and the Warthegau, KdF assignments took performers to France, Holland, Belgium, and Norway. Male entertainers earned the added perquisite of exemption from the draft in return for agreeing to the six weeks commitment. Yet the Wehrmacht's invasions of Greece, the Balkans and North Africa to shore up the faltering Italian armies, and in June 1941, the Soviet Union, presented formidable difficulties. Not only did KdF troupes face inclement weather, poor roads, and otherwise harsh geographical conditions, such as the North African desert that encouraged the Wehrmacht to ban the use of female performers, partisan attacks also compromised their safety. Moreover, the lack of theaters, opera houses, and concert halls in the field and in remote areas required additional adjustments when local facilities could not accommodate large troupes. Thus, instead of full orchestras and municipal theater companies, Strength through Joy used portable stages and small troupes of performers.[21] Nevertheless, by the end of 1941 when the invasion of the Soviet Union bogged down outside Moscow, Strength through Joy's troop entertainment had extended to all theaters of the war, including North Africa. Between September 1939 and late 1941, KdF staged 337,400

19   Alan Steinweis, *Art, Ideology, and Economics in Nazi Germany: The Reich Chambers of Music, Theater, and the Visual Arts* (Chapel Hill and London: University of North Carolina Press, 1993), 149–50.
20   "Anregung zur Freizeitgestaltung in der Wehrmacht," *Soldatenblätter für Feier und Freizeit*, ed. OKW Abteilung Inland, April 1940, BA-MA RW 6/447, 30–33.
21   Oberkommando des Heeres an OKW, Abt. Inland (II), 14 June 1941, BA-MA RW6/176, 553–4; Betr.: Stand der geistigen Betreuung der Truppe: Oberkommando des Heeres an OKW Abteilung Wehrmacht-Propaganda, OKW Abteilung Inland, 5 March 1940, BA-MA RW6/176; Deutsche Wehrmachtmission in Rumänien an OKW-Abt. Inland, Betr.: Geistliche Betreuung, 14 December 1940, BA-MA RW6/176, 256 b and c; Aussenstelle Wien 2. Bericht, 3 May 1941, BA-MA RW6/176, no. 437. See also Kater, *Different Drummers*, 117–18.

performances that reached audiences, which collectively numbered well over 126 million.[22] Given varying conditions, the diffusion of KdF's entertainment was uneven, yet the frequency with which its performers appeared at the front, in barracks, or in military hospitals solidified its claims to indispensibility.

Like its tourism, in which sensitivity to popular desires competed with its desire for a mobilized clientele, Strength through Joy took pains to ensure that its entertainment conformed to the expectations of the troops, while agreeing to observe the Wehrmacht's injunction that its performers obey the chain of command, adhere to military regulations, and settle for normal military provisions.[23] Aside from the occasional hazily defined request from commanders for "worthy" entertainment, troops expressed the general and unsurprising desire for entertainment that reminded them of home. Most often, soldiers requested small musical, theater, and dance groups that produced popular or folk entertainment rather than the masterpieces of "high" culture. Except for the occasional plea for church music, classical music carried little appeal, according to one Wehrmacht survey. Yodelers, magicians, humorists, poets who read from their own works, and musicians who played instruments such as harmonicas, accordions, and zithers went over particularly well. So did courses that introduced soldiers to a craft, woodworking being a prime example. Playing cards, games, periodicals, and radios that allowed the troops to pass their time off duty composed the remaining requests for sources of diversion. In Norway for obvious reasons, soldiers enthusiastically demanded organized winter sport competitions, in addition to other forms of cultural recreation. Despite the antipathy toward jazz, which the Nazi regime's cultural epigones scorned as "Jewish–nigger" music and the offal of American mass culture, Strength through Joy provided bookings for jazz musicians. Even the jazz-hating Goebbels succumbed to pragmatism, having appreciated the benefits to morale that accommodating popular tastes in wartime would bring.[24]

If entertainment was to bring to troops some of the comforts of home, the soldiers' requests for lectures, books, and other reading material revealed their desire to make sense of their present experience, conforming to Nazi ideology and their own prejudices. In addition to speakers who could discuss their war adventures, troops wanted experts, such as historians and geologists, who could introduce them to the foreign lands where

---

22 Die Deutsche Arbeitsfront Propagandaamt, *Bericht des Leiters der NS-Gemeinschaft KdF. Pg. Dr. Lafferentz zum Jahrestag der NSG KdF. am 27. November 1941*, 4.

23 Oberkommando des Heeres Gen. Z.b.v../H West Abt. (II) 28 February 1942, Betr.: Rechtstellung der in der Truppenbetreuung Eingesetzten Zivilpersonen, BA-MA RW6/178.

24 Kater, *Different Drummers*, 166.

they were stationed, and guidebooks that would aid them as they sought out sites in their free time. An indication of the degree to which soldiers' interests shared the regime's own imperialist and racist agendas, their book and lecture requests included topics such as Napoleon's conquest of Egypt, Germany and the Balkans, the resettlement of Germans in Lithuania and the Soviet Union, the Italian colonization of Libya, and Hans Grimm's influential work, *A People without Space* (*Volk ohne Raum*).[25] Their requests also prominently featured the antisemitic films, *Jud Süss* and *Der ewige Jude*, that had been released in 1940 to justify the deportations of Jews from Austria, Czechoslovakia, and Germany to Polish ghettoes.[26] Although mediated by their commanding officers, such desires suggest soldiers' receptivity to official antisemitism, or at minimum, the confluence of popular and official hostility toward Jews. That level of ideological engagement helps to explain the tenacity with which the Wehrmacht fought until the bitter end.[27]

Strength through Joy's desire to please yielded dividends in the troops' oft-expressed appreciation of its work on their behalf. Regardless, the demand for entertainment outstripped the supply of quality entertainers, creating problems that given expectations for a quick victory had not been foreseen. Despite the proliferation of orchestras, theater companies, and musical groups to meet the demand, the shortage of talented performers and the loss of KdF volunteers to conscription who normally did the bookings yielded complaints which Hinkel's office and KdF could not resolve.

25 Recommendations as to the entertainment needs of troops are found in the following: Deutsches Afrika-Korps Abt. I an das OKW, Betr.: Truppenbetreung in Afrika, 27 May 1941, BA-MA RW6/176, 433 a and b; Auszüge aus Winter – Erfahrungs berichten 1940/41, BA-MA, RW6/293, unnumbered. Wehrmachtbefehlshaber Norwegen an Heimatstab Nord, 13 December 1940, BA-MA RW6/176, 288; Leutnant Berndt an OKW WPr Gruppe V, 29 May 1941, BA-MA, RW6/176, 556–7; OKW/W Pr. Aussenstelle Brüssel an das OKW Wehrmachtsprogaganda 11f, 27 October 1940, Betr.: Filmlieferung, BA-MA RW6/292, unnumbered; W. Pr. IIfan OKW/WPr. Aussenstelle Paris, 21 January 1941, BA-MA, RW6/293, unnumbered; Die Deutsche Arbeitsfront, NS-Gemeinschaft "Kraft durch Freude," Reichsdienststelle, *Truppenbetreuung*, January–February 1942, Institut für Zeitgeschichte, Munich (hereinafter cited as IfZ), 72.34.

26 On the impact of the films, see Linda Schulte-Sasse, *Entertaining the Third Reich: Illusions of Wholeness in Nazi Cinema* (Durham and London: Duke University Press, 1996), 47–91; David Welch, *The Third Reich: Politics and Propaganda* (London and New York: Routledge, 1993), 76–82; and David Culbert, "The Impact of Anti-Semitic Film Propaganda on German Audiences: *Jew Süss* and *The Wandering Jew*," in *Art, Culture, and Media Under the Third Reich*, ed. Richard A. Etlin (Chicago and London: University of Chicago Press, 2002): 139–57.

27 On the ideological underpinnings of the Wehrmacht's murderousness, particularly the manner in which troops blamed their victims, see Omer Bartov, *Hitler's Army: Soldiers, Nazis, and War in the Third Reich* (New York and Oxford: Oxford University Press, 1991). Bartov has also argued that workers drafted into the armed forces differed little from soldiers from other backgrounds in their commitment to war effort. See his "The Missing Years: German Workers, German Soldiers," in *Nazism and German Society, 1933–1945*, ed. David F. Crew (London and New York: Routledge, 1994): 41–66.

Both faced the reluctance of entertainers, who were in a position to be choosy, to serve at the front or in otherwise undesirable locations, despite the handsome stipends they earned.[28] Some complaints from troops, such as the demand for first-run films rather than movies that had been released well before the war, were relatively mild.[29] Others, however, revealed the scorn which troops heaped upon acts that they considered substandard. Thus as early as the spring of 1940, the problem of incompetent performers became serious enough to bring a vehement response. Complained a KdF operative, soldiers stationed near Cologne hooted a performer and his accompanist, a poorly rehearsed female guitarist, after imbibing considerable quantities of beer. When commanded by a guard to cease until order was restored, the troops clapped sarcastically and then promptly departed. The base command, according to the source, did little to welcome the performers and the KdF staff who accompanied her, and even less to curb the soldiers' reprehensible behavior.[30] The problem only became worse the longer the war lasted. In 1944, a report from Gau Pomerania criticized the dancers, accordianists, and singers that KdF had "let loose on humanity" (*auf die Menschheit losgelassen werden*). They appeared so "work shy," no doubt a deliberately chosen expression to equate the performers with a cohort of concentration camp prisoners, that they had not undertaken even the minimum rehearsal. "A dancer who has nothing better to do than to show a few more or less graceful bounces of naked flesh for her compensation of forty marks is insane," the report huffed. The officer in charge of troop entertainment in the Pomeranian military district declared that he preferred to go without KdF events for a month rather than subject his soldiers to the "crap" (*Mist*) to which they had recently been subjected.[31]

Other reports of dissatisfaction with Strength through Joy's entertainment referred not only to the lack of talent of the entertainers, but also the desire of many performers to exploit a buyers' market by jacking up their fees. KdF's successful gambit before the war to regulate the fees for its services failed utterly as the scale of German imperialism confounded attempts to contain the cost of its entertainment. In Norway where long dark winters and boredom presented a chronic problem, KdF performances went unattended because in the view of the troops, the performers

28 Interview Herr Anatol von Hübbenet – Dr. Erica Schirmer am 28. August 1948 über Kurzwelle nach USA, "The German Labor Front's Cultural Program," BA-MA RW4/274, 285.

29 Armeeoberkommando 4 an die Reichspropagandaleitung, Hauptamt Film, 24 February 1941, BA-MA RW6/293.

30 Auszug aus einem Schreiben der Herrn Dr. Hans Künkel, Frankfurt (Oder, Brinbaumshülle 5–7), 12 April 1940, BA-MA RW6/176, 125–6.

31 Auszug aus dem Tätigkeitsbericht für Monat Februar Gau Pommern: Veranstaltung der NS-Gemeinschaft "Kraft durch Freude," 3 March 1944, BAL R56I/37, 31–32.

left something to be desired. Reported one source, many KdF-sponsored artists had gone a long time between jobs and their present contracts with KdF and the Chamber of Culture testified more to the business acumen of their agents than to their musical or artistic gifts. To add to the irritation, the demand for entertainers allowed them to negotiate salaries at levels well out of proportion to their career accomplishments. A promoter from Berlin, more interested in the profit he could gain from leasing autos to KdF troupes than in delivering quality entertainment was in charge of the local KdF office.[32] The torture of embarrassing performances by over-priced entertainers exasperated commanders, as was the case of the KdF musical group "Alvari." "It cannot be the task of a troupe to provoke gales of laughter from the soldiers and Norwegian civilians in attendance when during its performance it presents an aesthetically unpleasing picture of physical deformity."[33] Despite the aggravation that the overblown compensation of performers caused in the military, the propaganda ministry, and in the office of the deputy führer, Rudolf Hess, a solution proved elusive, even after March 1943 when Goebbels limited the number of venues where performances could be staged, excluding in particular the larger cities of occupied Europe.[34] Only in mid-1944 did Goebbels extract a promise from Ley that he rein in the inflation in performers' salaries, with meager results.[35]

Yet Strength through Joy's contribution to the German war effort remains unappreciated if evaluated solely according to its appeal to its audiences. Rather, KdF's fealty to the Nazi regime's racial and cultural objectives suggests a different, and more important, insight into its wartime role. KdF consigned its troop entertainment program to the Reich's imperial blueprint as it unfolded in the acquisition of living space; a vision that included the transformation of conquered territories befitting the culture-creating propensities of superior races. At its most defensive, Nazism's cultural campaign consisted of inoculating its soldiers against the alien influences of racial inferiors, a task that KdF took as seriously as satisfying soldiers' desires. The need to maintain morale conjoined uneasily with the high command's recommendation that the free time of soldiers,

32   Wehrmachtbefehlshaber Norwegen Abt. Ic. an OKW/Abt. Inland über Heimatstab Nord Ic, 27 April 1941; Betr.: Einsatz von KdF.-Spielgruppen, BA-MA RW6/176, 477–79.
33   Terr. Bef. Südnorwegen Abschn. Süd an das Höh. Kommando XXXVI, 13 January 1941; Betr.: KdF-Gruppe "Alvari," BA-MA RW6/176, 473.
34   Entscheidung des Reichsministers für Volksaufklärung und Propaganda, die Betreuung der Wehrmachtteile durch künstlerische Darbietungen betreffend, 10 March 1943, BAL R56 I/37, no. 41–2.
35   Der Stellv. Gauleiter, Gauleitung Moselland, Koblenz an den Stellv. des Führers, 3 March 1941,Vorlage für den Herrn Minister, Betrifft: KdF-Veranstaltungen, 16 April 1941, *APK*, nos. 066975 and 066974. See also Steinweis, *Art, Ideology, and Economics*, 152–3.

like that of workers, be carefully monitored. Because the Reich's cultural mission promoted the cultural wealth of the German nation, the quality of KdF entertainment and the caliber of soldiers' self-entertainment was depended on its "Germanness." Thus, despite the shortage of competent artists and the complaints that untalented ones generated, the propaganda ministry, the Chamber of Culture, and the Wehrmacht restricted the employment of foreign entertainers, including those who performed for Strength through Joy. Only written testimonials of political reliability, the prior submission of the performers' material, and the unavailability of ethnic German artists could circumvent that restriction. In addition to membership in the Reich Chamber of Culture and the possession of Aryan certification, performers had to prove longstanding ties to Germany, either through family members, spouses, or years in residence. That such restrictions proved unworkable, worthy of being ignored in the eyes of impresarios, does not detract from the dread that produced them.[36]

However objectionable, most foreign entertainers were at least citizens of neutral, satellite, or occupied states. Far worse from the perspective of the Wehrmacht and KdF was the pernicious influence of American or western European mass culture. Thus, KdF's woodworking courses encouraged representations of high art and discouraged "kitsch," described as tacky gift articles, mementoes, and sculptures influenced by passing fads, or more generally, the commercially manufactured and mechanically replicated objects of mass consumption.[37] Bonzo, the pudgy British cartoon dog that inspired popular and commercial reproductions, and the Walt Disney cartoon character, Mickey Mouse, whose blackness and associations with jazz represented the "negroization" (*Verniggerung*) of German culture to Nazis, epitomized the models to be avoided.[38] Ironically, KdF's inability to service some commands because of its finite personnel raised fears that troops could become tainted in the absence of sufficient "German" entertainment. Reported the deputy general command for East Prussia, the neglect of the troops' recreational needs allowed the penetration of insidious Polish influences.[39] In the protectorates of Bohemia and Moravia, even Strength through Joy's presence, as evidenced

---

36 Steinweis, *Art, Ideology, and Economics*, 156–7; BA-MA RW6/176 contains extensive correspondence regarding foreign entertainers.

37 "Freizeitschaffen: Weisungen zur volkstümlichen Holzwerkarbeit," *Tournisterschrift des Oberkommandos der Wehrmacht Allgemeines Wehrmachtamt-Abteilung Inland* 83 (1943), BA-MA RW6/444.

38 For a description of Bonzo, see http:www.bonzo.me.uk. On Mickey Mouse, see Miriam Hansen, "Of Mice and Ducks: Benjamin and Adorno on Disney," *South Atlantic Quarterly*, 92, no. 1 (Winter 1993): 33–4.

39 Stellvertretender Generalkommando I, Armeekorps (Wehrkreiskommando I) an die Gaudienststellen der NS-Gemeinschaft "Kraft durch Freude," 3 August 1940, BA-MA RW6/176, 128–30.

in the appearances of its theatrical troupes and variety shows, did not suffice given the barrenness of the country and the cultural backwardness of its people. Thus the troops needed approved forms of recreation that they could undertake themselves.[40]

Beyond immunizing German soldiers against the Slavs, the kitsch of Americanized mass consumption, and unregulated free time, KdF's leaders imagined themselves at the forefront of the Third Reich's construction of a new European community under German suzerainty. Germany would liberate Europe from Bolshevism and Americanism, renovating the continent through the magnificence of its culture and superior racial stock. Claimed Lafferentz, National Socialism represented the social liberator of Europe from Bolshevism with Strength through Joy serving as its cultural arm. KdF's service to the home front, its care of the cultural needs of Wehrmacht troops, and its generous efforts to entertain foreign workers, who would in turn benefit from their exposure to German artists, would cement a genuine European "community."[41] Such pious assertions, shared by much of the Nazi leadership, accorded in part with a longer tradition of "anticonquest." European explorers, scientists, traders, imperialists, and tourists justified their ventures by claiming their reciprocal relationships with non-European cultures, cloaking the violence that they unleashed with paeans to the "civilization" and "progress" which they had bestowed on benighted "natives."[42] The Nazi regime's decimation of millions by various means, however – atrocities visited this time on other Europeans – suggest that Strength through Joy's pretensions to the dissemination of Germany's superior culture appeared not so much to mask the Nazi regime's ferocity as to magnify it. The cultural transformation of the Nazi "New Order" required not just the transfer of populations and the subjection of others to forced labor, it also depended on the extermination of the destroyers of culture, the Jews.

From the Nazi perspective, cultural renewal was most urgent in Eastern Europe, the focal point of the Reich's drive for living space, for it

---

40 Wehrmachtbevollmächtigte beim Reichsprotektor in Böhmen und Mähren, Tätigkeitsbericht über die Arbeit der Abteilung im ersten Kriegesjahr, 16 September 1940, BA-MA RW 6/176, no. 158.

41 Bodo Lafferentz, *10 Jahre NS-Gemeinschaft Kraft durch Freude*, 1944, 20–3.

42 On the National Socialist version of European "community," see Mark Mazower, *Dark Continent: Europe's Twentieth Century* (New York: Alfred A. Knopf, 1999); 138–81; Hans-Dieter Schäfer, *Das gespaltene Bewußtsein: Über deutsche Kultur und Lebenswirklichkeit 1933–1945* (Munich, Vienna: Carl Hanser Verlag, 1981), 125–6; and Michael Burleigh, *The Third Reich: A New History* (New York: Hill and Wang, 2000), 407–32. For the notion of "anticonquest," see Mary Louise Pratt, *Imperial Eyes: Travel Writing and Transculturation* (London and New York: Routledge, 1992), passim. On the imperialist conceptions of French colonial tourism, see Ellen Furlough, "*Une leçon de Choses*: Tourism, Empire, and the Nation in Interwar France," *French Historical Studies*, 35, no. 3 (Summer 2002): 441–73.

was populated by racially inferior "subhumans" (*Untermenschen*), whom the regime slated for removal or extermination. Thus, echoing the tour brochures and monthly magazines of the prewar period, Strength through Joy's publications touted Germany's civilizing mission in Poland following Poland's collapse in the fall of 1939. Whatever culture remained in the Poland of the present, they claimed, resulted from the German migrations of the Middle Ages. The founding of Polish cities, the introduction of Christianity, Polish art and architecture, and even Poland's famous university in Krakow emerged from the cultural initiative and sophistication of Germans. According to Lafferentz, Strength through Joy's special task was to create a "stable order" by restoring German culture, thus undoing the material and spiritual damage that the Poles had inflicted in the centuries since the Slavs drove the Germans back.[43] For the occupied territories of western and northern Europe, which ranked higher in the Nazi racial hierarchy, KdF's cultural project veered unsteadily between the acknowledgment of the cultural achievements of defeated nations and assertions of German superiority. The tours that KdF organized for German troops in Paris and its environs, which took in sights such as Notre Dame, the Champs Elysées, the Opera, the Louvre, the Eiffel Tower, the Pantheon, Versailles, and the Loire Valley, certified the occupiers' pilgrimage to the signifiers of French high culture. At the same time KdF's excursions suggested the decline of French power in the face of the German ascendancy. KdF brought its international wing, the "Congress for Joy and Work," to occupied Europe to celebrate Germany's destruction of capitalistic–democratic doctrine, which purportedly treated workers only as the means of enriching a narrow elite. Yet whatever its claims to democratization, its opening ceremonies entertained dignitaries with the music of high culture, Beethoven, Mozart, Wagner, and Tchaikovsky.[44]

In reality, Lafferentz's conception of Strength through Joy as the avatar of German cultural expansion situated it in a broader cultural and propaganda offensive, which Hans Hinkel undertook in his dual role as director of the Reich Chamber of Culture and the propaganda ministry's troop entertainment office. In his book on the "Jewish quarters" of Europe from the Baltic to the Black Seas, which he compiled in the fall of 1939 after the Wehrmacht's conquest of Poland, Hinkel served notice that the

43 "Deutsche Kultur im Osten," NSG Kraft durch Freude, Gau Sachsen, *Monatsprogramm*, (November 1939): 4–7; "Deutsche Städte im Brennpunkt des Weltgeschehens: Das Zeugnis der Bauten und des Geistes Polens grosse Lehrmeister," NSG Kraft durch Freude Gau München-Oberbayern, *Kraft durch Freude* (October 1939): 2–5.
44 Gordon, "Warfare and Tourism:" 620–7; "Freude und Arbeit" Festkonzert im Konzertgebäude im Amsterdam, Auswärtiges Amt Politisches Archiv, Bonn (hereinafter cited as AA-PA), R99029, 4 November 1940.

acquisition of living space would mean the purge of Jewish–Bolshevik cultural influences in the east that the regime had accomplished at home.[45] His offensive expanded exponentially following the launch of the German invasion of the Soviet Union in June 1941, Germany's apocalyptic war par excellence. Bragged Hinkel in 1942, no fewer than 350 theaters and accompanying acting schools had formed in the Greater German Reich, not to mention the many others that had emerged in the German sphere of influence. In the "decisive battle against the Bolshevik enemy of all culture," Hinkel continued, ninety million Germans were ready to take the "greatest step in the revolution of our millennium." In recognition of Germany's arrival as the cultural center of a "new, free, and happy" Europe, Hinkel announced, KdF officially became the seventh office of the Chamber of Culture so that it could better fulfill its task of disseminating the best of Germany's artistic heritage.[46]

KdF's new status, which Ley had championed for months because it offered more financial support and a broader mandate beyond entertaining the armed forces, won the tepid support of Hinkel's immediate superior. Goebbels' backing apparently persuaded the führer to put aside his initial reservations. Although KdF as the purveyor of culture to the masses seemed a poor fit for the chamber, the scale of Germany's cultural imperialism brought a change of heart.[47] Symptomatic of the ambitions that soared in the wake of the Wehrmacht's conquests, Ley chafed at the limitations imposed on KdF, particularly the military's ban against the admission of civilians to performances for the troops, for he sought to address the cultural needs of German settlers as well.[48] Seeking to enlarge its purview, KdF personnel commandeered the playhouses, stages, concert halls, and opera houses of the Soviet Union soon after the invasion commenced, seeking to obliterate the culture-destroying pestilence of "Jewish Bolshevism." As early as July 1941, KdF had occupied a theater in the Lithuanian capital of Vilna. Consistent with the way it cannibalized the ideas and resources of the left at its founding in 1933, KdF showed little hesitation in availing itself of the first-class concert hall of the House of the Red Army to carry out its cultural mission.[49]

45 *Judenviertel Europas: Die Juden zwischen Ostsee und Schwarzem Meer*, ed. Hans Hinkel (Berlin: Volk und Reich Verlag, 1939).
46 Hans Hinkel, "Das Kulturzentrum des neuen Europa," undated, BAL R56I/37, 8–10.
47 Goebbels, *Die Tagebücher von Joseph Goebbels*, ed. Elke Fröhlich (Munich: K.G. Saur, 1996, 1998) part I, vol. 8, entries for October 1940, 361–2 and November 1940, 437; part II, vol. 2, entry for 22 November 1941, 342.
48 Notiz für Parteigenossen Passe. Betr.: Besuch von KdF-Wehrmachtveranstaltung durch Zivildeutsche in den besetzten Ostgebieten, 30 June 1943, *APK*, no. 066299 and 066300.
49 Oberkommando der Wehrmacht Abteilung Inland Aussenstellung Nordost, 17 July 1941 an OKW/Abt. Inland, BA-MA RW6/176, no. 574–5.

Purging the Ghosts of 1918: Entertaining the Home Front

The Nazi regime's support of Strength through Joy's continuation in wartime arose in part from the desire to avoid a repetition of 1918, when the collapse of civilian resolve brought the removal of the monarchy and the emergence of the Weimar "system."[50] As it did in the case of military entertainment, the propaganda ministry intervened in KdF's activities, which included promoting greater cooperation between KdF and small and medium-sized towns in advertising, staging, and financing of the performing arts. Despite the jurisdictional friction that arose between KdF and communal officials, the effort to assure the delivery of culture outside the largest cities testified to the regime's belief that maintaining morale meant assuring civilians that even in wartime, the "cultural property" of the nation would be theirs to enjoy.[51]

Geared from the beginning to bring culture to the masses to strengthen the popular commitment to the racial community, KdF's endeavors in the performing arts continued to promote low-cost access to high cultural productions. Works were selected not only because of their canonical status, but also because many testified to the racial status of Germans as culture "creators." Thus, in addition to promoting the operas of Bizet and Verdi KdF purveyed tickets to the plays of Goethe, Lessing, Kleist, and Schiller, concerts that featured Bach, Brahms, Schubert, and Beethoven, and the operas of Mozart, and Wagner. Its mobilization of soldiers, secretaries, and armaments workers to attend the Wagner festival at Bayreuth as "guests of the Führer," an undertaking which included an introductory lecture to the composer's work, proved hugely successful.[52] Although reproducing for its clientele the accepted repertory of the cultivated middle classes, one that included Italian and French opera, KdF fused

---

50 The need to strengthen the resilience of German civilians was explicitly stated in the document of October 1939, "Die Aufgabe der NS-Gemeinschaft 'Kraft durch Freude' während des Kriegeszustandes,"*APK*, no. 117 00023. This especially concerned DAF officials at the local level. Cf. Klaus-Michael Mallmann and Gerhard Paul, *Herrschaft und Alltag: Ein Industrierevier im Dritten Reich: Widerstand und Verweigerung im Saarland, 1935–1945* (Bonn: J.H.W. Dietz Nachf. Verlag, 1991), 142–2.

51 The agreement, approved in May 1941 by the interior ministry, the Reich Theater Chamber, and the propaganda ministry, is in the files of the Deutscher Gemeindetag, BAL R36/2361. A good example of the conflicts that arose is the memorandum from the mayor of Rathenow, 23 December 1941, Betrifft: Förderung des Kulturlebens in Rathenow – Verhältnis zu KdF., BAL R36/2361. The persistence of commercial tourism during the war as a means of maintaining a degree of normality, and thus morale, is a prominent theme in Semmens, "Domestic Tourism," Ch. 6.

52 *Meldungen aus dem Reich* (hereinafter cited as *Meldungen*), ed. Heinz Boberach (Herrsching: Pavlak, 1983): 15, 27 September 1943: 5806–11.

high culture and racism. KdF functionaries explained the popularity of Shakespeare with German audiences by reference to the British racist philosopher Houston Stewart Chamberlain, who argued that the English bard had brought German creativity to its summit. Performances of Ibsen lent themselves to equally racial interpretations, as did the lionizing of Wagner, whom KdF described as having taken German culture to a new level.[53]

Despite its steady stream of high culture, Strength through Joy's actors, singers, orchestras, puppeteers, trapeze artists, and film trucks staged variety shows, circuses, operettas, and other kinds of light entertainment. Although popular,[54] they at times provoked responses similar to those KdF received from the military: complaints about substandard quality and tastelessness. From Frankfurt am Main came the report that the jokes contained in a variety show were inappropriate for youth, who somehow received entry to the performance.[55] A report from Breslau, commenting on a KdF performance in a camp for relocated Volhynian Germans, that the scantily clad dancing girls in the show offended the modesty of the women and girls in the audience.[56] However welcoming the attitude of civilians to KdF's work, KdF regularly faced criticism that the prices for its performances were too high for workers, as well as the problem that it confronted in its troop entertainment: the scarcity of accomplished artists and performers.[57] Yet if KdF expended its energies unevenly, its volunteer promoters struggled tirelessly to perform their mission, even bringing relief to bombed out cities and towns. Furthermore, unlike tourism, the expense of which produced selective and reluctant support, business willingly subsidized KdF's stage performances. Because of restrictions on other KdF projects and the limitations on company outings, firms increased their purchase of blocs of tickets to concerts, cabarets, and other light entertainment, which they made available to their employees at little or no cost.[58]

Strength through Joy's civilian entertainment but halfheartedly addressed the recreational needs of the legions of foreign workers (*Fremdarbeiter*) pressed into service in Germany. Numbering close to eight million

---

53 NS-Kulturgemeinde-Amt Feierabend, Amt Deutsches Volksbildungswerk, *NSG Kraft durch Freude, Kulturelle Verantstaltung*, 1937/1938.
54 *Meldungen*, 4, 15 April 1940, 998–9. 6, 2 December 1940, 1824.
55 *Meldungen* 4, 27 March 1940, 920. The propaganda ministry was acutely concerned about off-color acts, as indicated in Goebbel's circular to local party officials of September 30, 1940 (Rundschreiben Nr. 188/1), LK Best. 714, no. 1230.
56 *Meldungen*, 3, 28 February 1940, 822.
57 *Meldungen*, 6, 5 December 1940, 1837–8; *Meldungen*, 4, 15 April 1940, 999.
58 *Heimatgrüsse: Werkzeitschrift der Betriebsgemeinschaft Gust. Rafflenbeul, Schwelm i. Westfalen, Wupperthal, Rosheim*, no. 20 (September/October 1942), 1, WWA N7/67, no. 6/3.

by 1944, the neglect of foreign laborers belied Lafferentz's claim that their presence signified the existence of a true "European community." Given their punishing hours, miserable wages, appalling working conditions, little to nonexistent medical care, and the abuse of overseers and police, the lack of recreation for foreign workers was arguably the least objectionable characteristic of their tenure. To be sure, the treatment accorded to foreign workers depended on their position in the regime's racial hierarchy. Western European workers received better handling than workers from Eastern Europe and especially the Soviet Union. In part, the conditions of their labor depended on timing, for regulations eased and working conditions improved after the German defeat at Stalingrad when the regime needed to improve the incentives for forced laborers. Nevertheless, even the best situated foreign workers suffered from discrimination, surveillance, and abuse, including the volunteers from neutral or allied states.[59]

Beyond those daunting liabilities, KdF's chronic understaffing and insufficient numbers of accomplished artists guaranteed that foreigners received short shrift. Furthermore, the lack of cultural accommodation became another means of enforcing segregation between Germans and foreigners, who were consigned to a lower position in the Nazi racial hierarchy. Firm "sport appeals," comradeship evenings, and cultural outings excluded foreigners, for including them would have promoted an unacceptable level of social interaction when the "honor" of labor applied exclusively to Germans. Similarly, KdF performances were off limits to the Ukrainians, Poles, and Russians who worked in German agriculture.[60] Instead, KdF entertained foreign workers separately and belatedly, usually providing them with foreign entertainers, thus undermining KdF's claim that the solicitude shown to foreign workers would expose them to German culture.[61] Even at the Volkswagen plant in Fallersleben that might

---

59   The best single study of *Fremdarbeiter* is Ulrich Herbert's *Hitler's Foreign Workers: Enforced Foreign Labor in Germany under the Third Reich*, trans. William Templer (Cambridge: Cambridge University Press, 1997). As for what happened to the enthusiasm of Spanish workers, Wayne H. Bowen's *Spaniards and Nazi Germany: Collaboration in the New Order* (Columbia and London: University of Missouri Press, 2000), 103–56, is illuminating.

60   WABW Bestand 10, no. 270, 12 July 1942; Notiz für Pg. Tießler, Betrifft: Besuch von KdF.-Veranstaltungen durch fremdvölkische Hilfskräfte, 30 September 1942, *APK*, no. 059287.

61   Kreisobmann Trier an die Gauwaltung der DAF, 4 May 1944. Betrifft: Arbeits- und Lagebericht der Kreiswaltung Trier für den Berichtsmonat April 1944, LK, Abt. 662, 3, 71–3. This reported on three performances by the "Vineta-Alikin Troupe" to foreign workers. An agreement between Ley and Fritz Sauckel, the plenipotentiary in charge of securing labor from the occupied territories that created a central office for the "care" of foreign workers did not occur until January 1944. See Tilla Siegel, *Leistung und Lohn in der nationalsozialistischen "Ordnung der Arbeit"* (Opladen: Westdeutscher Verlag, 1989), 91–2.

have showcased improvements in the quality of life of foreign workers to the credit of the European "community," KdF produced little to distinguish itself, limited as it was by the priorities of military production and an inadequate, wood-framed firetrap of a hall, originally built for mass meetings of Italian workers. To the extent that cultural events existed, they were allocated according to racial fitness and good on-the-job performance.[62]

Yet KdF's contributions in wartime extended beyond bolstering civilian morale through entertainment. To put the legacy of 1918 to rest required that it continue a function, albeit in different form, that its tourism performed before the war – training Germans to assume their roles as Europe's master race. The education that the military received would also be given to civilians. Uniting battlefront and home front in a common understanding of Germany's position would prevent the gulf of understanding that Nazi leaders saw as having contributed to Germany's collapse at the end of World War I. Strength through Joy's "People's Education" program emerged as the key to achieving that objective. KdF's other cultural programs had always integrated Nazi ideology, yet the People's Education program adopted traditional didacticism: courses, lectures, and workshops that would raise the ideological awareness of the racial community so that the *Volk* would be prepared for the challenges of empire.[63]

Ever in competition with the left, KdF sought to appropriate and nazify the adult education and university extension courses that the Socialists offered during the twenties. Rather than tolerating the passive reception of "dry knowledge" dispensed by distant lecturers, which according to KdF's literature characterized the educational endeavors of the Socialists, the KdF version of adult education emphasized seminars, small group discussions (*Arbeitsgemeinschaften*), and field trips to exhibits, museums, and factories. In addition to its centers in urban schools and universities, 325 of them by 1939,[64] the People's Education project also ran lectures and classes in the plants, in keeping with KdF's harmonizing of work and

---

62 Hans Mommsen and Manfred Grieger, *Das Volkswagenwerk und seine Arbeiter im Dritten Reich* (Düsseldorf: Econ Verlag, 1997), 749–50; NHH, Hann. 80, Lüneburg III, XXXIV, Gauleiter Ost - Hannover an Regierungpräsident Lüneburg 12 August 1941, 326; and Landrat Gifhorn an Regierungspräsident Lüneburg, 17 June 1939, 329. Cf. Klaus-Jörg Siegfried, *Das Leben der Zwangsarbeiter im Volkswagenwerk, 1939–1945* (Frankfurt, New York: Campus Verlag, 1988), 106–7.

63 Die Deutsche Arbeitsfront, NSG-"Kraft durch Freude," *Deutsches Volksbildungswerk: Freizeit Frohe Zeit*, Institut für Zeitgeschichte, Munich (hereinafter cited as IfZ), Db 76.06.

64 Laurence Van Zandt Moyer, "The *Kraft durch Freude* Movement in Nazi Germany: 1933–1939" (Dis.: Northwestern University, 1967), 210.

leisure. Much like the Beauty of Labor's improvements, People's Education would awaken the "creativity" of the *Volk*.[65]

Ironically, KdF did not formally assume control of adult education until 1936. Until Ley triumphed over Rosenberg, the educational apparatus of the left fell under the jurisdiction of the party's self-described cultural leader. Closely tied to the training and indoctrination of party leaders that district and county leaders supervised, the control over which Ley had aggressively sought, People's Education became another holding in the Labor Front leader's fiefdom.[66] In 1938, the last full prewar year, KdF's adult education claimed a diverse and substantial audience that consisted of nearly six thousand students and six thousand military personnel, over 13,000 business owners and employees, over 16,000 artisans, over 26,000 officials, over 42,000 workers, over 72,000 salaried employees, and over 22,000 housewives, household helpers, and pensioners. Its lecture series, workshops, field trips, and exhibits reached over 2.6 million attendees in the workplace and over 3.7 million in its centers.[67] Its rapid growth derived not simply from popular enthusiasm for its offerings, however. Rather, numerous hobby clubs found themselves summarily incorporated in the program, and instructed to cater to KdF's audiences.[68]

The People's Education project offered an array of inexpensive courses that catered to a variety of tastes, which ranged from the study of foreign languages, chess, photography, music, and cooking classes to history, art history, ethnography and folklore, geopolitics, and racial hygiene. Aside from classroom instruction, it led excursions to cultural sites, such as palaces and museums, and to sites of scientific and technological significance, such as subways, airports, and planetariums.[69] Unlike KdF's tourism, which approached sites of horror without acknowledging their

65   Ibid., 9. For a summary of the Volksbildungswerk, see *Unter dem Sonnenrad*, 153–61; Marrenbach, *Fundamente des Sieges*, 339–43; Moyer, "*Kraft durch Freude* Movement," especially 209–18; the Report on Strength through Joy, August, 1938 submitted by the American ambassador to Germany, Hugh R. Wilson, http://www.fdrlibrary.marist.edu/psf/box32/folo301.html, 72–82; and Fritz Leutloff, "From the University Extension to the German Popular Education Section of the National-Socialist Fellowship *Kraft durch Freude* (Functions and Aims of National-Socialist Education Work), *German Addresses for Committee VII, World Congress "Work and Joy: Rome 1938*, 5–7.
66   Anordnung Nr. 18/36, 9 June 1936, BAL NS 22/783.
67   Die Deutsche Arbeitsfront/NSG "Kraft durch Freude," *Arbeitsjahr*, IfZ 72.25, 18, 23. These figures refer to those who purchased "listener" cards, which allowed them access to lectures and courses for six months, for the price of 30 pf. See also Marrenbach, *Fundamente des Sieges*, 342–3.
68   *Deutschland-Berichte der Soualdemokratischen Partei Deutschlands* (Frankfurt am Main: Verlag Petra Nettelbeck, 1980) (hereinafter cited as *Sopade*), February 1938, 152–3.
69   *Unter dem Sonnenrad*, 153–61. The Volksbildungswerk offerings appeared regularly in KdF's monthly magazines and even its tour brochures, such as NSG Kraft durch Freude, Gau Sachsen, *Urlaubsfahrten 1937* (Berlin, 1937).

existence, the People's Education's participants actually visited the regime's penal institutions as an educational venture. A tour of a prison in central Germany, wherein the majority of prisoners were political detainees, emerged as one of its most popular outings. To be sure, some on the field trip complained that that Socialists and Communists did not deserve to be locked up with common criminals. Yet on the whole the response was positive, for the warden's description of the prison as a venue for the rehabilitation and education of its inmates reassured the students.[70]

In line with the anticommercialism that pervaded KdF's approach to tourism, People's Education promoted arts and crafts among its students, teaching them to create their own artisanal and artistic products to counter the corrosive impact of mass-produced kitsch. Periodically, it sponsored exhibits for participants to display their own work.[71] Acknowledged by domestic surveillance reports during wartime as extraordinarily popular, its faculty consisted of teachers, party and government officials, and other specialists, the vast majority of them volunteers, who lent their services to educating those whom the universities normally did not reach.[72] Despite its disproportionate concentration in cities and towns, the People's Education project sought to mobilize schoolteachers in the countryside to compensate for the wartime decline of "beautiful village" projects.[73] Their task included not just the prewar objective of mitigating the urban–rural divide, but also easing the discontent over the labor shortages that became especially acute during the war in rural areas. Sponsoring "village evenings" for rural folk, whom teachers encouraged to compose "village books" filled with local lore and letters from villagers serving at the front, People's Education reemphasized the rootedness of German culture while imparting to rural dwellers pride in their *Heimat* and a renewed sense of their importance to the economy.[74] Notwithstanding the seeming antimodernism of its rural program, the People's Education project disseminated radio programming to the countryside, while its communal evenings used slide presentations and films delivered by KdF film trucks. Its educational labor strove as well to convince villagers that the German struggle in the east justified the hardships that agriculture currently endured.

70 *Sopade*, April 1939, 465–7. On the hard line attitudes of most Germans toward crime and socially "deviant" behavior, see Robert Gellately, *Backing Hitler: Consent and Coercion in the Third Reich* (Oxford: Oxford University Press, 2000).
71 Die Deutsche Arbeitsfront/NS-Gemeinschaft Kraft durch Freude, *Ein Querschnitt durch den Arbeitsplan und die Arbeitswesen einer Volksbildungsstätte des Amtes Deutsches Volksbildungswerk*, undated, IfZ 72.31.
72 *Meldungen*, 2, Vierteljahresbericht 1939, 286; 2, 8 November 1939, 433.
73 NSDAP Gauleitung Moselland, Gaupropagandaamt Abt. Kultur, Rundschreiben 222/15, 10 November 1942, LK Best. 714, no. 1224.
74 *Dorfbuch und Dorfabend im Krieg* (Berlin: Verlag des Deutschen Arbeitsfront, undated), IfZ, 72.42a.

Explained one KdF monthly publication several months before the outbreak of war, the extension of German power in the present depended
on drawing from Germany's past, particularly its *Volk* culture. Thus the
village book contributed to the "historical work of greater Germany."[75]

The majority of the participants in People's Education classes selected
courses that brought them personal enjoyment or relaxation, such as
learning a craft, collecting stamps, or playing a musical instrument. Nevertheless, language courses, which KdF cruises stimulated before the war,
drew many enrollees, who were presumably captivated by the opportunities that Germany's expansion offered. After the conclusion of the Nazi–
Soviet Pact, which enabled Germany to attack Poland without fear of a
two-front war, even Russian became an attractive option.[76] Moreover, the
frequent museum excursions and lectures by well-traveled cognoscenti
transmitted the preconceptions and moral imperatives of imperialism.
During wartime, they substituted for the tourism that KdF had been
forced to suspend while pursuing the global and racial perspectives that
KdF tour organizers once expected their cruises would convey. Some lecturers spoke of Germany's destiny to reach the Black Sea, while others
explored the globe vicariously through the miracle of color film.[77] Native
Askaris, German-trained troops from what had been German East Africa
before World War I, recounted the benefits of German colonial rule, which
the Entente had sadly obliterated, while Carla Barthée, who once lived
among the Bedouins and Egyptian peasants, described their exotic, putatively unchanging, ways of life. Slide presentations described living among
"cannibals" in New Guinea while still others documented the different
racial types among the "Negroes" of the Cameroons, German East and
Southwest Africa, documenting in the process the perils of racial mixing.[78]
Armchair travel through the technology of slides became a major locus for
the popular discussion of Germany's imperial dreams which cut a cross
all levels of society, while Germany's alliances – which called into question its racial hierarchies – found an explanation through appropriate
comparisons. Thus, a slide lecture, "the new Asian," depicted a fierce,
aggressive, determined, but nonetheless modern, Japanese Samurai,
against an elderly Chinese in "traditional attire," who represented the

75 "Das Dorfbuch: Das Geschichtswerk Großdeutschlands," NSG Kraft durch Freude,
    Gau Salzburg, *Die Feierstunde: Monatshefte der NSG Kraft durch Freude* May 1939, 8.
76 *Meldungen*, 2, 8 November 1939, 433.
77 "Völkerwage und Völkerschicksale am Schwarzen Meer," 9 March 1941, WABW,
    Bestand 10, no. 271.
78 NSG Kraft durch Freude, Gau Steiermark, *Kraft durch Freude*, "Askaris erzählen von
    Deutsche-Ost," no. 9 (July 1939): 19; "Eine Frau allein unter Fellachen und Beduinen,"
    no. 28 (December 1940): 8–9; "Unter Goldgräbern und Kannibalen auf Neuguinea,"
    NSG Kraft durch Freude, Gau Steiermark, *Kraft durch Freude* no. 25 (November
    1940): 9; NSG Kraft durch Freude, Gau München-Oberbayern, *Kraft durch Freude*,
    "Deutscher Besitz im fremden Taschen: Unsere Kolonien in Afrika," (September 1937):
    9–16.

"impenetrable mask of timeless passivity."[79] KdF's attempt to extend Germany's "cultural property" to the masses while mitigating the war's hardships made as much of the real and vicarious mobility of Germans as it did the rootedness allegedly instilled by life in the countryside.

Consumerism, the Standard of Living, and Living Space

Residing in the capacious cultural and racial claims that underlay the Nazi imperial project lay the issues that, from the beginning, complicated the regime's priorities: mass consumption and the standard of living. In peacetime, radios and KdF vacation trips mitigated the constraints on consumption, for they testified to the Third Reich's ability to rescue Germany from the privations of Weimar, while forecasting an abundant future. For the duration of the war, however, the regime's pleas for sacrifice, modified by its tactical concessions to the home front, ensured that the Nazi brand of imperialism would grow especially murderous and exploitative. Territorial acquisitions and the defenselessness of "inferior" peoples offered the tantalizing prospect of redress for the shortages at home. Despite its comprehensive rationing at the beginning of the war, the Nazi regime adopted horrific measures in occupied Europe that, in addition to anchoring its program of racial reconstruction, muted domestic dissatisfaction. The Third Reich's draconian appropriation of foreign labor, partially to quiet discontent over the pressure on middle-class women to work, its commandeering of raw materials and food that callously disregarded the cost in human lives, its tolerance of commercial tourism, and its desire to keep civilians entertained testified to the Nazi leadership's belief that tolerable living standards preserved the fighting spirit that would guarantee the final victory.[80]

In the future, the master race would revel in material largesse after Germany won the war, no longer bound by the antimaterialism of the regime's prewar definition of the standard of living.[81] Speer's plans for

---

79 NSG Kraft durch Freude, Gau Steiermark, *Kraft durch Freude*, no. 19 (May 1940): 3–4.

80 On the effect of the war on consumption at home, see Richard Overy, "Guns or Butter? Living Standards, Finance, and Labor in Germany, 1939–1942," in R. J. Overy, *War and Economy in the Third Reich*, (Oxford: Clarendon Press, 1994): 259–314.

81 Although I have reservations about the continuities that he draws between the Third Reich and the postwar period, I am indebted to Michael Geyer's insights as to the role of consumption in the German war effort. See his essays, "The Stigma of Violence, Nationalism, and War in Twentieth-Century Germany," *German Studies Review*, 16 no. 2 (1993): 75ff.; "Restorative Elites, German Society and the Nazi Pursuit of War," in *Fascist Italy and Nazi Germany: Comparisons and Contrasts*, ed. Richard Bessel (Cambridge: Cambridge University Press, 1996): 134–64; and "Germany, or the Twentieth Century as History," *South Atlantic Quarterly* 94, no. 4 (Fall 1997): 663–702.

imperial Berlin included a cornucopia of pleasures, as he fended off proposals for avenues lined solely with government ministries:[82]

> A luxurious movie house for premières, another cinema for the masses accommodating two thousand persons, a new opera house, three theaters, a new concert hall, a building for congresses, the so-called House of the Nations, a hotel of twenty-one stories, variety theaters, mass and luxury restaurants, and even an indoor swimming pool, built in Roman style and as large as the baths of Imperial Rome, were deliberately included in the plans with the idea of bringing urban life into the new avenue. There were to be quiet interior courtyards with colonnades and small luxury shops set apart from the noise of the street and inviting strollers. Electric signs were to be employed profusely. The whole avenue was also conceived by Hitler and me as a continuous sales display of German goods which would exert a special attraction upon foreigners.

The east especially became in German eyes a massive reclamation project that involved the immigration of legions of good racial stock, the construction of settlements and roads that would transform Asiatic steppes from a cesspool of Jews and other "subhumans" (*Untermenschen*) into prelapsarian paradises. "The beauties of the Crimea, which we shall make accessible by means of an autobahn – for us Germans," intoned the führer, who strove to reiterate the connection between tourism and imperialism, "that will be our Riviera." "Crete is scorching and dry," he continued. "Cyprus would be lovely, but we can reach the Crimea by road. Along that road lies Kiev! And Croatia, too, a tourists' paradise for us. I expect that after the war there will be a great upsurge of rejoicing."[83] Ensconced in his East Prussian headquarters, Hitler fantasized about the blessings of modern technology, particularly in making the lives of German housewives easier:

> The mistress of the house must be set free from all the minor chores that make her waste her time. Not only must the children's play-gardens be near the houses, but the mother must not even be compelled to take her children there herself. All she

---

82 Albert Speer, *Inside the Third Reich: Memoirs*, trans. Richard and Clara Winston (New York: Macmillan, 1970), 160.

83 *Hitler's Table Talk 1941–1944: His Private Conversations*, trans. Norman Cameron and R. H. Stevens, ed. H. R. Trevor-Roper (New York: Enigma Books, 2000), 4–5. For an appreciation of the scale of the reconstruction in the east, and particularly its relationship to expulsion and genocide, see Debórah Dwork and Robert Jan Van Pelt, *Auschwitz: 1970 to the Present* (New York: Norton, 1996).

should have to do is to press a button for the woman in charge to appear immediately. No more refuse to take downstairs, no more fuel to carry up. In the morning, the works of the alarm-clock must even switch on the mechanism that boils the water. All these little inventions that lighten the burden of life must be set to work.[84]

Consistent with its mission, Strength through Joy's parent organization, the Labor Front, best embodied the regime's visions of abundance for the master race. It revealed the methods by which future bounty would secure the permanent integration of workers in the racial community. Not notably successful before the war in building working-class housing, Robert Ley used the prospect of victory to promote his cause. In September 1940, he garnered an additional title for himself, Plenipotentiary for Social Housing. Two years later, his power increased when Hitler appointed him commissar. Despite his battles with Franz Seldte, the labor minister, Walther Funk, Schacht's successor as economics minister, and Speer, the armaments minister, over the role of private industry and the cost of Ley's projects to the state budget, only military defeat stifled his ambitions for a postwar housing bonanza.[85] Ley's ceaselessly generated architectural plans envisioned working-class lives devoid of material hardship, a far cry from the architectural assumptions of the Weimar period. Small agricultural settlements once proposed as a solution to mass unemployment would occupy but a minor place, except those for housing miners and other workers in physically taxing trades, who required corporeal renewal. Instead, single-family homes with large live-in kitchens, ample bedrooms for large families, green spaces and gardens for recreation, and Volkswagens imagined the elimination of working-class ghettoes and the class conflict that accompanied them. Even the small rental flats that Ley proposed would bear no resemblance to the working-class tenements of the past. At low rents, reduced even further for child-rich families, the flats would provide comfortable spaces, central heating, and hot water.[86]

Although comparisons with underdeveloped nations had been a staple of the Third Reich's claims to have improved living standards, to which

---

84 *Hitler's Table Talk*, 347–8.
85 Funk an Ley, 3 June 1941, BAL, R43II/352b, 125–36; Seldte an Lammers, 29 April 1942, BAL R43II/1009a, 57–60. See also Ronald Smelser, *Robert Ley: Hitler's Labor Front Leader* (Oxford, New York, Hamburg: Berg, 1988), 173, 279–84, and Marie-Luise Recker, *Nationalsozialistische Sozialpolitik im Zweiten Weltkrieg* (Munich: R. Oldenbourg Verlag, 1985), 128–54.
86 Ley an Bormann, 10 May 1941, BAL R43II/1175 99–101; "Trotz Krieg sozialer Wohnungsbau: Dr. Ley über Einzelheiten des großen Bauprogramms," undated, BAL R43II/1175, 3.

the acquisition of Polish and Soviet territory only added, Ley provided the additional assurance that German workers were, and would continue to be, better off than their counterparts in Great Britain and the United States. Wages in England, according to the DAF's think tank, the Institute for the Science of Labor (Arbeitswissenschaftliches Institut or AWI), did not assure basic material comfort. Worse still, "next to the less than scarce nourishment," English workers lacked "above all the means to acquire small pleasures, cultural events, free-time entertainment and leisure travel."[87] Sensitive to the potential impact of widely publicized British proposals for the establishment of a comprehensive social insurance system after the war, Ley proclaimed the limitations prevalent in the 1942 proposals of the liberal economist William Beveridge. The Beveridge Report, he insisted, offered only a safety net for the unemployed rather than ending unemployment altogether. Not satisfied with attacking British social programs, Ley turned to Germany's principal nemesis in the standard of living contest. The New Deal in America, he claimed, was but a sham for it increased the power of Jewish industrialists and bankers while leaving poverty untouched. It produced an oxymoron, "a planned economy without real planning." In turn, Ley's housing program composed but one element of a massive state-financed and administered welfare state, which would parcel out rewards according to individual merit and racial fitness.[88]

For the military, entertainment, tourism, and consumption became not merely ancillary to combat, but the very ends of warfare. Freed of the need for self-restraint, the German invaders satisfied their material desires at the same time that they carried out the regime's agenda. Given its relatively high prewar living standards, occupied Western Europe not surprisingly provided rich opportunities for acquisition. Far from generating pangs of conscience, desires for adventure and the satisfaction of immediate needs coexisted easily with despoliation, however appalling the juxtaposition appears in retrospect. Pleasures became the spoils to which the racially superior were entitled.[89] Until the stalling of the German advance in the Soviet Union, the Reich's rapid conquests of Poland, France, and the low countries encouraged touristic analogies: "Up to now," reported one soldier in May 1940 after the Wehrmacht overran France, "it has been a great big Strength through Joy trip," as good an illustration as any of the

87 Propagandaamt der Deutsche Arbeitsfront, *England – eine Plutokratie* (Berlin: Verlag der Deutschen Arbeitsfront, 1941), 125, IfZ, 76.01.

88 Ley, *Große Stunde: Das Deutsche Volk im Totalen Kriegseinsatz* (Munich: Franz Eher Verlag, 1943), 38–43; *Roosevelt verrät Amerika!* (Berlin: Verlag der Deutschen Arbeitsfront, 1942). For a comparison of Ley's proposed welfare state and Beveridge's see Recker, *Nationalsozialistische Sozialpolitik*, 151–2.

89 See especially Daniel Jonah Goldhagen, *Hitler's Willing Executioners: Ordinary Germans and the Holocaust* (New York: Alfred A. Knopf, 1996), 265.

way in which KdF tourism had gripped the popular imagination.[90] For Germans in Paris, the city represented the tourist site par excellence and a prime venue for consumption. Be it art at the Orangerie, the dancers at the Moulin Rouge, or dinner at elegant hotels that a wealthy international clientele had once frequented, Paris offered the Wehrmacht bounty for the taking. The undervaluing of the franc encouraged shopping sprees that would have been unimaginable at home.[91] Refugees in Flanders fleeing from the invading German armies in the spring of 1940 received little sympathy from an enlisted man, who focused more closely on what his comrades could wrest from their conquest. "I'm sorry for the kids and the old people," he said, but "it can't be changed. We don't suffer from any need. There is a world of difference between here and Poland. What we want we can get. We simply take it. Everything is gone and the houses are open. The population has had to get out and only some of the peasants remained behind."[92]

Battlefield experiences spawned descriptions from soldiers that resembled the contents of guidebooks, albeit with an emphasis on militarily relevant geographical or climatic conditions.[93] Once defeated by German armies, occupied Europe presented an unlimited source of tourist sites for soldiers, many of them working-class, who had never traveled outside of their homeland. In addition to snatching up their Baedeckers, they also became the eager recipients of the tour guides that KdF and the DAF provided them. The guides explicitly promoted the regime's racial biology, even in Western Europe with populations that from the Nazi perspective compared more favorably than those of Eastern Europe and the Soviet Union. Thus, a 1940 guide to Paris that the People's Education project published interspersed virulent antisemitism with more mundane descriptions of "must see" sights and observations as to the character of the French. Calling attention to the third arrondisement where large numbers of foreign Jews lived, the guide described the dirt, disgusting cooking smells, overcrowding, and foreign-looking attire that were supposedly observable there. The usual strategy of Jews in France, the book intoned, was to move quickly into better neighborhoods and acquire more wealth. Had it not been for the German presence, the overwhelming economic power

90 Quoted in Klaus Latzel, *Deutsche Soldaten – nationalsozialistischer Krieg? Kriegserlebnis – Kriegserfahrung 1939–1945*, 2nd ed. (Paderborn, Munich, Vienna, Zurich, 2000), 134. According to Latzel, the analogy of "travel" became the lens through which Wehrmacht troops first experienced the war.
91 Burleigh, *Third Reich*, 411; Latzel, *Deutsche Soldaten*, 135–8.
92 Otwin Buchbender and Reinhold Sterz, eds., *Das Andere Gesicht des Krieges: Deutsche Feldpostbriefe 1939–1945* (Munich: C. H. Beck Verlag, 1982), 56.
93 Burckhard Dücker, "Reisen in die UdSSR 1933–1945," in *Reisekultur in Deutschland: Von der Weimarer Republic zum "Dritten Reich,"* ed. Peter J. Brenner (Tübingen: Max Niemeyer Verlag, 1997): 279.

of the Jews would have remained unshaken. The guidebook concluded by praising the institution of racial laws after the defeat of France, as well as the deportation of Jews without French citizenship to concentration camps.[94]

The quintessential apparatus of tourism, the camera, which KdF had done much to popularize through the snapshot contests it sponsored in its monthly magazines, became instrumental to deepening the racial stereotypes among soldiers that justified the Third Reich's draconian population policies, especially in Poland and the Soviet Union. Photos and movie cameras preserved the daily routine of the troops in the field, who by using those instruments depicted defining moments in their lives and the male comradeship that elevated national over class or regional identity. They also provided visual testimony to the savagery of German empire building. Amidst moments of levity and boredom, an unsparing pride seeped into a putatively impersonal and representational medium as photos and movies depicted hangings, shootings, deportations, mass graves, and the constant humiliation of racial "inferiors," particularly Jews.[95] The language of tourism ineluctably crept into the efforts of the Wehrmacht to maintain morale and thus the troops' willingness to fight. Photo albums, claimed the Wehrmacht High Command with nary a trace of irony or remorse, provided a perfect opportunity for soldiers to compose a souvenir, a lasting memory of their "special war experiences."[96]

The degree to which consumption saturated German imperial expectations emerged clearly in its "drive to the east" (*Drang nach Osten*), where the German experience with the poverty of eastern Europe sharpened racially grounded perceptions of Germany's "high" standard of living similar to those that KdF's cruises to Italy and Portugal once encouraged. Assuring an adequate food supply for German soldiers and civilians contributed to the apocalyptic murderousness of Barbarossa, and especially the Holocaust, which built upon aggressive plans already being carried out in Poland to modernize "backward" Slavic lands.[97] Any moral scruples

---

94 Oberleutnant Dr. Schulz, *Paris deutsche gesehen* (Berlin-Grunewald and Leipzig: Verlag Hermann Hillger KG., 1940), 51–3.

95 See Dieter Reifarth, Viktoria Schmidt-Linsenhoff, "Die Kamera der Täter," and Bernd Hüppenauf, "Der entleerte Blick hinter der Kamera," both in *Vernichtungskrieg: Verbrechen der Wehrmacht 1941–1944* (Hamburger Edition HIS Verlag, 1995): 475–503 and 504–27 respectively; *The German Army and Genocide: Crimes against War Prisoners, Jews, and other Civilians, 1939–1944*, ed. Hamburg Institute for Social Research, trans. Scott Abbott (New York: New Press, 1999); and Ernst Klee, Willi Dreßen, and Volker Rieß, *"Schöne Zeiten": Judenmord aus der Sicht der Täter und Gaffer* (Frankfurt am Main: Fischer, 1988).

96 "Freizeitgestaltung der Truppe: Vorschläge und Anregungen," *Tournisterschrift des Oberkommandos der Wehrmacht* 63 (1942), BA-MA W6/440, 4–5.

97 Christian Gerlach, *Krieg, Ernährung, Völkermord; Deutsche Vernichtungspolitik im Zweiten Weltkrieg* (Zurich and Munich: Pendo, 2001); Götz Aly and Susanne Heim, *Vordenker der Vernichtung: Auschwitz und die deutschen Pläne für eine neue europäische Ordnung* (Hamburg: Hoffmann and Campe, 1991).

among SS personnel that might have impeded extermination quickly dissipated when transports to death camps filled with Jewish victims provided booty for camp administrators and their wives, stimulating a lust for princely lifestyles that knew no difference in gender. The exaction of tribute, the imposition of grossly unequal exchange rates, and the outright plunder of furs, jewelry, cameras, oriental rugs, among other valuables, whether by the Wehrmacht, the Gestapo, or the SS, regularly accompanied mass murder.[98] Even for German pioneers with no direct responsibility for mass killings, many of them young women who assisted in the resettlement of ethnic Germans, the proliferation of German shops with colorful window displays assured them that civilization had replaced the repulsive Poles and Jews who had once lived there.[99] The lower living standards of the east magically transformed criminal brutality into beneficence and liberation in what was in reality a "community of spoils" rather than a national community.[100]

Especially in the Soviet Union, where civil war and the products of Stalinism, rapid industrialization, collectivization, and famine had created far worse misery than that witnessed by KdF tourists in Naples or Lisbon, consumption framed the racist assumptions of soldiers, already intensified by the rhetoric of the Reich's struggle with "Asiatic–Jewish Bolshevism." Working-class troops differed little from middle-class soldiers in their views.[101] In firm newspapers, which provided space for the "retinue" called up to military service so they could share their experiences with their comrades on the home front, letters mocked the "workers' paradise" that the Bolshevik Revolution claimed to have created. Frequently resorting to the justifications of "anticonquest," troops cast themselves as liberators even as they expressed incomprehension and contempt for

98 See Gudrun Schwarz, *Eine Frau an seiner Seite: Ehefrauen in der "SS-Sippengemeinschaft"* (Berlin: Aufbau Taschenbuch Verlag, 2001), especially 112–69; and Frank Bajohr, *Parvenüs und Profiteure: Korruption in der NS-Zeit* (Frankfurt am Main: Fischer, 2001), 75–136. Examples of the wanton expropriation of Jewish goods abound in Ilya Ehrenburg and Vasily Grossmann, eds., *The Complete Black Book of Russian Jewry*, trans. David Patterson (New Brunswick and London: Transaction Publishers, 2002). For particularly good examples, see 13, 109, 115, 162, 198–9, 220, 313, and 352.

99 See Elizabeth Harvey, "Die deutsche Frau im Osten: Geschlecht und öffenticher Raum im besetzten Polen 1940–1944," *Archiv für Sozialgeschichte*, 38 (1998): 191–214; and "'We Forgot All Jews and Poles': German Women and the 'Ethnic Struggle' in Nazi-Occupied Poland," *Contemporary European History*, 10, no. 3 (2001): 447–61.

100 This is the apt expression of Frank Bajohr, *Parvenüs und Profiteure*, 187.

101 There is now a substantial literature on the racism of German troops. In addition to Bartov, *Hitler's Army, The German Army and Genocide*; Latzel, *Deutsche Soldaten*; and Heer, *Vernichtungskrieg*; see Alf Lüdtke, "The Appeal of Exterminating 'Others': German Workers and the Limits of Resistance," *Journal of Modern History*, 64, supplement (December 1992): S46-S67. To magnify the propaganda impact, the regime published collections of soldiers' letters, such as Wolfgang Diewerge, *Deutsche Soldaten sehen die Sowjet-Union: Feldpostbriefen aus dem Osten* (Berlin: Wilhelm Lempert-Verlag, 1941).

those they had subjugated. For Otto Conrads, drafted out of the West-phalian firm Rafflenbeul to serve on the eastern front, Bolshevism had created nothing but barbarism. "Still," he insisted, "order will once again be returned here when Bolshevism is destroyed. For only tears, need, and misery are the milestones of this Jewish doctrine."[102] After a detailed cat-aloguing of conditions in what he disparaged as the "peasant and worker paradise," another worker from the Brüninghaus steel firm concluded with the plea: "May the Lord grant that this struggle, for us the most dif-ficult ever, soon end victoriously, so that then the last strike for the paci-fication of the world can be accomplished."[103] According to the Krupp employee turned corporal, Heinz Gerig, "these Soviet people have no idea to what extent they've been deceived, since up until now they've had no insight into the life of even the most ordinary man in a culture state (*Kulturstaat*). What is taken for granted in Germany, the theater, the cin-ema, light music, the coziness and cleanliness of a German home, and so forth, these people don't have the vaguest idea about."[104] Like the soldier stationed in the Ukraine who was astounded that a Russian family he met did not know a single Christmas song, the consequence, he noted, of twenty-five years of Bolshevism,[105] Gerig had seemingly absorbed an important element of the Nazi *Weltanschauung*, the culture-destroying power of "Jewish Bolshevism." In contrast to the miserable living con-ditions of their enemy, soldiers expressed satisfaction with not only their room and board, but especially with the cultural events that allowed them to transcend their surroundings temporarily, especially those offered by Strength through Joy.

Detailed descriptions in soldiers' letters of housing, furnishings, cloth-ing, and cleanliness (or the lack of it), particularly the way their contents paralleled the observations of KdF tourists in southern Italy or Portugal, further illustrated the degree to which the Reich's sensitivity to consump-tion had not been misplaced. Travel, be it through the invasion of civilian tourists or through that of the German military, anchored the regime's legitimacy. Crossing beyond Germany's eastern frontier, according to one soldier, meant entering a different world, in which a dwelling that would have been considered a hovel at home was "a first-class villa here."

102 "Aus unseren Zweigwerken," *Heimatgrüsse: Werkzeitschrift der Betriebsgemein-schaft Gust. Rafflenbeul, Schweln i. Westfalen, Wupperthal, Rosheim*, September/October 1942, 11, WWA N7/67, nr. 6/3. For similar comments, see the letters in Buchbender and Sterz, *Andere Gesicht des Krieges*, 72–5, 81–7.
103 "Von der Heimat für die Front," Stahlwerke Brüninghaus-Friedrich Thomee-A.G. Werdohl, WWA, F103 no. 10 (February 1942), 6.
104 *Krupp/Zeitschrift der Kruppischen Betriebsgemeinschaft* 33, no. 5(1 February 1942): 55, HA Krupp.
105 Walter Kempowski, *Das Echolot: Ein kollektives Tagebuch Januar und Februar 1943*, vol. 1, *1. bis 17. Januar 1943* (Munich: Albrecht Knaus Verlag, 1993): 425.

Whoever possessed two rooms ranked as a "plutocrat."[106] "A table, a bench, two chairs, and a bed; those are the only furnishings," remarked the Krupp employee Willi Laurenz. The occasional photo provided the only decoration in the Ukrainian peasant hut that he encountered.[107] Comparisons between the living standards in Germany and the Soviet Union cut across social boundaries, uniting soldiers, workers, party members, and the middle classes, and they became the grist for morale-building popular exhibits, which the regime circulated.

One particular display in Essen in 1942, "Workers' Paradise, and Worker Homeland," documented the primitive living conditions of Soviet workers. As an adjunct to an exhibit staged in Minsk during the same year, one that circulated a forty-eight-page brochure and a short, but riveting, film to accompany it, the Essen exhibit testified to the irresistible propaganda that the regime's attention to the standard of living could generate. An image of a filthy, dark, one-room hovel for a Soviet working-class family with two shabbily-dressed parents and four grimy, undernourished children accompanied a photo of a comparable flat in the Krupp compound that housed the company's employees. The Krupp apartment contained a spacious German live-in kitchen, a bedroom for the parents, a smaller bedroom for each of the children, and a bathroom. Seemingly cognizant of the standards propagandized by the Beauty of Labor, the flat radiated brightness and squeaky cleanliness, conveying as well the confluence of moral and racial judgment.[108]

Until late in the war, Hitler's belief that only living space would provide the basis for a prosperous Germany was regularly acted upon until military reverses, surrender, and the Allied occupation redefined the terms of reconstruction. During a midday rumination in the summer of 1942, the führer spoke of delivering the English Channel islands to Ley so that Strength through Joy could use them as collectively as a "marvelous health resort."[109] Communal and commercial tourism interests, aware of the expanding horizons and soaring expectations that the war had spawned, projected Strength through Joy's rapid postwar growth. According to the tourism director of Heidelberg, KdF would likely to become the largest travel agency in the world. Workers in a victorious postwar Germany would naturally come to a greater sense of entitlement, and thus

---

106 "Von der Heimat für die Front," 8 June 1943, WWA, F 103.
107 *Krupp* 33, no. 6 (1 March 1942): 67–8.
108 *Krupp*, 34, no. 2 (1 November 1942): 14. The brochure was titled *Das Sowjet-Paradies: Ausstellung der Reichspropagandaleiter der NSDAP: Ein Bericht in Wort und Bild* (Berlin: Zentralverlag der NSDAP, 1942). The film went by the same title. See also Latzel's remarks on the dehumanizing uses of "cleanliness," *Deutsche Soldaten*, 179.
109 *Hitler's Table Talk*, 584.

the overall quality of Strength through Joy vacation trips would have to appeal to a less spartan, more materialistic clientele.[110]

Had the Third Reich triumphed, it is unlikely that KdF would have prospered without abandoning its original raison d'etre. And unless a victorious Third Reich mutated into a less expansionist version of itself, a scarcely imaginable prospect, KdF's synthesis of spartanism and luxury might well have succumbed to the exactions of permanent war. Even before 1939, Strength through Joy's disproportionately middle-class constituency and its inclination to promise comfort and even "luxury" sat uneasily with its anticommercial and antimaterialist frugality. What is certain is that the defeat of the Third Reich and the emergence of two Germanys with diametrically opposed political and economic systems resurrected the modes of consumption that Strength through Joy sought to circumvent.

110 Hanns Fischer an Fiehler, 8 April 1943, Hanns Fischer an Otto Bennecke, 30 November 1943, BAL R36, no. 2495.

Epilogue

The End of "German" Consumption: Consumerism and Tourism in the Postwar Germanys

Strength through Joy's resort at Rügen is for the most part a ruin. Unfinished at the outbreak of war, the regime hastily completed some of its buildings during the cataclysm to shelter the victims of air raids or the refugees fleeing the Soviet armies. Following Germany's defeat in 1945, the Soviet military government dismantled materials for reparations or for the construction of settlements associated with the expropriation and redistribution of landed estates. Island residents plundered bed linens, silverware, and beach chairs that Strength through Joy acquired in preparation for the resort's opening in the spring of 1940.

During its forty-year existence, the German Democratic Republic used Prora as a military installation, designating part of the ruin for detonation practice, and the remainder for barracks, athletic facilities, and entertainment centers for the National People's Army units stationed there. In addition to barring civilians from the Prora inlet and concealing the remains of the resort behind a thicket of trees, undermining in the process Clement Klotz's design, the GDR took hold of the island's tourist establishments that once catered to the middle and upper classes. Managed by the GDR's travel bureau or the travel service of the trade unions, those properties became vacation hostels for union members and employees of the large state-owned companies (Kombinate) created in the seventies to further centralize the economy.[1] Since unification in 1990, the resort has found new uses, including a museum that documents its Nazi and East German past.[2] Yet as a symbol of KdF's demise and that of the regime that sustained it, the KdF-Seebad Rügen will likely never serve the purpose for which it was once intended.

1 Hasso Spode, "Tourismus in der Gesellschaft der DDR: Eine vergleichende Einführung," in *Goldstrand und Teutonengrill: Kultur- und Sozialgeschichte des Tourismus in Deutschland 1945 bis 1989* (Berlin: Verlag für universitäre Kommunikation, 1996): 16.
2 Jürgen Rostock and Franz Jadniček, *Paradiesruinen: Das KdF-Seebad der Zwanzigtausend auf Rügen*, 3rd ed. (Berlin: Ch. Links Verlag, 1995), 90–108; "Inside the Holiday Camp Hitler Built," *The Observer*, 12 August 2001.

The collapse of the Third Reich and Germany's occupation and division by Allied forces brought Strength through Joy's dissolution. The destruction of its headquarters by Allied bombardment, the Allied Control Commission's designation of the German Labor Front as a criminal organization, and the confiscation of the DAF's assets deprived KdF of the legal standing and resources to continue. In any case, more basic concerns than tourism and leisure moved to the foreground. Hunger and the loss of life, the collapse of political authority, and the destruction of transportation and housing by air raids left thousands displaced and homeless. The millions of ethnic German refugees expelled from eastern Prussia, Czechoslovakia, Hungary, and other parts of Eastern Europe had to be absorbed. Finally, the incompatible proposals among the Allies for promoting economic recovery, the rebuilding of government, and the punishment of former Nazis increased the likelihood that two Germanys would emerge from one, further complicating postwar reconstruction.

In light of such hardship, most Germans dealt with the Nazi past in evasive or exculpatory ways. Although Nazism enjoyed substantial popularity during its twelve-year rule – at least until the defeat at Stalingrad and air raids brought the war home to civilians – Germans who had not directly encountered the regime's repression accepted little responsibility for the grim consequences of their support for the Third Reich.[3] Rather, when they confronted the past at all, they cast themselves as victims of Nazism and the Allies both, who having endured the Third Reich now struggled to rebuild in the present.[4] Although assuming radically different forms in the two states that emerged in 1949 after the collapse of inter-Allied cooperation, the trope of suffering shaped the founding myths of the German Democratic Republic and the Federal Republic of Germany. In East Germany, Nazism's persecution of the KPD became essential to legitimating the Socialist Unity Party (SED) at the expense of a broader conception of victimhood that acknowledged the Nazi regime's crimes against the Jews. The anticommunism of the West German state, by contrast, integrated the experiences of German women raped by Soviet soldiers and the horror stories of Germans expelled from Eastern Europe into a narrative of German persecution by Nazi and Soviet "totalitarianism."[5]

---

3   On the significance of Stalingrad in influencing popular perceptions, see Martin Brozsat, Klaus-Dietmar Henke, and Hans Woller, eds., *Von Stalingrad zur Währungsreform: Zur Sozialgeschichte des Umbruchs in Deutschland* (Munich: R. Oldenbourg, 1988).
4   See Norbert Frei, *Vergangenheitspolitik: Die Anfänge der Bundesrepublik und die NS-Vergangenheit* (Munich: C.H. Beck Verlag, 1996).
5   On the myth of antifascism in the GDR, see Sigrid Meuschel, *Legitimation und Parteiherrschaft in der DDR* (Frankfurt am Main: Edition Suhrkamp, 1992), 29–40; and especially Jeffrey Herf, *Divided Memory: The Nazi Past in the Two Germanys* (Cambridge, Massachusetts: Harvard University Press, 1997). For the West German side, see Elizabeth D. Heinemann, *What Difference Does a Husband Make? Women and Marital Status in Postwar Germany* (Berkeley and London: University of California Press, 1999),

As the founding myths of East and West Germany soon revealed, the two states defined themselves against each other, especially by the manner in which each claimed to have broken from the Third Reich. Finding its roots in the anti-Nazi resistance movement that culminated in the failed assassination plot against Hitler on July 20, 1944, the Federal Republic cast itself as the liberal democratic alternative to the Third Reich and to the Stalinism of the GDR, which it structurally equated with the Nazi regime. The GDR, on the other hand, positioned itself as the embodiment of the best German traditions, particularly socialism. With the "fraternal" assistance of the Soviet Union, the "workers' and peasants' state" rooted out the class bases of Nazism that survived in West Germany with the collusion of NATO, or so the SED maintained. The evasions in the East and West German myths, the reluctance and even refusal to acknowledge social, institutional, and attitudinal continuities with the Third Reich, belied assertions as to a rupture between the Nazi regime and the postwar experience.[6]

Nevertheless, the manner in which the postwar Germanys dealt with consumption broke decisively with Nazism. Leaving aside the obvious point that the destruction of Nazism shattered Strength through Joy along with it, neither German state provided fertile ground for the "German" consumption that KdF once embodied. KdF "solved" the Nazi regime's guns-and-butter dilemma until the realization of a prosperous German empire, while its success derived from satisfying the, by comparison, modest consumer expectations of the thirties. The postwar rump states on the other hand embraced consumerism, albeit in contrasting ways, as the

especially 75–107; Atina Grossmann, "A Question of Silence: The Rape of German Women by Occupation Soldiers," in *West Germany under Construction: Politics, Society, and Culture in the Adenauer Era*, ed. Robert G. Moeller (Ann Arbor: University of Michigan Press, 1997): 33–52; and "Pronatalism, Nationbuilding, and Socialism: Population Policy in the SBZ/DDR, 1945 to 1960," in *Between Reform and Revolution: German Socialism and Communism from 1840 to 1990*, ed. David E. Barclay and Eric D. Weitz (New York and Oxford: Berghahn Books, 1998): 443–65; and Robert G. Moeller, *Protecting Motherhood: Women and the Family in the Politics of Postwar West Germany* (Berkeley and London: University of California Press, 1993), 8–37. For the conduct of Soviet soldiers and its impact on the Germans in the Soviet zone, see Norman N. Naimark, *The Russians in Germany: A History of the Soviet Zone of Occupation, 1945–1949* (Cambridge, Massachusetts and London: Belknap/Harvard University Press, 1995), 69–140. On the expulsion, see Robert G. Moeller, *War Stories: The Search for a Usable Past in the Federal Republic of Germany* (Berkeley and London: University of California Press, 2001). Finally, Harold Marcuse's *Legacies of Dachau: The Uses and Abuses of a Concentration Camp, 1933–2001* (Cambridge: Cambridge University Press, 2001) is invaluable for tracing the long-term evolution of the founding myths of the Federal Republic, including the impact of unification in 1990.

6 Because the scholarship on the Federal Republic is more extensive than for the GDR, the challenge to its founding myths is better developed. See Robert G. Moeller, "Introduction: Writing the History of West Germany," in *West Germany under Construction: Politics, Society, and Culture in the Adenauer Era*, ed. Robert G. Moeller (Ann Arbor: University of Michigan Press, 1997): 1–30.

signifier of material well being and as the tangible evidence of discontinuity with the past. As heirs to the mass consumption regimes of the prewar period, Fordism and socialism, against which Nazism defined itself, the Federal Republic opted for market-based consumption while the GDR pushed for state ownership and central planning. As rivals in the competition over which could provide their citizens with a better material existence, they personified the broader competition between the West and the Soviet Bloc. If in the end the Federal Republic succeeded while the German Democratic Republic failed, West Germany's "victory" confirmed the correctness of East Germany's ruling elite, for the Socialist Unity party recognized soon after the GDR's founding that its survival depended on "delivering the goods." To be sure, the East German dictatorship, which engaged thousands of paid and unpaid informants to spy on seventeen million citizens, became notorious enough to invite comparisons with Nazism.[7] Regardless, the GDR's competition with West Germany, staged within the constraints of the postwar order, bore little resemblance to the Third Reich's imperialist solution to consumption. In the postwar climate, in which consumer expectations mounted amidst desires for security and the good life, the German Democratic Republic, like the Soviet Bloc, tried to prove that the socialist mode of consumption, achieved through central planning and the equitable distribution of goods, would outperform the inequality-producing chaos of capitalism.

The Federal Republic: Social Market Economy, Consumer Democracy, and Commercial Mass Tourism

West Germany's incorporation into the American-dominated Atlantic alliance ensured that the Federal Republic's economy would diverge from that of the Third Reich. Accepting a once exclusively American notion, that consumer choice composed the essence of democratic citizenship, West Germany's "economic miracle" (*Wirtschaftswunder*) of the fifties and sixties testified to the centrality of consumption to its recovery.[8] Despite its neoliberal underpinnings, which allowed less state intervention and regulation than the social democratic welfare states elsewhere in

---

7 Karl Wilhelm Fricke, *MfS Intern: Macht, Strukturen, Auflösung der DDR-Staatssicherheit* (Cologne: Wissenschaft und Politik, 1991), 21, 44.
8 On the influence of the United States on postwar Western European reformers, see Victoria de Grazia, "Changing Consumption Regimes in Europe, 1930–1970: Comparative Perspectives on the Distribution Problem," in *Getting and Spending: European and American Consumer Societies in the Twentieth Century*, ed. Susan Strasser, Charles McGovern, and Matthias Judt (Cambridge: Cambridge University Press, 1998): 79.

Western Europe, West Germany asserted the state's responsibility for assuring the well being of individuals, while simultaneously rejecting Nazi and communist "collectivism."[9] The West German "social market economy," the prime mover of which was Konrad Adenauer's economics minister, Ludwig Erhard, self-consciously broke with the Third Reich's policies of autarky, monopoly, and producer goods. Instead the Federal Republic would join the military and trading bloc of the West, stimulate consumer production, and provide a generous social safety net.

The "economic miracle" coexisted with the social conservatism of the ruling Christian Democratic Union (CDU). Seeking to restore the "private" sphere that the Third Reich's "totalitarian" control invaded, while compensating for the disruption of families during the war and the delayed return of German POWs from the Soviet Union, a distinctive consumerism shaped the reconstruction of the family and "proper" gender roles.[10] Married women would become "rational" consumers, who by attending to the material needs of their families through responsible shopping would bolster West Germany's economy and secure the Federal Republic's status as the "legitimate" Germany allied with the West. A prosperous capitalist democracy with social benefits generous enough to guarantee the "good life" complemented the Hallstein doctrine, which enshrined the Federal Republic's refusal to recognize the GDR or maintain diplomatic relations or trade with states that did. West Germany imagined itself as a beacon to oppressed East Germans, which would erode the legitimacy of the SED in the eyes of its own citizens.[11]

Countervailing trends challenged the hegemony of those assumptions almost from the moment that the conservative consensus solidified. Yet rather than retarding the growth of a full-blown consumer culture, they stimulated it. By the early fifties as the conservatism of the Federal Republic became entrenched, West German youth, attracted to American movie and pop stars, jazz, rock music, and fashion, ushered in a "getting and spending" ethos that provided individual and collective meaning. Despite the dismay of conservatives in politics, culture, and business who expended pots of ink on the corruption of youth, the Federal Republic's

---

9　Mark Mazower, *Dark Continent: Europe's Twentieth Century* (New York: Alfred A. Knopf, 1999), 182–211. Mazower, however, places less emphasis on the inherent anti-communism in Western European plans for postwar reconstruction than I do.

10　On Ludwig Erhard's career, as well as those of other neoliberal economists during the Third Reich, see A. J. Nicholls, *Freedom with Responsibility: The Social Market Economy in Germany 1918–1963* (Oxford: Clarendon Press, 1994), 60–121. On the critical role that West German women were to play in the economy, see Erika Carter, *How German Is She? Postwar West German Reconstruction and the Consuming Woman* (Ann Arbor: University of Michigan Press, 1997).

11　On West German political culture in the fifties and sixties, see Christoph Kleßmann, *Zwei Staaten, eine Nation: Deutsche Geschichte 1955–1970* (Bonn: Bundeszentrale für politische Bildung, 1988), 58–62.

Atlanticism and the seductive presence of American troops on West German soil encouraged the acceptance of mass production, self-service shopping, and the accumulation of goods as constitutive of individual identity. Unlike Weimar when the debate over Americanism fueled the right's assault against the republic, conservative misgivings belied the degree to which consumer prosperity legitimated the Bonn republic, despite the favorable perception of the Third Reich that West Germans held until the sixties.[12] Regardless of the anticapitalism and anticonsumerism enunciated by the student protests of the sixties, which emerged at the moment that the long postwar boom began to stall, West Germany remained a liberal democracy through energy crises, stagflation, and globalization. Consumer goods shaped the identities of West Germans and defined significant moments in their lives.[13] As a draw for ethnic Germans from Eastern Europe and refugees from the GDR in the late eighties, furthermore, West Germany's "magnetic" effect, which derived from the strength of its currency and its glittering consumer culture, hastened the disintegration of GDR and the Soviet Bloc.[14]

The Atlantic-oriented market economy of West Germany discouraged approaches to work and leisure of the sort that Strength through Joy once advocated. Although until the late sixties, employers adhered to ingrained notions of the "plant community" in an attempt to maintain labor discipline, the Beauty of Labor's effort to aestheticize the workplace and structure the recreational choices of workers to ensure work discipline meshed poorly with the altered business environment.[15] The reemergence

---

12 On West German youth and their consumption, see Maria Höhn, *GIs and Fräuleins: The German–American Encounter in 1950s West Germany* (Chapel Hill and London: University of North Carolina Press, 2002), especially 60–84; and Ute Poiger, *Jazz, Rock, and Rebels: Cold War Politics and American Culture in a Divided Germany* (Berkeley and London: University of California Press, 2000). Other valuable works on the emergence of West German consumer culture include Arne Andersen, *Der Traum vom guten Leben: Alltags- und Konsumgeschichte vom Wirtschaftswunder bis heute* (Frankfurt, New York: Campus Verlag, 1999); and Heide Fehrenbach, *Cinema in Democratizing Germany: Reconstructing National Identity after Hitler* (Chapel Hill and London: University of North Carolina Press, 1995). On the memories of Nazism in West Germany, see Axel Schildt, *Moderne Zeiten: Freizeit, Massenmedien und "Zeitgeist" in der Bundesrepublik der 50er Jahre* (Hamburg: Hans Christians Verlag, 1995), 307.
13 See the introduction in *1968: The World Transformed*, ed. Carole Fink, Philipp Gassert, and Detlev Junker (Cambridge: Cambridge University Press, 1998): 1–27. On the anthropology of consumer goods, see John Borneman, *Belonging in the Two Berlins: Kin, State, Nation* (Cambridge: Cambridge University Press, 1992), 231–5.
14 Hartmut Berghoff, "Konsumregulierung im Deutschland des 20. Jahrhunderts: Forschungsansätze und Leitfragen," in *Konsumpolitik: Die Regulierung des privaten Verbrauchs im 20. Jahrhundert*, ed. Hartmut Berghoff (Göttingen: Vandenhoeck and Ruprecht, 1999): 8–9.
15 On the continuities in the behavior of business leaders, see *Deutsche Unternehmer zwischen Kriegswirtschaft und Wiederaufbau: Studien zur Erfahrungsbildung von Industrie-Eliten*, ed. Paul Erker and Toni Pierenkemper (Munich: R. Oldenbourg Verlag, 1999), especially Erker's introduction, 1–18. The authors modify the argument

of the moderate left in the Social Democrats and the trade unions, albeit a left that by 1958 abandoned all pretense of Marxism, assured material gains for labor over the long term that undermined the premises of Nazi labor policy. The establishment of a liberal democracy that gave the Social Democrats a voice further guaranteed a different climate than that of the Third Reich. Despite the conflicts that emerged between management and labor over the conduct of employers during the Third Reich, business slowly grew to the idea of conciliating their workers, instead calling them "coworkers" (*Mitarbeiter*) or "employees" (*Arbeitnehmer*). While rejecting the class associations of "worker," they also abandoned the Labor Front's designations of "leader" and "retinue" with their implicitly fascist notions of hierarchy and obedience. With its new approach to labor relations, West German business drew inspiration from American-style public relations to project an image of social responsibility, which in turn allowed employers to suppress the memory of their accommodations to the Third Reich.[16] Whereas under Nazism beautiful workplaces, lunchtime concerts and art exhibits, sports programs, and clean bodies conferred status in the racial community, sizeable wage gains, employee representation on corporate boards through "co-determination," and restored political rights defined citizenship in the Federal Republic. With workers earning the wherewithal to exercise consumer choice, authoritarian attempts to discipline consumption and "harmonize" work and leisure fell by the wayside.

To be sure, "consumer choice" mattered little until the late fifties and early sixties. Although the currency reform of 1948 ended the black market and put goods on the shelves, the search for basic necessities and long hours in service of reconstruction constrained the lives of most West Germans, who in any case trusted the state more than the market to provide for them.[17] Despite the early re-formation of German tourism associations, the vacation travel of most consisted of visits to relatives or sites close to home.[18] As the "economic miracle" took hold, however, popular

of Volker Berghahn, *The Americanisation of West German Industry 1945–1973* (Cambridge: Cambridge University Press, 1986), who charted a less problematic transformation in the attitudes of employers.

16 See S. Jonathan Wiesen, *West German Industry and the Challenge of the Nazi Past, 1945–1955* (Chapel Hill and London: University of North Carolina Press, 2001), 190–2, and Wiesen again, "Coming to Terms with the Worker: West German Industry, Labour Relations and the Idea of America, 1949–60," *Journal of Contemporary History* 36, no. 4 (2001): 561–79.

17 See Michael Geyer, "In Pursuit of Happiness: Consumption, Mass Culture, and Consumerism," in *Shattered Past: Reconstructing German Histories*, Konrad H. Jarausch and Michael Geyer (Princeton and Oxford: Princeton University Press, 2003): 275–86.

18 My discussion of West German tourism is drawn from the following: Andersen, *Traum vom guten Leben*, 177–92; Alon Confino, "Traveling as a Culture of Remembrance: Traces of National Socialism in West Germany, 1945–1960," *History and Memory*

consumption patterns changed dramatically, displacing the class-defined consumption and spartan spending habits of the interwar and immediate postwar periods. Rising incomes and shorter workdays contributed to that trend, but so too did the extension of paid vacations as the outcome of both industry wage negotiations and state legislation. By the mid-sixties, all workers up to the age of thirty-five received a minimum of fifteen days of paid time off. By 1982, the average paid vacation for all employees was 34 days, with nearly half receiving six weeks or more.[19] As a result, consumers defined their own choices in travel, leisure, and the arts, rendering irrelevant the mediation between consumers and the market that Strength through Joy once offered.[20] Influenced by television and ultimately by air travel, more West Germans expanded their horizons to the entire globe, even if most vacationed in Austria, which posed fewer language difficulties.[21] The disposable income of West German youth, which sustained a culture defined partially by the possessions that money could buy, encouraged young people to opt for forms of entertainment similar to those that the Nazis had once anathematized or tried to "Germanize."

The contributions of the Third Reich to the postwar boom in mass tourism cannot be overlooked. The surge in tourism among former soldiers derived from the exposure to foreign lands, which the quest for living space engendered. Combining contradictory desires, the recovery of youthful adventures, and the experience of domination on the one hand and the assurance to foreigners as to the decency of German soldiers on the other, the tourism of veterans fused remembrance with evasion.[22] Moreover, the attraction of specific tourist destinations, Italy especially, owed much to Strength through Joy's having popularized them during the thirties. Although postwar travel to Italy became overtly hedonistic – the quest for pleasure and relaxation in the land of sun and sex rather than the self-improving pilgrimage to sites of classical culture – KdF's cruises

12, no. 2 (2000): 92–121; Christine Keitz, *Reisen als Leitbild: Die Entstehung des modernen Massentourismus in Deutschland* (Munich: Deutscher Taschenbuch Verlag, 1997), 258–301; Rudy Koshar, *German Travel Cultures* (Oxford and New York: Berg, 2000), 172–6; Axel Schildt, *Moderne Zeiten*, 180–202; and the essays on West German tourism in Hasso Spode, ed., *Goldstrand und Teutonengrill*.

19 Schildt, *Moderne Zeiten*, 182; *Die Arbeiter: Lebensformen, Alltag und Kultur von der Frühindustrialisierung bis zum "Wirtschaftswunder,"* ed. Wolfgang Ruppert (Munich: Verlag C.H. Beck, 1986), 156.

20 Rather than emphasizing the currency reform of 1948 as the launching pad of the West German recovery, recent scholarship has delayed the "economic miracle" by about ten years. See especially Michael Wildt, *Am Beginn der "Konsumgesellschaft": Mangelerfahrung, Lebenshaltung, Wohlstandshoffnung in Westdeutschland in den fünfziger Jahre* (Hamburg: Ergebnisse Verlag, 1995), and *Vom kleinen Wohlstand: Eine Konsumgeschichte der fünfziger Jahre* (Hamburg: Fischer, 1996).

21 Andersen, *Traum vom guten Leben*, 177.

22 On this theme, see Confino, "Traveling as a Culture of Remembrance": 107–11.

and the pleasure-seeking that took place on them left their legacy.[23] Finally, as the institution that best embodied the Third Reich's struggle to find its own path to high living standards, KdF's virulent anticommunism and that of the regime that founded it influenced the Cold War culture of the Federal Republic. The experiences of nearly thirteen million German soldiers in the east during the war,[24] the stuff of countless newspaper articles, reinforced perceptions as to the linkage between communism and impoverishment.

Nevertheless, the stereotypes associated with KdF's tourism during the Third Reich returned with greater force in the postwar period as discriminating consumers tailored their leisure plans to their own tastes. Strength through Joy's one-time popularity among salaried employees and workers succumbed to a generalized contempt, which reproduced images of mute, undiscriminating hordes once expressed by the better-off "private" tourists of the thirties. Rising incomes and increasing automobile ownership, especially among wage earners, and the multiplication of travel and leisure choices encouraged consumers to map their own itineraries and eschew collectivist options. Thus workers could escape the discipline of company-sponsored trips or the package tourism of the political parties.[25] Moreover, the rivalry between the Germanys discredited Strength through Joy from another direction. Whereas KdF once proved its anti-Marxism by nationalizing workers through workplace beautification, tourism and other forms of recreation, popular attitudes in the postwar period perceived little difference between Strength through Joy and the state-subsidized leisure of the GDR. Given the official and popular inclination to "forget" the deep reservoir of consent enjoyed by the Third Reich and especially Hitler, West Germans equated the regimented mass tourism of KdF with the tourism of the left.

In fact, the trade unionist tourism that did reemerge in West Germany was ambivalent from the outset about organizing its own package tours, often choosing to negotiate rebates from commercial travel agencies. Although ricocheting thereafter between sponsoring its own travel and relying on commercial tourism, the increasingly commercial character of West German social tourism paralleled the outcome of left-sponsored tourism elsewhere, even in France where the Popular Front's two-week paid

23   Birgit Mandel, "'Amore ist heisser als Liebe': Das Italien-Urlaubsimage der Westdeutschen in den 50er und 60er Jahren," in Goldstrand und Teutonengrill ed., Spode, especially 149–50.

24   The German Army and Genocide: Crimes against War Prisoners, Jews, and Other Civilians, 1939–1944, ed. Hamburg Institute for Social Research, trans. Scott Abbott (New York: New Press, 1999), 8. This figure is found in Michael Geyer's foreword.

25   Schildt, Moderne Zeiten, 379; Axel Schildt and Arnold Sywottek, "'Reconstruction' and 'Modernization': West German Social History during the 1950s," in Moeller, ed., West Germany under Construction: 424–5.

vacation anchored the principle of leisure as a social entitlement.[26] By the late sixties, trade union and Social Democratic tourism lagged behind the commercial variety except in a few localities, a casualty of the West German Social Democrats' abandonment of Marxism and the erosion of once tenacious working-class subcultures and consumption patterns.[27] Like the working-class consumer cooperatives, which declined precipitously by the sixties, social tourism no longer found a place, for it evoked lifestyles that Nazi repression and the war permanently disrupted.[28] In all likelihood, the social tourism that emerged in the GDR provided West Germans with yet another justification for rejecting collectivist travel.

Only one element of Strength through Joy, the Volkswagen, survived in West Germany's hothouse consumer culture. Having outlasted labor shortages, inadequate raw materials, and the threat of dismantling as reparations the Volkswagen plant at Wolfsburg recovered by producing transport vehicles for the Allies. Because the British occupation needed dollars with which to feed the population of its zone, it allowed Volkswagen to export its autos, albeit to a limited extent at first so as not to compete with British auto manufacturers.[29] Thereafter, the Volkswagen "Beetle" became a badge of the West German "economic miracle," an individual and family status symbol. With the West German auto industry as a whole, it became the prime mover behind the flowering of West German tourism in the late fifties and sixties until inexpensive air travel emerged

26 Schildt, *Moderne Zeiten*, 191–2; Keitz, *Reisen als Leitbild*, 272–85. On France, see Ellen Furlough, "Making Mass Vacations: Tourism and Consumer Culture in France, 1930s to 1970s," *Comparative Studies in Society and History* 40, no. 2 (1998): 247–86.

27 Ironically, the SPD gained more working-class support in West Germany than it had at any time previously, according to Jonathan Sperber, who calls into question the long-standing scholarly claim that the SPD became a broad people's party in the course of the twentieth century. See his "The Social Democratic Electorate in Imperial Germany," in *Between Reform and Revolution: German Socialism and Communism from 1840 to 1990*, ed. David E. Barclay and Eric D. Weitz (New York and Oxford: Berghahn Books, 1998): 167–94. Yet the identities and consumption patterns of the interwar period evaporated. See Schildt, *Moderne Zeiten*, 311–13, and Josef Mooser, *Arbeiterleben in Deutschland 1900–1970* (Frankfurt am Main: Suhrkamp, 1984), 180–236.

28 See the revealing table in Michael Prinz's, "Von der Nahrungssicherung zum Einkommensausgleich: Entstehung und Durchsetzung des Selbsthilfemusters: Konsumvereine 1770–1914 in England und Deutschland," in *Europäische Konsumgeschichte: Zur Gesellschafts und Kulturgeschichte des Konsums (18. bis 20. Jahrhundert)*, ed. Hannes Siegrist, Hartmut Kaeble, Jürgen Kocka (Frankfurt/New York: Campus Verlag, 1997): 727. See as well Brett Fairbairn, "The Rise and Fall of Consumer Cooperation in Germany," in *Consumers against Capitalism? Consumer Cooperation in Europe, North America, and Japan*, ed. Ellen Furlough and Carl Strikwerda (Lanham, Maryland: Rowman and Littlefield, 1999): 295–7.

29 See Hans Mommsen and Manfred Grieger, *Das Volkswagenwerk und seine Arbeiter im Dritten Reich* (Düsseldorf: Econ Verlag, 1997), 949–93; and Heidrun Edelmann's essay on the Volkswagen general director Heinrich Nordhoff, in *Deutsche Unternehmer* ed. Erker and Pierenkemper, 44–5.

as a competitor. Once relieved of the restrictions on its exports, the Volkswagen penetrated markets in Western Europe and in the United States, thus demonstrating the benefits of integration with the West. The degree to which the quintessential product of West German mass consumption competed effectively against American-made products in the homeland of the mass-produced automobile differed clearly from the twenties, when American imports, investment, and mass culture spawned fears of Germany's submergence.

Although exhibited after unification in 1990 in a manner that effaced its origins in the Third Reich,[30] the Volkswagen Beetle's postwar success resided in part on prewar meanings, for its image as a family car originated in its homey depiction in Strength through Joy's periodicals. In contrast to the Nazi regime's failure to deliver a single auto to its subscribers, however, the Volkswagen symbolized the Bonn republic's ability to produce a high material standard of living. To be sure, with the support of a diverse coalition of political interests including the SPD, Volkswagen resisted the privatization that Ludwig Erhard demanded. It won protection against foreign penetration and competition that in part derived from its privileged status in the Third Reich, while West German courts protected the company from the claims of those who saved for an auto during Nazi rule. To this day, the state of Lower Saxony remains partial owner of the company.[31] Yet rather than having proven the führer's "motorization of the masses," the Beetle stood for the democratization of consumption facilitated by a liberal capitalist democracy and an anti-autarkic Atlantic trading bloc. As the best example of the astonishing dissemination of technology since the early twentieth century, the automobile constituted the most recognizable signifier of prosperity. As a signifier of liberty, furthermore, West Germans increasingly understood travel as a right equivalent to other social and welfare rights contained in the West German Basic Law. In contrast to the constraints on East Germans, in which the authorities curtailed travel even before the construction of the Wall, West Germans, driving in their automobiles on highways that Hitler had left unfinished, experienced freedom.[32]

---

30 Thus, the German Historical Museum in Berlin, under the heavy influence of the Christian Democratic government of Helmut Kohl, prominently displayed a green "Beetle" as a symbol of the "economic miracle" without acknowledging its connection to the führer's dream of motorizing the masses.

31 See Simon Reich, *The Fruits of Fascism: Postwar Prosperity in Historical Perspective* (Ithaca and London: Cornell University Press, 1990), 186–201.

32 On the Volkswagen's meaning for consumers, see Alon Confino and Rudy Koshar, "Régimes of Consumer Culture: New Narratives in Twentieth-Century German History," *German History* 19, no. 2 (2001): 156–7; and Andersen, *Traum von guten Leben*, 155–75.

The German Democratic Republic:
Unsatisfied Desires, the Failure of Socialist
Consumption, and the Subversion of Tourism

Although occupying territory that Allied bombing damaged less extensively, the German Democratic Republic faced hurdles after its formation
that put it at a comparative disadvantage to the Federal Republic. Hand-
icapped by limited natural resources except for its polluting brown coal,
confronted with a shortage of skilled workers despite the influx of refugees
from the east, deprived of Marshall Plan aid, and bound to the less developed economies of the Soviet Bloc, the GDR did well to generate modest
rates of growth in its first decade.[33] Although seriously debated in the first
three years after the war, alternatives to the Soviet-style reconstruction of
the eastern zone evaporated. Despite the KPD's transformation into a
mass party, the Soviet's dismantling of industrial plans and rolling stock
and the rapes by Soviet soldiers undermined its popularity and reinforced
its dependence on its protector from afar. In fact, the eastern zone's communists pursued a separate socialist state more intransigently than their
Soviet benefactors, who envisioned a united and neutral Germany and
acceded to the GDR's founding only when the Cold War precluded that
option. Having forcibly incorporated the SPD in 1946 after failing to
achieve the electoral majority that it wished, the Communist-dominated
SED remained wedded to the KPD's practices of the twenties and thirties,
which presupposed the revolutionary agency of the working class with
the party as its vanguard. Instinctively disliking disorder and distrusting
the masses, whom it deemed complicit in elevating Hitler into power, the
SED propagated an official myth that linked fascism to finance capitalism and Nazism to West Germany. While celebrating the Soviet Union's
"fraternal" liberation of Germany from the Third Reich, the SED's majority infused its hostility to "cosmopolitan" capitalism with antisemitism,
purging from the party's ranks those who recognized that antisemitism,
not just anti-Marxism, fueled Nazi ideology.[34]

---

33 See Mary Fulbrook, *The Two Germanies 1945–1990: Problems of Interpretation*
    (Atlantic Highlands, New Jersey: Humanities Press International, 1992), 53; Martin
    McCauley, *The German Democratic Republic since 1945* (London: Macmillan, 1983),
    42; Hermann Weber, *Die DDR 1945–1990*, 2nd ed. (Munich: R. Oldenbourg, 1993),
    11–12.
34 On the development of the SED's self-understanding the literature is rich. See Meuschel,
    Legitimation und Parteiherrschaft, 9–122; Eric D. Weitz, *Creating German Com-
    munism, 1890–1990: From Popular Protests to Socialist State* (Princeton: Princeton
    University Press, 1997), 311–86; Alan Nothnagle, *Building the East German Myth:
    Historical Mythology and Youth Propaganda in the German Democratic Republic,
    1945–1989* (Ann Arbor: University of Michigan Press, 1999); and Herf, *Divided Mem-
    ory*. As Weitz's discussion indicates, the relationship between the SED and the Soviet

The economic realities that the German Democratic Republic encountered and communist myths, derived from the Soviet experience, which valorized heavy industry as equivalent to modernization, produced a different economy from that of the Federal Republic, yet one that soon incurred the resentment of the GDR's citizens. As early as 1952, the SED's inability to prevent the exodus of young, highly skilled East Germans to West Germany, frustrated by the state's discrimination against the private economy and desirous of a better standard of living, provoked it to seal most of the GDR's borders. By the summer of 1961, the SED was forced to erect the Berlin Wall, a humiliating decision that closed the one remaining escape hatch.[35] Yet, despite the elimination of market-based consumption, the contradictory practices of state-owned consumer goods stores, the constraints against innovation, and the SED's hostility to uncontrolled consumer desires, which in its view reduced individuals to the possession of things, the party knew that consumer goods would ensure its legitimacy.[36] Highlighted in the five-year plan that followed the workers' uprising of June 1953 and the seven-year plan announced in 1959, the SED proposed sizeable increases in consumer production. The accelerated production of goods beyond that of the basic necessities was to realize a socialist utopia, in which the operative principles were distribution according to need and consumption in line with basic material comfort. To be sure, the party's expectation that the GDR would overtake the Federal Republic in per capita consumption remained chimerical.

Union is sharply debated. See Dietrich Staritz's interpretation in *Die Gründung der DDR: Von sowjetischen Besatzungsherrschaft zum sozialistischen Staat* (Munich: DTV, 1984) and Weitz's response, 316–17n. and 347.

35 Kleßmann, *Zwei Staaten*, 321.

36 The scholarship since the collapse of the GDR has increasingly recognized the GDR's consumerist ambitions, thus complicating the stereotypes long applied to East Germany. See the masterful book of Ina Merkel, *Utopie und Bedürfnis: Die Geschichte der Konsumkultur in der DDR* (Cologne, Weimar, Vienna: Böhlau Verlag, 1999), which has become the standard work on this subject. Work on consumption, however, continues to proliferate, as the following articles indicate: Katherine Pence, "'You as a Woman Will Understand': Consumption, Gender and the Relationship between State and Citizenry in the GDR's Crisis of 17 June 1953," *German History* 19, no. 2 (2001): 218–52, and "Schauenfenster des sozialistischen Konsums: Texte der ostdeutschen 'consumer culture,'" in *Akten, Eingaben, Schaufenster: Die DDR und ihre Texte: Erkundungen zu Herrschaft und Alltag*, ed. Peter Becker and Alf Lüdtke (Berlin, 1997): 91–118; Raymond G. Stokes, "Plastics and the New Society: The German Democratic Republic in the 1950s and 1960s," in *Style and Socialism: Modernity and Material Culture in Post-War Eastern Europe*, ed. Susan E. Reid and David Crowley (Oxford and New York: Berg, 2000): 65–80; Elizabeth A. Ten Dyke, "Tulips in December: Space, Time and Consumption before and after the End of German Socialism," *German History* 19, no. 2 (2001): 253–76; Jonathan Zatlin, "The Vehicle of Desire: The Trabant, the Wartburg, and the End of the GDR," *German History* 15, no. 3 (1997): 358–80; and Mark Landsman, "The Consumer Supply Lobby – Did It Exist? State and Consumption in East Germany in the 1950s," *Central European History* 35, no. 4 (2002): 477–512.

Nevertheless, the SED's sensitivity to popular opinion remained the leitmotif of its forty-year lifespan.[37]

Despite the SED's efforts after 1961 to satisfy the material wishes of a population that it virtually imprisoned, consumer goods production in the GDR suffered from uneven distribution, chronic shortages of goods against demand, poor quality, and selling practices that no one would have mistaken for the shopper-friendly environment of the Federal Republic. Worse still, from the perspective of the SED's legitimacy, was that having promised a high standard of living to rival that of the Federal Republic, the state incurred heavy debts by importing the goods from the West that its citizens preferred. The alternative, paying or trading for the imports, was not feasible because the GDR had few marketable goods to export.[38] By the seventies, the SED moderated its egalitarianism and commitment to collectivized consumption in the attempt to meet the need for goods in ways that conveyed personal distinction and more refined notions of taste. The differentiation of consumer goods outlets according to those that sold Western goods and those that did not, a process that the Honecker government accelerated, privileged some East Germans at the expense of others.[39] From the perspective of East Germans, the SED's assurances as to the fair allocation of consumer goods and its repeated claim that prosperity lay around the corner created a moral economy, in which the shoddiest West German goods became the glue of relationships and symbols of social capital. The liabilities inherent in the GDR's consumption policy grew more evident with the normalization of relations between the Germanys in the seventies. Access to West German television and increased travel between East and West Germany, although much more restricted for East Germans, allowed the movement of goods and images that advertised West Germany's glittering consumer culture.[40]

37 Kleßmann, *Zwei Staaten*, 313. Even the Five-Year Plan proclaimed in 1951, which emphasized industrial production, envisioned that by 1955 the prewar standard of living would be exceeded. See Hermann Weber, *Geschichte der DDR* (Munich: DTV, 1985), 214.

38 Mike Dennis, *The Rise and Fall of the German Democratic Republic, 1945–1990* (Harlow, England: Longman/Pearson Education, 2000), 146–8; Mary Fulbrook, *Anatomy of a Dictatorship*, 145; and Klaus Schroeder, *Der SED-Staat: Partei, Staat und Gesellschaft 1949–1990* (Munich and Vienna: Carl Hanser Verlag, 1998), 219–23. The best discussion of East Germany's economic weaknesses and their relationship to the need to raise living standards is that of Charles S. Maier, *Dissolution: The Crisis of Communism and the End of East Germany* (Princeton: Princeton University Press, 1997), 59–107. Although contemporary observers sometimes touted the GDR's economic progress, the disparities in the standard of living between it and West Germany were too obvious to ignore. See Stephen F. Frowen, "The Economy of the German Democratic Republic," in *Honecker's Germany*, ed. David Childs (London: Allen and Unwin, 1985): 32–50.

39 Merkel, *Utopie und Bedürfnis*, especially 243–50.

40 On East Germans and their consumer goods, see Daphne Berdahl, *Where the World Ended: Re-unification and Identity in the German Borderland* (Berkeley, Los Angeles,

To compete over which German state best delivered the "good life," one in which the German Democratic Republic could never win even during the sixties when its consumerism seemed efficacious, the SED had no choice but to accentuate the positive. Thus, it emphasized the social benefits that the state did provide, which granted cradle-to-grave security. In addition to the subsidized educational opportunities that allowed youths of working class or peasant background to climb the social ladder, the SED guaranteed jobs, comprehensive maternity and medical benefits, careers for women according to the principle of equal pay for equal work, state-mandated paid vacations and a subsidized leisure and tourism program.[41] On the surface, the SED's desire, or more accurately its need, to play "catch up" while remaining suspicious of the unsatable desires spawned by Western style consumption resembled the approach of Strength through Joy. Yet lacking the Nazi regime's means of solving the consumption problem by dint of postwar geopolitical realities, the GDR's leisure and tourism could not approach KdF's success in making credible its promise of an abundant future. As the smaller and poorer of the two postwar German states, the GDR's failures received regular confirmation from the lifestyles of West Germans across the border.

Recognizing the impossibility of travel to the West, organized tourism in the GDR occupied a track separate from Nazi tourism and that of the Federal Republic. While the surge in tourism became evident in the Federal Republic by the early sixties, mass tourism did not emerge in the GDR until late in that decade. After the GDR sealed its borders, increased living standards, and extended paid vacations to a minimum of fifteen days, a favorable climate for popular travel took hold. The main promoters of organized mass tourism in East Germany consisted of "People's-Owned Companies" (Volkseiniger Betriebe, or VEB), the Kombinate, and especially the Free German Trade Union Federation (Freier Deutscher Gewerkschaftsbund or FDGB). Evoking the leftist vacations of the twenties, the FDGB dispatched workers to vacation hostels, which now included the expropriated palaces and estates of nobles. The ties between the FDGB and East German industries and partners in the Soviet bloc nations enabled vacation travel to spas or hostels outside of the GDR.[42]

London: University of California Press, 1997), 104–83. See also Ten Dyke, "Space, Time and Consumption": passim.

41 This is especially evident in the life stories of the GDR's founding generation. See Lutz Niethammer, *Die Volkseinige Erfahrung: Eine Archäologie des Lebens in der Industrieprovinz der DDR* (Berlin: Rohwohlt, 1991), and the article-length English version, "Zeroing in on Change: In Search of Popular Experience in the Industrial Province in the German Democratic Republic," in *The History of Everyday Life: Reconstructing Historical Experiences and Ways of Life*, ed. Alf Lüdtke, trans. William Templer (Princeton: Princeton University Press, 1995), 252–311.

42 *Urlaubsfreuden durch den Feriendienst der Gewerkschaften: Ein Wegweiser durch die schöne Kur- und Ferienorte der Deutschen Demokratischen Republik*, ed. Freier Deutsche Gewerkschaftsbund, Bundesvorstand, Feriendienst der Gewerkschaften

In one of the last years before the GDR's collapse, some 3.2 million persons had taken vacations to VEB-sponsored hostels or resorts, with an additional 1.8 million having traveled through the services of the FDGB. The Free German Youth (Freier Deutsche Jugend, or FDJ) added to those numbers as the second most important purveyor of mass travel, for it saw tourism as a means of indoctrinating its membership in the virtues of socialism.[43] Unlike Strength through Joy, which received no financial contribution from the state to supplement the resources of the Labor Front, the East German party and state subsidized vacation packages. Whereas in West Germany, KdF-style mediation lost out to prosperity and to the individualism of a full-blown consumer culture, it lost out in the GDR to the state's intervention in providing what KdF had once been unable to offer: well-subsidized vacation trips that guaranteed the opportunity to travel to even the lowest paid workers and their families. In contrast to the Third Reich, which during the thirties promoted a "synchronized" commercial tourism that it subsequently tolerated during the war, the GDR eliminated the private travel industry. The SED's mass organizations not only closely regulated leisure activities independent of tourism, such as sports, hobbies, and the fine arts; their recreational offerings also received heavy subsidies.

Moreover, the GDR's effort to keep its population from emigrating and prevent the corrupting influences of Western style consumption from intruding necessarily meant different tourist sites than those KdF favored, as well as a different tone for spots that had been popular before the war. In addition to plant and FDGB vacation hotels, domestic tourist sites consisted of earlier vacation locales, such as the Baltic resorts, stripped of their former commercialism.[44] Because travel to KdF's prime destinations – Madeira, Italy, Greece, and Norway – was impossible, East Germans traveled to the beaches of Bulgaria, to Lake Balaton in Hungary, and to the mountains in Czechoslovakia, Poland, and Romania. Or they visited cities such as Warsaw, Prague, and Budapest after the introduction of visa-free travel in the late sixties and early seventies. Despite the Soviet government's restrictions on individual travel, the Soviet Union became a frequent choice of destination for tourists from the GDR. With the advent of jet air travel, a small number of East Germans ventured beyond Europe,

(Dresden: Tribüne Verlag, 1955): 9–18, 27–8. I extend my appreciation to Randall Bytwerk for lending this brochure to me. The literature on East German tourism remains limited. For a start, see the following essays in Hasso Spode's collection, *Goldstrand und Teutonengrill*. In addition to Spode's essay, "Tourismus in der Gesellschaft der DDR: Eine vergleichende Einführung," they include Gundel Fuhrmann, "Der Urlaub der DDR-Bürger in den späten 60er Jahren:" 23–50; and Gerlinde Irmscher, "Alltägliche Fremde: Auslandsreisen in der DDR": 51–67.
43   Schroeder, *SED-Staat*, 579–80.
44   *Urlaubsfreuden durch den Feriendienst der Gewerkschaften*, 41–169.

availing themselves of package tours to Mongolia or Cuba.[45] To be sure, the FDGB's ships, the *Fritz Heckert* and the *Friendship among Peoples* (*Völkerfreundschaft*) resembled the working-class cruises that KdF strove to achieve right down to the SED's rhetoric of democratizing a privilege. Yet, in addition to confining their destinations to the Baltic and Black Sea ports, the GDR's cruises did not become the public relations centerpiece of its tourism as did the cruises for Strength through Joy. Not only did the number of ships not increase compared to those of KdF, the number of passengers they transported declined significantly from 1960 to 1970, never reviving thereafter.[46]

The GDR's chronic defensiveness meant that much of its tourism for domestic and foreign consumption sought to anchor its lineage and accomplishments, while proclaiming its distance from Nazism. Thus, competing with the consumerism of West Berlin, the SED reconstructed the GDR's part of Berlin by merging classical architecture with the principle of social solidarity, creating a built environment that testified to East Germany's high living standards.[47] The SED constructed or reconfigured sites of commemoration according to its founding myths, its shifting conceptions of its relationship to German history, and its need to invent a symbolic landscape for a previously nonexistent state. As was true in the Federal Republic,[48] memorializing sites of Nazi horror conveyed the GDR's dissimilarity with the Third Reich, while giving voice to those whom it believed deserved recognition for opposing fascism. Unlike its cousin to the west, however, an equally "artificial" creation, such sites became more conspicuous in the GDR. Because the SED could not compete with West Germany in cementing its legitimacy through consumer goods, even if the GDR seemed prosperous relative to the Soviet bloc, visual signs of the past allowed it to remind visitors of what the party had accomplished.[49] Concentration camps such as Sachsenhausen, Buchenwald, and Ravensbrück paid tribute to communist resisters, Germany's Soviet liberators, and the GDR's official break as the "workers' and peasants' state" from the legacies of Nazism, which in the SED's view survived in the Federal Republic. The SED's claim to inherit the best German cultural traditions, reflected in its early lionizing of Goethe and Bach, resulted in the restoration of historical sites connected with them. In the eighties, the SED's desire to include in its self-representation once troublesome

45 See Irmscher, "Alltägliche Fremde," 53–7.
46 Ibid., 52, and Fuhrmann, "Urlaub der DDR-Bürger," 40.
47 Carter, *How German Is She?* 118–30.
48 See Marcuse, *Legacies of Dachau.*
49 While I agree with Sarah Farmer's article, "Symbols that Face Two Ways: Commemorating the Victims of Nazism and Stalinism at Buchenwald and Sachsenhausen," *Representations* 49 (Winter 1995): 97–119, especially 99, she overlooks the most fundamental reason as to why the SED invested so much in them.

historical figures, such as Martin Luther and Frederick the Great, required an additional investment in sites of memory. The "Luther City" of Wittenberg honored the progenitor of the Reformation, who during the forty years of the GDR's existence went from being castigated as the "traitor to peasants" to a humanist whose contributions to German culture the SED claimed to inherit.[50]

By the late eighties, the GDR's accumulated failures in producing a socialist version of the "good life" to rival the commercial consumption of the Federal Republic brought its dissolution. The SED's consumerist promises, especially during the Honecker years, and the acceptance of vacation travel as a popular entitlement exacerbated popular frustrations. The SED's pledges conflicted with the realities that the West German media and West German relatives regularly transmitted, while the proscriptions against travel outside the socialist nations for all except the privileged removed whatever luster remained to the SED's claim to have extended vacations to all. Despite the large clientele that the GDR's collectivist tourism embraced, the popularity of camping suggests that increasing numbers of East Germans shared the anticollectivist ethos of West German tourists, complementing the private commodity exchanges of ordinary citizens, which occurred beyond the government's official venues of purchase.[51] For its part, the SED could not resolve the contradictions in its approach to consumption, veering between state-managed collective entitlement on the one hand and the encouragement of private desires on the other. While creating hierarchies in the distribution of consumer goods, the SED propagandistically adhered to the egalitarianism of "real existing socialism." While tolerating the travel that existed independently of state-owned industries and SED mass organizations, especially camping, it limited the production of Trabants (Trabis) and Wartburgs, suspicious of individual freedom of movement. Notwithstanding the triumphalism of its collectivist tourism, it never possessed enough facilities to meet the demand, even if its proletarian character was more straightforward than that of KdF.[52]

Nevertheless the limited mobility granted to East Germans led to the GDR's collapse in 1989, for the GDR's tourists instigated the implosion of the socialist mode of consumption. In the summer and fall of 1989 as the SED condemned reformism in the Soviet Union, Poland, and

50 For commemoration in the GDR in addition to Farmer's article, see Rudy Koshar, *From Monuments to Traces: Artifacts of German Memory, 1870–1990* (Berkeley, Los Angeles, London: University of California Press, 2000), 187–98, 211–18, and 267–85.
51 On camping, see Koshar, *German Travel Cultures,* 177–8; Schroeder, *SED-Staat,* 582; Fuhrmann, "Urlaub der DDR-Bürger," 38, 41–2; and Merkel, *Utopie und Bedürfnis,* 324. On the inability of East German mass organizations to provide meaning through consumption, see Geyer, "In Pursuit of Happiness:" 300–1.
52 Zatlin, "Vehicle of Desire": 363.

Hungary, thousands of East Germans left on camping trips, reemerging near Hungary's newly opened border with Austria so as to escape to West Germany. Or they abandoned their Trabis and Wartburgs in Prague to crowd into the West German embassy until their government finally granted them permission to emigrate.[53] Unable to compete with the Federal Republic, the GDR's days were numbered once the state opened the GDR's border on 9 November, allowing East Germans to gaze on West Berlin's bountiful shopping districts. Unlike Strength through Joy, which had deepened Nazism's popular acceptance, tourism in the GDR had accomplished the opposite.

Contrary to the founding myths of the Federal Republic and the German Democratic Republic, the defeat of the Third Reich in 1945 was no simple "zero hour" (*Stunde Null*), a radical break with a troublesome past. Nevertheless, the postwar experience of consumption in West and East Germany underscored Nazism's lethal distinctiveness, which Strength through Joy embodied. Both a short-term compensation until living space could be secured and a harbinger of future bounty, KdF advanced the regime's imperial ambitions. Adhering to those strategies, it propelled Nazism's inhumanity by reinforcing racial exclusion at home, abetting racial hierarchies abroad, and channeling consumer desires into expansionism. In the end, the resources of a global military alliance were required to defeat the Third Reich, which until then retained the backing of its racially acceptable citizens. Despite the inequalities and exploitation inherent in market-based consumption or the ugly repression and economic failures of state socialism, the Nazi campaign to achieve a higher standard of living achieved a distinctiveness all its own, a war of unparalleled destruction.

---

53 See the news clipping from the West German newspaper, *Die Welt*, 21 August 1989 in *DDR-Das Ende eines Staates*, ed. Paul Jackson (Manchester and New York: Manchester University Press, 1994), 50–2.

Index